HOLY WOOD

MOVIES DOING THE BIBLE

PHIL SCHEIDT

Copyright © 2020 Phil A. Scheidt

All rights reserved. No part of this book may be reproduced in any form without the permission of the author.

ISBN: 978-0-578-63688-7

www.HolyWoodBook.com

This book was copyrighted in November of 2018, but due to the illness and death of the author's wife it was not published until 2020

Edited by Deb Strubel and Jim Watkins
Proofreading by Rebecca Scheidt and Nancy Scheidt
Cover and Interior design by John Reinhardt Book Design

Printed in the United States of America

Portions of this book are works of fiction. Any references to historical events, real people, or real places are used fictitiously. Other names, characters, places and events are products of the author's imagination, and any resemblances to actual events or places or persons, living or dead, is entirely coincidental.

However, when the name Phil Scheidt appears in this book it is referring to the author who is in fact a terrible golfer who had trouble getting dates in college.

Wawasee Theater
(A Pet Friendly Theater)

Each fall the Wawasee Theater presents a series of vintage films from the past. This year the theater is proud to present:

Movies Doing the Bible

Each week starting Monday, September 3rd and continuing until Christmas there will be a single or double feature on Monday evening at seven and Saturday afternoon at one. The series features films that are based on Bible stories or characters described in the *Bible*.

As in all of the series the theater presents each fall, these screenings not only allow audience participation, but encourage it. Be prepared to laugh because it can get rowdy sometimes.

Since the films in these series date back to the 1940s the admission price is lowered accordingly to twenty-five cents.

The first film to be shown will be:

The Bible: In the Beginning

STARRING:

George C. Scott as ...... Abraham

Ava Gardner as ...... Sarah

John Huston as ...... Noah

Peter O'Toole as ...... The Three Angels

(Seriously, Count em — Me, Myself, and I)

Location

FICTIONAL TOWN OF WAWASEE, INDIANA
WAWASEE THEATER (BUILT IN 1915)

Cast of Characters

Members of the Audience

The Sunday School Teacher, **DEB** is an attractive fifty-year old blonde who works as the head of Christian Education at a local church. She teaches a Wednesday Bible study and Sunday school for adults.

The Professor, **JIM** is her forty-five year old husband who wears a beard that is starting to turn grey. He and Deb own a horse farm in Indiana. With a background in biology, the college professor's hobby is mixing DNA as he breeds animals.

The Talking Mule, **CHESTER** is the result of Jim combining the DNA of a mule, a Standard Poodle and a parrot. (Chester has sired over one hundred similar mules)

The Talking Horse, **CHARLEY** is the result of Jim combining the DNA of a horse, a Standard Poodle and a parrot. The parrot mixture was accidentally doubled resulting in Charley occasionally repeating things, to Deb's embarrassment, that he hears Deb say to Jim.

The Business Man Turned Politician, **RONALD RINK** is an overweight seventy-year old divorced businessman who loves to post on social media.

The Woman Who Returns to Indiana, Seventy year old **TIFFANY CLAYTON** is a former New York widowed politician who returns home to Indiana after losing an election.

CAST OF CHARACTERS

- **The Tall Guy Who Won't Sit Still, DAVE** is a tall recently divorced forty-year old man who attends Deb's church. He normally sits behind Jim and Deb.
- **The Middle Aged Single Woman, CINDY** sometimes sits behind Dave in the theater and has trouble seeing the screen when he moves.
- **The Defrocked Minister, LES** knows the Bible very well. He used to pastor the church where Deb works before he was fired for falling down in the pulpit when he was drunk during a Christmas Eve service. He stands in the back of the theater and yells at the screen when he sees absurdities.
- **The College Couple Dating, IAN** and **Avery** are freshmen at the local college who meet outside the theater before the first movie and discover they are in the same class on the Old Testament.
- **The Golfer, JOE** is a doctor who drinks and smokes. He often sits with Dave, and plays in a golf group with Rick, Dave, and Jim on Saturday mornings.

Employees of the Theater

The Usher, TEDDY is Deb and Jim's son. He attends Deb's Sunday school classes and works in the theater. Teddy is an all-state wide receiver for Lilly High School who as a naïve freshman, earned the nickname "Splash," when he threw a cooler of Gatorade on the head coach, not knowing you only do this when the team wins.

The Theater Owner, RICK is very wealthy despite still being in his thirties and is still a member of Deb's church, despite being Les's son.

The Ticket Seller, ERICA is a beautiful high school cheerleader who has a crush on Splash. After the box office closes she watches movies with Rick at the back of the theater.

The Popcorn Girl, CHARLOTTE is also a cheerleader and is Erica's best friend. She works in the concession stand. When she has no customers, she looks around the corner into the auditorium and watches the movies. When the stand closes she joins Rick and Erica at the back of the theater. She and Erica occasionally lead cheers during the films.

The Projectionist, JASON passes the plate at Deb's church on Sunday mornings. Occasionally he yells at the screen along with Les, except one time when he fell asleep in the projection booth.

WSOD is a radio and television station that is on and off the air since the days of Noah.

"The Salty Dog," JON COATS is a WSOD radio and television personality who is on and off the air since the days of Noah. He occasionally dies from disasters while on the air.

Deb's Rating Scale

ENTERTAINMENT

★★★★★ Great film
★★★★ Good film
★★★ Just a film
★★ A film you watch to help you sleep
★ A DVD you gift to someone you don't like

ACCURACY

★★★★★ Very accurate even though it may include small errors
★★★★ Accurate but with a few significant errors
★★★ Follows general story line, but has many errors
★★ Doesn't follow story line or has egregious errors
★ A DVD you gift to someone you don't like

Coming Attractions

No Code Sections: An Introduction xvii

I. Talking Snakes: Movies About Adam and Eve

Introduction 3

As Told in:

1. The Bible: In the Beginning 1966. 7
2. The Private Lives of Adam and Eve 1960 11
3. Genesis: The Creation and the Flood 1994. 17
4. What Difference Does It Make?. 23

II. Cloudy With a Chance of Rain: Movies About Noah

Introduction 27

As Told in:

5. The Bible 2013 29
6. Noah 2014. 31
7. Noah's Ark 1999 45
8. What Difference Does it Make?. 53

III. She Ain't Married, She's My Sister: Movies About Abraham

Introduction 57

As Told in:

9. The Bible: In the Beginning 1966......................... 61
10. The Bible 2013 65
11. Abraham 1994 69
12. What Difference Does it Make?........................... 75

IV. Please Pass the Salt: Movies About Sodom and Gomorrah

Introduction 79

As Told in:

13. The Last Days of Sodom and Gomorrah 1962............... 83
14. The Bible 2013 93
15. Noah's Ark 1999 99
16. The Bible: In the Beginning 1966........................ 105
17. What Difference does it Make?.......................... 109

V. Cheaper by the Dozen: Movies About Jacob

Introduction 113

As Told in:

18. Jacob 1994.. 117
19. What Difference Does it Make?.......................... 125

VI. Family Feud: Movies About Joseph

Introduction 131

As Told in:

20. Joseph 1995... 133
21. Joseph and the Amazing Technicolor Dreamcoat 1999...... 139
22. What Difference Does it Make?.......................... 143

VII. Surf's Up: Movies About Moses

Introduction 147

AS TOLD IN:

23. The Ten Commandments 1956 151
24. The Bible 2013 161
25. Exodus, Gods and Kings 2014 167
26. What Difference Does it Make? 177

VIII. Mother-In-Law: Movies About Ruth

Introduction 181

AS TOLD IN:

27. The Story of Ruth 1960 183
28. The Book of Ruth: Journey of Faith 2009 191
29. What Difference Does it Make? 197

IX. Having a Bad Hair Day: Movies About Samson

Introduction 201

AS TOLD IN:

30. Samson and Delilah 1996 203
31. Samson and Delilah 1949 211
32. The Bible 2013 221
33. What Difference Does it Make? 225

X. Skullduggery: Movies About David

Introduction 229

AS TOLD IN:

34. The Bible 2013 233
35. The Story of David 1976 239
36. David and Goliath 1960 243
37. David 1997 251
38. David and Bathsheba 1951 259
39. King David 1985 267
40. What Difference Does it Make? 277

XI. Married with Wives: Movies About Solomon

Introduction 281

As Told in:

41. Solomon 1997. 283
42. Solomon and Sheba 1959 291
43. What Difference Does it Make? 299

XII. Prophecy World: Movies About Daniel

Introduction 303

As Told in:

44. The Book of Daniel 2013. 307
45. The Bible 2013 315
46. What Difference Does it Make? 321

XXIII. Hide and Seek: Movies About Esther

Introduction 325

As Told in:

47. The Book of Esther 2013. 327
48. Esther 1999 333
49. Esther and the King 1960 341
50. One Night with the King 2006 351
51. What Difference Does it Make? 361

XIV. Please Don't Let Me Be Misunderstood: Movies about Jesus

Introduction 365

As Told in:

52. The Jesus Film 1979. 369
53. The Passion of the Christ 2004. 373
54. Jesus Christ Superstar 1973 377
55. Jesus of Nazareth 1977. 383
56. The Greatest Story Ever Told 1965. 395
57. King of Kings 1961. 409

58. Son of God 2014 417
59. Killing Jesus 2015 425
60. What Difference Does it Make? 437

    This is the End: An Epilogue 439
    Why I Wrote Holy Wood 445

HANDOUTS

Part I

Snake in the Grass 451
Where's My Sweater? 452

Part II

Date Setting 455

Part III

Rama Lama Ding Dong 457
Three Day Event 458
It's Déjà Vu All Over Again 459
Leap of Faith 460

Part IV

Don't You (Forget About Me) 463
I'm Proud to be a Sodomite 464

Part V

I will Hate that Strawberry Field Forever 467

Part VI

Three's a crowd 469
Brotherly Love 470

Part VII

Let My People Shoot Fireworks on the Fourth of July 471
Hard Hearted Pharaoh 472
Seven Sisters 472
Westward Ho 473

It's His Party 474
Alternative Facts.. 475

Part VIII

Family Law 479
Four Queens and a King 480

Part IX

Three Little Pigs Find Three Mile Island on the Third Day 481

Part X

One Little Murder and I'm Jack the Ripper..................... 483
Everybody Out For Volleyball!.................................. 484
And the Winner of the Mister Israel contest: Saul!............ 485
"Round and Round" 485

Part XI

"I'm Really Rich!"... 487

Part XII

Ten Card Stud... 489

Part XIII

Hide and Seek... 493
I Hate Those Guys 494
I Can See Clearly Now... 495

Part XIV

Eight Days a Week 497
Happy Birthday to You 497
No Room at the Holiday Inn 500
My Wife Doesn't Understand Me 501
Warning... 503
Alternative Facts Part Deux 503
Palm Saturday... 504

Acknowledgments 507
References 509

No Code Sections

AN INTRODUCTION

"I think we have time to take one more call," as Jon Coats, whose radio name is "The Salty Dog," closes out WSOD's annual tax show. "Terry from Palm Harbor, you are on live with our CPAs, what is your tax question?"

"I don't have a question, I just want to thank you for doing this, and tell you that I look forward to this show every year."

"Well thank you Terry and I also want to thank Phil Scheidt and his CPA friends who have done this show for the past thirty years. Stay tuned for the WSOD Afternoon Show."

As Jon and Phil are saying goodbye in the lobby, Jon asks, "Phil, I hear you're writing a book, is it about income taxes?"

"No, the book I am writing compares films about Bible stories to the actual stories in the Bible."

"Phil, we've known each other for over thirty years, and you know I love you, but to be honest, this sounds like a very boring book."

"Doesn't a show about income taxes sound boring? Every year we do this show and we almost always get calls like the last one today and the phone lines stay completely lit during the entire show. Salty, do you understand why this show is so popular?"

"Obviously it's me."

"No, Salty. The main reason this show has a large following is that I have told the other CPAs on our panel to never quote code sections and do everything they can to make this show as funny and entertaining as possible. I am writing this book using a similar formula of informality and humor. The structure and presentation of this book is possibly different from any book that has ever been written."

"Come on Phil, that's a pretty big claim!"

"Obviously it is. But in terms of structure, have you ever heard of a book that discusses material in the Bible that does not use a single Bible reference or quotation? Not only that, have you ever heard of a review that uses fictional characters to point out errors and absurdities they see in films?"

"No to both questions, but first of all, I never realized you are a Bible scholar, second, how will people know the errors these characters point out are actually errors, and finally, who are these characters you're talking about?"

"Jon, first of all, I am not a scholar, but I do know how to read. Second, the errors the characters point out is backed up with references on the book's website, and finally, these characters include employees of the theater where the movies are being shown, as well as members of the audience, including four couples, a drunken former minister, a talking mule, a talking horse and a single digit handicap golfer."

"You have a talking mule in this book? That's absurd!"

"Absolutely! But you know what else is absurd? One film shows Noah contemplating slitting his twin granddaughters' throats because they are born girls. So my response is to include the use of a few absurdities when writing about Bible movies."

"Are any of the films accurate?"

"A few of them are actually well done, including two musicals. Oh, before I go, I almost forgot to tell you Salty, you also appear in this book."

"Me? You have me in this book?"

"Both you and the station make guest appearances throughout the book, from before the flood of Noah to the time of Christ."

"The station is on the air all this time?"

"Well Salty, not quite. The station gets destroyed and you get killed twice in this book."

"How do I get killed?"

"The first time you get killed is when you get washed away as you are reporting on rising water by a shoreline during the time of Noah, and the second time is when you are a disk jockey in Sodom, playing songs like 'Great Balls of Fire.'"

"What exactly, are you trying to accomplish? Are you trying to make me look like an idiot?"

"Not just you Salty. I occasionally poke fun at both the right and left political spectrums, and I even poke fun at myself. For example, in poking fun at the right, I describe the Pharaoh of Egypt posting his feelings about his encounter with Moses on social media using the moniker, '@makeegyptgreatagain.'"

"My goal is to point out that there are hundreds of errors in these films and do it in a way that will make readers laugh and have fun reading the book, just as I had fun writing it. If I am really successful, a few readers will understand that some of these errors really do matter. I hope they find this boring topic entertaining just like our listeners find our tax show entertaining. Gotta run Salty, I still have some returns I need to finish."

"This does sound like a very different kind of book. Wait! I get killed twice? Do I suffer?"

"Gotta run Salty!"

Talking Snakes

MOVIES ABOUT ADAM AND EVE

An Introduction

AS ADAM AND EVE are packing their animal skins to take with them as they leave the Garden, Adam says, "Eve, hurry up, we have to be out of here by sundown."

"I'm getting ready as fast as I can, Adam."

"Does this leopard skin make me look fat?" She asks.

"Well maybe a little, but we need to get going."

"I probably should wear the sheep skin."

"Whatever! Let's get going."

"Adam, there are four kinds of snakes I hate. Big snakes, little snakes, sticks that look like snakes, and especially, talking snakes."

"Eve, speaking of talking, will you please stop talking so much? If you had done less of that, we would not be leaving the Garden."

"Adam, we don't talk much anymore. Are you seeing somebody else? Do you still love me? You never take me anywhere except to elephant races."

"Eve, not now, we are about to get struck by lightning!"

"Wait, Adam. I think I left the stove on."

"Eve, do you see that guy with the flaming sword? We're being evicted! We have to hurry. You always make me late for everything!"

As they are leaving the Garden, the Cherubim waves the flaming sword, saying, "Get out and stay out! And don't come back thinking you will get your damage deposit returned."

Millenniums later, in the town of Wawasee, Indiana, a series of movies about Bible stories is about to begin. The matinee is always the cheapest way to see a movie, and Ian, a freshman at the Wawasee extension of the state University system, doesn't have much to spend, so this afternoon he is standing at the ticket booth when he sees a pretty girl walking toward the theater.

"So, you're going to follow the professor's advice and watch these Bible films?" he says to her.

"How do you know that?"

"We're in the same 'Old Testament' class; I was sitting in the back row when you walked in yesterday. The professor's suggestion about writing a paper on these films for extra credit is a good idea and easy to do, so here I am. By the way, my name's Ian."

"I'm Avery. So why do you think this would be an easy term paper? Are you some kind of minister?"

"Far from it, but my parents were Bible thumpers and I grew up on stories like . . ."

Before Ian can finish the sentence, a nice looking couple walks into the theater leading a miniature horse and a miniature mule.

"Did you just see what I saw?" Avery asks.

"You saw it too?"

Together they rush to the ticket booth and Avery asks the girl behind the window, "Did a small horse and mule just walk into the theater?"

"I guess you have never been here before. They belong to Jim. He is an animal breeder, and his wife Deb works at the local church. The mule's name is Chester and the horse is named Charley. Do you believe in talking animals?"

"Not really," Ian replies.

"Well you're about to. By the way, my name is Erica. My father Rick is the owner. He built special seating for Charley and Chester because he plays golf with Jim. Teddy, the usher, is Jim's son, and Jason, the projectionist, is Rick's brother."

Ian points to himself, "I'm Ian, and this is Avery. It sounds like we are in a hillbilly movie theater."

Erica laughs at Ian's comment, "Do you have a sense of humor?"

"It looks like we will need one," Ian says as he turns to Avery, "Would you like to sit with me?"

"Sure."

"One more thing," Erica says. "There is a man named Les who once was a minister. He sometimes drinks a little too much in his apartment above the theater and gets a little loud when he comes down to the auditorium, everyone here is used to him."

"This should be quite an experience," Avery says as they walk into the theater.

1

Talking Snakes

As Told in
The Bible; In the Beginning
1966

THE FILM STARTS at creation, with John Huston narrating the creation account in Genesis, as the film shows images that reflect the various stages of Creation week, ending with the creation of Adam and Eve.

Deb and Jim are seated with their animals near the front of the theater. "I like how this begins," Deb says. "These are beautiful images."

God puts Adam and Eve in the Garden of Eden and tells them they can eat any fruit they wish except for the fruit of one tree, warning them that they will die if they eat that fruit. They look at the tree and Adam walks away, but Eve gazes back at it for a few seconds, before she follows Adam.

"That girl has a look about her," Jim says. "This might not end well."

"Eve isn't created rebellious," Deb says. "She is innocent and naïve. It appears she is going to be blamed for what is about to happen."

That evening, they lay down together and God tells them to be fruitful and multiply. Late at night they are asleep under a tree when Eve hears a voice softly calling her.

"Eve." The voice quietly says.

"She hasn't been named yet!" Les yells in the theater. **"How does she know the voice is calling her?"**

"He's right," Ian says, "Eve isn't named until after their encounter with Satan."

"So what do you think Adam calls Eve?" Avery replies.

"Babe, Honey, Sweetheart are possibilities, but if it were me, I would call her 'Avery.'"

"You flirt! We just met twenty minutes ago!"

She wakes up and walks away from where Adam is lying and toward the tree with the forbidden fruit. As she walks through the woods she hears the soft voice again saying, "Eve."

"Hold your horses, I'm coming!" Charley yells.

As Eve approaches the tree, there is movement visible behind the beautiful flowers that cover the tree, but at this point there is no conversation. Meanwhile Adam wakes up and sees that Eve is missing.

"Adam!" Jim jokes. "You better call 911."

"I like the image of the tree," Deb says. "It's beautiful!"

"Maybe we should plant one."

Back at the tree, the audience sees it has only one piece of fruit which appears to be an apple. By this time Eve is standing under the tree.

"Just one apple? Must be a bad crop," Jim says.

"I ate the rest of them," Chester says grinning at Jim.

"The idea that the fruit is an apple is wrong," Ian says. "Whatever it was, it no longer exists."

The serpent talks to Eve and convinces her to eat the fruit; she takes a bite and moans in apparent pleasure just before Adam walks up to the tree and sees Eve, who tells him, "The serpent hath said that we shall not die, that our eyes shall be opened and we shall be as gods. Taste it. There's no harm."

"It is disobedience," Adam says.

"The serpent speaks with forked tongue," Chester jokes.

"It will make us wise," She says, handing him the apple.

"An apple a day keeps the serpent away!" Charley responds. "Take a bite."

Then Adam opens his mouth and bites down on the fruit.

"He is so easily tempted he will probably remove the 'Do not remove' tag from their mattress when they move in their new home," Ian says.

"She doesn't even wash the fruit," Avery comments.

"True, but at least it's organic."

"This is all wrong!" Deb says. "Adam is not asleep during the encounter; he is standing next to Eve the entire time; he never says a word while she does all the talking."

"So, why doesn't he say anything?" Jim asks.

"He's obviously henpecked. Eve is clearly in charge of this family since she does all the talking to the serpent."

God confronts the couple and hears their excuses for disobeying him. When God curses the serpent a shadowy figure falls from the tree and slithers away, appearing as a large snake.

"A snake! Why is he always a snake?" Les yells.

God pronounces curses on the couple, and as thunder rumbles, they run out of the garden to a barren rocky landscape, ending this part of the story.

As they are walking toward their truck which is parked down the street, Deb says, "The film changes what is said when God confronts them for eating the fruit. The first thing Adam does is try to deflect blame from himself by blaming God for giving him the woman."

"Makes sense to me," Jim jokes. "How does he do that?"

"He says to God, 'The woman you gave me gave me the fruit.' So, in other words, Adam is blaming God for giving him Eve."

"So, is the serpent a talking snake?"

"No way! He is an angel. The term 'serpent' is used to describe the angel's character, not his appearance. He is probably very attractive. I imagine if I was single and on a dating site I would answer his post."

"Not if you see my post first, Deb."

"Of course not, Jim," She says as she grabs and pats her husband's hand.

"So, how do you rate this film?"

"It's entertaining, so that deserves a three. But accuracy would only be a two."

2

Talking Snakes

As Told in

The Private Lives of Adam and Eve

1960

THIS FILM FEATURES eight people who end up on a bus traveling to Reno. The film stars Marty Milner as a husband named Ad, who is chasing his wife named Evie, played by Mamie Van Doren, who boards the bus to Reno to get a divorce. Mickey Rooney stars as an arrogant rich man named Nick, who has been through several marriages and is getting on the bus to Reno to get yet another divorce. He is joined by his soon-to-be-divorced current wife, Lil, played by Fay Spain, who wants to save their marriage. There is a teenage girl, played by Tuesday Weld, running away from home and a traveling salesman with a wandering eye who flirts with Weld, who is also on the bus. Paul Anka is a young singer named Pinkie, who starts out driving a car to Reno, but ends up on the bus, and the final person on the bus is the "kindly old bus driver" who narrates the movie.

The last stop the bus makes before reaching Reno is Paradise, Nevada, a small town with only four buildings, which include a casino owned by Nick, a lunch room, and garage owned by Ad and Evie. The bus continues on its trip, but a storm hits California making it dangerous to travel, and because the road gets washed away, they end up in a small church that is near the road.

That evening, Ad and Evie talk and end up falling asleep on a church pew together where they share a dream that takes them back to the Garden of Eden, where they are the original Adam and Eve. In a similar production process to *The Wizard of Oz*, the film changes from black and white to color. The dream starts with a creation account which includes the narrator saying, "And God created love and sex." Followed by, "but the devil in hell sent a spirit of rebellion into the world."

> *"Really? I don't have the Bible memorized, but I know it doesn't say that," Deb says.*

Adam, who is wearing a small brief, is shown waking up in the Garden. He explores the garden and then starts naming the animals he sees.

> *"I'm glad I'm not doing that," Jim says. "I have all kinds of problems remembering names."*

> *"I didn't hear you," Deb says. "You have trouble remembering what?"*

> *"I can't remember."*

> *"So you can't remember what you can't remember."*

> *"This could go on all night," Chester says. "Don't laugh Charley, you'll only encourage them."*

Meanwhile in hell, the devil is surrounded by several beautiful women. The devil, played by Mickey Rooney with horns and wearing a set of red tights, is naming each girl after a day of the week. The two scenes alternate between the Garden of Eden and hell until Lil walks up to Adam while he is naming animals. She flirts with Adam and he names her "Lilith" as the devil and his girlfriends watch from a nearby hill, where the devil is invisibly coaching Lilith on seducing Adam. Lilith attempts to get Adam to eat the forbidden fruit but fails.

> *"Is Lilith in Genesis?" Jim asks.*

> *"Lilith is not mentioned in Genesis but she can be traced back to other sources as a female demon or the first wife of Adam," Deb responds.*

"Picturing the devil living in hell, having horns and a tail, and wearing red tights is hysterical, but totally inaccurate."

"Rooney is great in this role!" Jim says.

The dream sequence continues with the couple in the garden after Eve has been created. Adam now having a surgical scar in his side meets Eve, who has strategically placed long blond hair, standing waist deep in a nearby lagoon. They swim together as they get to know each other.

"So, what's your sign?" Jim jokes, referring to a pickup line in a bar.

"Adam has a surgical scar? Really?" Deb laughs.

"Maybe there was a cosmetic surgical adjustment that compressed the scar into a belly button."

"There would not be a scar if God does the surgery."

The couple spends time together talking, and eating food from the Garden. During that time, Adam warns Eve not to eat the forbidden fruit and then walks off to name more animals, leaving Eve by herself. This leads to the encounter between the devil and Eve who is near the forbidden tree and wants to eat an apple which is shown to be the forbidden fruit.

"Clearly, the forbidden fruit is not on any tree today, or people would be eating it," Deb says.

She continues to explain to Jim, "If that is the case there are millions of trees in existence today growing the forbidden fruit. This stupid idea of it being an apple is probably the reason the lump in your throat is called an 'Adam's apple.'"

"I ate an apple and learned to talk," Charley tells Chester.

"For me, it was the pear in the tree with the partridge in it," Chester responds.

While Eve is holding the apple and talking to herself, Mickey Rooney, still playing the devil, appears wearing a snake suit. This suit features a giant snake head which exposes Rooney's face and includes a tail that wags while he talks to Eve.

"A snake! Why is Mickey Rooney shown as a snake?" Les yells.

Deb and Jim start laughing. "This is hilarious!" Jim says.

"You think it's funny having a tail?" Chester says. "Try it some time, especially when you are sitting down."

Mickey tells Eve it is okay to eat the fruit, so she does. Meanwhile, a thunderbolt alarms Adam and he goes looking for Eve.

"Here's another movie that shows this scene wrong," Deb comments. "Once again, the film doesn't show Adam next to Eve."

Once he finds her, he takes a bite of the apple, and the movie switches from color back to black and white.

"Jim knows better, but I need to explain to you and Charley that this scene is really wrong," Deb pats Chester's head.

"I know," Charley says. "Who in the world would believe a snake can talk? Snakes can't talk."

"Yeah!" Chester agrees. "Other than parrots, we're the only animals that can talk."

"No, what I want to point out is that the devil does not appear as a snake."

The film continues with them in their new home outside of the garden, which is in a cave where they are trying to make a fire. When the fire makes smoke, Adam stands up coughing and he bumps his head on the ceiling of the cave. A hole in the ceiling is the result, and mud falls down covering his head and body. Eve laughs and tells Adam that he has invented a chimney and that he is all muddy.

"This is interesting," Deb says. "The root of the Hebrew word for Adam can be red or earth. So the name 'Adam' can literally be red mud, with which he is covered. The producers do a good job with this."

Eve has Adam moving around large rocks which is their furniture when she gets Adam to admit he feels Eve is responsible for them now living in a cave. She cries, but they kiss and make up, and Adam calls her Eve for the first time. The film continues by showing they still have arguments.

"Adam calls the woman Eve just before they leave the garden," Deb says.

The dream flashback continues as it shows Lilith causing marital problems for Adam and Eve, but the problems end with the couple embracing and the dream sequence ends.

Ad and Evie wake up the next morning and realize they both had the same dream. They agree to reconcile and to read the Bible together. Along with the six other people, they walk out of the church and the film ends.

As they leave the theater Deb tells the others. "This film is tongue in cheek, and obviously not meant to present the story accurately, but it is fun to watch."

"Especially Van Doren," Jim says.

"Jim, how would you feel if I look at a Tom Cruise movie and check him out?" Deb reminds Jim. "Fairs fair."

"While you get to see me the first thing every morning?" Thinking about what he just said, Jim adds, "Never mind, sorry Deb. In the meantime, how do you rate this film?"

"I love the film and give it a five for entertainment, but I have to give it a one for accuracy."

3

Talking Snakes

As Told in

Genesis: The Creation and the Flood

1994 TELEVISION MOVIE

CHARLOTTE IS MAKING another batch of popcorn when her uncle Joe walks into the lobby with Dave.

"Hi, Uncle Joe. Did you guys have a good golf weekend?"

"We sure did. I had a hole in one! We played twenty-seven holes on Saturday, so it was a great weekend, but Honey, I'm still exhausted from that five-hour drive."

"Well, enjoy the film, I've heard it's relaxing."

This Italian film, narrated by Paul Scofield, and music composed and directed by Ennio Morricone, begins with a child telling his mother he is afraid of the dark. There is the sound of wind, and as the camera stops focusing on the child's face, it shows that the scene is in a tent. The child asks what the new day will bring, and an old man, also in this large tent, wakes up and tells the child that "No one can know what is still hidden."

The old man, the child's grandfather, who is obviously Middle Eastern, talks to the boy and starts telling the story of creation.

As he tells the story, the sounds of soft flute music and sheep baaing is played in the background, while the movie shows scenes of the successive creation days. The soundtrack is now accompanied by the sounds of a Middle Eastern woman chanting.

> "There's not much action so far," Jim says. "I'm getting a little bored."

Various images of the Bedouin camp and surrounding areas are shown, still accompanied by soft music, as the tribesman begin their move across the wilderness. A cobra raises its head, apparently watching the Bedouins on their journey.

> **"A snake! Why is Satan always a snake?"** Les yells.
>
> *Ian stretches, raising his arms, "This movie is very relaxing." He then lowers his arms, with one now behind Avery who is sitting next to him.*

The film shows tranquil scenes which include someone's hand picking raspberries, and a child asleep at the base of a tree.

> *"Deb, I feel like I am going to join that kid in a nap," Jim says.*

After a few minutes of these scenes, the narration continues to quote Genesis, reciting how the first man is put in a garden, and told not to eat the forbidden fruit because he will then know what is good and what is evil, and that gaining that knowledge will kill him.

> *Jim yawns and turns to Deb, "Speaking of knowledge killing Adam, that Hitchcock film, 'The Man Who Knew Too Much' is on the late show tonight. But I doubt I can stay awake for it after watching this."*
>
> *"I agree, I'm really having trouble keeping my eyes open. By the way, the Bedouin misquotes that passage. The knowledge doesn't kill. Notice Eve doesn't change until Adam eats the fruit."*

It's still dark in the campsite, just before daylight. A child says, "So many stars." And one of the men says, "Look, that one is Ishtar. It is the star of the morning."

"Remember, our professor just talked about this today," Ian says to Avery. "Christ is the morning star, commonly known as Venus, while Ishtar is a Babylonian fertility goddess. Each of the main planets and some of the constellations have biblical meanings."

"Isn't that Astrology?" She asks, and then yawns.

"No, astrology is a corruption of Biblical astronomy. But I don't agree with using the name of a Babylonian goddess for the planet that represents Christ."

Scenes at the campfire continue to the sound of a flute, as the old man continues to recite Genesis, while images of that story continue.

Joe is an avid golfer. Now that he no longer plays football, he eats, breathes, and sleeps golf. Sleeping golf can be a problem for Joe because he suffers from narcolepsy, and sometimes he has sleepwalking episodes during what he calls, "golf nightmares." He is now fast asleep in the movie theater and dreaming he is on the first tee box of the course where he plays golf.

In his dream, he places the ball on a worn out wooden tee, but it won't stay on the tee and falls off. This happens repeatedly as other foursomes start lining up behind his group waiting their turn to tee off. After a dozen attempts, the ball not only falls off the tee, but it rolls over a six-foot retaining wall at the front of the tee box and then into a ravine.

As the dream continues he walks around to the front of the retaining wall, and looks back, seeing dozens of men patiently waiting for him to tee off. When he climbs down into the ditch in front of the tee box, he trips, falling on his face, and he is now laying in hundreds of white golf balls, some of which are now bouncing and pelting him in his face. He can't tell which ball is his.

Erica runs into the lobby when she hears, Charlotte scream, "Uncle Joe, are you all right?" Erica looks down at Joe who has sleepwalked into the popcorn machine at the concession stand, knocking it over, and spilling popcorn all over the floor of the lobby while the popcorn maker, despite laying on the floor, is still spitting out kernels of fresh popcorn straight into Joe's face.

Rick and Dave see Joe walking through the theater and immediately recognize what is happening and run to stop him, but they are too late. They arrive at the stand in time to see Joe waking up and wiping popcorn oil off his face and groaning. Rick smiles and looks down, "Have a nice nap?"

They help him up, and after cleaning up the mess, they take him to the coffee shop next door.

Adam and Eve are also asleep, but then Eve gets up and walks away, waking Adam. The only sound heard by the theater audience is the grandfather reciting the account of the woman and the serpent. Adam follows Eve, but there is no depiction of the encounter or of them eating the forbidden fruit, neither is there any conversation heard between them.

"They need to get marriage counseling so they can learn to communicate with each other like we do!" Chester jokes to Charley.

"How can the film leave out eating the fruit?" Deb asks.

"That fruit must be out of season in the middle east," Jim sits up having almost dozed off. "What was that noise in the lobby? Where's Joe?"

As the grandfather speaks, the scene switches back to a campfire where he is now talking to the entire tribe. The grandfather continues the account and quotes Adam saying, "The woman gave me that fruit and I ate some of it. And now, now I know fear. I am alone. Now I know good and evil."

"Well?" Jim looks at Deb. "Does Adam say any of this?"

"This is misquoted badly," she responds. "He never mentions being alone and knowing good and evil."

While the grandfather recites the curses on the first couple, the scene switches to the next morning when the tribe is moving camp again, fighting a strong wind. The old man then recites the verses describing Adam and Eve being expelled from the garden, ending that part of the film.

In the theater, the film ends in a different way. Up in the projection booth, Jason is waiting for the black dot to appear on the screen, signaling the end of that roll of film, but he misses both the first and second dot because he has fallen asleep. The audience sees the screen turn bright white to the sound of film flapping in the projection booth. Everyone looks back at the booth and sees Jason passed out on the window ledge that opens into the theater.

Rick goes running up, thinking Jason has had a heart attack. "Jason, are you okay?"

"Sorry Rick, I just had trouble keeping my eyes open while watching this movie. Guess I fell asleep."

A few other people are also dozing off until Charley shouts, **"I have a headache Jim!"**

"You had to put in parrot DNA," Deb says. "Who knows what else he might say?"

As they leave the theater, Deb says, "I'm not sure what version of Genesis we heard, but it is different from any version I ever read."

"In what way?" *Jim asks.*

Before she can respond, Teddy, who is walking to the truck with them says, "The film omits the encounter between Eve and the Serpent."

"That's right Teddy," *Deb says.* "Several of the verses recited in the film leave out or change important information. For example, the film leaves out the words 'you gave to me' referring to Eve. The film also leaves out the words 'because you listened to your wife' which is the first reason Adam is cursed."

She continues, "Singular and plural pronouns are changed which have significance. You will strike 'their' heel is recited instead of 'his' heal and become like 'me' instead of like 'one of us' are among the changes in this film."

"Anything else?" *Jim asks.*

"Yes," Deb says, sliding into the seat. "The curse on the serpent implies the ultimate defeat of the serpent will be an ongoing process rather than a single event."

"So Deb, what are your ratings?"

"I give it a three for entertainment based on the beautiful scenery and music, but I can only give it a two for accuracy. I'm sleepy. I can't wait to get home and fall asleep while you rub my feet."

Jim yawns, "Me too. Can you drive?"

4

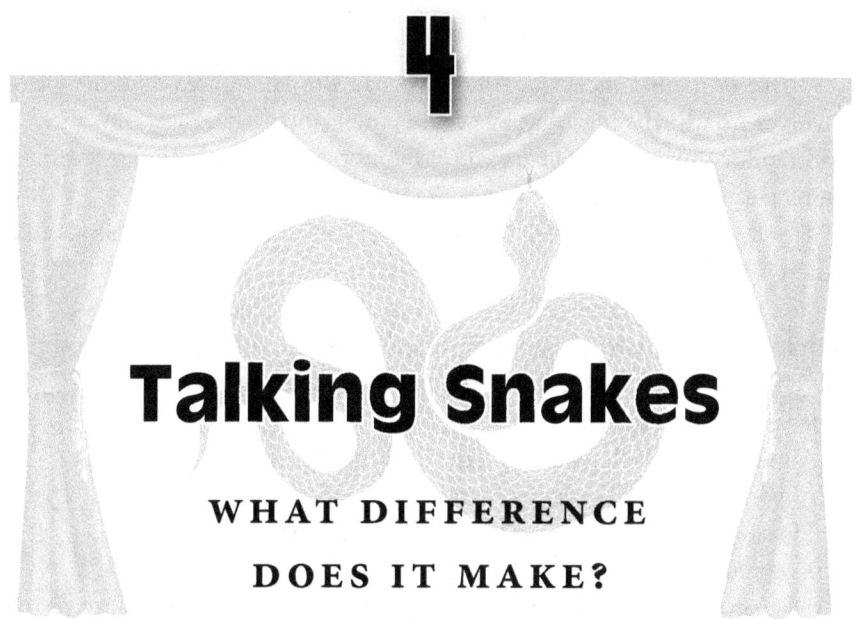

Talking Snakes

WHAT DIFFERENCE DOES IT MAKE?

THE FOLLOWING SUNDAY, Deb is leading her Sunday school class.

"We have a new attendee today in our class. Avery, would you care to introduce yourself."

"Hi, my name's Avery. I am from Temple Terrace, which is in Florida. I am in my first year at the college. Ian invited me to come today."

"Hi Avery," everyone responds.

Deb starts the class by describing what they watched in the films about the story of Adam and Eve, and the differences they see from the Bible stories. "Does it make any difference? Does anyone have a problem with the way Eve is presented when she talks to the serpent?"

Jason raises his hand, "It seems everyone thinks that the downfall of man is Eve's fault. There are a few words in the passage that seem to go right over the heads of almost everybody who has ever read this account. Adam is standing right next to her the whole time! He is more responsible than Eve for their expulsion from the garden by not speaking up and taking charge of the situation. This misunderstanding is obviously the result of how paintings and movies distort the image of this encounter."

"This is a pervasive concept. Our minister wasn't even aware of this when I told him," Deb tells the class. "That's good Jason. Don't stop."

"There is a misconception that Eve has the encounter and then she involves Adam. The idea that Eve causes their downfall has given women a bad rap for thousands of years and no doubt has resulted in many women being treated very badly."

"He should tell the serpent to take a hike," a woman says. "It sounds like Adam is a wimp."

"You're right," Deb says. "I'll be giving out a handout that discusses the implication of Adam being right there with Eve during that encounter. Let's move on. I want you to have some fun with a one question quiz. Class, please describe a pencil."

A man says, "Well, it's about five to six inches long."

A woman adds, "It's made of wood."

Ian says, "It has a metal tip that holds an eraser."

Avery adds, "It has a pointed end with dark grey material."

Deb says, "I have asked this question many times and you all gave me the response I have always received. However, if an ancient rabbi were to be asked to describe a pencil, the response would be, 'It is something you write with.' Brad Scott uses this example in a video called 'Esau and the Tares.'"

"The Genesis scroll is originally written in Hebrew by men who think like ancient Hebrews as opposed to writers who think like people today in our western civilization. There is a big difference. There would be no description of its appearance. Hebrew thinking emphasizes function over form. Once you understand that concept, you will understand that the term 'serpent' is not describing the appearance of Satan, but it is describing his function or character."

"Are you saying the serpent is not a snake?" A woman asks.

Jesus is described as, "The lion of Judah," Deb responds. "Does that mean he looks like a lion? Many times in the Bible an animal is a metaphor, I believe this is an example of that. You should now understand that you do not need to believe in talking snakes in order to believe the story in Genesis." Deb concludes by telling the class this concept is also discussed in today's handouts.

"Great job Deb," a man says as they walk out of the classroom toward the sanctuary. "I never had a response to people who tell me they can't believe a snake talks."

part II
Cloudy with a Chance of Rain

MOVIES ABOUT NOAH

An Introduction

"GOOD MORNING! This is your WSOD Morning Show, and I am your host, Handsome Harry. With me in the studio this morning is Blonde Barb. Our weatherman, The Salty Dog, and Buxom Betty are out on assignment, so we will check in with them later."

"We have two main stories to bring you this morning. Everyone knows that Noah has been building a giant vessel he calls an ark for many years, in fact, for many decades. Well, somehow he managed to get animals to come to the construction site a few weeks ago and the people of the nearby towns were astounded to see all these creatures gathering at his ark."

"It was quite a show!" Barb says. "I was there last week and saw animals I didn't even know existed. I even saw squirrels eating bird food. What's that all about?"

"Well Barb, things have changed out at the ark. For the last several days Noah and all the animals are nowhere to be seen. It appears they are all in the ark, but we can't verify that. We have our reporter, Clark, with a crew out at the ark. Clark, can you tell us what's going on?"

"It just started raining, but other than that, absolutely nothing, Harry. As you know we knocked on the door yesterday and asked if Noah would come out and talk to us, but the only thing we heard were the words, 'No comment!' and what sounded like a chimpanzee laughing."

"I can tell you Harry, a crowd is starting to gather here and unlike previous crowds, no one is laughing. This rainstorm has suddenly become violent, and I don't even know if the road will be open to return to the studio because of reports of street flooding we are hearing. I think people in this crowd are taking Noah's warning seriously."

"Well Clark, you and your crew be careful. We will get back to you shortly."

Back at the studio, Sam says, "With all this rain, you know someone has to be having a hurricane party. Let's join Betty at a party on the bank of the Euphrates."

"Hi Betty. With this storm, I understand why you guys didn't come in to the studio. How's the party?"

"Everyone's having a great time! They all had a little too much to drink last night, but the bottles are not empty yet, so they are still going at it. We can see the Salty Dog and the weather crew across the river. I feel sorry for the Dog being out in this!"

A drunken voice behind Betty yells, **"Let's go water skiing!"**

"Well, you guys have a great time. Speaking of rain, it's time for our WSOD weather. Let's go out to Salty who's on the other side of the Euphrates River."

Salty is standing in strong wind gusts, struggling to stay upright while he is knee deep in water.

"Hey Dog, you told us three days ago this would be a cloudy day with a 10 percent chance of rain. What happened?"

A house that can be seen across the river, behind Salty, suddenly gets washed away, while a voice can be heard shouting, **"Let's party! We need more beer!"**

"Was that Betty I just saw floating in the water?" Barb asks.

"She'll be fine, she was an Olympic swimmer," Harry comments.

"Salty, did I just see building material fly behind you in that wind? You need to get out of there!"

"I can't Harry. The entire crew was washed away three minutes ago, and I now have a tripod set up to automatically film myself. I'm surrounded by water, so there is nowhere to go. These winds are really getting high and now the water is waist deep."

"Salty, duck!" Harry yells out as a trashcan flies by, just missing his head.

The last thing the viewing audience sees is a surfer on a large wave, which washes the Salty Dog away just before the screen goes blank.

A husband is watching the show when his wife yells to him that water is coming in under the kitchen door. "Put a towel under it!" he shouts. As he is watching the report, the last thing he hears Harry say, before the television shorts out is, "Do you think Noah was right?"

5

Cloudy With a Chance of Rain

As Told In
The Bible
2013 TELEVISION MINI SERIES

THUNDER AND LIGHTNING are heard and seen at night as the ark floats on turbulent seas beginning this television series. Noah recites the six-day creation account to his frightened family inside the ark. While he tells his family that Adam and Eve disobeyed God, a snake is shown watching Eve remove fruit from a tree.

"A snake! Why is he always a snake?" Les yells.

After reciting those events Noah walks out on the deck and looks out over the water and a rainbow is shown as this part of the introduction ends, and the narrator introduces the series.

"The special effects of the flood are well done," Deb says. *"I'm looking forward to seeing the series, but I already saw two errors."*

"Obviously, showing a snake as Satan is one," Jim says. *"What's the other?"*

"The film shows a rainbow over an empty ocean. The rainbow doesn't appear until after the ark lands."

"I guess that's why leprechauns don't survive the flood. The rainbow appears too early and drowns them," Jim jokes.

"Why would a rainbow drown lepers?"

"I said 'leprechauns.' It's because their pot of gold is at the bottom of the ocean."

"It's too bad the series doesn't spend more time on Noah," Dave says. "I like how they show how afraid the family is inside the ark. Deb, how do you rate this?"

"My rating for this opening scene is accuracy three and entertainment five."

6

Cloudy With a Chance of Rain

As Told in
Noah
2014

THE WORDS, "In the beginning there was nothing" appear on the screen in this film about Noah as it starts.

"*This doesn't start out well!*" Deb says. "*There is no mention of God.*"

The first image is that of a green snake, followed by the words, "Temptation led to sin," and then an image is shown of a hand picking a piece of fruit off a tree.

"*A snake! Why is he always a snake?*" Les yells.

"*It's in the snake's union contract!*" Dave yells. "*They can't have a non-snake play Satan.*"

"*They must have a powerful union,*" Jim says.

The audience is told that Cain is sheltered by a band of fallen angels, called "The Watchers," after he kills Abel and flees to the East. Cain's descendents become an evil civilization that fills the entire earth. Meanwhile, Noah is the last in a line of descendents from Seth, who defend and protect what is left of creation.

> "Fallen angels could not have supported Cain because they were in a spiritual prison," Deb says.

> "Some of them might have gotten out on parole," Dave says.

> "Another problem with this is that Adam and Eve have many children, it is very unlikely the only people alive are the descendents of Cain," Deb says as she laughs.

Noah is a child when his father is killed by evil men who want his land. Noah escapes and now is grown with sons of his own. He is with Ham and Shem when he finds an animal that is dying from a wound inflicted by men who hunt animals for food.

> "Most likely, all people were vegetarians before the flood," Deb says.

> "So they would not 'm-e-a-t' together?" Jim jokes.

The hunters attack Noah, but he kills them and returns to his wife, who is caring for their third son, a boy named "Japheth." That night he has a nightmare that everyone is under water, drowning, and realizes the world is going to be destroyed by water.

> "God tells Noah what he is going to do," Deb says, "He doesn't give Noah a dream for him to interpret. The film is also showing Japheth as a boy when he is actually married before the flood."

> "Maybe he is married to a cougar," Jim says. "She might be thirty years old and is too busy doing laundry to appear in the film."

The next day, Noah takes his family to see his grandfather, Methuselah. They travel through a world that is an ecological wilderness, with only the dead stumps of trees remaining.

> "I like how they do this scene," Deb says. "While I believe trees existed, it shows a good visual of a corrupted and doomed planet."

They find a wounded young girl named Ila and, together, they flee from a group of men, who chase Noah and his family into a valley.

"I guess Ila must become a daughter-in-law of Noah," Deb says. "But she would have been so before Noah was told about the flood."

In the valley they encounter and talk to large creatures called "watchers," who look like they are made of rock. One of the watchers tells Noah they fear men, who try to kill them and explains the Creator formed them on the second day.

"Talking rocks?" Dave shouts. ***"That's realistic!"***

"They're just stoned," Jim jokes.

"Who, Noah and his family?"

"No, the fallen angels. They must have gotten high to counter the fear that men would disassemble them, sell their parts for pet rocks, and skip the remaining stones across the Pacific."

"Maybe they were afraid they would be buried up to their waist on some island out there," Chester joins in.

"Some of them did end up on Easter Island," Charley responds, "but their arms are hanging from the roof of Mammoth Cave in Kentucky."

"I think the top of those Easter Island heads were used for Lazy Susans," Jim chuckles. "None of them have foreheads."

They were not originally stone beings, but were angels made of light. They pitied Adam and Eve and watched over them after they sinned, and tried to help them. But the Creator punished the angels for interfering and turned them into stone beings that could talk. Having that ability, they taught mankind all they knew of creation.

"So how much can a rock remember?" Chester asks.

"It depends on the size of its hard drive," Charley responds.

"I guess they are supposed to be the Nephilim," Deb says. "The whole idea that fallen angels help Adam survive as opposed to God is horrible. It's basically saying that demons nurture the first family and get punished by God for doing so."

"Are these angels supposed to be the giants?" Jim asks.

"Baseball or football?" Dave asks.

"No," Deb says, "the giants that show up in the Bible."

"You mean those teams are named after the Nephilim?" Dave jokes.

"In this movie, it appears the rock men are giants, but the actual giants are not angels, they are descendents of human mothers."

"Who are the fathers?"

"Some people believe the fathers are angels and other people believe they are powerful human leaders. What matters is the Nephilim are not angels."

A watcher guides Noah on their trip and tells him that the men of that age hunted and killed the watchers, except those who were protected by Methuselah, who is armed with a flaming sword that is capable of incinerating evil men when he stabs it into the ground. The watchers begged the Creator to take them home, but they only received silence as a response.

"So, Methuselah protects fallen angels?" Les yells.

"Let me get this straight," Dave says. "The fallen angels are actually repentant and God ignores their repentance. That's nonsense."

"Also," Deb adds, "this film does not describe how the fallen angels follow Satan in their rebellion against God. Clearly fallen angels are portrayed here as nice guys."

Noah arrives at the mountain where his grandfather lives and they drink tea, giving Noah a vision of animals rising from beneath the water to the surface where a vessel is on top of the water. After that, Methuselah gives Noah a seed from the original Garden of Eden.

"So," Les yells, "Noah gets the idea to put the animals on the boat because of tea Methuselah makes?"

"This was the first Tea Party!" Dave yells back.

"But I think there was a little more than tea in that drink!" Jim shouts.

> "The Bible says nothing about Methuselah, so this is contrived," Deb says. "God tells Noah to save the animals."

Noah returns to his family with the watcher, who is still with them, and tells them the world will be destroyed, but his family has been chosen to save the innocent, referring to the animals on Earth.

> "Saving the animals was not the primary purpose of the ark," Deb says. "It was to save Noah."

Noah plants the seed Methuselah gives him and when he wakes up the next morning, watchers arrive who seize the watcher who has been helping Noah. Noah asks the other watchers to help him, but they refuse until water bubbles to the surface forming four streams which spread out over the land. Plants immediately appear and become a forest of trees.

> "This is another fictional scene," Deb says. "But, it does show how rivers might have flowed in the original garden, so it's great imagery. However, Noah never asks fallen angels to help build the ark."

The streams continue to flow across the wilderness, attracting birds to the water, which follow the streams of water to their source where the watchers are now helping Noah build the ark.

> "It is possible that Noah hires workers to help build the ark," Deb says, "but angels turned into stone men certainly don't."

> "Maybe the stone men are non-union labor," Jim jokes.

Noah and his wife burn a small amount of plants that emit smoke that puts the birds to sleep as they settle in their cages in the ark that is being built. Snakes are next to arrive, slithering across the landscape in a great multitude.

> **"Hey Les!"** Dave yells, **"Check out all the snakes! Maybe they are Satan's kids."**

> **"If all the birds are asleep, then where will they later get the raven and the dove?"** Les yells back.

> **"They get them from Rent-a-Bird!"** Dave shouts.

Noah and his family encounter a tribe of people led by a man named Tubal Cain. When they threaten Noah and try to force Ham to become a soldier for them, the watchers make it clear they will protect Noah and his family.

> "Noah is never threatened while he builds the ark, at least according to the story," Deb says. "It is possible he preaches to the people of that time for one hundred and twenty years, but there is nothing said about a man named 'Tubal' who tries to draft Ham."

> "I wonder if Noah passes the plate at each service," Jim jokes. "Maybe they want their money back after one hundred and twenty years."

Tubal starts making weapons and gathering an army so they can crush the watchers which he calls 'giants.'

> "As I said earlier, the 'giants' are another name for the Nephilim," Deb says. "The word, 'watchers' is not used in the flood narrative."

Right after he mentions the word 'giants,' a herd of animals journey near their camp, frightening the people in the clan, as hundreds of animals migrate to the ark. When the animals arrive, they climb into the ark and then fall asleep.

> "The animals are awake during the flood," Deb says. "God tells Noah to store food for them."

> "Chester!" Charley says, "I don't see any mules in that group. How did you get here?"

> "Connections," he answers. "Literally, as there would have been horses and donkeys on the ark!"

Ham and Japheth need wives, so Noah visits the nearby town and finds a brutal violent civilization that has degenerated into cannibalism. He returns without girls for his sons, and Ham gets very upset.

"All three sons have wives before the flood!" Les yells.

"I do like how they show the violence of that era," Deb says.

Noah tells his wife that he, she and their sons are all wicked, so once the ark is built, they will die along with everyone else.

"Speak for yourself, Noah!" Dave yells.

"This is completely false!" Deb says. *"Noah is righteous! He never says anything like that!"*

Ham runs off into the forest, and Ila follows him, while Noah's wife visits Methuselah. She tells Methuselah that Ila is barren and the other two boys do not have wives, so there will be no one left to repopulate the world.

"Again, the film is showing two of the sons not having wives," Deb says. *"And, once again, Methuselah is never mentioned in the story."*

Meanwhile Ham is now in the city where he falls into a pit. As he looks around at the skulls and dead bodies, he meets a girl named Na'el, and gives her food. He takes the girl back toward the ark, but she gets ensnared in a trap that Ham cannot open.

"Ham actually has a wife at that time, and she would really get mad if he shows up at the ark with Na'el," Dave says. *"My ex once accused me of bringing another woman to our house."*

"So, did you?" Jim asks.

"No, I never even thought about it. After spending ten years with my ex, the last thing I needed was more drama."

As Ila walks through the woods, she encounters Methuselah, who is on his knees collecting berries. He blesses her by touching her stomach and all of a sudden, a strong breeze occurs, which apparently ends her condition of being barren. Shem calls to her, and she runs to him and passionately kisses him as they embrace.

"Apparently, the film is indicating that Methuselah dies in the flood," Deb says. *"It is most likely that Methuselah dies shortly before the flood begins. It is unlikely he has mystical powers to make a girl fertile. It's also unlikely that Ila becomes pregnant at the beginning of the flood since they will be on the ark over a year and there are no babies born on the ark."*

Back at the ark, as Noah shuts the door to the ark, he sees gathering clouds.

"The ark is shown with its door in the front. It is actually in the side," Deb says.

"The side is the emergency exit," Jim jokes. "Airbags shoot out as it crashes in the sea."

A raindrop falls on Noah's face. Tubal also sees the rain and addresses his people, telling them they will kill Noah and the giants, and take the ark for themselves.

"Noah and his family are in the ark for seven days before the rain starts," Deb says.

Before the townspeople reach the ark, Noah sees Ham and the girl, but cannot help Ham free her from the trap, so he tells Ham to leave her.

"Ham is in the ark with his wife when it begins to rain," Deb says.

"Noah must be hamstrung," Jim chuckles.

The people of the city attack the ark and the giants fight them off, but Tubal kills one of the giants with what looks like a mortar shell blown to the stomach and then sticks a spear into the dying rock man.

"Are you telling me they have some form of gunpowder before the flood?" Les yells.

The giant dies and is then taken to heaven in a bright light. As the other giants fight and kill the attackers, they too are killed and taken to heaven. While Noah repels invaders, Tubal sneaks on the ark.

"There is no battle at the ark!" Les yells. **"Noah is sealed inside!"**

"Hey Tubal!" Dave yells. **"You're on standby, you have to wait to get on board."**

"I can't believe someone from the town gets on the ark!" Jason yells from the projection booth.

"The angels that rebel don't get taken back to heaven," Deb says. "To this day they are still in prison."

Giant geysers erupt around the ark, killing the attackers and Methuselah, who is eating a berry he just found in the forest.

"I like the way they show the geysers," Deb says. "Many people think the earth is flooded just by rain, but part of the flood is from underground water."

Waves break over the ark and almost wash Noah away as he is hanging out the front gate of the ark, holding onto a rope, but he makes it inside the ark and when things calm down, and the screams of people outside the ark are heard no more, Noah tells his family the creation story.

"I'm telling ya, Noah is inside the ark for seven days before the flood starts!" Les yells.

Noah then tells his family that mankind will end since Noah assumes Ila is barren. At this point in the film the only people in the ark are Noah, his wife, their three sons and Ila, plus, hidden in the bowels of the ark, Tubal, who is being helped by Ham since Ham feels Noah let Na'el die.

"There are eight people on the ark!" Les yells.

"OK!" Jim says. "That makes seven. We're getting close to eight."

Ila is not feeling well. When Noah's wife makes her some herbal tea, she discovers that Ila is pregnant, so Noah's wife, Shem, and Ila go to Noah and tell him the good news. He immediately says that is impossible because she is barren. Ila explains to Noah that she went to Methuselah, and Noah figures out that his grandfather helped her to conceive.

"Another Tea Party!" Jim jokes.

"Maybe Methuselah advised her that if she wants to get pregnant maybe they should try having sex," Dave jokes. "That's what I told my ex."

"At least you are not paying child support," Jim says.

"My ex said she did not believe in having sex before marriage," Dave says. "I didn't know until it was too late that she didn't believe in having sex during marriage either."

"No one gets pregnant on the ark," Deb interrupts.

Noah becomes furious! "Have you any idea what you've done?" He screams in her face. "Do you know what this forces me to do?" He then walks off in a rage and prays, telling God that he will not fail him. As his family walks out to him, Noah tells them if the child is a girl, she must die, and he will personally kill her at birth.

> *"If my former father-in-law killed his daughter,"* Dave jokes, *"I wouldn't be shelling out $2,000 a month in alimony."*

> *"Noah is righteous,"* Deb says. *"He would never murder an innocent baby!"*

A bird flies to the ark with no mud on its feet, indicating there is no land anywhere. In order to protect their baby from Noah, Ila and Shem have built a raft they will use to escape from the ark, but Noah's wife tries to talk them out of leaving, saying they will run out of food and water. She says they should wait and then send out another bird.

> **"Hey Mrs. Noah!"** Les yells, **"The entire world is covered with fresh water!"**

> **"But it's not bottled water,"** Dave yells back.

> *"They do not try to build a life raft to try to escape from Noah!"* Deb says.

Ila says they will wait no longer, as she sees Noah walking around on the ark. What she cannot see going on deep in the ark, is Ham talking with Tubal, telling him that he must help him kill his father. When Ham hesitates, Tubal takes out a knife and violently slits the throat of one of the sleeping animals.

> *"That must have been a unicorn,"* Dave jokes. *"That's why there are none of them around today. Just the floating bodies of dead leprechauns."*

> *"The film says there are two of each animal in the ark,"* Deb says, *"This is wrong, there are either seven or fourteen of all clean animals, and none of them die on the ark."*

> *"Why so many?"* Jim asks.

"They will need clean animals to eat and sacrifice. Also, there is not anything to support the idea Ham would ever think about killing Noah," Deb says.

As Shem is ready to set sail, Noah appears on an upper deck and throws some material that ignites their raft in flames, and then he cuts the rope to the raft, ending his son's plan to leave the ark. Noah is convinced it is his job to make sure every living human on earth dies.

"Noah never would think that," Deb says. "Noah is the only righteous man on the planet."

Ham yells to his father that the animals are awake and eating each other, and then he leads Noah to a spot where Tubal waits to kill him. As Ila screams from delivery pain, Noah and Tubal fight in the bowels of the ark. Ila delivers twin sisters. Shem says he will protect his daughters so now there are three people on the ark that want to kill Noah.

"None of the wives have a baby while they are on the ark," Deb says. "Plus, nobody on board wants to kill Noah!"

The ark shakes violently as it crashes into the top of a submerged mountaintop, interrupting the fight. After Tubal falls to the floor, Noah approaches him to finish him off when Shem hits his father from behind.

"*What?*" Les screams. "**Shem hits Noah?**"

Tubal hits Shem, saying, "He's mine," but before he can kill Noah, Ham stabs Tubal in the back.

"Total fiction," Deb says, "There is no one on the ark other than Noah and his family."

Noah, with a knife in his hand, hears the crying babies, goes up to the deck and sees Ila holding her twin girls, and menacingly walks toward her.

"*Hey Noah!*" Chester yells. "**Aren't you supposed to be hiding in a closet waiting for them to open the door?**"

"**I thought he would be waiting in the toilet stall!**" Charley yells.

"If he's going to be a murderer, he needs a more exotic weapon," Chester shouts. *"Maybe he should hit the babies over the head with an accountant's calculator."*

"Or an abacus!" Charley yells.

"Noah needs some kind of mask!" Dave joins in. *"Maybe a brown grocery bag with the numbers 0 dash 16 written above the eyeholes like some football fans wear!"*

Before Noah can kill the girls, Ila begs him not to slice their throats while they are still crying. He allows her to comfort them as his wife walks up on the deck of the ark. The babies are now asleep, so Noah raises his knife to kill them, but as he lowers the knife, he kisses them instead, and walks away, sparing the girls.

"Those baby girls were never on the ark!" Les yells.

"Right!" Dave yells back. *"It they were, God would have told Noah to pack diapers!"*

A dove returns to the ark with an olive branch.

"The first and third dove trips are missing," Deb says.

Later, when the waters have receded, Noah picks some grapes, makes wine, gets drunk, and passes out on the beach naked. Ham walks around an outcrop on the beach and discovers him lying face down, and Shem and Japheth walk around and see their father too. Shem and Japheth cover their father, but Ham watches from a few yards away and is contemptuous of his dad.

"It doesn't happen this way," Deb says. *"Ham actually goes to his brothers and tells his brothers about their father. Also, none of this happens on a beach."*

Ham decides to leave and says goodbye to Ila, telling her he is glad everything is beginning with her.

"This totally changes the genealogy of the three sons," Deb says. *"Each of the sons already has a wife. They won't marry their nieces."*

As Ham walks away, Noah walks over to Ila, who is sitting on the beach, and she comments that even though Noah is now separated from his family because of what happened on the ark, in the end he showed love and mercy.

"At least Noah's not paying alimony!" Dave yells.

"Noah never gets separated from his family," Deb says.

As the survivors start over by farming, in the distance remnants of the flood can be seen in the plains below, while scenes of animals nurturing their newborn are shown.

"I like the imagery in this scene," Deb says. "It conveys the hope of a new beginning."

Noah's wife is digging in the dirt when Noah walks up to her, and she ignores him. He touches her hand, kisses her head, they embrace and make up.

"For three hundred and fifty years you're going to hear about this Noah!" Dave jokes loudly. "Every time you argue, she's going to say, 'Well, you were going to slit our grandbabies' throats.'"

"Noah and his wife never have a fight in the original story," Deb says.

In the final scene the family gathers at the top of a ridge overlooking the water in the distance. Noah wraps a snakeskin around his arm and blesses the children, telling them to be fruitful and multiply.

"A snakeskin! Why does it have to be a snakeskin?" Les yells as he leaves.

"God gives the multiplication directive to Noah, not Noah to his granddaughters," Deb says.

As they leave the theater Jim asks Deb what she thinks of the film.

"If you take out the errors, I would like it. It's entertaining, well acted, and has great visual effects. But I don't like how they make so many changes and never show God speaking to Noah. My ratings for this film are accuracy one and entertainment five."

7

Cloudy With a Chance of Rain

As Told In
"Noah's Ark"
1999 TELEVISION SERIES

NOAH AND HIS FAMILY have survived the destruction of Sodom as the story of Noah's life before the flood, continues.

"Sodom was destroyed after the flood!" Les yells. "This show has the fire and sulfur before the Flood!"

Jon Voight plays Noah, Mary Steenburgen plays his wife, Naamah, and F. Murray Abraham plays Noah's cousin, Lot, in this television series about events in the book of Genesis. In a tranquil countryside, Noah and his wife contemplate how their lives will change since they no longer live in Sodom. Noah says that someday this story will be written down "so future generations will know what happened." But Naamah says the writers will "change things" and might even "say they weren't even there."

"She's right about that," Les yells. "They weren't."

As Noah and his family travel to a new home they encounter an itinerant peddler, played by James Coburn, who is on his way to Sodom to sell merchandise. After Noah tells him Sodom is destroyed, Noah and Naamah buy hats from the trader.

> "You can't help but like Coburn," Deb says. "I like the comic relief he provides, but Noah cannot tell him Sodom is destroyed, because it hasn't happened yet."

> **"That's what I just said,"** Les yells back.

Ten years later, Noah's sons are no longer children and they go into the nearby village looking for wives. Their trip introduces people in the town including a future wife of one of the boys and ends with a mob wanting to sacrifice the girl to a pagan god. One woman in the crowd says they should add Noah and his wife to the group to be sacrificed, so Naamah hits her on the head with a frying pan.

> "This part of the series is very entertaining without being contradictory," Deb says. "Some of it is very funny, especially the frying pan scene."

As Noah walks in the field, God talks to him and tells him to build an ark. So Noah and his sons begin building the boat while the townspeople come out and laugh at him. One evening, Noah asks God to help him, because four people cannot do this alone. The next morning, the family arrives at the construction site and finds dozens of stacks of precut lumber that they can use to build the ark.

> "I guess God calls Building Supplies Are Us," Dave jokes.

> "It takes decades to build the ark," Deb says, "and God doesn't provide the lumber."

> "How do you know?" Jim asks. "Maybe God just got a new credit card and wanted to take advantage of the discount to new customers."

God also provides written instructions on how to assemble the precut material.

> "That's a nice thought, but it doesn't happen that way," Deb says.

> "Have you ever read assembly instructions?" Jim laughs. "They never help."

Some unsavory men come to the construction site and demand food. It appears a fight is about to happen when their leader, Lot, recognizes Noah and embraces his cousin.

"So Lot is now a bandit leader?" Les yells.

"He looks pretty old for not being born yet!" Dave shouts. **"Maybe he is his own grandfather!"**

When Noah asks Lot how he could have become a murderer, Lot tells him he had no choice after Sodom was destroyed because he had no job or money.

"This is a terrible way to picture Lot!" Deb says. "A murderer?"

"You've got to understand," Dave jokes. "He has no money. He has to continue paying support for the maintenance of the salt statue of his ex-wife."

"Very funny Dave."

Later, Noah walks in his sleep and is awakened by God, who shows him the ark he finished building for Noah.

"So basically," Deb says, "this film has God doing most of the construction."

"Well it does save dozens of years," Jim says.

"At the price of accuracy."

"And, it is cheaper than paying union wages."

God tells Noah Sodom was a warning. He destroyed Sodom with fire and now he will destroy the world with the water of his tears that he will cry for forty days.

"He doesn't destroy Sodom before the flood!" Les yells.

"This is completely reversed," Deb says. "The end will come by fire in the future."

Noah begs God to give mankind another chance.

"Noah doesn't try to intercede," Deb says.

Noah gives Naamah a tour of the completed ark and shows her a part of the ark that will hold snakes and she gets upset and says she doesn't like them, and never will.

> **"Snakes!"** Les yells. **"Why would you save snakes? I don't blame you, Naamah!"**

> "I'm sure Noah's wife never objected to any of the animals," Deb says. "However this is a cute scene."

Pairs of animals travel to the ark, including a pair of cattle, and many of those animals walk through the village while families are having conversations about Noah, and that he must be mad. They are amazed to see this parade of animals in their street.

> "I like this scene," Deb says. "I have to believe the people of that day think Noah is crazy and are surprised to see the animals traveling to the ark."

Noah and his family wake up the next morning and see the animal pairs, including a pair of sheep, grazing around the ark and begin walking up the ramp, into the boat.

> **"Cattle and sheep will not go in as pairs!"** Les shouts in the audience.

> "Most people don't understand that clean animals go in by sevens," Deb says. "As much as I like this part of the film, Les is right."

The ark is completed and a new moon shines at night over the landscape where the ark rests with the door in the side open, and showing light from the inside. Noah is praying, and God tells him he will start the flood tomorrow.

> "They correctly show the door in the side of the ark," Deb says, "but they don't show that Noah and his family are sealed in the ark for seven days before the flood begins."

> "Maybe they have pizza ordered," Dave jokes.

> "Or they didn't cancel the newspaper and hold the mail until the next day," Jim says.

Meanwhile back in town, the villagers, led by Shem's father-in-law, are angry that the animals cause damage as they walk through the town on their way to the ark. The townspeople walk to where Noah and his family are waiting outside their home and when they threaten Noah, a tiger and two lions appear and scare them off.

> "The townspeople can't approach Noah," Deb says. "Noah and his family are locked in the ark."

When Noah tells the villagers it's going to rain, they mock him until the sky darkens and heavy rain begins. Noah and his sons bring the last animals into the ark as the rain starts.

> "The animals have been inside for seven days," Deb says.

Noah's sons paddle into town on rafts to get their girlfriends, but Shem has to punch his girl in the face to knock her out because she refuses to go with him back to the ark.

> **"All eight of them are in the ark!"** Les yells. **"They have been there for a week!"**

As the flood water continues to rise they return to the ark, climb on board and raise the ramp, sealing the ark.

> **"That was seven days ago!"** Les yells again.

People and animals start drowning in the flood.

> "They do a good job with the flood scene," Jim says.

The storm ends and the ark is now floating at night on a calm ocean lit by a full moon.

> "This film never shows water coming from beneath the earth," Deb says. "That is one thing I like about the Russell Crowe version, it shows geysers."

Inside the ark, Noah finds Naamah getting ready to throw tarantulas and cockroaches overboard, but Noah won't let her do it.

> "While that is a good idea, it never happens," Deb laughs.

Life aboard the ark is shown, including the sons having to feed the animals, clean large amounts of manure from the pens, and the girls having to do laundry.

> "That part is left out of the Bible," Dave says, "but they certainly have to do those things. That's a good addition."

The peddler who sold Noah pots, pans and hats has a raft that he navigates with a paddle wheel and he approaches the ark.

> **"The flood kills everyone!"** Les yells. **"What's he doing alive?"**

The peddler comes aboard and sells items to the eight people on board. After they trade food for merchandise, he paddles away and life continues on the ark until a fleet of ships sail up to the ark led by Shem's father-in-law. The survivors of the flood, now pirates, want to attack the ark.

> **"They're all dead!"** Les yells. **"Plus, where do they get boats?"**

> **"They probably find a couple empty lifeboats from the Titanic!"** Jason yells.

Lot is leading this group, and he yells to Noah that's he has deteriorated a long way since Sodom and that he has loved every minute of it. He then tells Noah to surrender the ark.

> **"Lot hasn't been born yet!"** Les yells.

> "How can this film show Lot becoming a pirate?" Deb asks. "God doesn't save him so he could end up this way."

The attack begins by the pirates throwing steel grappling hooks on the deck of the ark and climbing up the side of the boat while Noah and his family fight them off. Even the women fight as Naamah hits one pirate in the head with a frying pan.

> **"A frying pan!"** Les yells. **"What's with Noah's wife and a frying pan?"**

> "I don't know whether to laugh or cry," Deb says. "This story has been changed so much it upsets me, but on the other hand the film has very funny moments."

> **"Les!"** Deb yells. **"It's ok. I like the frying pan scenes."**

The animals join in the fighting when a bear and a gorilla confront Lot.

Despite laughing, Deb manages to say, "There is no fight on the ark!"

Lot gives up the attack and jumps off the ark, telling Noah he will return. Once Lot climbs back on his boat, the pirates start catapulting balls of fire onto the ship, causing fires to break out on the ark. Noah asks God for help and a tornado appears, approaches the pirate boat and kills those on it. Lot laughs as he is sucked to his death inside the tornado, and then waves break over the ark, putting out the fires.

"This is really over the top," Deb says. "Lot is a righteous man that God spares. He doesn't become a pirate who laughs as God kills him."

"So," Jim laughs, "pirates don't attack the ark?"

"I assume you're joking."

After the attack God tells Noah he is thinking about destroying him and his family and then tells Noah he hasn't made up his mind. When Noah calls to the Lord, he doesn't respond.

"This is the opposite of what the story says. God remembers them in the ark in a protective way," Deb says.

As the days wear on, Noah starts to go mad while the rest of the family deals with boredom, and once again Noah prays for a sign and receives silence in return. Days later Noah sends out a raven, which returns later to the ark. That night Noah prays and God responds, telling Noah he has decided to let them all die.

"Really?" Deb says. "That's a terrible portrayal of God. It makes it appear that God puts them through all this with no set plan. Plus Noah doesn't go mad and certainly has no unanswered prayers."

"Does the raven return to the ark?" Jim asks.

"No, that's also wrong."

When Noah starts dancing and whistling instead of praying with tears to God, the world is given another chance as God says Noah's reaction touches his heart, and that he will give Noah a sign tomorrow if he sends out a dove.

"God never considers killing Noah," Deb says.

Days after sending the dove out, it returns carrying a small olive branch. In the distance they see a rainbow.

"Those poor leprechauns!" Dave jokes.

"The series condenses this," Deb says. *"Noah sends a raven out which does not return, and then he sends the dove out three times. They also show the rainbow too soon."*

The ark crashes into what will become a mountain top and the animals are released to repopulate the earth. Noah, as captain of the vessel, performs a marriage ceremony for his three sons and their girlfriends. After they get married, the sons and their wives leave Noah.

"The sons are married before the flood begins," Deb says. *"Plus, they don't leave Noah immediately after the flood."*

As the film ends, God tells Noah he needs man as much as man needs him, and he will not destroy man again.

As they leave the theater, Jim tells Deb, "This is an entertaining version of this Bible story."

"I agree," She responds. "They change a lot of things, but there are some funny scenes. However, having Lot appear before the flood and then having him killed as he attacks the ark is totally absurd. But, there are good actors and good special effects, so the film has some good points, but sticking to the Bible is not one of them. My rating for this film is accuracy zero and entertainment five."

8

Cloudy With a Chance of Rain

WHAT DIFFERENCE DOES IT MAKE?

SUNDAY SCHOOL gets started a little late this morning because a heavy rainstorm floods the parking lot.

"Well, this is certainly appropriate," Deb says, "but we still have time to talk about some movies. Most of us have had a chance to see the films about Noah, and I believe it's clear there are some big differences between the Bible story and the films. So the question is, 'What difference does it make'?"

"Dave, does it make any difference?"

"One difference I see in one movie is the characterization of God. The television series *Noah's Ark* makes it appear God makes mistakes. I have a real problem with that."

"Speaking of characterizations," Jason says, "having Noah portrayed as a man who would even consider slitting his granddaughters' throats is very troubling."

"I agree, but if we remember these films are meant to be entertainment as opposed to accurate Bible presentations, we can understand why they do what they do, even if we think it is wrong to change the story," Deb says. "Next week we will start looking at films that deal with Sodom and

Gomorrah. In the meantime, I have a small handout relating to the timing of events in the flood narrative. Have a great week!"

part III

She Ain't Married, She's My Sister

MOVIES ABOUT ABRAHAM

An Introduction

TIME: Present day
LOCATION: WSOD Television Studio

"IT'S SEVEN O'CLOCK and welcome to The WSOD Morning Show. I'm Harry and with me are Betty and the Salty Dog. Together, we will bring you news, weather, sports, as well as special features to get your day started."

"Before we get to the news, this being an election year, we thought we would start your day with some funny quotes politicians have made in recent years. For example, there is a famous quote by Dan Quayle to Representative Claudine Schneider of Rhode Island when he was complimenting her on her command of the French language, then adding, 'I was recently on a tour of Latin America and the only regret I have is that I didn't study Latin harder in school so I could converse with those people.' The representative later admitted Quayle was clearly joking, but some national media reported this as a serious statement."

"Attacks are not limited to twisting quotes," Betty says. "They include everything you do, and your mistakes will be remembered much more than your accomplishments, especially if they are funny. Here, let me give you a few other comments and quotes."

"Here's one by George Bush, 'For seven and a half years I've worked alongside of President Reagan. We've had triumphs. Made some mistakes. We've had some sex, uh setbacks.'"

"And this by Al Gore, 'A zebra does not change its spots.'"

"Australian Minister Keppel Enderbery announced, 'Traditionally, most of our imports come from Overseas.'"

"'Stand up, Chuck, Let'em see ya.' Joe Biden told Missouri State Senator, Chuck Graham—who is in a wheelchair."

"These are all funny," Harry says. "But Salty you covered an election four thousand years ago between Abraham and an Assyrian named Ronald Reagan. I'm going to read an excerpt from the debate you moderated."

"SALTY: 'Mister Reagan, we all know that God promised great blessings to Abraham, but when he went to Egypt he pretended that his wife was his sister so he would not get killed. Would you say that Abraham did not show faith that God would protect him by what he did'?"

"REAGAN: 'Well, facts are stubborn things.'"

"SALTY: 'Again, isn't it also true, that years later, Abraham went to Gerar, and told King Abimelech that his wife Sarah is his sister in order that he would not get killed'?"

"REAGAN: 'Again, facts are stubborn things.'"

"SALTY: 'Mister Reagan, what do you have to say to Abraham about this'?"

"Reagan: "At the risk of repeating myself, 'Well Abraham, there you go again.'"

"ABRAHAM: 'Ronnie, I have to admit that you are right. It took me awhile to trust God completely. In fact God had to test me one last time before he knew I trusted him.'"

"REAGAN: 'Abe, I love hearing you say that. Sir, I concede this election. I have more important things to do anyway, like bomb Russia.'"

"As we all know," Betty says, "Abraham was one of the greatest men who ever lived, yet he had his faults and this should be very comforting to the rest of us who have flaws."

"Except me!" Salty says.

> *Speaking of great men, a member of the Wawasee town council walks up to the ticket booth and says, "Hi Erica, I thought I would start watching this series of films you have here."*
>
> *"Hi Mister Rink, it's a pleasure to see you again, I hear you're running for mayor."*
>
> *"News gets around fast, but this is not fake news. Yes, I am running, and I promise, nobody will be as good a mayor as I will be."*

AN INTRODUCTION

"Well good luck mister soon-to-be-mayor!"

Ronald walks into the lobby thinking, "Well, I guess I better start watching these films if I want to show voters I know all about the Bible."

9

She Ain't Married, She's My Sister

As Told in
The Bible: In the Beginning
1966

THIS MOVIE, stars George C. Scott, when he is still named Abram. God tells him to leave his father and go to a new land, where God promises him he will make him into a great nation. Abram leaves Ur with his wife, Sarai, and his nephew, Lot, and they take their tribes and herds with them to Canaan.

> *Jim goes to the concession stand and buys some popcorn from Charlotte. As he returns, he asks Deb, "Anything wrong so far?"*
>
> *"Just one thing," she says. "They show Abram leaving his father in Ur when they actually leave Ur together and go to Haran, where Abram eventually leaves his father."*
>
> *"Maybe they have an **urgent** reason to leave," Chester says and starts laughing while stomping his hooves.*

Abram prospers in the new land, traveling all over Canaan feeding their herds. During this time, Hagar is introduced as Sarai's handmaiden. Despite their prosperity, there is not enough water to satisfy the animals of both tribes, so Abram tells Lot they must split up, giving Lot the choice of where he will go. Lot chooses to go toward the plains of Jordan, near the cities of the plain. Abram warns him not to go there, but Lot argues they can be protected by the city walls.

> "This is another set of errors," Deb says. "Lot never mentions the cities and Abram does not warn him about them."

> "Does Lot mention being in a safe place?" Jim asks.

> "No, they make that up too, but they do so show it is Abraham's decision to split up and he gives Lot the choice of lands to go to. That part is accurate."

Abram goes to a mountain top where God blesses him and promises Abram that all the land he sees will be given to him and his descendents. Abram responds he has no children, but God tells him in a vision that he will have many descendents, starting with Isaac. The vision includes prophecies about his descendents.

> "The timing of this vision is wrong," Dave says, sitting behind Deb.

> "I agree," Deb responds.

> Ronald types on his phone, "I'll have more descendents than this guy. Nobody will have more descendents than I will!"

The film describes the birth of Ishmael, the renaming of Abram and Sarai, the story of Sodom and the separation of Hagar and Ishmael from Abraham. (The film's version of the destruction of Sodom is told in the next part, "Please Pass the Salt.")

> "You've been quiet Deb," Jim says.

> "This has all been pretty good."

Abraham is asleep when a voice softly calls his name, waking him up, and telling him to take his son to the mountains and offer him as a burnt offering. Abraham responds by questioning if God would want him to behave like the Canaanites "who lay their firstborn on fires before their idols? Art thou truly the Lord my God?" he asks.

"God ought to be ashamed!" Chester jokes.

"Abraham doesn't ask this," Deb says.

At first Abraham shouts "No!" and won't do it, but in the morning, he takes Isaac with him to the land of Moriah.

"The film leaves out the two servants and the firewood they carry," Deb says.

"I'm going to ask you about that on Sunday," Dave leans over the seat.

As they journey, they pass what is left of Sodom, and Abraham tells Isaac what happened there. Isaac asks if the children were also killed, and then a snake is shown coming out of a small skull.

"Not another snake!" Les shouts.

Abraham walks through the ruins, talking about how insignificant men are compared to God, and before they continue their journey, he tells Isaac they must always obey God.

Ian puts his arm around Avery, "I went to Israel with my folks last summer and visited the area around Beersheba which is south and west of Jerusalem. Sodom would have been near the Jordan River to the east, so there is no way Abraham and Isaac would walk through its ruins on their three day journey to the mountain."

Avery snuggles up against him. "Are you sure Isaac was sacrificed at present day Jerusalem."

"I'm not certain, but that is the common belief."

"Maybe they were following Sarah's map. I know how my mom is with directions."

"The same way dads can be when they don't remember what they are supposed to bring home."

"Like in this case, Isaac?"

"I imagine Sarah would be really upset if Abe came home without him."

They arrive at the top of the mountain, and Isaac asks, "But where is the ram for the sacrifice?" Instead of answering Isaac, Abraham binds the frightened child and lays him on the pile of wood they brought to burn the sacrifice.

> "The film really messes this up," Deb says. "Isaac asks where the lamb is, not a ram. Also, Abraham doesn't ignore him, he responds that God will provide a lamb."

> "I'm glad he isn't going to sacrifice a mule," Chester says.

> "That would be quite an insult," Charley jokes. "You're supposed to sacrifice something useful! Not something you would take to Goodwill."

Abraham lights the wood, takes out his knife and holds it in the air, ready to kill Isaac, when God stops him, telling him he now knows Abraham will obey him. Isaac sees a ram caught in a bush, and they sacrifice the ram, and as they walk down the mountain, the movie ends.

> As they walk by the concession stand and say goodnight to Charlotte, Jim asks Deb,

> "So how does this film do with the story of Abraham?"

> "The film does a pretty good job on what it covers, but it does leave out the two times Abraham passes Sarah off as his sister. That's a pretty important part of the story. I give it a five for entertainment and a four for accuracy."

10

She Ain't Married, She's My Sister

As Told in
The Bible

2013 TELEVISION MINI SERIES

THE FIRST EPISODE of this series briefly describes Noah in the ark, and then starts with the story of Abraham. As Abraham is standing on a mountain, he hears a voice saying, "Abraham, leave your home and go to the land I give you."

"His name is not Abraham, it's still Abram!" Les shouts from the back of the theater.

God promises a blessing, so Abraham tells his wife Sarah that God has spoken to him and they need to leave for another land.

"Her name is not Sarah, it's still Sarai!"

"I think Les is drunk again," Deb says.

"When isn't he?" Jim asks.

Abraham speaks to Lot, and his wife who doesn't want to go, but they all leave for Canaan. Once they arrive, fights break out between Lot's men and Abraham's men, so they split up. (Certain events from this part of the series are told in the next part, "Please Pass the Salt.")

The series shows the interaction between Abraham, Sarah, and Hagar that results in the birth of Ishmael, and describes the love Abraham has for his son, which leads to conflict in the family.

"This is all pretty good," Ian says.

Fourteen years pass, and then Abraham hears a voice call his name, and he looks at a hilltop where he sees three men standing. The three individuals approach, and Abraham bows down, recognizing that one of them is the Lord. One of the angels asks about Sarah and Abraham answers that she is in the tent. The angel tells him his wife will have a son within a year. Sarah hears this and laughs, and then the Lord walks into the tent and asks her why she laughs.

"Don't you ever knock?" Chester yells.

"The Lord actually asks Abraham why Sarah laughs, he doesn't ask her," Deb says.

"You know Deb," Jim says, "You always used to laugh at my jokes, but you don't anymore."

"Sorry Honey. Maybe I just need a hearing aid."

"Maybe he just needs funny jokes," Chester whispers to Charley.

The visitors are leaving and when Abraham asks where they are going, one of the angels tells him they are going to decide the fate of Sodom. The series then continues by describing what happens to Sodom, and then the separation of Ishmael. (The events from this part of the series through the destruction of Sodom are told in the next part, "Please Pass the Salt.")

"This part is done well," Deb says.

Ten years pass and the narrator tells the audience that Abraham has been tested, and that he must prove his faith, again and again. Abraham is out in a meadow, and with thunder in the background, he utters the word "Sacrifice." Then he bitterly says, "No. Have I not shown you enough faith?"

"He never says anything like that!" Les shouts.

Nevertheless, Abraham goes back to the camp and tells Isaac to come with him. He packs up some wood and they climb to the top of the mountain that is next to the camp, which is still visible below.

"Do you see that?" Les yells. *"You can still see the camp from the mountain top! It's a three day journey to that mountain!"*

"Maybe they just climb slow!" Dave yells, *"and it takes them three days to get to the top."*

"Maybe its three days by way of Sodom," Joe yells.

"They also forget to take the two servants," Jason joins in from the projection booth.

"Not to mention a road atlas," Teddy jokes to Rick and Erica as they stand in the back of the theater.

At the top of the mountain, Isaac asks where the lamb is, and Abraham assures him that "The Lord will provide a sacrifice." Meanwhile, down below, Sarah finds out Abraham did not take a lamb and she realizes he is going to sacrifice their son. She gets upset and looks up at the top of the mountain, where Abraham is preparing the altar, and as she walks around the camp, she ends up weeping.

"She's nowhere near that mountain!" Les yells. *"It's a three-day trip!"*

Abraham grabs Isaac. He struggles as he starts getting tied up and asks his father what he is doing.

"He doesn't struggle!" Les yells.

"Maybe he thinks Dad wants to wrestle!" Dave shouts.

His father puts him on the altar, and as Isaac begs for mercy, Abraham takes out his knife and asks his son to forgive him. He holds his knife in the air and he hears a voice say, "Abraham!" as he thrusts the knife down, barely missing his son and stabbing the firewood. He looks at a nearby peak where he sees the Lord standing in a crimson robe, and then walking away.

"I hate it when someone talks on my backswing," Joe yells.

Abraham turns and sees a lamb walking up to them.

"Is this a bad time?" Chester jokes, imitating what the lamb might say to Abraham.

"It isn't a lamb!" Les yells.

"He's right," Deb says, "It's actually a ram. This whole scene is wrong. Isaac doesn't struggle, Abraham doesn't ask Isaac to forgive him, and God doesn't simply yell out Abraham's name from another mountain top wearing what looks like a dark red Ku Klux Klan outfit."

Sarah runs up the mountain and her husband appears alone on a cliff above her, and she starts crying thinking Isaac is now dead, and that her husband has killed him.

"Honey, I'm home," Jim jokes, imitating Abraham yelling down to Sarah.

Isaac then steps up next to Abraham, and she realizes he is still alive. The episode ends with Abraham taking Isaac down the mountain to meet Sarah. As Abraham extends his hand to help Isaac climb over a rock, Isaac ignores him and keeps climbing down while Sarah stares daggers at her husband.

"I guess he'll be sleeping on the couch for awhile," Jim says as they get up to leave.

As Chester and Charley climb into the trailer, Jim asks Deb, "What do you think of this episode?"

"I would say it's well acted and is interesting, so I can rate it four for entertainment, but I have to give it a one for accuracy."

11

She Ain't Married, She's My Sister

As Told In
Abraham
1994 TELEVISION MINI SERIES

THIS TURNER PRODUCTION begins while Abram, starring Richard Harris, is still living with his father in Haran. He is assisting a sheep giving birth to a lamb, while Lot's wife is in labor, being assisted by Abram's wife, Sarai, who is played by Barbara Hershey. The film introduces Lot, Terah, and Nahor, who is in the business of selling pagan god statues. After the lamb is born events are shown that lead up to Abram, Sarai, and Lot leaving the country to settle in a different land. As God gives instructions, his voice is replaced by Abram reciting the promises that God makes to him.

> "This is a different way of showing God speaking to a man," Deb says, "I like how this is done."

Abram and Lot depart with their livestock and servants across a barren wilderness, finally arriving at a river. Abram sees a man approach the river and brings him into his camp. The man is an escaped slave from Damascus, and the servants of his master immediately appear at the camp and want to take him back to his master. Abram pays the men so that the servant, Eliezer, can be free, and he joins Abram and his family.

> "Eliezer has an important role in Abraham's life," Deb comments. "I'm glad he is a part of this film."

> "Why is he so important?" Jim asks.

> "He is very close to Abraham, in fact Abraham sends him to get a wife for Isaac."

The film has them arriving in Canaan and settling in a fertile valley and prospering until a drought hits the land, killing much of the livestock, so they go to Egypt. When they arrive, Eliezer warns Abram that the Pharaoh loves beautiful women, and that he will kill Abram to have Sarai, while still obeying their law that no one can take another man's wife.

> "The film adds this, but it a nice addition," Deb says.

They arrive at the border but they are not allowed to enter Egypt until a man notices how beautiful Sarai is, and then they are allowed to enter. The man takes Sarai to the Pharaoh, played by Maximilian Schell, and he assumes Sarai is Abram's sister. He not only welcomes Abram but gives him livestock and allows him to stay in the fertile land of the delta.

> "This part is distorted," Deb says. "The film downplays Abram's willingness to pass Sarai off as his sister."

> "She ain't married, she's my sister," Chester and Charley start singing.

Once outside the palace, Abram sends Eliezer back inside to see if there is a way to rescue Sarai.

> "There is no plan to rescue Sarai," Deb says.

The film shows the interaction between the pharaoh and Sarai, including the illnesses of the Egyptians, before the pharaoh finds out Sarai and Abram are married and subsequently orders Abram to leave and to take his wife, and everything he was given, with him.

"The film adds material but it does not contradict the story," Deb says. *"I like how the film does this."*

Abram returns to the land they were living on in Canaan and the drought has passed. They discover a source of water, and make a treaty with Mambre, a neighbor. The story continues several years later when Lot's men and Abram's men fight over water for their herds. Lot tells his uncle there is not enough water for both groups and he wants to go where there are greener pastures near the Jordan River, and he will also have the benefit of living closer to cities where he can get a better price for what they sell.

"The split is not Lot's idea," Deb says.

"I wonder why some films miss this?" Jim responds.

Lot settles near Sodom, which gets attacked by an alliance of four kings. Sodom loses the battle and the kings take Lot and his tribe north as slaves. When Abram hears of this, he and Mambre join forces to fight the four kings and rescue his nephew. It takes two battles, but Lot and his followers are rescued, and once again the tribes split as Lot chooses to stay in Sodom.

"There is actually just one battle," Deb says.

When Abram returns, he goes out at night and prays. In the prayer, Abram tells God that Eliazer will be the only one that can be his heir, but God tells him that Eliazer will not be his heir because the number of stars he sees will be like the number of descendents he will have through his own son. Melchizedek visits Abram's camp the following day and brings Abram bread and wine.

"The timing is wrong," Deb says. *"He meets Mel before he leaves Sodom."*

"Anything else?" Jim asks.

"Yes, it leaves out Abram tithing to him."

The film shows Sarai asking Hagar if she will bear a son for Abram, the servant agrees, a few weeks later she is pregnant. The story continues showing how circumcision is introduced as a covenant, and the angels visiting Abraham, telling him that he and Sarah will have a son. Then the angels tell Abraham they are going to visit Sodom.

"You've been pretty quiet for over an hour Deb," Jim says.

"They have been doing a great job! I can't criticize any of this."

The two angels walk through Sodom and see the depravity of the people. They meet Lot, who invites them to come to his home. A mob approaches Lot's house and demand the angels be brought out to them. Lot goes out to them and tells them to take him and his daughters but to not take the angels. The angels appear and blind the mob and lead Lot and his family out of the city at night, telling them not to look back, which unfortunately, Lot's wife does, as Lot and his daughters are entering a cave for protection. (There are several errors in this scene, all of which are in other movies on this subject, and they are pointed out in the next part, "Please Pass the Salt.")

A year later, Isaac is born, and as he grows into a boy of about six, he looks up to his brother, Ishmael, who loves him. There is a feast that night, and near the campfire, Ishmael, who is now a teenager, is wrestling with another young man in the tribe. After winning that match, there is another event where Ishmael puts Isaac on his shoulders and he wins yet another competition.

Later that night Sarah talks to Abraham and tells him she believes Ishmael will be a threat to Isaac and insists that Abraham send him and his mother away. Abraham steps out into the night and returns to the tent saying he believes what she asks is God's will and he sends Hagar and Ishmael away. They travel through the wilderness until they run out of water and are dying of thirst. An angel appears to Hagar and conveys God's promise to Ishmael, and water springs forth from a cliff wall, and they survive.

"You're still being pretty quiet Deb," Jim says. "I guess you still aren't seeing any errors."

Without turning to Jim, Deb says, "This feast is celebrating Isaac being weaned. He looks like he is six years old."

"I guess that is a little old," Dave says from the seat behind them.

"Not for me," Ronald posts. "I was twelve."

"It doesn't show Ishmael acting like a brat and mocking Isaac, and it doesn't show God telling Abraham to send them away," Deb says

while continuing to watch the screen. "Other than that, its all good." Deb turns to Jim and adds, "You must be thinking I'm not paying attention."

Six years later, God tells Abraham to take Isaac to the mountains of Moriah and offer Isaac as a burnt sacrifice. Abraham is greatly distressed and asks "Why?" and starts weeping. The next morning Abraham takes his son and two servants out of the camp and they leave for the journey to the mountains.

"Most people won't accept that Abraham now has enough faith not to question God," Deb says. "He doesn't ask why or start crying."

They arrive at the mountain and Abraham takes his son to the top and prepares to sacrifice Isaac. He has his knife ready to kill the child when an angel appears and tells him not to kill the child. Abraham looks at the angel, and then looking around, sees a ram in a thicket that he can sacrifice in Isaac's place.

"The film gets the ram right, but it doesn't show it caught by its horns in the thicket," Deb says.

As they walk down the mountain God pronounces another blessing on Abraham and the film ends.

As they leave, Deb doesn't wait for Jim to ask what she thinks about the movie. "I really like this film. It has very few errors and everything is well produced with wonderful actors. This is a great film, I love it! I give it a five for both entertainment and accuracy."

"I couldn't agree with you more," Chester says.

12

She Ain't Married, She's My Sister

WHAT DIFFERENCE DOES IT MAKE?

ABOUT TWENTY PEOPLE are in the Sunday school class that Deb teaches that weekend, including Dave. Deb gives a brief description of the movies to the class and then Dave asks a question.

"Deb, as we were watching *The Bible*, you commented that George C. Scott doesn't take the two servants with him and Isaac as they make their trip to the mountains to sacrifice his son. Why is that important?"

"They need two witnesses that can attest as to what happens on that trip."

"Deb, you also mentioned the other night that Abraham hid the fact that Sarai is his wife twice, and you said this is important. Can you also explain that?"

"It is very important! Abraham is not a finished product during these times. He did not have faith that God would protect him, and especially Sarah."

Deb looks at the class, "What is the most important theme of the story?"

"That Abraham wants to get rid of his wife?" Dave jokes.

The class laughs.

Ian raises his hand.

"Ian?"

"Faith?"

"That's right. Does Abraham have faith throughout his life, or does he drop the ball once in awhile?"

A woman in the front says, "I think he drops the ball more than once. He lies about Sarah twice."

"I think the most telling thing is that God gives Abraham his blessings six times before he asks him to sacrifice Isaac," Deb says. "Only then does God say that he knows Abraham fears God."

"This demonstrates that Abraham's faith has to grow before he is worthy of the blessings he receives," Deb says as she concludes the class. "I have four handouts for you. The first handout deals with why a ram is sacrificed instead of a lamb. The second one deals with the concept of the 'third day,' and the third one deals with patterns in the Bible, and the fourth handout is about Abraham's faith. Have a great week everyone!"

part IV
Please Pass the Salt

MOVIES ABOUT
SODOM AND GOMORRA

An Introduction

IT'S BEFORE DAWN in Sodom and the Salty Dog is starting the Morning Show on WSOD. As he does every morning, he begins the show by playing the opening sample on the song "V. Thirteen" by the group "Big Audio Dynamite."

"Good morning Sodom and Gomorrah, good morning sinners. No, that wasn't your radio set on the bleep again."

Salty Dog fades down the song and screams into the microphone,

"Good morning Sodom and Gomorrah!"

"This is the Salty Dog broadcasting to you from the lowest spot on this planet where this signal can be heard from Assyria to Egypt."

"Today we are celebrating a great festival and people are coming from all the cities of the plain to party here in Sodom. But, while all these people are coming here, there is an undocumented immigrant named Lot who is leaving our fair city. He was last heard telling some relatives that the city is going to be destroyed by fire and we are all going to be burned up!"

"I feel we should recognize this man and play some songs for him as he leaves our fair city. I am going to ask listeners to call the station and we will play the first ten songs listeners request to honor Lot as he leaves town. So give me a ring."

The phone lines light up and Salty Dog punches line 1.

"Is this the Salty Dog?"

"You are on the air."

"This is the mayor and I have a request."

"Anything for you, Mister Mayor, what song should we play for Lot?"

"I would love to hear 'The Doors' sing 'Light My Fire.'"

"Great choice, we will play Mister Morrison."

"Caller on line two, you are on the air at WSOD. What would you like to hear?"

"How about Tori Amos, 'Fire to Your Plain'?"

"You got it! Line three you are on WSOD with the Salty Dog. What do you think we should play?"

"I Love the group Modest Mouse. How about 'Fire it Up'?"

"I love it! Caller number four, your choice."

"This is a no brainer. Jerry Lee Lewis, 'Great Balls of Fire.'"

"Next up we have Gomer from Gomorrah. What do you want to hear to honor Lot, Gomer?"

"How about AC/DC, 'This House Is on Fire'?"

"Well Lot thinks it will be you, Gomer."

"Caller six you are on WSOD with the Salty Dog. What should we play for Lot?"

"Morrissey, 'Hair Dresser on Fire.'"

"It must be that hair spray. We still have four more songs we can play. Lucky number seven, you are next on WSOD."

"Queen, 'Put Out the fire.'"

"My producer tells me our eighth caller knows lot. Let's hear what he has to say. Caller number eight, tell us about Lot."

"He is my father-in-law. I have been telling my wife for years her dad is nuts. Last night was really weird. He comes in warning us to leave the city. We all laughed and said, "What? Leave before the party?"

"What song should we play for your father-in-law?"

"Play R.E.M., 'It's the End of the World as We Know It.'"

"Ninth caller, what do you think we should play?"

"Since we are running out of time, how about, 'Eve of Destruction' by Barry McGuire?"

"Wow, number nine, this is getting depressing! Last caller, do you have a more cheerful request?"

"Let's hear something for the Parrot Heads out here. How about Jimmy Buffett's, 'Party at the End of the World'?"

"We will play all of those and more, but first I want to play my favorite song in honor of our celebration today. The name of the song is 'Loaded' by Primal Scream. This song starts out with an audio sample where we will hear Peter Fonda, from the movie, 'The Wild Angels,' expressing what we all feel today."

Peter Fonda is heard until he recites the last line of the audio sample,

"We're gonna have a good time, we're gonna have a party."

After the word "party" radios tuned to WSOD, from Assyria to Egypt, receive only static.

Please Pass the Salt

As Told in
The Last Days of Sodom and Gomorrah
1962

IN THIS FILM, Stuart Granger as Lot, a widower with two daughters, leads his tribe to settle in a barren part of the desert that is near the cities of Sodom and Gomorrah.

"Already shaking your head?" Jim says to Deb.

"This starts off wrong. Lot chooses to go to this area because it is very lush and fertile."

The story begins by telling the audience there is political intrigue in Sodom's palace. The city is ruled by a queen, whose brother played by Stanley Baker, wants to kill her so he can become king. The movie shows that Sodom is a city that has become wealthy by selling salt and slaves.

Lot and his tribe arrive at the river Jordan. While his people rush to the water, Lot sees a valley filled with dead and dying slaves. There, he meets a prophet who has been speaking out against the sins of Sodom. Soon after this, the queen of Sodom, accompanied by soldiers, slaves, and citizens of the city walk out to the Jordan to meet Lot and his people who have arrived at the other side of the river. Lot crosses the river to meet the queen, and she gives barren land to Lot and his tribe if they agree to provide wheat to Sodom for the next seven years.

> "This film adds a lot of material to the story," Ian jokes.
>
> "Is there anything wrong with additions?" Avery asks.
>
> "No, actually I am enjoying this so far."

In closing the deal, the queen gives Lot a beautiful slave woman, and she comes to the Hebrew camp, complaining about the clothes she will be wearing and the luxury she will be losing by leaving Sodom. While the intention is that she will spy on Lot, she will eventually become his second wife.

> "I never heard that Lot will have a second wife," Jim says.
>
> "He doesn't, I think the movie must add a pagan wife so no one will feel sorry for her when she is turned to salt."
>
> "Do you really think movie audiences feel sorry for anyone anymore?"
>
> "Probably not."
>
> "I never feel sorry for horses that end up in a glue factory," Chester says.
>
> "I hope you end up as the only mule on a Borax twenty-mule team," Charley responds.

Lot plans to improve the land by building a dam which will supply water to grow wheat.

> "I hope he can get all the environmental permits," Jim says. "It took almost a year for us to get a permit to build a fence for Chester so he could have his own space."
>
> "I remember," Chester says. "I had to live with a bunch of horses for eleven months."

The film shows two slaves escaping Sodom and crossing the river for sanctuary. The queen's brother leads soldiers to capture them and Lot wounds him while protecting the runaway slaves. Lot orders the other soldiers to go back to Sodom and has one of his daughters tend to the wounded brothers' wounds. As she is tending to him, they very quickly embrace and kiss as the scene ends.

> *"Talk about easy!"* Les yells.

> "So much for her being a virgin," Ian says, "although she does try to resist him, for at least five seconds."

> "What do you mean?" Avery asks.

> "Later in Genesis, Lot will offer his two virgin daughters to the mob that want to rape the angels."

The movie introduces Ishmael as a Hebrew who is in love with Lot's other daughter. He approaches Lot and tells him he wants to marry his daughter, and Lot gives him his blessing.

> "She won't be a virgin much longer," Jim says after hearing Ian. "So, I wonder who Lot's two virgin daughters are?"

> "Maybe they will remain chaste," Deb responds.

> "I'll give them the benefit of the doubt. So, is that Abraham's son?"

> "No, Ishmael would be less than fourteen years old. Plus, that would make him her cousin."

> "What's wrong with that? My parents are cousins. There is a lot of line breeding in my family." Charley says.

> "Line breeding? Is that similar to line dancing?" Chester responds.

> "Yes. If it's danced to 'I Walk the Line' by Johnny Cash."

In the meantime, Lot falls in love with the girl the queen gives him, and he wants to marry her. She warns him she is not a nice person and someday she may betray him and want to go back to Sodom, but Lot isn't worried that might happen, and he marries her anyway.

> "I think it's important that Lot's wife is a Hebrew," Deb says. "Her punishment is an example to other people in God's church."

> "He better get a pre-nup," Joe says to Jim. "I've had three drawn up over the years. I should have had a fourth."

"Are you still living in your office?"

"No, number four finally remarried. I gave her new husband a set of headphones as a wedding gift."

"Does he like music?"

"No, these are for sound suppression."

"So, why did your first three wives leave you?"

"Because I smoke and drink."

"What about your fourth wife?"

"Because I started smoking and drinking again."

"So why did you marry your fifth wife?"

"Because she smokes and drinks."

"I just heard Dave is finally divorced and he is now paying alimony."

"He better save some money for weekends when we bet on our golf game."

The wedding ceremony is interrupted by news that the tribes from the desert are riding toward Sodom. All the women and children take refuge in the city while the men prepare to fight on the side of Sodom to protect their interest in the land. There is a long battle scene, and Lot's people eventually defeat the desert tribes by destroying the dam they built, which washes the enemy tribes away with a flood in the valley.

"Deb, I can see you're getting upset," Jim says looking at his wife.

"How can the film show this? Lot is captured!" Deb says. "He ends up being rescued by Abraham."

"No one likes a loser who is captured in battle," Ronald types on his phone. "I like winners."

The queen of Sodom is grateful for their victory, and she invites all of Lot's people to come into Sodom and have shelter and food. Lot accepts her offer and says they will stay until their camp is rebuilt. However, the water that washed away the enemy exposes a salt vein which pollutes the water, so Lot and his people can no longer be farmers, and they move into Sodom permanently. Lot becomes the Prime Minister of Sodom as a reward for saving Sodom from the desert tribes.

"Lot never becomes Prime Minister of Sodom!" Les yells.

"What about Gomorrah?" Dave yells.

"Neither one!" Jason yells. *"He's an undocumented worker and cannot hold political office!"*

"He could in the US!" Joe shouts.

"Not in Wawasee if I become mayor!" Ronald posts.

The film describes events in Sodom that show that Lot will become part of their culture, and culminates with a fight in which Lot kills the queen's brother. The queen taunts Lot by telling him that he has a lust for blood since he not only kills her brother, despite him begging for mercy, but he kills thousands of tribesman by opening the dam and wiping them out in the battle that saves Sodom, even though the battle was already won. She tells Lot, "You are a true Sodomite, Lot. Welcome."

"Lot is saved because he is righteous!" Deb says. *"This is absurd!"*

Lot feels ashamed and sentences himself to prison.

"Our entire congress should do that!" Jason yells.

"I agree," Ronald says. *"Drain the swamp!"*

"I'm in the Jailhouse now," Chester sings.

"I have sinned!" Dave jokes as he imitates television ministers that get caught doing bad things.

As Teddy walks down the aisle, he tells his parents, *"Wait till you see what's next."*

Once in his cell, Lot prays and begs God to forgive him for leading his people to Sodom and for becoming part of their society, and then he breaks down weeping. Two angels, who look like old ancient prophets, appear to Lot.

"Wow, this is crazy," Dave thinks out loud.

Hearing Dave, Deb says to Jim, "Crazy is a nice word for this. In the original story, the angels are so beautiful that the men in Sodom want to rape them. There is no way anyone would think these two guys would inspire a mob to want to have sex with them. They look like they are a pair of ninety-year olds."

"Maybe the entire population of Sodom is over ninety years old," Jim replies. "They drive around in golf carts, play bingo, pickleball, shuffleboard, and then go line dancing every night."

"Because you're mine, I walk the line," Charley sings.

"I've heard those old folks really get it on at those places," Chester says, "maybe long haired angels, who look like old hippies wearing sheets, get these old men really excited."

"Yeah, that's about the only way I could see a mob wanting to rape them," Jim says.

The angels tell Lot that Jehovah will destroy the city before sunset for being corrupt and corrupting his chosen people.

"The city is destroyed at sunrise, not sundown," Deb moans.

Lot asks if God will kill the innocent as well as the guilty, but one angel tells Lot the innocent had the chance to speak out, but did not, so they will die also. Then Lot negotiates on behalf of the Sodomite people, asking if ten righteous people can be found, will the city be spared.

"Doesn't Abraham negotiate with God?" Jim asks.

"That's right. Lot doesn't negotiate with the angels," Deb replies.

"Not to mention that the negotiation takes place nowhere near the city," Dave adds sitting behind Deb. Then he stands up to stretch, blocking the view three rows back.

"Sit down!" *A girl behind Dave yells.*

"Lot has no idea how to make a good deal, nobody knows how to make better deals than me." Ronald taps on his phone.

"And you!" *The woman yells.* **"Turn off your phone!"**

The angels tell Lot the city will be spared if ten righteous men can be found. However, if Lot cannot find ten righteous people, and he has to leave the city, he should not turn back and look at Sodom when it is destroyed. The angels disappear, his chains fall to the floor and the jail door magically opens, allowing Lot to walk out of his cell. He meets friends who are looking for him and Ishmael in the prison, when Ishmael walks up to them and tells them that his chains fell off too.

"Ishmael is not part of this story and neither he nor Lot are ever in prison," Deb says.

Guards appear, and tell them not to leave. Lot tells them to let them pass, but they refuse and draw their swords. Lot raises his hand and says, "In the name of Jehovah." With that, there is a boom of thunder and the guards are blinded, allowing them to escape.

"Lot is not in prison!" Les yells at the screen. **"It's the mob that is blinded, not some prison guards!"**

"Les is right, the mob is blinded at Lot's house, not in prison," Deb says.

Up in the balcony Ian tells Avery, "The story of prisoners having shackles fall off is in the New Testament, not in Genesis."

Lot goes out to the palace courtyard and warns the crowd of judgment coming to Sodom while his followers go among the crowd and talk to fellow Hebrews, warning them to leave. Meanwhile the rest of the crowd is laughing at Lot as he speaks. Lot tells the Sodomites that if ten of them will follow the Hebrews out of Sodom, the city will not be destroyed. The queen allows Lot to leave and take his Hebrews with him, as well as any Sodomites who wish to leave, none of whom decide to leave.

"None of the Sodomites are warned, much less, given an opportunity to escape," Deb says.

"Maybe they pass around coupons for cab rides out of Sodom," Jim jokes.

As Lot leads his people though the courtyard, the prophet that Lot found among the dead bodies asks him if the city is really going to be destroyed.

When Lot says yes, he responds, "A sight I have longed to see. Goodbye Lot." The prophet stays there and does not follow them out of the city.

> **"What?"** Les yells. **"He's going to just wait inside the city as it gets destroyed?"**
>
> "You better settle down Les," Joe says. "It's bad for your heart."
>
> "I just had an EKG at your office, I'm fine."
>
> "Yeah, Les is right, that doesn't make any sense," Charlotte says to Erica as they go back to the lobby to close the popcorn stand.

Lot approaches his daughters and tells them they must leave with him. Neither move until Ishmael walks up and one daughter walks away with him. Then the other daughter says she will leave with Lot because she hopes to see her father someday suffer, and she wants to be there when that happens. Lot's wife, who had been standing with the daughters, follows Lot through the city, as he frees all the imprisoned slaves, and adds them to his entourage that is leaving the city.

> "There's no entourage," Les says quietly.

The guards place a beam across the doors of the city which locks the gates from the inside, but there are no guards present as Lot and his followers approach the doors. The door miraculously opens to the inside, breaking the beam, allowing Lot and thousands of his followers to walk out of the city.

> "Lot is leading thousands of followers to an unguarded gate. Why can't a few of them just remove the beam from the door?" Charley asks.
>
> "They just don't have any mule sense," Chester responds.

Comments that can be heard as the procession walks through the gates include, "It's another Miracle." "It's the hand of Jehovah." "Jehovah has opened the gate."

> "I went out to get leftover popcorn for Chester," Deb says. "Is this the same movie? This looks like the scene where Moses leads the Israelite slaves out of Egypt."

"It's still the same movie, only now there are thousands of people escaping Sodom," Jim replies.

"Thousands? It is only Lot, his wife and two daughters that escape."

"So why is Lot's wife leading the group?" Chester says as he eats the popcorn that Deb is holding for him.

"She has to be in front so people can see what's left of her as they pass the salt," Charley tells her.

"It's amazing that none of thousands of former slaves don't turn around and take a peek as they walk out," Chester says. "These are humans we are talking about."

Lot's wife leads the procession out of the city and up a mountain trail. Meanwhile an earthquake begins to destroy the city while lightning strikes the buildings. While there are a few small fires, the city is shown being destroyed by collapsing buildings.

"Those buildings look like cardboard boxes," Joe says.

Lot's wife looks back just in time to see an explosion that destroys the rest of the city, and she is turned to salt. Lot's two daughters and Ishmael comfort him as they lead him away from the salt pillar, and the movie ends.

"Ishmael's not there!" Les says quietly.

As they leave the theater, Jim simply says, "Deb?"

"I'll give it a three for entertainment, but zero for accuracy, for want of a lower number."

As Charlotte and Erica leave the theater after it closed, Charlotte says, "Isn't it great we both made the cheerleading squad?"

"I am so excited! I really appreciate Rick giving free admission to members of our squad who show up tomorrow night in their outfits."

"That will be so cool! I wish we could sit with them."

"At least we can join them for the last part of the film after the stand closes."

"I have a feeling Splash won't take his eyes off of you. You look great!"

"What are you talking about?"

"You know he has a crush on you, don't you?"

"No way!" Erica laughs. "He hardly ever says a word to me."

"Splash is incredibly shy!"

"He is a high school all-American wide receiver, how could he be shy?"

"Trust me, he likes you."

"Boys can be so stupid! He needs to say something!"

The girls start laughing and go to the parking lot.

14

Please Pass the Salt

As Told In
The Bible
2013 TELEVISION MINI SERIES

THE TELEVISION SERIES tells the story of Sodom, and explains why Lot, Abraham's nephew, is living there in the first place. Abraham and Lot originally enter Canaan together but Lot's herdsmen fight Abraham's herdsmen because the area is too small to support both men's animals. Lot's wife pressures Lot to tell Abraham what they talked about, which is that they need to split up into two separate tribes.

Lot tells Abraham that they should split up, but Abraham argues that they should stay together and that God will provide for them. However, Lot's wife yells that this is a god they cannot see. Lot then explains to his uncle that they are going to leave. When Abraham asks where he wants to go, Lot tells Abraham he will settle in the greener pastures next to Sodom. Abraham warns Lot that those lands are dangerous, but he reluctantly allows Lot to leave, and they hug as they say goodbye to each other.

"Is this another film that is off to a bad start?" Jim asks Deb.

"This is the exact opposite of what is told in the story. It's Abraham's idea to split up and he offers Lot the choice of which land he wants. Also, his name is still Abram, not Abraham."

Jim shrugs. "I can understand how two families living together would not work out. I remember when your brother and his family stayed with us for three weeks. I couldn't wait for your relatives to leave. No wonder this family needs to split up. Talk about the smell of dead fish after three days."

"My relatives? You say my relatives are a problem?" Deb pauses. "Now that you mention it, we are talking about my brother. I guess they were there too long. I couldn't wait for them to leave either."

"Jim, I heard you figured out a way to shut off the plumbing to the guest bathroom," Dave comments. "Very clever!"

A year later one of Lot's men comes to Abraham's camp and tells him that Lot is a prisoner.

The next part of the series describes Abraham rescuing Lot.

"This part is pretty good," Jim says.

Fourteen years later, Abraham now has a son named Ishmael, when he is visited by three angelic beings. After he feeds them, the angels tell Abraham they are going to decide the fate of Sodom, and leave his camp. While they walk toward Sodom, Abraham negotiates with them and they finally agree that if ten righteous people are found in Sodom, the city will be spared.

"I like this part too," Jim says. "I especially like the actors that portray the angels."

During the negotiation, the scene changes to a street in Sodom where one of the angels is asking Lot to protect them from the people living there. He has been beaten and has an open wound on his head that is dripping blood down his face.

"Angels don't bleed!" Les yells.

The scene now switches back to the negotiation.

"Thirty, twenty. What if there were ten righteous men?" Abraham asks.

Back in Sodom, Lot takes the angels to his house where he shelters them. The mob in the street hears the sound of a wooden bowl fall to the floor inside the house and then a man starts pounding on Lot's door.

"Open the door! Maybe those are school girls selling cookies?" Chester jokes.

"Are those guys wearing short sleeve white shirts and ties?" Charley asks. "Maybe they are there to share some good news."

"Lot feeds the angels unleavened bread before the mob shows up. That is significant. Also the series leaves out what the mob wants to do to the angels," Deb whispers to Jim.

"Why is unleavened bread significant?"

"It gives a clue to the timing of this event."

The angels look at each other in fear, but then throw their shoulders back and walk toward the door, no longer afraid, while Lot is outside telling the mob the angels are his guests. The angels remove their robes and reveal they are wearing shining armor.

"They must be changing into their superhero outfits," Jason mutters while changing reels.

"The reason the mob wants them is because of their glorious appearance," Deb says. "The series doesn't show them appearing glorious when they arrive in Sodom."

They step out the door and have Lot move aside. The angels look up at heaven, and then look back to the crowd causing them painful blindness which results in men screaming and holding their hands to their eyes. As the angels escort Lot through the city, one of them says to Lot, "For Abraham's sake, the Lord is saving you."

"The angel never says that," Charlotte says to Erika as they take a break. "God saves Lot because he is the only man in town who is not an obnoxious evil pig."

"Sort of like the boys in our history class?" Erica jokes.

Meanwhile, Jim looks at Deb. "I see you are not happy with this scene either."

"This part of the series is completely wrong. Lot spends all night in the city trying to get his relatives to leave. As dawn approaches he and his wife still have not left, and they practically have to be dragged out of the city."

As they continue to walk through the city to the gate, they confront another mob which attacks them. One of the angels has two swords hung on his back. He draws the swords and attacks the mob, killing them, as he engages in martial arts moves, stabbing one Sodomite with one sword and another with the other sword, spinning and jumping in the air as he does so. By this time that angel is also bleeding.

"Angels don't bleed," Les Yells at the screen, **"and there are no martial arts fights!"**

As the audience watches the martial arts continue on the screen, a cheerleading chant breaks out in the back of the audience.

"Fly like a butterfly, sting like a bee."

"Touchdown, touchdown, 123."

Charlotte, Erica and all the cheerleaders, repeat the cheer over and over again, kicking their legs in unison in the back of the theater. Meanwhile, Teddy marches up and down the aisle in his usher uniform, acting like a drum major as he struts with a borrowed baton, blowing a whistle in tune with their cheer.

The angels look up to heaven and fire starts raining down on Sodom, while Lot and his three family members are still there.

Deb rolls her eyes. "They aren't even in the city when the fireballs start."

Not finished fighting, one angel continues to attack the inhabitants with his two swords, while the other angel takes out his sword and hacks his way through another group of Sodomites.

The cheerleaders lead another cheer.

"L-E-T-'S-G-O, Let's Go!"

> "L-E-T-'S-G-O, Let's Go!"

> "I guess they are urging Lot to leave," Jim says.

> "Swords! Really?" Jim turns around says to Joe. "Why not just blind those guys too?"

> "These angels are definitely war heroes!" Ronald types. "At this point the angels are responsible for approximately twenty-four dead Sodomites. And the Sodomites? All they have accomplished is two superficial wounds to the angel's heads. Those Sodomites are losers! I'm surprised they don't surrender."

The angels tell Lot to get away because the city is being punished. As the angels run out of the city with Lot and his family, they warn them not to look back.

> "Why are the angels running out of the city?" Jim asks, "That's pretty dumb when they can fly first class."

Once they are away from Sodom, Lot's wife looks back toward the city, with the result that Lot and his two pre-teen daughters see her turn into a pillar of salt.

> "So, she becomes a lost pillar of salt?" Jim asks.

> Dave, who is a parrothead, says, "No, a Lost Shaker of Salt."

The narrator tells the audience that Lot and his daughters flee to the mountains and never see Abraham again, as this part of the series ends.

> Deb gets up to leave. "They actually go to Zoar and they are there when the cities get destroyed. After that they go to the mountains. Of course, they leave out what happens at the mountain."

> "I think that's best left out," Jim says

> "I think we all had a good time," Deb says. "I especially enjoyed watching Teddy and the cheerleaders."

> "Your rating?" Jim asks.

> "The series is very entertaining, so that deserves a four. But I can only give the accuracy a two."

As they leave the theater, the four of them, and the cheerleaders all sing,

"Wastin' away again in Margaritaville, searching for my lost shaker of salt."

Please Pass the Salt

As Told in
Noah's Ark
1999 TELEVISION SERIES

THE FIRST EPISODE of the series starts with the vision of a pagan god and the sound of one crowd chanting "Gomorrah! Gomorrah!" while another crowd chants, "Sodom! Sodom!" The crowds are watching men from each city engage in a battle, killing each other, while a Bible verse appears on the screen, saying the world is full of violence. On top of a hill, Jon Voight, as Noah, observes the carnage and walks away. Lot, played by F. Murray Abraham, is one of the men who survive the fighting, and he approaches his cousin, Noah, who is kneeling down over a mortally wounded man, giving him water. After the battle, there is a party, and Lot asks Noah if he is going to stay for the orgy. Noah tells Lot that he will not stay and that he is only there to do his duty to God, as a citizen of Sodom, by helping the city of his birth.

> *"This is wrong!" Les yells. "Noah and Lot are centuries apart!"*
>
> *"And they aren't cousins!" Jason yells from the projection booth.*

> "How in the world can this film show Lot living before the flood?" Deb angrily says. "I'm leaving!" She starts to stand up to leave, but Jim stops her.
>
> "Honey, you can't leave. You promised Chester some popcorn."
>
> "Ok, I'll stay for Chester. You owe me, buddy."
>
> "Thanks Deb. Can you get me some popcorn now?"
>
> *Deb stands up again, but this time she walks to the concession stand.*

During their conversation, Lot is shown to be a degenerate who does not believe in God, but despite that, the two men love each other. Noah leaves and invites Lot to go with him, but Lot stays at the party.

> "This is crazy!" Jim says. "I thought Lot is righteous."
>
> "He is," Deb moans. "The film gets a **lot** wrong here!"

Noah arrives home to his wife, Naamah, played by Mary Steenbergen, and his three young sons, who ask their father how many men he killed, and if he brought them any swords, or maybe an enemy ear, from the battle. He tells the boys he didn't kill anyone. His wife tells the boys to let their father rest. As he rests in his bed, God talks to him, telling him there is not much time, and that he is to meet him on top of a mountain.

Just before Noah leaves, Lot's wife, played by Carol Kane, barges into their home and demands to know where her husband is and why he didn't return from the fighting. She is admittedly "hot-tempered."

> "I'm glad I stayed," Deb admits, "I'm actually starting to enjoy this film. It has a great cast."
>
> "Wow, Lot's wife is a nasty one!" Joe says. "She reminds me of my wife number three."

When Noah arrives at the mountain, God tells him he is going to destroy Sodom and Gomorrah, and that Noah needs to take his family and leave. Noah asks if there is a way to save the town, and God says if he can find fifty righteous people there he will save it. Noah counters by asking if the number could be ten, and God agrees.

"Not that it matters," Deb says, "but Abraham negotiates with God over Sodom, Noah does not negotiate with God over Sodom."

"You're not going to believe this," Ronald speaks into his phone. "Noah is negotiating with God about Sodom. Plus he's a lousy negotiator; nobody negotiates better than I do."

"Turn your phone off Ronald!" Les yells. **"It's bad enough watching these errors without you giving us a replay."**

Noah returns to Naamah, and they try to put together a list of ten people. Noah mentions Lot, but his wife says she would hardly consider Lot righteous. Noah counters that he is a good friend and a cousin of Naamah, so he is family. They cannot come up with any other names, so the final list is made up of Lot and his wife.

"Really?" Deb says as she brings popcorn back. "So it is Noah and his wife who determine who is righteous in Sodom? Really?"

"You're cute when you get angry," Jim replies.

"Patronize me again and I will really show you angry," Deb jokes.

Noah tells God who is on his list, and God replies that he is not too happy that Lot and his wife are included. God tells Noah that he, his family, Lot and his wife must leave Sodom by noon the next day and that Sodom will be destroyed that night. They are not to look back as they leave. Noah visits Lot and passes on God's instructions.

"First, Noah is not there," Deb says. "Second, if he was there he would not make a list, third, if he did make a list, God would not be unhappy that Lot is on the list, fourth, Lot is supposed to leave by morning because the destruction will occur during the day, and finally, angels give Lot the instructions to leave."

"But, they are told not to look back! That's correct!"

"OK!" Deb laughs, "It's not all wrong. We need the cheerleaders to lead a cheer about getting that part right."

Jim jumps into the aisle and shouts, "**R ,I, GHT!**

Got it right,

Got it right,

ALL RIGHT!"

Jim finishes by doing a split, looking up and smiling at Deb.

The film shows the separate escapes that Noah and his family and Lot and his wife take from Sodom. During their escape, Lot tells his wife he didn't know what happiness was until he married her, but then says, "Now it's too late."

"These scenes are really funny!" Ian laughs.

Noah and his family arrive at a mountain top when balls of fire start flying in, heading toward the city.

"Great special effects," Jim says.

"The problem is the destruction is during the day," Deb replies.

"I'm glad they make this change, these effects are terrific."

"This film is omitting Abraham, Lot's two daughters and the angels."

"W, R, ONG!" *Jim cheers.*

In an effort to explain why Lot's wife turns around to see the destruction, the film shows Lot's wife, who hates the town people, crying out, "They're burning! They're burning! I've got to see it." She tries to turn around but Lot holds on to her. She yells at him, "You never let me do anything I want. I never have any fun." Then she elbows Lot in the side, allowing her to escape his grasp, and turns around saying her last words, "I never have any fun." One of the fireballs land next to them and she is turned into a pillar of salt.

"There are two possible reasons she turns around," Deb says. "But hatred of her neighbors is not one of them. I'll go over those Sunday."

Lot looks at what's left of her and says kindly, "Oh my dear." He then removes a ring on her finger, breaks off the finger of salt, and smiles saying to the salt statue, "I warned you." He kisses her salt arm, which falls off, and he walks away.

"It could have happened!" Jim laughs.

Deb softly shakes her head in agreement. "If she is that nasty, it might have."

The destruction of the city continues with hundreds and hundreds of fireballs flying into it, until it is annihilated. All the men, women, children, rats, cats and camels are consumed in the fire, ending this segment of the series.

"What do you think, Deb?" *Jim asks.*

"Since zero is the lowest rating I can give, I will give the film that for accuracy. But, otherwise, I love it, so I will give it a five for entertainment."

16

Please Pass the Salt

As Told in
The Bible: In the Beginning
1966

ABRAHAM HAS BECOME very wealthy and now is old when three men walk across the field and visit him in his tent. As these men approach, they seem to fade out and reappear, clearly a sign these are special individuals. Abraham bows down to them and finds out they are traveling to Sodom. As they leave Abraham's tent, he realizes the angels are going to destroy Sodom. He negotiates with the angels and gets the one in charge to agree not to destroy the city if ten righteous people can be found in the city.

> "This film has some great actors," Jim says. "I love George C. Scott as Abraham."

> "The angel's first appearance is a neat scene," Dave says.

Lot is at the gate of the city when two of the angels come toward him. In this movie, as in some other productions, the angels are wearing robes that cover their features and hide their faces.

> "How could individuals, who might be lepers, incite a mob to want to rape them?" Jim asks.

> "Clearly they are attractive," Deb responds, "or they would not attract a mob."

> "Maybe those Sodomites are Klansmen and think the angels are from a different lodge," Dave jokes.

Lot recognizes them as angels and escorts them into the city, where they observe people involved in terrible behavior of a sexual nature. When Lot and the angels arrive at Lot's house, a mob gathers and wants the angels given to them, and they are all blinded as a result. The angel, played by Peter O' Toole tells Lot, "Whatsoever thou hast in the city, bring them out of this place, for the Lord hath sent us to destroy it. Take thy wife and thy two daughters which are here, lest thou be consumed in the iniquity of the city."

> "Too many thees and thous for me," Jason says to Rick as he walks down to Charlotte's popcorn concession to get a drink. "Why do some of these films have to speak in King James English?"

While Lot and his family walk through the blinded mob, they are warned not to look back. As they walk out of the city while it is still dark, it appears that everyone in the city is now blind.

> "Once again, a very important element of the story is missing in this movie," Deb says. "There is no mention of any family members other than Lot's wife and two daughters."

> "These films all miss this," Jim agrees. "They are showing Lot and his family leaving Sodom at night without any delay, as opposed to Lot going to see other relatives during the night and delaying their departure until the morning."

> "Very good Jim!" Deb says.

> Teddy sits down with them since the movie is almost over. "The film has them going to the mountains and not to Zoar. None of the movies show that either."

> "The road map went up in smoke!" Dave says. "What do you expect?"

The next morning they are walking up a rocky barren landscape, completely devoid of life, and the city can be seen in the distance.

"This is a very lush area, similar to the Garden of Eden, not some barren desert," Deb says.

"Maybe someone forgot to turn the sprinklers on," Jim jokes.

As they are climbing a mountain, the area lights up and they hear rumbling sound behind them, causing Lot's wife to turn around and she is changed into a pillar of salt, ending this segment of the movie.

As the five of them get into the truck, Jim asks Teddy what he thinks of this film.

Teddy responds, "Dad, this movie is almost as old as you are, but it's still a pretty good film."

"What is your rating Deb?" Jim asks.

"I give it a three on entertainment, which would be a four if it didn't use King James English, and I will rate accuracy a four."

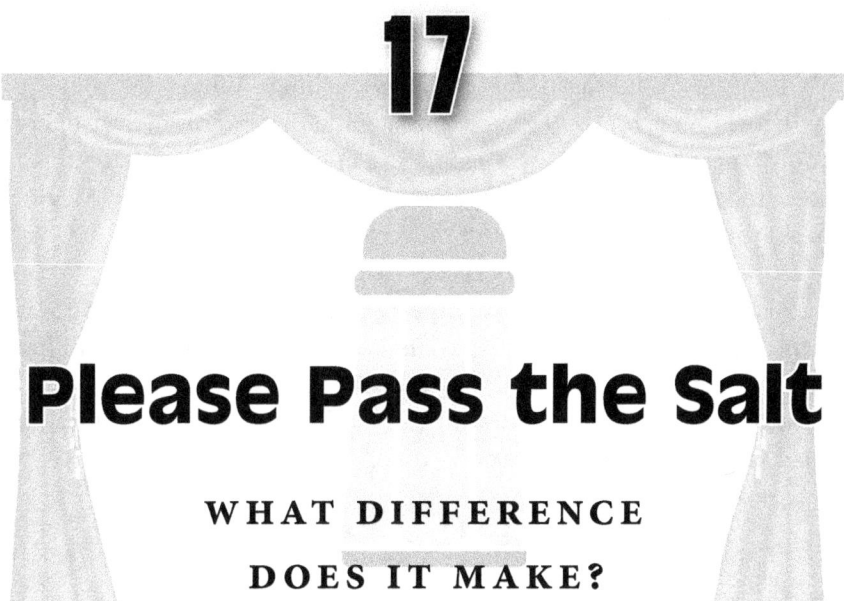

17

Please Pass the Salt

WHAT DIFFERENCE DOES IT MAKE?

NEXT SUNDAY, Deb is telling the class about the cheerleaders in the theater.

"The entire audience was laughing. It was hilarious. The next thing I know my husband is cheering."

She then starts the discussion on the movies and asks, "Is there anything all these films leave out?"

Dave answers, "None of these films show that the area around Sodom is well-watered like the Garden of Eden. This was a beautiful place, not just a barren wilderness."

"I agree," Joe jokes. "There must be a dozen gated communities with great golf courses and low homeowner fees."

"Yeah," Ronald says. "Just like the one I built on Lake Wawasee."

"Except they wouldn't charge $500 for a round of golf," Joe says. "Nobody charges more for golf than you do."

"I bet Sodom has a nice park where you can go on carriage rides pulled by a camel," Jason laughs.

"Not to mention theme parks with waterslides," Ian joins in.

"They probably allow watering lawns seven days a week," Rick says.

By this time everyone is laughing.

"Seriously," Deb says, "something else is missing."

"Okay, Deb," Dave says as he continues laughing. "What is it?"

"There is one error that is made consistently. That error is the size of Lot's family. There are possibly ten people in Lot's family and I discuss this in one of today's handouts. If this is true it is easy to understand why Mrs. Lot turns around, she's worried about the rest of her family."

"There is one other misconception that is universally accepted. While sexual sins are serious, there is another sin that Sodom commits that leads to the city's destruction, That sin is discussed in the other handout I have for you today. One we all need to address."

"Next week we will have only one film to discuss and that will be a film about Jacob. Have a great week everyone!"

part V
Cheaper by the Dozen

MOVIES ABOUT JACOB

An Introduction

LIKE MANY SMALL TOWNS, Wawasee has a weekly newspaper. Nancy Coats has an advice column in that paper called, appropriately, "Dear Nancy." The following four letters arrived at the newspaper office on the same day.

Dear Nancy,

You won't believe what happened to me. While I was traveling abroad, I met this beautiful girl and fell in love. Since her father had to approve of the marriage, I had to work seven years for him to have her become my wife. While there was no marriage ceremony, there was a great bachelor party at the end of the seven year indenture. He arranged a honeymoon suite for us at a local resort, but then he substituted his other daughter to share my bed by cutting off the power and bringing her to me in the dark. Quite frankly, I was too drunk to notice. The next morning I discovered her incredibly ugly sister smiling at me when I woke up.

My question is, which of these three people do I kill, the father, the ugly daughter, or my bride who went along with this charade?

Signed, So many choices

. . .

Dear Nancy,

Last night was a horrible night. I met the man of my dreams seven years ago and we were finally going to have our honeymoon after seven years. Before he took me to the hotel, Dad told me my mom just had a heart attack and I had to go home immediately. When I told him I had to get Jacob, he said he would get him for me. When I got home, my mother was okay, so I went back to the hotel. I quietly opened the door and heard my husband having sex with another woman, so I left and cried all the way home.

My question is, couldn't he have at least waited an hour?
Signed, Tired of Waiting Too

. . .

Dear Nancy,

You're not going to believe this letter is real. My sister, Rachel was to be given to Jacob yesterday. Unfortunately, I had too much to drink or someone possibly put a date rape drug in my wine. All I remember is waking up the next morning in a hotel room—and I was with Jacob! Even worse, he took one look at me and then he chugged a two-liter bottle of cheap wine which made him sick. After he finished throwing up, he told me to get the hell out of the room.

My question is, do you think I had sex with him?
Signed, Innocent Until Proven Guilty

. . .

AN INTRODUCTION

Dear Nancy,

I tried to avenge a relative and now I am in a real mess. My favorite nephew, Esau, was totally screwed by his brother, Jacob, on two occasions. I decided to teach Jacob a lesson and get rid of an ugly daughter in the process. I had to get Jacob drunk and use a knockout drug on Leah to accomplish this, but once I turned the power off at the hotel. I was able to bring her to him in the dark. Remember, Ben Franklin once said, "In the dark all cats are grey," so I was confident this would work. When Jacob confronted me the next morning, I told him I could not exchange Rachel for Leah because he didn't work an additional year to get the "Product Protection Plan."

Now Jacob is trying to decide which of us he wants to kill. My question is, how can I make sure it isn't me?
Signed, Scared Stiff

Nancy, assuming these are prank letters from some Deke at the local fraternity house, tosses the letters in the trash.

Cheaper by the Dozen

As Told in
Jacob
1994

The lights had just dimmed as the film is ready to begin. A woman walks down the aisle and is having trouble finding a place to sit, when she spots the light from a cell phone shining on an empty seat. Stepping in front of people as she makes her way across the row, she accidently steps on the foot of the man holding the cell phone just before sitting down next to him.

"I think you just broke my toe."

She sits down and says, "Shush! You're yelling and disturbing people. Sorry, but your foot will be fine in a few days. At that point, what difference will it make?"

The film they will be watching is part of *The Bible Collection*, distributed by TNT. It begins in a sandstorm while Abraham is still alive and his sons, Ishmael and Isaac, are grown. Sheltered from the storm in a tent, Isaac and his wife, Rebekah, are having a conversation where the audience is told that Isaac favors Esau and his wife favors Jacob. Rebekah reminds Isaac about Jacob holding Esau's heel when the twin boys were born.

> "I like this introduction," Deb says, "it gives a lot of background in a very short time."

After the sandstorm, Jacob sees that one of the men in their camp is very sad, so he asks the tribesman why he is upset. The man tells Jacob his son is dying. Jacob goes into the tent and picks the child up and comforts him. He then makes lentils for the child and the boy recovers.

> "Jacob is a medicine man? I never heard that before," Jim says.

> "We don't know why Jacob makes that food," Deb says, "or have any reason to believe the food would heal a sick child. But, this is an interesting addition to the story."

Esau returns from a successful hunt, carrying his kill. He is hungry and, after he tells Jacob about his attraction to Canaanite women, he asks Jacob for food.

> "There is no way Esau starts making locker room talk when he returns from hunting. He is extremely weak and tells Jacob he feels like he is about to die."

> "I've seen guys at horse races walk to the hot dog stand that look hungrier than this guy," Charley says.

> "Men are never too tired to talk about women," Jim says to Deb, "but, I can understand how hungry he might be, you know how I am when I miss lunch."

> "Not to mention the ten o'clock donuts, the two o'clock cookies, the four o'clock ice cream and a half pound of cheese with our glass of wine before dinner. But think if you went two or three days without anything to eat, you might get as hungry as Esau."

Jacob refuses to give Esau the food he cooked saying it is for the sick child.

> "Wait a minute!" Jim says. "The kid just ate and is feeling better."

Esau argues there's enough food for the child and him, to which Jacob responds that Esau should not just think of himself and wait. Jacob reminds Esau that he is the firstborn and should be more caring. Esau says, "Firstborn be damned." Jacob tells Esau that since the inheritance means so little to him, then he should give it to him and then he could eat all the porridge he wants, so Esau agrees to the deal.

> Les yells, *"One minute he is saving the food for the sick kid, but now he will give Esau all the food he wants for a bigger inheritance!"*

"That's a lousy deal!" Ronald posts. "Esau should insist the recipe be included."

Later, Esau marries a Canaanite woman and is building a stone house in the camp where his parents live.

"There is no mention of Esau building a house," Deb says.

"Does that make a difference?" Jim asks.

> *Teddy hears this question as he walks by and leans over and whispers to his father, "It makes a big difference Dad. Mom's going to talk about this on Sunday."*

Isaac sends Esau out to hunt game, promising to bless him when he returns. While he is gone, Rebekah tells Jacob to impersonate Esau. Jacob argues with his mother and tells her that would be wrong. Rebekah argues back that Jacob should have been the firstborn during the birth process.

> *Deb notices the error immediately. "Jacob doesn't argue that this is the wrong thing to do, he argues that he will get caught and cursed instead of blessed."*

Jacob goes into the tent to give Isaac the food and receive the blessing. The following is a partial dialogue.

JACOB: "Father, I am here"
ISAAC: "Is it Jacob or Esau?"
JACOB: "Your firstborn."
ISAAC: "Are you truly my son Esau?"
JACOB: "Yes, I am your son."

"Did you notice that?" Deb says.

"Notice what?" Jim says.

"Jacob doesn't lie to his father that he is Esau. The film is not showing how devious Jacob is."

"In our day and age, Jacob would make a great politician," Ronald texts on his cell phone to his daughter. "I have to remember how he answers questions when I run for mayor."

Beep beep beep. His daughter texts back, "Daddy, forget being mayor, you could someday become president."

"I'll make this country broke again, but make millions in the process."

Esau goes into the tent to receive the blessing and finds out Jacob got there first and stole the blessing.
Esau: "Have you no blessing left for me?"
Isaac: "God saw me bless Jacob. He allowed it to happen. I—I cannot change that."

"So, it's God's fault?" Les yells.

"The film doesn't show Isaac saying Jacob is deceitful," Deb says.

"It seems like all these films want to sugarcoat lead characters," Jim replies.

Isaac sends Jacob to Aram to get a wife from the daughters of Laban. As he leaves, his mother gives him a gift for his future bride, so he leaves with a rich dowry to offer Laban. Esau's Canaanite brother-in-law goes after Jacob and steals the dowry as Jacob escapes.

"I see an error," Charley says. "He actually steals his diary."

"There's a lot of good stuff in there," Chester says.

"No one steals a dowry or a diary," Deb says. "This scene is not in the story."

Jacob stops to rest and wakes up late at night. He sees a bright star in the night sky and a golden stairway descending to the top of the hill as he hears a voice telling him he will be blessed.

"Three things are left out in this part of the film," Deb says. "It doesn't show Jacob anointing the stone with oil, it doesn't show the Lord standing above the ladder, and it doesn't show angels going up and down the ladder."

"What's the point of having the ladder if no one is going to use it?" Jim jokes.

Chester hears the question and turns to him. "The union will not allow the angels to climb more than ten steps."

Jacob arrives at Haran and meets Rachel, giving her a kiss after he helps her water her sheep. Rachel runs into town and tells her father that his sister's son has come to their city so Laban tells his daughter to bring Jacob to his home.

"Laban actually runs out to meet him," Deb says.

Jacob walks into the house and passes out before he can embrace his uncle.

"Once he meets Jacob, Laban kisses him and brings him back to the house," Deb points out.

Jacob falls in love with Rachel, and he negotiates with her father how long he must serve him in order to have her as his wife. Laban mentions Leah must be married first. However they agree that Jacob will get Rachel after seven years.

"This part is wrong," Ian tells Avery. "Laban doesn't mention Leah needing to be married first."

Seven years later, Laban realizes that he has been blessed because Jacob is working for him, so he hatches a plot to keep Jacob there seven more years. He substitutes Leah for Rachel on the wedding night. The wedding occurs, and Jacob goes into the wedding chamber, which is slightly lit, kisses his bride, and consummates the marriage.

"There's no wedding described in the story, just men having a feast," Ian says.

"I hope Rachel's having a bachelorette party with a male stripper," Avery jokes.

"That's funny just thinking about how the policeman would slowly remove his robe," Ian laughs.

"In the film, Jacob has kissed Rachel many times. Wouldn't a man notice he is kissing someone different?" Deb asks.

"Remember, he hasn't been with anyone for seven years. He wouldn't care who it is," Jim responds.

"Men are such pigs!"

"Oink oink," Ronald laughs.

The film covers the twenty-year period that Jacob has eleven sons and a daughter, during which time Jacob leaves Laban and the story of the division of the livestock is told.

"This part of the story is very well done," Deb says. "I don't see any contradictions."

"As opposed to medium rare," Jim jokes but then agrees. "It is well done."

A member of Esau's tribe informs Esau that Jacob is coming home, so Esau takes men out to meet Joseph with the intention of killing him. Esau is riding with a few men and sees the campfire where Jacob is cooking the sacrificial lamb and tells his men they will attack Jacob the next day.

As Deb returns with more popcorn for Chester, she sits down and tells Jim, "This part is completely wrong. Jacob sends messengers to Esau, telling him that he is coming home with all his livestock and servants. Esau doesn't come out because of a warning from his own people."

Before the brothers meet, Jacob wrestles with an angel in a two-minute scene.

"They actually wrestle most of the night," Deb says.

Jacob gets hold of the angel and won't let him go until the angel blesses him. The angel responds that, "I've not come to bless you, but to make sure you don't escape."

"What?" Deb says. "Really? Where does this come from?"

Jim responds. "Escape from where?"

"Maybe the heat," Dave says.

"This is not right! He wants to be let go because it's close to sunrise."

In the morning, Jacob, hurt in the wrestling match, struggles to limp across the river at the same time Esau and about fifteen of his people ride to his camp.

"It's actually four hundred men that are with Esau," Deb says.

"Those extras get $8 an hour," Jim says. "Union labor costs a lot of money."

Esau rides to the camp and has his men surround it. He rides up to Jacob and speaks harshly to him, as Jacob bows down before his brother. Esau dismounts and holds a sword near Jacob's throat, saying he came here to kill him.

"This is a shame, the film has stayed with much of the story, but this part is wrong," Deb says. "Esau actually runs to meet him, kisses him and weeps."

Esau tells Jacob he cannot kill him and they embrace. Esau invites Jacob to follow him to Seir, but Jacob says they have to rest and will follow them later. Esau responds, "Very well, you'd better take shelter. A storm is coming."

"The film deletes some comments but adds Esau's warning," Deb says. "This is a good addition because it has an obvious double meaning, a rainstorm, and the future conflict between their descendants in the generations to come. This may be my favorite line in the movie."

The film ends with Jacob taking his family to Shechem, where he purchases land for one hundred sheep.

"The ending is interesting," Deb says as they leave the theater. "All the versions I read say he purchases the land with money, but the Septuagint says he buys it with sheep. I'm not sure why there is a difference."

"It probably has to do with financing," Jim smiles. *"With sheep, he has a higher down payment, but with money he gets a lower interest rate."*

"So Mom, do you like this movie?" Teddy asks as they leave the theater.

"It's another good effort by the folks at TNT. I would rate entertainment a strong five and accuracy a four."

19

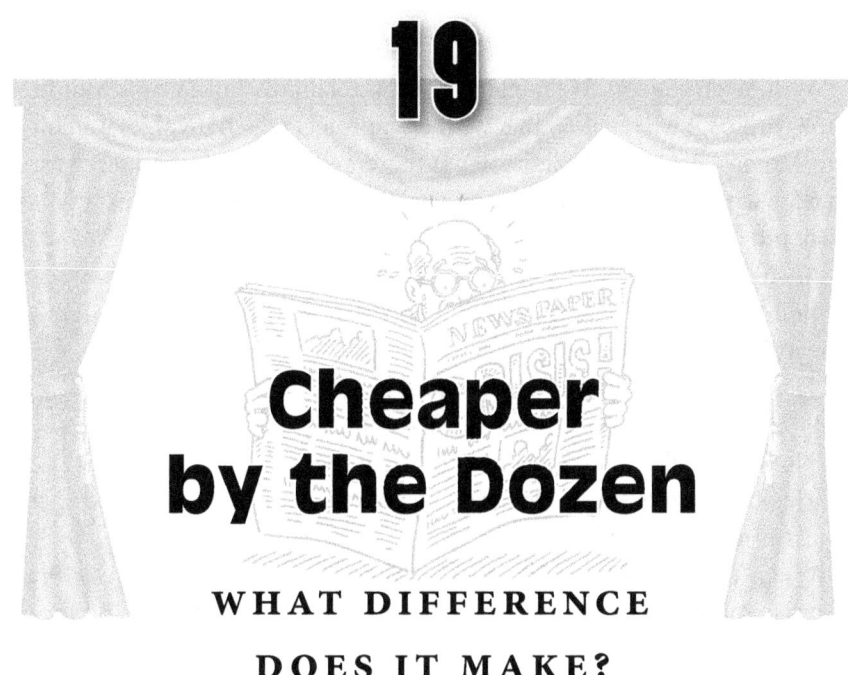

Cheaper by the Dozen

WHAT DIFFERENCE DOES IT MAKE?

AS PEOPLE ARE SITTING down in Sunday school class, Deb says, "I would like to introduce a new member to our group. Class, this is Tiffany Clayton. She has recently moved back to Indiana from New York where she once was a state senator."

Ronald recognizes her as the woman who stepped on his foot in the theater and says, "I guess it's time we get properly introduced. My name is Ronald." He extends his hand to Tiffany, who unfortunately has built up a high charge of static electricity from the carpet in the room. As their hands touch, the static discharges into Ronald's hand, causing him to yell, "What's this? Are you wearing some kind of joke ring?"

"I'm so sorry Ronald, I've had this problem of static buildup all my life. In fact, that is the reason I lost my job before I went into politics. I could not work around computers because my body would discharge static electricity and delete files occasionally when I would touch the keyboard. One time I accidently deleted thousands of e-mails from my boss's server by simply turning on his computer."

"I bet he was shocked!" Dave jokes.

"Well," Deb pauses, "Welcome to our class, Tiffany. Since this is your first time with us, I will explain that we have a project which involves watching the 'Movies Doing the Bible' series at the Wawasee Theater and discussing in class what we see in those films. There was only one movie this week so it should be a short class."

As she opens her Bible, Deb says, "There are two topics that I would like to point out about the film *Jacob*. The first one involves Esau building a house. Does anyone see a problem with that?"

"He doesn't have a contractor's license?" Ronald frowns as he is still rubbing his hand. "Trust me, that can be a real problem."

"No Ronald, that's not one of them. Anyone else?"

"He's building the house before he gets married," Dave says. "Now the house is marital property."

When the class stops laughing, Deb wipes tears from her eyes, "Brad Scott, of Wildbranch Ministries, points out in a video that many Bible parables involve a house and a field. It is very important to understand that Esau represents a man who lives in a field as opposed to Jacob, a man who lives in a house. Living in the field as opposed to living in a house is a bad thing, because the field represents the world with all its corruption as opposed to a house which represents safety. Our handout today goes a little deeper into this subject."

"The second thing in this film I would like to talk about today regards a legend. There is an object in this story that is possibly in the world today. That is the stone that Jacob rests on when he is in the wilderness."

"Talk about a lumpy mattress!" Dave jokes.

"For several centuries, every king and queen of England, including Queen Elizabeth II, has been crowned sitting on a throne that is above a particular stone. Tradition says this stone is the same stone that Jacob sleeps on at Bethel. However, there is evidence the stone actually came from Scotland. This stone was recently transported to Scotland, and I watched the ceremony which was quite a spectacle. It's a shame the stone in the film is not similar to that stone, since there is so much written about it. Names attributed to this stone include 'Stone of Scone' and 'Liafail,' as well as several other names."

At that moment, Jim walks into the room. "Sorry I'm late, did I miss anything?"

"Did you get in nine holes, Jim?"

"No, it started to rain."

"Next week we are going to have a special treat. Since we will be looking at films about Joseph, we will get to see the musical about the story of *The Amazing Technicolor Dreamcoat*. This is one of my favorite films of all time. Have a great week everyone."

part VI
Family Feud

MOVIES ABOUT JOSEPH

An Introduction

THE SALTY DOG introduces the show to the studio audience's applause.

"Live from our recently rebuilt WSOD studio, welcome to 'The Phil Show.' Once a week Phil Scheidt, an accountant during tax season and a relationship advisor during the summer, helps dysfunctional families by giving them advice on national television. But you, in the studio audience, get to see this live and hear for yourselves the problems that lead to dysfunction."

"Today we are honored to have Jacob, his two wives, their two maids, his twelve sons and his daughter with us."

Phil walks on to the stage with his Poodle named Prince, where the guests are sitting in front of a fireplace.

More applause from the studio audience as Phil asks his guests, "So what's the problem?"

"Well for one thing, all of us not named Rachel, Joseph or Benjamin are second class citizens," Leah says.

"Jacob makes it plain he doesn't love me and never comes near me unless he wants another kid. And guess what? If I'm not available, rather than wait, he will jump into one of the maid's tents. The three of us are nothing but baby machines."

"Have you ever had to clean up after thirteen kids?" Bilhah, one of the maids says. "Zilpah and I have to do all the work while constantly listening to Leah nagging Jacob, 'You don't love me! You think I'm ugly.' That's all we hear out of her. She's driving us all to the funny farm!"

"That's not the only issue here," Simeon wearily says. "Dad constantly reminds me and my nine brothers that we are second class citizens compared to Joseph and Benjamin, who all of us know, can do no wrong."

Judah shouts, "Who has to go out and spend weeks at a time in the field taking care of Dad's sheep? We do. Who stays home, takes naps, and makes notes about his dreams, taunting us with them later? Joseph! Who else?"

Phil asks Jacob, "What's this I hear about a coat? What's that all about?"

"Well," Jacob says, "Joseph is a great son to have. Other than Benjamin, the rest of them are idiots. They are constantly screwing up and poking each other in the eyes. I thought if I give Joseph this magnificent coat that they would take it upon themselves to behave more like Joseph and then they could get coats if they would stop acting like morons."

"So, how has that worked so far?" Phil asks.

"I think it's working out really well," Jacob replies. "He looks great in that coat. It looks like a tartan from the McDonald clan."

"Aye. It's a good one, idn't it?" Joseph smiles.

"Yeah, it's working out well for Joseph!" Dan joins in. "But what about the rest of us?"

"What can I say?" Jacob moans, "You guys still act like imbeciles, but I have ten more coats stashed away. Some day? Who knows? Maybe you will all get coats."

"Come back next week," Phil says. "The family is planning a vacation in Egypt and we will get to hear how that turns out."

Phil walks off the stage to applause as Prince runs over to the guests wanting to have his tummy rubbed.

Family Feud

As Told in
Joseph
1995 TELEVISION MINI SERIES

As Erica enters the theater to get ready for work, she walks over to Charlotte. "He did it! He asked me to help him clean the auditorium after the last movie."

"Are you talking about Splash?"

"Yes, while it's not an actual date, it's a start. This is so great!"

"Make sure you tell him you're thirsty afterward, or he may just walk off. He is sort of clueless when it comes to girls."

"I can't wait."

The film that night is one of several TNT series shown on television in the nineties about characters in the Bible.

"I like these films," Deb says as they walk into the Wawasee Theater. "It's obvious they try to stick to the story, but still be entertaining."

"But, don't they add and omit things?" Jim asks.

> "As long as the additions don't contradict the story and the omissions are not important to understanding the story, it's fine with me."

At the beginning of the film Joseph, played by Paul Mercurio, is at a slave market in Egypt waiting his turn to be sold. Potiphar, played by Ben Kingsley, is at the market and purchases Joseph to be a field hand at his home. Lesley Ann Warren is Potiphar's wife, sees how handsome Joseph is, and without hesitation, tries to seduce him. When she fails, she accuses Joseph of trying to rape her, an accusation Potiphar doesn't believe, so he asks Joseph what really happened. Joseph tells his side of the story which is shown as a flashback of his life up to that time.

> *"This is a great introduction," Deb says. "All three of these actors are perfect for their roles, the flashback is a great way to start this film, and what is shown is totally accurate so far."*

> *"I hear Martin Landau will play Jacob," Jim responds. "I'm looking forward to seeing him in that role."*

The flashback begins with Jacob leading his family through Canaan and arriving at Shechem. Before getting into Joseph's story, the film tells the story of Dinah, who is Joseph's sister, going into the city of Shechem, drinking too much at a feast, and then finding a room to sleep it off.

> *"Smart girl," Rick tells Charlotte. "She doesn't drink and drive."*

> *"She could lose her chariot drivers license if she gets hit with a DUI," Joe says.*

Shechem is not only the name of the city, it is the name of the son of Hamor, the ruler of the city. The son follows Dinah to the room where she is sleeping and rapes her.

> *"The film changes this," Deb says. "Dinah is not in the city, she goes out to meet girls who live in the country."*

The next day Hamor goes out to Jacob and does all the talking in an attempt to smooth things over.

> *"Actually, he and his son both do the talking," Deb says.*

> *"How do you talk your way out of that?" Jim asks.*

"By agreeing to have all the men of the city cut off their foreskins."

"They'll take my foreskin out of my cold dead hands," Chester says.

"You don't have hands," Charley reminds Chester.

"They better not walk up behind me. After they feel my hot live hooves on their threeskins, they won't be cutting anything off of anybody."

Once the men of Shechem are weakened, Simeon and Levi lead a group of their men to kill the men in the city, and then burn Shechem.

"According to the story, Simeon and Levi do all the killing and then the other sons loot the city," Deb comments, "also, they don't burn the city."

The film now continues telling Joseph's story to Potiphar about how he ends up in Egypt. All the brothers are out in the field at night, eating one of the lambs they are supposed to be protecting. Joseph not only won't eat any of the lamb, but he tells on his brothers to his father. The brothers get yelled at, and Joseph gets the famous coat of many colors.

"This is a good example of an addition that doesn't contradict the story. It is possible something like this could have happened," Deb says.

"It sure goes a long way in showing why the brothers would hate Joseph," Jim agrees.

Jacob tells his wives that Joseph will receive the birthright and inheritance before his brothers sell him into slavery.

"That's not true, is it?" Jim asks.

"No, that's never mentioned."

Jacob sends Joseph out to his brothers' camp. When he doesn't find them where he expects they would be, he wanders around looking for them, when he meets a man who tells him his brothers went to Dothan.

"Alabama?" Chester Jokes.

When Joseph looks in that direction and turns back toward the man, he is no longer there.

"Maybe he is a famous magician," Charley comments.

> "Didn't a magician once make the whole state of Alabama disappear?" Chester asks.

> "I bet Georgia football fans wish that would happen."

> "This is actually another good addition, the man doesn't really disappear in the original story," Deb says. "But this reinforces the idea that God is responsible for what is going to happen without contradicting what's told."

Joseph finds his brothers, and they decide to kill Joseph by putting him in a pit where he cries out to them throughout the night. But a caravan comes by the next morning, and they instead sell Joseph into slavery.

> "There is a change for dramatic effect here," Deb says. "The brothers sit down to eat a meal and then the caravan appears. They don't listen to Joseph's pitiful calls to his brothers all night."

The flashback ends with Joseph telling Potiphar that his brothers sell him into slavery, and he goes on to explain that Potiphar's wife attempts to seduce him. Potiphar believes him and has Joseph put in prison instead of killing him. While Joseph is in prison he is joined there by the Pharaoh's cup bearer and baker. The baker is shown to be an obese bully.

> "This guy has been eating too many of his doughnuts!" Ronald starts texting on his phone. "Look how fat he is!"

The cup bearer, however, is very nice to Joseph.

> "I remember this. One of these guys gets released," Ronald continues to text. "I bet it will be the baker. The cup bearer is toast. Nice guys finish last."

> Deb comments, "The story does not describe the personalities of these two men so the producers have the option of making one obnoxious if they want to, but the original story doesn't say the baker bullies Joseph. This is another good addition."

When these two men find out Joseph can interpret dreams, the cup bearer describes his dream to him, and Joseph tells the cup bearer that in three days he will be released from prison and restored to his former position in the court. Then the baker tells Joseph his dream and instead of Joseph giving him the bad news, he is reluctant to tell the baker his fate. Then he softens it by telling the baker this is what he believes will happen.

> "This part isn't true," Deb says. "He doesn't hesitate to tell the baker what's going to happen."
>
> Jim smiles, "Joseph would make a great CPA since everyone knows they have no reluctance to tell their clients bad news. I know Phil doesn't."
>
> Dave comments, "Phil once told me about a dentist walking into his office and saying, 'Your people must hate to see you as much as my people hate to see me.' The dentist threw his books on Phil's desk and walked out without turning around or saying goodbye."
>
> Deb jokes, "I guess if Joseph is a CPA he would tell a client who is about to be audited, 'I believe you owe money to the IRS, but you might not. In the meantime, please pay me while you still have money left.'"

Joseph tells the baker the Pharaoh will hang him from a gallows.

> "It's actually a tree," Deb says. "Also, the film leaves off Joseph asking the cup bearer to remember him when he gets back in the Pharaoh's court."
>
> "Does that matter?" Jim asks.
>
> "It will. I'll talk about that in class."

Two years later, the pharaoh has dreams that cannot be explained, and then the cup bearer remembers Joseph, so he calls him to interpret the Pharaoh's dream. The Pharaoh does not believe his interpretation and puts Joseph back in prison for the night.

> **"He doesn't put him back in Jail!"** Les yells.
>
> "He immediately makes him the second most powerful man in Egypt," Deb says. "Les is right."

Joseph takes over Egypt's administration and when the drought starts, the film switches back to Jacob and his family. The film explains that ten brothers make the trip to Egypt to buy grain. The film shows that they are all sent in order to protect each other and their money on the way there, and the grain on the way back.

> "Why all ten brothers went is not explained in the original story but it makes a great deal of sense," Deb comments. "I really like this addition."

When the brothers arrive they meet Joseph but do not recognize him. The film shows the details of how Joseph manipulates events to see the reaction of the brothers. Once he sees they have changed, he reveals himself and sends for his father.

> "The film does not show Joseph listening to them admit their guilt, which is pretty important, but the reunion is well done," Deb says.

> "If they are a typical family, they will all be fighting the next day," Dave jokes.

Jacob not only sees Joseph, but sees his grandsons as well. He blesses them, which ends the film.

> As they leave the theater Jim says, "I have a feeling you like this version."

> "Despite a few small errors, this is an excellent film, one of the best I have ever seen. It definitely deserves a five for both entertainment and accuracy."

> "I agree, it's an excellent film."

> "It's a great film," Chester also agrees.

21

Family Feud

As Told in
Joseph and the Amazing Technicolor Dreamcoat

1999

AN ASSEMBLY at a children's school outside of London is the centerpiece of this film. The film, based on one of Andrew Lloyd Webber and Tim Rice's first musicals, begins with children walking into an auditorium, followed by the faculty. Once everyone is seated, Maria Friedman walks down the middle aisle and almost trips as she makes her way to the stage. She begins singing and Donny Osmond is introduced as Joseph as he walks into the auditorium singing "Any Dream Will Do," at which time, Maria gives him the coat of many colors. The entire production is song and dance, featuring many types of music. Even though this presentation is a film, all the scenes appear as if this is a live performance.

Maria, who appears throughout the film, walks through an opening at the back of the stage into a set that appears to be a Middle Eastern landscape where Jacob's family is introduced. The song the brothers sing shows the animosity that all of Joseph's brothers, including Benjamin, hold against Joseph. This bitterness leads to a plan to kill Joseph, but instead, they end up throwing him into a well, pull him out and selling him into slavery.

> "I don't think Benjamin is part of the plot for two reasons," Deb says. "Joseph and Benjamin are close, plus Joseph is seventeen at the time this happens which would make Benjamin as young as ten."

> "You're right," Jim agrees. "Since Joseph is seventeen at the time and not out with the brothers, I think it is safe to assume Benjamin is not out there either."

> "Maybe he has football practice," Teddy jokes.

> "Joseph or Benjamin?" Jim asks.

> "Both of them, high school and pee wee."

The brothers return to Jacob and sing to him that Joseph died saving their lives from a vicious goat which would killed them all except for Joseph's bravery.

> "It is a wild beast," Deb says laughing. "It's not a goat."

> "Maybe so," Jim laughs, "but this song about a ferocious goat killing Joseph is hysterical!"

> "You just can't trust those goats," Charley says. "He must be one wild and crazy goat."

> "Had he not sacrificed himself we would all be dead," Chester starts singing along with the song in the film.

Joseph is sold to Potiphar and he does well until Joan Collins, as Potiphar's wife, tries to seduce him in a song and dance presentation. Potiphar walks in on them and has Joseph thrown in jail.

> "The film gets this part wrong," Deb says. "Potiphar doesn't walk in and find them together."

While in jail, Joseph musically interprets the dreams of the baker and the butler. When the baker tells his dream to Joseph and receives the news that he will be executed, Osmond sings to him, "Don't rely on what I've said, but I've never been wrong before."

"That is so funny!" Avery laughs. "I'm always right, too."

"I thought you were a liberal," Ian says.

The next scene introduces an Elvis impersonator as the Pharaoh, who has dreams he cannot interpret, so he has Joseph brought to him to tell him the meaning of his dreams. After Joseph interprets the dreams, he becomes the number two man in Egypt.

"I love this," Deb says. "It's worth buying the DVD just for this scene."

Back in Canaan, Jacob and his family are starving because of the famine that Joseph predicted to the Pharaoh is happening there. The sons travel to Egypt and encounter Joseph where the family is ultimately reconciled.

The final scene shows Joseph riding a chariot to meet his father, and once they meet the film ends with Joseph singing "Any Dream Will Do."

> *As they leave the theater, Jim and Deb are both smiling and agree they love the musical while Chester and Charley are singing "Any Dream Will Do," as they climb into the trailer.*
>
> *Getting into the truck to drive home, Jim says, "This film is both entertaining and informative. I just love Maria Friedman in this movie."*
>
> *"Not only that," Deb responds, "but it's way more accurate than most of the movies we have watched so far. The only problem is that I would not want to show this in Sunday school because of the revealing costumes some of the actresses wear, but I still happily give this a four for accuracy and a five for entertainment."*
>
> *They drive off, also singing along with Chester and Charley, "Any Dream Will Do."*

Family Feud

WHAT DIFFERENCE DOES IT MAKE?

IN SUNDAY SCHOOL, Deb describes the films to the class for the benefit of those who were not able to make it to the theater that week. The class discusses the small differences that are in each film and agree these differences don't hide any important messages in the story of Joseph, or don't have any significant contradictions.

At the end of the class Deb says, "I have two handouts today. The first one deals with events that appear in the Old Testament and later get mirrored in the New Testament. Some of these events can be called Messianic moments. The second handout deals briefly with Benjamin's age."

"Next week we will see films on Moses, and these films will definitely give us plenty to talk about. Have a wonderful week everyone."

part VII
Surf's Up

MOVIES ABOUT MOSES

An Introduction

IN THE WEST WING of the palace, the pharaoh's cabinet is in executive session as they start discussing the pharaoh's posts on social media.

"It's disgraceful!" The vizier says.

"I agree! We are the laughing stock of the world," the chief treasurer sadly says. "Not only that, our kingdom is now bankrupt!"

"From Assyria to Carthage," the chief scribe adds, "every slave that owns a tablet is now laughing at us."

"Our former slaves are even sharing his posts on tablets they plundered from us as they left," the chief overseer comments.

"Let me read you these posts!" the vizier says.

> **@makeegyptgreatagain** Moses, what a loser, shows up today with his buddy, Aaron. He wants special treatment for our guest workers. He wants to take them on three-day trip. No way can they take up to a week off while the hard-working citizens of Egypt continue to work.

> **@makeegyptgreatagain** This is nothing but extortion. He pollutes Nile and then demands special treatment. Says Nile is now blood, but I think it is actually tomato juice. I think I'll have a Bloody Mary.

@makeegyptgreatagain Things keep happening, we just don't win anymore, but we will. Our country is out of control; however, we do have enough frog legs to feed everyone for months.

@makeegyptgreatagain We have to be much smarter or this is never ever going to end.

@makeegyptgreatagain Why would the Hebrews follow this guy Moses out of our great country. What a lightweight! He is meek and doesn't even speak well. No ego. Show me someone without an ego, and I'll show you a loser.

@makeegyptgreatagain Well, they left. Good riddance! If these people can stay poor for so many generations, maybe these aren't the kind of people we want in our country. Taking care of them has resulted in tremendous fraud and abuse. Well that's ending!

@makeegyptgreatagain Tomorrow will be amazing! Just amazing. We are going to chase these people completely out of Egypt. Let's see if they can swim across the Red Sea! This is no shallow stream that they can just walk over.

@makeegyptgreatagain We have great generals. Believe me! The losers are trapped. The incredible men and incredibly hot women of our military will wipe them out!

@makeegyptgreatagain The Red Sea is now divided into two great walls of water. Our fantastic gods of Egypt have arranged it so we can slaughter Moses and his buddies on the other side, so we don't even have to bury their bodies in Egypt.

AN INTRODUCTION

@makeegyptgreatagain That wall of water looks great for surfing! When the army returns we will all play volleyball and surf!

@makeegyptgreatagain We have a great military, not one of them surrendered. No losers in this bunch! Any time you go to visit the Red Sea, remember our entire army, which is at the bottom of that great body of water.

@makeegyptgreatagain This is a great victory. The wonderful people of our military got rid of these people. They are out of Egypt and will not return. I will build a great wall to keep them out! Nobody builds walls better than I do. Plus, we will make Israel pay for the wall.

@makeegyptgreatagain Don't listen to the fake news! We actually won, and we will rebuild our military.

@makeegyptgreatagain I have two words to say to all the fake gods of Egypt, "You're fired!" These gods do nothing for Egypt. They are a disaster! They let this loser, Moses ruin our great country.

@makeegyptgreatagain Now that the loser gods are gone, I would like to introduce our new gods. Egypt will be much more efficient with just two gods. You will be amazed at how good they are! They will do incredible things for us. Meet our new gods, Covfefe, and his wife, Hillary!

@makeegyptgreatagain WE ARE GOING TO MAKE EGYPT GREAT AGAIN! Mark my words!

The vizier puts down his tablet, and with that, all the cabinet members start chanting,

"Two pence! Four pence! Six pence a dollar! All for Mike Pence, stand up and holler!"

The cheering can be heard all the way down Egypt's National Mall.

> Cindy has lived in Wawasee all her life, and now at the age of forty-two realizes it is unlikely she will ever marry or have children, despite being so pretty in high school that she was homecoming queen. Owning the candy shop the beautiful blue eyed brunette inherited from her parents has been an eighty-hour occupation since the shop also includes a restaurant where judges and lawyers, who work in the courthouse across the street, gather for lunch.
>
> She recently started reading the Bible and decided to start watching the films that are being played in the Bible marathon at the theater down the street. After saying hi to Erica, a high school girl she has known since the cheerleader was a baby; she goes into the crowded theater and sits down behind Dave, who is depressed over his divorce and is is slumping down, not revealing that he is quite tall and will block Cindy's view as they both watch the movie.

Surf's Up

As Told In
The Ten Commandments
1956

The *Ten Commandments* is by far the most well-known production of a Bible story in history. Undoubtedly, more people have seen this film than any other Bible movie, especially since it is shown on television every year at Easter. Cecil B. DeMille directs this movie and also narrates the introduction and occasional segues throughout the film. As the film begins, he reads what seems to be a passage from Genesis.

"And God said, 'Let there be light. And there was light. And man was given dominion over all things upon this earth. And the power to choose between good and evil. But each sought to do his own will.'"

> *"That's not in Genesis,"* Les yells from the back of the theater. *"Someone made that up!"*

> *"I recognize the first verse as being from Genesis, but the rest of what he's saying is not in the Bible,"* Deb comments.

> *"I think he is quoting from First Cecilonians,"* Dave says

"It does have a King James sound to it," Jim says. "I wonder if he talks like that to his wife?"

Dave jokes, "Why doest thou always hath a headache at bedtime?"

The story begins with astrologers telling the pharaoh of Egypt that a baby has been born who will lead the slaves out of Egypt, saying that a star in the heavens is a sign of his birth. Fearing such an event, the Pharaoh orders that all Hebrew male babies be killed.

> "Oops! The film is using the wrong Testament," Deb says. "There is a story in the New Testament about Herod killing male children to keep a new king from rising, but that's not what's happening here. The Pharaoh orders the babies to be killed because there are too many Hebrews, and he fears they will eventually overpower the Egyptians."

In a Hebrew home, an Egyptian soldier stabs a baby to death with a sword, and walks away while the mother sobs.

> "Very dramatic and heart wrenching," Deb says, "but that's not what happens. The Pharaoh orders the babies to be thrown into the river. It's possible he does this for the amusement of the Egyptians, who might enjoy watching Israelite babies fed to crocodiles."

"Does it really matter how the Egyptians kill the babies?" Jim asks.

> "Actually it does. Remember that the first plague on the Egyptians, forty years later, is the Nile being turned to blood. That plague could be a reminder of what Egyptians did to those babies."

In the area where the slaves live, an Israelite woman puts a baby in a basket and floats it down the Nile where it is found by an Egyptian princess and her attendant. The princess saves the child and adopts him, naming the baby "Moses." As an adult, Moses, played by Charlton Hesston, will be shown to be a great general and Nefretiri, an Egyptian woman in the palace, played by Anne Baxter is in love with him. She is not the only one who loves him, the pharaoh loves him even more than Ramses, his own son.

> "Nefretiri must be a misspelling of Nefertari," Deb says. "There is no one known by either name in the story."

Pharaoh orders Moses to build a city. While he is supervising the construction, he saves the life of an old woman, who is actually his mother, before she is about to be crushed between two huge stones. At this time he meets Joshua, a Hebrew stone mason, who is played by John Derek. Moses, acting on what he observes and seeing that mistreating slaves is inefficient, gives the temple grain to the slaves as well as giving them a day of rest every seventh day.

"Why not giving them Labor Day too?" Jim asks.

Deb answers, "Moses is never told to build a city, and he certainly did not have the authority to give the slaves a day off."

The film starts with the assumption that Pharaoh orders the Hebrew babies killed because there might be a potential ruler in that group. So, the film cannot have Moses, or anyone else, know that he is a Hebrew. However, the attendant knows, and when she finds out Nefretiri wants to marry Moses, she tells her that Moses is a Hebrew and threatens to expose Moses out of loyalty to Egypt. Nefretiri kills the woman as a result of her threat and when Moses walks in right after the murder, Nefretiri tells him the details of his birth.

"You mean I'm gonna get circumcised!" *Charley jokes loudly.*

"Out of my cold dead hooves," *Chester yells back.*

Moses is in the mud pits, where he stomps on straw with other slaves to make bricks, so he can experience what it is like to be a Hebrew. He is there long enough to have several days of beard growth.

"Moses goes out to observe the Hebrews not to join them," Deb says. "He only goes out there twice in two days."

"I remember reading this," Dave says. "He kills the overseer on the first day and is confronted by the Hebrews on the second day."

Moses sees Joshua being whipped and kills the Egyptian overseer, played by Vincent Price. Joshua realizes Moses is the deliverer when he finds out that Moses is a Hebrew. He thanks God that the time of the delivery of the Israelites has finally come.

"This doesn't happen," Les yells. *"The Hebrews reject Moses when he kills the Egyptian."*

Edward G. Robinson, as Dathan, sees this conversation and reports to Ramses, played by Yul Brynner, that Moses is the deliverer.

"Deliverer?" Dave yells. *"Is he going to drive a brown chariot and wear a brown uniform?"*

"No," Joe responds, *"he will become an OB-GYN."*

"These are two of the greatest actors of that period," Jim quietly says to Deb. *"I love watching them. They are perfect in these roles."*

After Ramses is told about Moses, he takes Moses out to the desert and sends him into exile. DeMille narrates as Moses struggles to cross the hot desert to Midian.

"He's quoting First Cecilonians again," Dave jokes.

"It's definitely not from Exodus," Deb says. *"Moses flees Egypt, he isn't expelled."*

Moses is weak and dehydrated, unable to walk much further when he arrives at a well. Despite his exhaustion, he quickly dispatches evil shepherds who are trying to drive girls away from the well as they are watering their father's sheep. Moses is invited back to the girl's camp where he meets Jethro, their father. Jethro gives Moses the choice of his daughters to marry, and he chooses Zipporah, played by Yvonne DeCarlo.

"I hope he gets a pre-nup," Dave says.

"I always get a pre-nup," Ronald posts. *"I have great lawyers, nobody has better lawyers than I do."*

"Did you have a pre-nup, Dave?"

"No, and now I'm paying her every month. Speaking of ex wives, didn't you remarry your first wife after you divorced number two?"

"Yeah, I did," Joe says sadly.

"Why would you marry her again?"

> "We weren't done fighting yet."
>
> "The film leaves out a significant event that happens after he drives the mean shepherds away," Deb says.
>
> "What's that?" Jim asks.
>
> "The film doesn't show Moses watering the sheep. There is more to this story than just a fight scene. I'll have a handout on this Sunday."

Forty years pass, and Moses is happily married, content to be herding his father-in-law's sheep. Joshua visits Moses and this encounter begins the next part of the story, which is Moses being called to lead the Israelites out of Egypt.

> "Joshua doesn't visit Moses in Midian," Deb says.
>
> "If he does I hope he doesn't stay more than three days," Chester answers. "You know how guests stink up a stable after three days."
>
> "Maybe he is taking a vacation on credit card points and accidently runs into him," Charley jokes.
>
> "What kind of a theater is this?" Cindy thinks. "Are these people and those two animals going to talk all night?"

Moses climbs a mountain and encounters the burning bush. He bows down at the beginning of the conversation and asks God his name. When told and given his assignment, he humbly asks how he can lead the Hebrews out of slavery. During the conversation he looks directly at the burning bush and he bows down again at the end of the scene.

> "Moses never stares at the bush and the film leaves out an important part of this encounter," Deb comments. "The film doesn't show Moses not wanting to get involved."
>
> "He doesn't?" Jim asks.
>
> "No, Moses argues that he has a speech defect and asks God to send someone else. He wants no part of this."
>
> "Can you imagine Charlton Heston stuttering?" Charley asks.

"They will take this staff out of my co-co-cold, d-d-dead, h-h-hands," Chester jokes.

While Moses is still in Midian, the scene switches to Egypt. The dying Pharaoh still loves Moses and utters his name with his dying breath.

"This is not true. There is nothing in the story about the pharaoh loving Moses," Deb says. "In fact he orders Moses killed."

Moses returns to Egypt and confronts Ramses, who is now Pharaoh. Moses does almost all the talking, and doesn't show a speech defect as he tells the Pharaoh to, "Let my people go."

"Aaron actually does most of the talking," Deb says.

Nefretiri is married to Ramses but she still loves Moses, and attempts to seduce him. Moses is not interested. So, she gets angry, telling Moses she can soften Ramses' heart or harden it. Moses then says that God might use her to harden Ramses' heart.

"It's God that hardens Pharaoh's heart, she has nothing to do with it," Deb says.

Pharaoh won't set Israel free, so the plagues are unleashed, starting with the Nile being turned to blood. In the film all the plagues, except the boils and locusts, are either presented or referred to. The plague of hail, like the other plagues, arrives without warning.

"Pharaoh is given a warning about the plague of hail that will come the next day," Deb says. "There are some Egyptians that heed the warning and shelter their livestock."

The final plague, the death of the firstborn, is the result of Ramses ordering the death of the firstborn sons of Israel.

"This is made up," Deb says. "Pharaoh never issues such an order."

At midnight, before Pharaoh can kill the children the next day, the angel of death, in the form of green mist, arrives in the night sky next to the moon in the first quarter. The mist moves around Egypt, killing the firstborn on contact.

"**Hello!**" Les shouts. "**Passover is always on a full moon!**"

"Les is right," Deb says. "This plague introduces the first Passover. Showing it on a quarter moon is a huge mistake!"

"Don't they all die at midnight?" Jim asks. "This green mist lollygags for hours, like its floating through a flea market."

"Drift like a mist, float like a flea!" Joe jokes.

The next morning is a glorious day for the Hebrews, as the Pharaoh relents and lets the slaves free. They journey toward the Red Sea, but Pharaoh, at of the urging of Nefretiri, goes after them.

"Once again, his wife has nothing to do with this," Deb says. "It's God who hardens Pharaoh's heart."

The Israelites arrive at the Red Sea, just slightly before the Egyptians do in the middle of the day. The pillar of fire first appears at this moment, preventing the Egyptians from attacking the Israelites.

"The film leaves out the pillar of cloud and the pillar of fire that leads them out of Egypt," Deb says.

In order to escape the Egyptians, Moses faces the sea, holds out his staff and the sea parts on the shore where they are standing and rapidly separates from them toward the eastern shore.

"Let's see if I have this right," Jim says. "The east wind parts the sea, but it separates from the west."

"This is a great miracle, it's like God has a giant vacuum cleaner that he holds on the other shore," Les yells.

"Is that former minister drunk?" Cindy thinks, remembering the scandal when Les was fired.

As the sea parts, Dave sits up and completely blocks Cindy's view and she recognizes Dave as a regular customer at the lunch counter. At the same time a baby starts crying in the theater.

"Whose baby is that?" Avery asks.

"That's Mrs. Clayton's grandson," Ian answers. "She's babysitting."

"Am I having a bad dream?" Cindy thinks. "This theater is becoming a house of horrors. I can't see or hear anything. Plus, some guy won't turn off his cell phone."

"Even though the parting includes an error," Jim says, "the special effects of the parting sea are terrific!"

Moses leads the Israelites across the dry seabed in daylight, as some of them happily sing, and they reach the other side of the Red Sea during the day. Once some of them are across, Moses stands on a high point where the remainder of the people can see him as they walk toward the eastern shore.

"This is completely wrong," Deb says. "They cross the seabed at night, walking into a wind that is strong enough to keep the sea parted. This isn't easy, especially when you think of taking children and animals through a path illuminated only by the moon."

"So if this scene were shown accurately, Moses would be standing on the opposite shore as an inspiration to those still walking through the sea and no one would be able see him?" Jim asks.

"Unless Moses' staff divides into two light sticks and he waves them over his head like an airline ground crewman guiding a plane to the gate," Dave laughs.

"I still wouldn't be able to see him if I was walking behind you Dave," Cindy thinks.

Once the Israelites are safely on the other shore, the pillar of fire dissipates, allowing the Egyptians an opportunity to follow their former slaves through the Red Sea. Ramses orders his army to follow the former slaves and the army all drowns when the sea crashes down on them as they attempt to follow the Israelites.

"Look Charley, they are showing horses drowning," Chester says. "At least the film doesn't have mules as stand-ins."

"I'm calling PETA!" Charley responds.

Weeks later, Israel gathers at the Mount Sinai where Moses receives the Ten Commandments. While Moses is on the mountain, the Israelites make

SURF'S UP

a golden calf and prepare to provide a human sacrifice to it, that sacrifice being Joshua's girlfriend.

"There's no mention of a human sacrifice," Deb says.

Moses comes down the mountain, sees what is going on, and orders those who are with God to get behind him. After they do, he throws the tablets down, breaking them on the golden calf. An earthquake occurs, causing a giant sinkhole with flames coming out of it to open up, and all the bad Israelites fall into it to their death.

"This isn't what happens," Deb says. "That calf is an idol that represents the true God as opposed to being a pagan god."

"I know that much," Jim says. "But isn't there a sinkhole that swallows them?"

"Not during this event. When Moses comes down to the camp he throws the tablets at the foot of the mountain and burns the calf. He orders the Levites that support him to get behind him and then tells them to kill the other people in the camp. The people that die are killed by Levites, not by falling into a sinkhole."

DeMille starts narrating again, explaining that the Israelites have to spend forty years in the wilderness to prove they can keep God's commandments.

"Oh great!" Deb says, "More quotes from Cecilonians."

"They stay in the wilderness because of the bad report of the spies!" Les yells.

"Les makes a good point," Deb comments. "This is actually very important because the date they bring back the bad report will be cursed."

On the top of a mountain Moses, with his close friends and family, observe the Israelites going into Canaan. He acknowledges that he cannot go in, and his wife tells him that wherever he goes she will go.

"Isn't that from the book of Ruth?" Jim asks Deb.

"Yes. But Ruth says that hundreds of years later to Naomi."

However, Moses tells her to go in with the people, and the movie ends.

"I wish my ex would have left that easily," Dave yells.

"We have seen this film so many times," Jim says as they leave the theater, "but this time I would like to hear your rating. You have to admit, this is a good movie."

"It is fun to watch," Deb agrees. "I easily give it a five for entertainment and a two for accuracy."

"It is a fun movie," Chester says, "I could watch it every year."

24

Surf's Up

As Told In
The Bible

2013 TELEVISION MINI SERIES

THE TV SERIES *The Bible* starts with a flashback where the pharaoh's daughter tells Moses, "You were so many."

"This is very accurate!" Deb says.

Moses is growing up in the palace when he discovers his identity. After he is told, he goes out to a construction site and observes an overseer beating a Hebrew. He picks up a brick and uses it to kill the Egyptian. There are slaves around him performing work, and they see this happen.

"Moses actually looks around to make sure that no one sees him before he kills the guy," Deb says. "There should be no slaves in sight."

One slave tells Moses to escape and he will bury the body, but the body is discovered and it is holding a piece of jewelry that everyone knows belongs to Moses.

"It's that watch!" Chester says. "He is always misplacing it."

"That is a lousy job of burying a body!" Charley says.

> "If one of my workers dug a hole that bad, I would fire him," Ronald posts. "I know how to dig great holes, nobody digs better holes than I do."

> "The series makes two serious errors in this scene," Deb says. "Moses thinks nobody sees him kill the overseer. Plus, the slaves want nothing to do with Moses. They are not going to help him escape."

After Moses leaves Egypt, he is shown coming out of his tent to investigate the light from a burning bush. He sees the bush, and God speaks from it telling Moses he is the God of Abraham, Isaac, and Jacob, to which Moses replies, "You are real?" God replies, "I AM."

> **"Nice meeting you!" Dave yells.**

> **"Really?"** Les screams loudly. **"When God says, 'I AM,' he's not answering a question. He is telling Moses his name!"**

Moses doesn't remove his sandals and stares at the bush during the entire encounter.

> "Moses has his face to the ground the entire time," Deb says. "He doesn't just stare at the flaming tree. However, I like how the film shows this tree, it's beautifully done."

God tells Moses he is sending him to lead his people out of Egypt, and Moses responds, "How can I set them free?"
"I will be with you," is the response.
Moses says, "With your power, I will set them free."

> "Once again, Moses is not shown arguing with God that he should send someone else," Deb says. "This series has him almost volunteering."

> "I was told in the army to never volunteer," Jim says.

> "Well, Moses does not volunteer for this either," she responds.

> "I know a mule who volunteered to go in the army. He was never heard from again," Charley says.

> "He is now a mascot at West Point," Chester responds.

> "I thought he got eaten by a goat."

"*You're confusing him with Buffalo Bill.*"

When Moses returns to Egypt he meets Aaron in Goshen.

"*Aaron actually travels out to meet him,*" Deb says.

Moses then meets Miriam, his older sister, who now has two young children.

Les yells, "**That woman is over eighty years old!**"

"**Her husband can't keep his hands off of her,**" Joe yells back. "**They just don't show the other sixty kids.**"

Moses meets with Pharaoh and says to him, "Let my people go."

"*This reminds me of the Peter, Paul and Mary song titled, 'Let My People Go,' but Peter, Paul and Mary don't complete the sentence,*" Deb says, "*and neither does Moses in these films. The rest of the sentence gives the reason they are to be let go, and that is to go into the wilderness to have a feast to the Lord. They are only asking to be freed for a few days.*"

"*I thought it is just to be set free,*" Jim responds.

"*You and almost everyone else think this, partially because of these films.*"

The ten plagues are about to begin. Moses and a few Israelites hide in bushes on the other side of the Nile while Pharaoh is bathing. Moses stands up, holding one staff while Aaron strikes the water with another staff. The river turns red around the Pharaoh and he comes out of the Nile covered in blood.

"**Where's the pool guy? He needs the filter cleaned!**" Dave yells.

"*Actually, Moses not Aaron, uses his staff to strike the river,*" Deb says, "*and the Pharaoh is not swimming.*"

All ten plagues are shown or referred to, however the ninth plague, darkness, is depicted as falling on Goshen. The implication is that all plagues through number nine affect the Israelites as well as the Egyptians.

"Only the first three plagues fall on the Israelites," Deb says. "It is very important that the ninth plague not fall on Israel."

"Why is that?" Jim asks.

"It's important that the Egyptians, who are in darkness, see Israel living in light."

There is no depiction of the softening and hardening of Pharaoh's heart during the plagues. He is only shown yelling no several times.

"He actually goes from yelling no to being willing to let the slaves go, but not out of Egypt," Deb says. "The Pharaoh not only will acknowledge the existence of God, but he will eventually admit sinning against God and Moses."

The series shows the plague as the death of firstborn sons, resulting in Moses being brought to Pharaoh the next day.

"The tenth plague falls on all the first born, including the livestock, not just the sons," Ian says. "Also, Moses meets Pharaoh at night, right after the death angel leaves."

"He must have his days and nights mixed up," Avery replies. "Mom told me I had that problem when I was a baby."

"I bet you were a cute baby, just look at you now."

The series omits the pillar of cloud and the pillar of fire leading the Israelites out of Egypt. The pillar of fire is not shown between the army and the former slaves, which keeps the Egyptians from attacking the Israelites before they can cross the Red Sea, since they are within sight of each other.

"Why can't men on chariots catch the slaves when they are only a few hundred yards apart?" Jim asks.

The series shows a wonderful vision of the Red Sea parting. However, Moses is shown parting the sea by striking it with his staff.

"This doesn't happen," Deb says. "Moses doesn't thrust his staff into the seashore, like an Apache plunging his spear into the ground in some western."

A strong wind blows, but does not appear to part the sea. The Israelites are shown crossing the Red Sea during the day, but the series shows that it is dark deep beneath the parted Red Sea.

> "The film gets it half right," Deb says. "The Israelites are shown crossing in darkness."

After Israel escapes the Egyptians, Moses climbs a mountain, as he struggles against stormy conditions. At the top of the mountain, tablets drop out of the side of the rock, and Moses takes them down to Joshua. The episode ends, showing Joshua, forty years later, preparing to attack Jericho.

> "So, what do you think about this episode?" Jim asks as they walk out the theater.

> "It's very entertaining, so I will give that part a five, but the errors make the accuracy worth only a three."

25

Surf's Up

As Told in
Exodus, Gods and Kings
2014

EXODUS, GODS AND KINGS also attributes the killing of Hebrew babies to the fear that a leader has been born who will overthrow the Egyptians. The Pharaoh orders all the firstborn Hebrew boys to be killed. However, Moses gets rescued and Miriam, the sister of Moses, is brought into the palace to help raise him along with Ramses, the son of Pharaoh.

> "They kill the babies to control the population. Isn't that right Deb?" Jim asks.

> "That's right," she says. "You're learning!"

Moses, played by Christian Bale, is told his father was a great general. Everyone thinks he is the cousin of Ramses, and now he is an important advisor and friend to Pharaoh. He is also a fighting general who is very popular with the masses of Egypt.

> "Total horsefeathers! Even I know that," Charley says. "When Pharaoh finds out Moses kills an overseer, he orders Moses killed without even talking to him."

The action starts early in the film and it features Moses in a bloody battle scene where he saves the life of Ramses. After the victory, Pharaoh orders Ramses, his son, to go to Pithon and learn what happens there, so he can someday be a better ruler. Moses suggests to Ramses that he go instead. Once there, Moses arranges to talk with the elders of the Israelites. Among them is Nun, the father of Joshua, who is depicted as a leader of the elders.

> "Wow! Where does this come from?" Deb asks? "First of all, that's not the reason Moses goes to see the Hebrews, and second, Nun is never mentioned in the Bible except as being the father of Joshua."

> "Sounds like this is all nunscence," Jim jokes.

When Moses meets with the elders, there is a hint that they recognize him as the revolutionary leader to come. Joshua arranges a second meeting where Moses is told of a prophecy about a revolutionary leader that will lead them out of Egypt, and that Moses must be that guy. Moses rejects this idea and leaves the building angry and confused. As he walks down an alley, Moses is accosted by two Egyptian guards. He kills one and injures the other. The surviving guard informs the viceroy of this. The viceroy is also told by two evil Hebrews of the conversation that Moses has with Nun, and that Moses is a Hebrew. This is all reported to Ramses, who expels Moses from Egypt, despite the fact that he still likes Moses.

> "Mule feathers!" Chester says. "There is only one Egyptian Moses encounters, and that guy is beating a Hebrew. After he kills the Egyptian, the Hebrews don't want anything to do with Moses, they reject him when he tries to talk to them. He then escapes Egypt because Pharaoh is going to kill him."

> "How do you know all this?" Charley asks.

> "I have big ears and heard Deb commenting on other films. Plus, I have mule sense."

Moses arrives in Midian and saves the girls at the well from shepherds who try to drive the girls away. Moses marries one of the girls and stays in Midian for nine years, during which time he is portrayed as an agnostic.

> "He is actually in Midian for forty years," Deb says.

"Is he ever described as an agnostic?" Jim asks.

"No way!"

"Wow! That Zipporah is incredibly hot for a shepherd girl," Jim says as he stares at the screen.

"She obviously spends a lot of time at the drugstore cosmetic counter," Deb responds. "By the way, zipper your lips."

"She sure is," Dave whispers to Jim, agreeing with him.

The nine-year period in Midian ends with Moses climbing a mountain on a rainy day and getting engulfed in a mudslide that covers his entire body except his face. While lying on his back in the mud he sees a bush spontaneously ignite into flames and an eleven-year old child walks up to Moses. Looking at him in the face, Moses asks the child for help because his leg is broken and then asks, "Who are you?"

The child responds, "Who are you?" and Moses replies that he is a shepherd.

The child—in the role of God—tells Moses he needs a general and that he thinks Moses should go to his people and see what is happening to them, adding, "Are they not people in your opinion?"

Once again Moses asks the child, "Who are you?"

The camera zooms in on the child's face and he responds, "I Am."

> The film stops, the lights come on and Rick walks on the stage and speaks to the audience.
>
> "Most of you know Chester and Charley, and that Deb teaches them from the Bible. Chester watched the DVD of this film Thursday and told me about this scene and asked if we could stop the film and see how the audience reacts to how this movie presents God in this scene. Quite frankly, I found it offensive and told Chester to go for it. If anyone is unhappy that we are doing this, at the end of the movie Erica will be in the lobby with coupons for three future movies and popcorn you may have if you are upset that we interrupt this film. Chester, you and Charley may come up now."
>
> Chester and Charley walk up on the stage, and Chester asks the audience, "What things did you just see that are total 'Mulefeathers'?"

"All of them!" *Teddy yells.*

Chester looks up to the balcony, and says, "Ian, what did you see that was wrong?"

"I heard a child say he is 'I AM,'" *Ian answers.* "There is no way that can be true because God never talks to a man as a child."

Chester, continuing to look in the balcony says, "I see a hand up, what did you see?"

"Ian's right," *Avery says.* "Also, the real Moses lies on his stomach and won't look at God, while this Moses lies on his back and looks the child in the eyes. The real Moses takes his sandals off because he is standing on holy ground. This guy is just buried in mud."

"Besides that, Moses goes to God, God doesn't come to him," *Les shouts.* **"Moses says 'Here I am,' not, 'Who are you'?"**

Turning to the third row, Chester says, "I see a hand sticking up from behind Dave. Tell us what you just saw."

"I couldn't see much because Dave won't sit still," *Cindy says* "but there is no way the bush catches on fire while he is already there. Moses goes to investigate the bush that is already burning."

Charley asks, "Joe, did you notice anything, or are you still thinking about five putting number eight the other day?"

"Yeah, Moses says he is a shepherd."

"That's the only thing in this encounter that is shown right!" *Dave laughs, slapping Joe on the back.*

"Ronald, can you stop texting on your cell phone long enough to tell us if you noticed anything, while you were annoying everyone in the theater?"

"Yeah," *Ronald responds,* "God thinks Moses should go to Egypt! What, he can't make up his mind? Leaders need to lead!"

"Why would God have to ask who Moses is?" *Erica asks.*

"Since when does Moses get a broken leg?" *Charlotte joins in.*

"And why is God asking if Moses considers the Hebrews people?" Tiffany, who is holding her crying baby, asks. "Would Moses think they are deplorables?"

"I was taught Moses spends forty years learning humility," Teddy says. "Why would God now want him to be a general?"

"Splash is right," *Someone yells.* **"By the way Splash, great game Friday!"**

Teddy turns to the man and bows.

"God wants a general?" *Jason yells.* **"Are the Hebrews like toy soldiers in some kid's toy box?"**

"Let's have a show of hands. How many like this scene?" Chester says.

Not a hand goes up.

"Point made," Chester says.

*As he and Charley return to their seats, the theater is quiet until Charley blurts out, **"I have a headache, Jim."***

The lights go down and the film resumes, showing Moses leaving Midian.

Moses tells his wife and son he is leaving for Egypt, but before that, he gives his shepherd's staff to the boy. He takes his sword and rides away from his family and crosses a shallow part of the Red Sea on his horse.

"He has two sons!" *Les yells.*

"He takes his wife with him," *Dave cries out.*

"Yeah, he takes his staff and doesn't even own a sword," *Jason adds.*

"So why does he later need to part the Red Sea?" *Les yells again.* **"He could just take them to the shallow part."**

"You'll see, he gets lost," *Chester responds.*

Once Moses returns to Egypt, he goes to a stable and confronts Pharaoh who treats Moses as a long-lost friend. They get into a discussion about how the slaves should be freed or get paid. The Pharaoh tells Moses the slaves cannot handle freedom.

"There are some things too difficult to handle," Dave says.

"Sort of like asking a mule to juggle bowling pins,'" Charley says.

After Deb stops laughing at the visual of a mule trying to juggle, she says, "Moses never argues with Pharaoh."

There is almost no discussion of God except when Pharaoh asks, "Which god?" Moses does not answer that question and they part, knowing they will soon be enemies.

"Moses doesn't want to tell him God is an eleven-year old child," Charley says.

Shortly after that encounter, Pharaoh orders that Moses and his family be killed. Since they can't be found, Pharaoh hangs a slave family and warns the Hebrews that he will kill additional families every day until they turn over Moses. In the meantime, Moses trains freedom fighters and they raid the Egyptians in additional fighting scenes.

"None of that happens," Deb says. "No order to kill families, no freedom fighters or raids on Egyptians, none of this."

When the fighting fails to free the slaves, the child tells Moses he is doing it all wrong, and that he will take over from now on.

"He tells Moses he wants a general that will fight!" Ian tells Avery. "Now he is angry the fighting isn't working?"

The first plague, the Nile being turned to blood, is caused by crocodiles attacking people in boats. The film continues to show the plagues except the lice and the darkness.

"These are great special effects," Jim says.

"But it doesn't show Moses striking the water with his staff," Deb says.

"Well something gets those gators mad," Chester says. "Did they lose to FSU?"

"Those are crocodiles, not gators," Charley says. "You have been watching too much football!"

When the plagues aren't working, Moses yells at the child because the plagues are affecting everyone.

"Only the first three plagues affect the Israelites," Les yells.

"Yeah, Moses is really going to yell at God!" Teddy tells Rick at the back of the theater. "That would be like me yelling at you."

"Splash, you would be on restroom duty in a heartbeat."

During the final plague, Moses is shown to be outside, instead of being inside his house.

"Moses and all the Israelites are in their homes," Deb says.

"Unless he and his wife have a fight and she locks him out," Dave says. "My ex did that once."

Ramses goes to Moses the next day and orders them out of Egypt.

"The Pharaoh calls for Moses to come to him at night, just after the final plague," Ian says.

"I just love how smart you are!" Avery responds.

The Israelites are now allowed to be released. In this part of the story, God is omitted, not even answering Moses when he asks for help on what to do. As a result, Moses leads them to the wrong spot in their flight from Egypt.

"I told you, two left turns then a right, not two right turns and then a left," Charley jokes.

"Although I think he eventually would end up in Atlanta. All flights go through there."

"This is a different kind of flight," Chester explains.

Once at the Red Sea, late in the evening, Moses sees a shooting star that appears to reach ground far off in the distance. The next morning the sea has gotten shallow enough to cross, the apparent effect of a meteorite plunging into the sea, causing the sea to recede long enough for the slaves to escape. The wall of water can be seen far to the south and it will soon return as a tsunami.

"So much for the parting of the Red Sea," Deb says. "It's just going to be a big tidal wave."

"Dudes! Get your surf boards!" Chester says. "Surfs coming up!"

There is no east wind that causes the sea to stay divided and the Israelites cross during the day, which involves them wading in water waist deep in several areas.

"So much for crossing on dry ground between divided waters," Deb says.

"Is that important?" Jim asks.

"It is to Paul, who pictures this crossing as a type of baptism."

"Isn't there a film where Jesus is only immersed to his knees?" Jim asks,

"Yeah there is, we'll see that in a few weeks."

As the wall of water is returning, Moses goes back to meet Ramses just before the tidal wave arrives. They both get caught by the huge wave but both survive, with Moses ending up on the east shore and Ramses the west shore.

"What are the odds?" Charley says. "The entire Egyptian army is wiped out, but these two guys survive?"

After the events at the Red Sea, Moses returns to Midian, bringing all the tribes of Israel to his home.

"Honey, I'm home," Chester says. "I brought some friends with me for dinner, is it okay?"

Charley mimics the wife in a falsetto. "Great! How many did you bring?"

"About two million."

"Give me about two hours to put on my makeup," Charley answers in the falsetto.

Once at Midian, Moses climbs the mountain and meets with the child. During the meeting, Moses inscribes the Ten Commandments on tablets and the child brings him something to drink.

"*Do you want a refill?*" Chester asks. "*Is that diet or regular?*"

"*God is not going to wait on Moses,*" Deb says.

The period at the top of the mountain includes the following dialogue between Moses and the child while Moses writes the commandments.
THE CHILD: "What do you think of this?"
MOSES: "I wouldn't do it if I didn't agree."
THE CHILD: "These laws will guide them in your stead."

"*So,*" Deb says. "*God is asking Moses what he thinks of the Ten Commandments and Moses replies he wouldn't write them down if he doesn't agree with God.*"

"*I guess Moses is the greatest type setter of all time,*" Jim responds.

"**Moses doesn't write the Ten Commandments!**" Les yells.

In the final scene, which takes place years later, Moses is with the Israelites as they travel through the wilderness. He is now very old and riding in a covered wagon. He picks up the cover and looks outside the wagon and sees the child walking next to the wagon. The child stops walking and the movie ends.

"**God travels with them spiritually with the Ark of the Covenant in a wagon,**" Les yells.

After the film ends, Rick goes over to Erica and asks her, "How many coupons did you give out?"

"*Only one,*" Erica answers.

"*Wow! I'm glad it was just one. Who took the coupon?*"

"*Ronald. He said this is too good a deal to pass up.*"

"*Let's have your ratings Deb,*" Jim asks as they leave.

"*The film is well done from an entertainment point. Great acting, action, and the special effects, especially the visuals of Pithon, are incredible, so I give entertainment a five. It has huge accuracy issues so I rate the accuracy at one.*"

26

Surf's Up

WHAT DIFFERENCE DOES IT MAKE?

DEB HAS A BUSY week preparing for Sunday school while watching these films, but she still finds time to write down a few things to ask the class, as well as prepare several handouts. When everyone arrives and takes their seats, she starts by asking how many people had seen any of the movies. Everyone had seen *The Ten Commandments*, and most of the class had seen at least one of the other films. Three people, including Dave and Ian, had seen all three films.

Deb starts the class by explaining one of the things she pointed out to Jim in the movies. She explains that the Egyptians throw the babies into the Nile instead of stabbing them, and that this could be part of the reason God turns the Nile into blood. She goes on to explain the rest of the reason.

"All the plagues relate to Egyptian gods, and they are used to show that God is more powerful than they are."

"Let's talk about omissions that are important. I saw some omissions that all three productions make. Can anyone name any of them?"

"I know one of them," Dave says. "They do not show that the Egyptian priests duplicating the miracles of turning the Nile to blood and producing frogs."

"That's right. Does anyone have any ideas how they do those things?"

Jason speaks up. "Obviously, their duplications have to be tricks, like pulling a rabbit out of a hat. They can't turn the Nile to blood since it has already happened. They must have done tricks on a smaller scale."

"Do you think God could prevent their tricks from working?" Deb asks.

Charlotte says, "Sure."

"Is it possible he allows these tricks to work in order to harden Pharaoh's heart?"

"Certainly," Erica says.

Deb tells the class, "By the way, one of today's handouts deals with hardening Pharaoh's heart. Any other omissions?"

Ian raises his hand. "Another omission is that none of them show the warning of the hail plague before it arrives resulting in some Egyptians protecting their livestock because they believe the warning."

"That's good, Ian."

"What does Moses repeatedly say to the Pharaoh? I'll give you a hint. There is a song title which includes these words."

"Let my people go," three people say at once.

"Do the movies leave anything out when they have Moses repeat these words?"

This time there is silence in the room.

"In every film as well as the song made famous by Peter, Paul, and Mary, the purpose of the freedom is left out. They are to be freed so they can hold a feast in the wilderness. This purpose is so important it is mentioned six times. The first handout explores this in more detail."

Deb continues, "Have you ever wondered why Moses spends forty years in Midian? Why doesn't he just free the slaves before he leaves Egypt?"

"Let me guess," Dave says, "there's a handout on this too."

"You're right," Deb says. "There are six handouts today. There is a great deal of material in this story that isn't mentioned in the films, so these handouts barely scratch the surface of what movie viewers miss. Enjoy the service which starts in five minutes. I hope you can all find good seats."

part VIII
Mother-in-Law

Ernie K. Doe. 1961

MOVIES ABOUT RUTHS

An Introduction

AS DAVE AND JOE walk into the theater, Joe says, "I hear your former mother-in-law can be difficult."

"Mildred can be way more than difficult. She constantly thinks she is entitled to cut in line and use her deceased husband's handicapped pass to avoid walking across a parking lot, despite being perfectly healthy. Every time we took her to dinner, she always made us late because her time was more important than ours. Speaking of dinner, did I ever tell you what it was like going to a restaurant with her?"

Not waiting for an answer, Dave continues.

"One time we went to a restaurant we hadn't been to in three years. As we walk into the lobby, Mildred announces in a sing-song manner for all to hear, **'We're Baaaack!'**"

"Now the question is, would anyone remember us after three years? If we walk in with Mildred, the answer is yes!"

"After being told it's an hour wait or first-come first-served at tables at the bar, Mildred walks over to a bar table and stands next to the patrons sitting at it to claim it when they leave. 'Don't mind me,' she says to those victims, 'go ahead and enjoy your dinner.'"

"Mission accomplished! All conversation ceases at that table, and we sit down within five minutes."

"Mildred orders the all-you-can-eat fried shrimp and my ex orders lobster. It is bad enough that my ex sends her order back four times, but after Mildred eats a dozen of the huge shrimp, she then orders a second helping and proceeds to stash it in her purse."

As Dave is relating his story, a car pulls up outside the theater and parks in the handicapped parking spot. A woman gets out of the car and then cuts in line at the ticket booth, telling the people in line she is too handicapped to stand in line. As she enters the theater, she announces in a singsong manner for all to hear, **"I'm baaack!"**

About four in the morning, in a one-bedroom apartment, Dave suddenly wakes screaming so loudly that all the tenants in the complex can hear. **"Noooooooo!"**

As Dave realizes he has had another nightmare about his former mother-in-law, he asks himself, "I wonder how Ruth would have dealt with Mildred?"

27

Mother-in-Law

As Told in
The Story of Ruth
1960

RUTH IS A LITTLE GIRL living in Moab, at the beginning of this film, when her father sells her to the local pagan temple where she will become a child sacrifice. The six-year old girl thinks this is a great honor, so she looks forward to dying for the god, Chemosh. As the leaders of the temple prepare to sacrifice her, they discover a blemish on her arm that miraculously appears which disqualifies her as a sacrifice. One of the other girls says, "Look, I have no blemishes," and happily runs over to the priests to be killed. Since Ruth cannot be sacrificed, she grows up in the temple and becomes a priestess who worships Chemosh and prepares little girls to be sacrificed.

> "She's such a cute little girl," Jim says. "Do you think any of this actually happens?"
>
> "No, none of this really happens in the story; this is imaginary. Well-written, but imaginary."
>
> "Sort of like fake news?"
>
> "Not quite the same. Remember, I said well-written."

"So," Chester says, "Ruth could actually be from Chicago and it would not contradict anything in the story?"

"That's right."

Hearing this conversation, Ronald texts, "There's a better chance of that than Tiffany being shot at in Bosnia."

"The movie takes a whole reel of film on something that never happens," Jason tells Rick as he starts the second reel in the booth.

Now that Ruth is grown, the film introduces Naomi and her family. The film shows that the father and two sons have a thriving business in Moab fabricating gold crowns and religious artifacts. One son is married and the other son, Mahlon, played by Tom Tryon, is still single.

"Doesn't the father die before either of his sons get married?" Jim asks Deb.

Teddy hears this question as he is walking by with his flashlight and he leans over and whispers to his father, "That's right Dad."

Deb says, "There is nothing known about how the father and the two sons die. What is known is that the husband dies before his sons get married."

Mahlon meets Ruth and in the next few scenes he teaches her about God and now that she is converted, she will no longer participate in child sacrifice. The father and the two sons are blamed for corrupting Ruth, and they get thrown in prison, where Mahlon's father and brother get killed. Ruth devises an escape plan to free Mahlon. She has a servant walk into the quarry at night, he taps Mahlon on the shoulder, and together they climb some steps and crawl towards a wall to where Ruth is waiting.

"This plan is pure genius! All they have to do is climb out of the quarry. It's brilliant!" Chester says.

"I never would have thought of doing that," Charley responds.
"Humans are so smart!"

"Are you guys being sarcastic?" Jim asks

Chester and Charley respond singing to a calypso beat, "Oh no, not us, we would never make such a fuss."

Before Mahlon can get to the wall, a guard stabs him in the back. After the servant pushes the guard away they escape to a hilltop, where Mahlon dies, but not before he marries Ruth.

"Ok, another reel and the film is now at verse five," Jason mumbles to himself.

"Of course, nothing like this is in the story," Deb points out, "but it is interesting and a good addition."

Naomi and Ruth travel west to Bethlehem carrying their possessions on two donkeys while attempting to escape from Moab. Soldiers follow them but are not able to catch them, so in frustration, the Moabite soldiers poison a well while they are in Israel.

"I hear those Moabite soldiers are really tough, sort of like our Navy Seals!" Jim jokes.

"That's not what happens," Deb says. "They are not trying to escape from Moab or Moabite soldiers. They leave because the drought in Israel is over."

Stuart Whitman, as Boaz, makes his entrance as a Judean leader who forces a captured Moabite soldier to drink the water from the well the Moabites poisoned.

"This is more fiction," Deb says. "There are no Moabite soldiers in the story."

"I thought Boaz is much older than Ruth," Jim says.

"Stuart Whitman is only thirty-two years old when this film is made. He's way too young to play this role. It's clear in the story that Boaz is much older than Ruth."

"Maybe this is what Boaz sees when he looks in a mirror," Jim stands up and jokes. "A seventy-year old man who thinks he looks like he is thirty."

"Suck in that gut Jim!" Chester jokes.

Naomi arrives in her home town of Bethlehem and introduces Ruth to Eska, an old friend of hers. When Eska finds out Ruth is from Moab, she warns Naomi they should not be seen too much since Ruth is from Moab. Eska tells Naomi that the well at her former house, which she and her husband owned before they left Israel to go to Moab, is now dry. After Naomi walks away Eska tells her friends that Ruth is from Moab, and the women gasp in revulsion.

"Wow! They're not very friendly," Jim says.

"This is completely wrong," Deb says. "The people of Bethlehem are excited to see Naomi return."

Once they settle in Naomi's house, they are without money, so Ruth goes out to the fields to glean wheat. Once she is there, Boaz sees Ruth gleaning in his field while he mentions to one of his men that there is a drought.

"The reason Naomi returns to Israel is that the drought is over!" Les yells.

When Boaz sees this beautiful woman gleaning his field, he starts talking to her, but when he finds out Ruth is from Moab he talks harshly to her, apparently losing interest.

"What a jerk!" Charlotte says to Erica as they take a quick look at the movie.

Meanwhile, in the back row of the balcony, Avery says to Ian, "If you had talked to me like that, we never would have had a second date."

"What are you talking about?" He asks.

"I'm talking about how Boaz talks to Ruth. He is really mean. He's actually not mean in the story."

Boaz rides off after talking to Ruth, and it is obvious he does not want her in his field.

"Boaz actually praises Ruth for the way she treats Naomi," Deb says. "He calls her 'daughter,' and tells her to stay close to the other young women and not leave his field."

That evening, Boaz has a servant take food to Naomi's house, but they refuse the gift.

"I don't understand why they would refuse free food."

"I know I wouldn't," Chester says.

"He actually instructs the harvesters to leave extra grain for Ruth to pick up. He doesn't send her a care package," Deb says. "I don't understand why this is changed."

Ruth decides to go to another field where she meets her dead husband's closest relative. While unnamed in the narrative, he is named in this movie and "Tob" wastes no time in going after Ruth. He falls in love with her at first sight and sends servants to restore Naomi's house in an attempt to impress Ruth.

"Maybe this is like one of those songs that The Salty Dog plays backwards," Jim says. "I think the film presents the story in reverse order."

"That's right," Deb says. "Boaz wants Ruth and the close relative does not."

The film shows that the people in Bethlehem hate Ruth; to the extent a woman actually hits her. Boaz comments, "I have never seen the people so aroused."

"I've aroused a lot of women in my day," Ronald texts. "Nobody is better at arousing women than I am."

"Nothing like this happens," Deb says.

Meanwhile, after Naomi and Ruth leave Moab, the Moabite king is angry, so he sends two soldiers to sneak into Israel. Once they find Ruth they try to get her killed by telling the Israelites she was a priestess of Chemosh before she came to Bethlehem. Boaz is a judge and tells his fellow judges that if she is guilty he will judge her himself. As he leaves the room he mutters to himself, "This is absurd!"

"My thoughts exactly," Deb says.

"And mine," Dave says.

"Mine too," Chester says.

There is a trial and Ruth proves that they are spies by showing they cannot name the tribes of Israel, with the result that Ruth is found innocent and the spies are sentenced to be stoned to death.

"Some secret agents they are!" Joe yells. *"They don't kill anyone before the hero kills them in some macabre way and then jokes about the way they get killed after the villains are dead."*

"Yeah," Jason yells. *"Like 'Those Moabites got mobbed.'"*

"Even the Moabite soldiers poisoned that well," Dave responds. *"These guys could at least plant a bomb on a chariot."*

It is now time for the harvest festival. Ruth and Naomi arrive, and Tob comes up to them and tells Ruth he is going to tell the elders the next morning that Ruth will be his bride. Tob has been drinking too much and passes out while he and Ruth dance during the celebration. As the party winds down, Ruth follows Naomi's instructions and walks over to where Boaz has fallen asleep. He wakes up and finds Ruth standing there right after she arrives.

"She's lying down at his feet!" Les shouts.

He tells Ruth he loves her, and she responds that she has known this all along. They kiss and agree they want to get married. When Ruth mentions that Tob has the right to marry her, Boaz assures her that he will work it out because Tob will be more interested in possessions than her, and he will use that knowledge to get Tob to step away.

"What's he going to do, steal Tob's chariot and hold it for ransom?" Dave yells.

"Maybe he has friends that are Moabite mobsters who will cut off the head of Tob's mule and put it in a floral arrangement before the wedding," Joe responds.

"One less mule would not make Tob step away," Charley yells. *"Now a horse head would be a different matter!"*

"Boaz actually tells Ruth he will perform the duty of a close relative if the other one won't," Deb says. "There is no indication he will try to manipulate the other relative."

But, it turns out that Tob wants her more than Boaz realizes. He even refuses an offer of all Boaz's property in exchange for Ruth. She and Boaz are disappointed, but he tells Ruth she must marry Tob according to the law.

"The relative never offers to give up his possessions," Ian says. "Unlike him, I would give up everything in my suitcase for you, which is all I own."

"Don't forget your phone," Avery says.

"Now that might change things."

She elbows him in the side, "I would give up mine."

"But yours is an old flip phone."

The next day, during the wedding feast, Ruth announces she does not love Tob and that she was with Boaz the previous night resulting in Tob getting angry.

"Lighten up Tob," Joe yells. **"It was a bachelorette party and Boaz was just imitating a dancing policeman."**

Tob loses all interest in marrying her, so Boaz claims the right as the second closest relative. He tells Tob to give him his sandal, according to the ancient custom, and Tob responds by angrily throwing his sandal at Boaz.

"High and outside!" Rick jokes to Charlotte. "He would never make it to the minors."

"You've been pretty quiet Deb," Jim says. "Any comments?"

"The film shows this wrong."

"What do you mean? Are you saying he doesn't want her for some other reason?"

"When the relative finds out that Ruth is part of a package deal involving Naomi, he declines to redeem the land because he does not *want to ruin part of his inheritance, which would happen if he and Ruth have a child. This film has him offering his land for Ruth, which is the exact opposite of what happens. He lets her go because he doesn't want his family to lose his land."*

Boaz walks with Ruth to the elders, and they swear that nothing other than talk happened between them and they ask permission to be married. The chief elder pronounces that they are married and the movie ends.

"You must love these 60's movies," Jim says to Deb as they leave the theater.

"There is a simplicity to them that can be charming, so this film is clearly a four as far as entertainment, but I only give it a two for accuracy."

28

Mother-in-Law

As Told in
The Book of Ruth: Journey of Faith
2009

THIS A SHORT FILM, only about an hour and a half long. The first fifty minutes show events leading up to Naomi returning to Bethlehem with Ruth.

"*I like this film so far,*" Deb says. "*I haven't seen a single mistake and it's a very entertaining movie.*"

As the women arrive in Bethlehem, they comment about the wheat in the market.

"*I spoke too soon, this is an error,*" she says.

"*I do that all the time on the golf course,*" Jim says. "*Joe will hit a long drive and I will yell, 'Great shot!' Then the ball goes out of bounds. Les and Dave will just stare at me making me feel like an idiot for making such a bad call. So what's wrong in this film?*"

"*The timing of events is wrong. There are two spring harvests, barley and wheat. They actually arrive at the beginning of the barley harvest.*

The story concludes at the wheat harvest. These two harvests are on very significant days. The barley harvest occurs around Passover and the wheat harvest occurs around Shavuot."

"Shavu what? I don't get it," Jim responds. "What's Shavuot?"

"That is the day on the Hebrew calendar we call Pentecost."

"Are you telling me the Jews keep Pentecost?"

"They have been keeping it for over thirty-five hundred years, only with a different name. They don't think of it in Christian terms, but they still recognize that day as being holy."

"What's with all these Jewish holidays?"

"There are seven major feast days that reveal God's plan for mankind."

"Isn't that just for Jews?"

"No, these days help Christians understand God's timetable as well."

As Naomi and Ruth walk around Bethlehem one of Naomi's old friends is very excited to see her.

"The other film does this scene differently. What is the true reaction of the people in town?" Jim asks.

"Actually, the entire town is excited to see her," Deb says.

The women are destitute, so Ruth decides to glean fields, taking grain that is not picked by harvesters home to Naomi. She goes to a field that Boaz owns to do the gleaning.

"I guess it's a good thing for Ruth she ends up gleaning a field that Boaz owns," Jim comments to Deb.

"This is not just a matter of luck, as the film shows. Ruth has an ulterior motive for wanting to glean Boaz's harvest."

"What is the motive?"

"She wants to get noticed by Boaz, and Naomi supports her in this. Some people might think Ruth is a gold digger but she is actually a

wheat gleaner. She wants to get noticed by a male relative of her dead father-in-law, as opposed to just any man in Bethlehem."

"What difference does that make?"

"If she hooks up with Boaz, who is a close relative, the land that was owned by Naomi's dead husband must be redeemed to Ruth."

When Boaz first sees Ruth, he asks who she is. The man in charge does not know, but another man identifies her as Ruth, however he does not mention her as being from Moab. Boaz fires one of his supervisors and the supervisor tells Boaz he will report this to his uncle. Boaz is obviously attracted to Ruth, and he approaches her and tells her to work only in his fields. In the conversation between Boaz and Ruth, she asks why he is being so nice to her. Boaz responds that it's because he sees people as they are and not who they were.

"What else can he say?" Dave asks. "Do you expect him to answer, 'Because you're really hot'?"

"I bet that's one of your pickup lines," Joe says.

"Believe me, that one doesn't work."

"This sounds wonderful, but it doesn't happen that way," Deb says. "Boaz, as well as the entire town of Bethlehem, knows who Ruth is and how well she treats her mother-in-law."

Boaz instructs his servants to provide grain to Ruth. The next scene introduces "Neb" as Elimelech's brother, and Boaz's uncle. Neb is angry at Boaz because he gives extra grain to Ruth, who is a foreigner, saying he will bring death to Israel for doing so. They almost get into a fight, and Neb threatens Boaz that someday he will need him, but he will not be there.

Les sits down next to Deb and whispers to her, "This makes Boaz a cousin of her first husband. An uncle would share 25 percent of the DNA of Ruth's first husband and a cousin would share 12.5 percent of his DNA, so Neb would be the closest relative."

"I remember asking you about that many years ago while doing Sunday school. Thanks for remembering."

Les returns to his seat.

In the film, Boaz never refers to Ruth as "Daughter."

"Boaz calls her Daughter every time he talks directly to her," Deb says.

Naomi tells Ruth that Boaz is obviously in love with Ruth, and Ruth admits she loves Boaz. Naomi instructs Ruth on what to do that night at the harvest festival. At the end of the festival Boaz goes to sleep on a pile of straw and Ruth goes to him and lies down at his feet. When Boaz wakes up, they each declare their love for each other, but Boaz can't figure out how to get Ruth as his wife since the closer relative has first dibs. Unfortunately, the closer relative is Neb, who is angry at Boaz. Then, according to the narrator, God shows him a way.

"Boaz knows exactly how to proceed as he is talking to Ruth," Deb says. *"The narration is wrong."*

The film shows the meeting with the elders is put off at least part of a day, if not an entire day.

"The meeting occurs in the same day he talks to Ruth," Deb comments.

Boaz hatches a plot. He sends a servant to tell Neb that he is going to give Ruth half his grain. In response, Neb convenes the elders in order to have Boaz stoned for doing such a horrible thing.

"This is a horrible sin. Everyone must pay their fair share to the government," Tiffany yells. **"You don't just give it to some bimbo!"**

"I thought the Israelites are supposed to be kind to the poor, including foreigners," Jim asks. *"Is this a crime?"*

"Not that I am aware of," Deb answers.

Boaz admits he is going to buy the land and save the house of Elimelech from destitution. Neb argues that since he is the closest relative, he should redeem Naomi. But then he finds out he has to have children with Ruth instead of Naomi.

"That is not a deal breaker," Ronald posts. *"She's hot!"*

> "I would much rather be with you than with some twenty-five year old," Jim says romantically to Deb.
>
> "There is no way you would ever have the chance to find out," Deb says. "Remember, twenty-five year old girls would never even see you because to them, you are invisible."
>
> "What about that waitress who is so nice to me?"
>
> "I hate to break it to you. She's not being that way because she finds you attractive."
>
> Later that night, when Jim looks in the bathroom mirror sucking in his gut, he thinks to himself, "I bet she does."

Once Neb finds this out, he throws his sandal at Boaz, signifying he is passing his responsibility of redeeming the land to Boaz.

> Jim looks at Deb and says, "This is all wrong. First, Boaz convenes the elders, and second, there is no plot. Finally, the reason 'Neb' refuses to marry Ruth is because he is concerned about his inheritance, not because he hates the idea of marrying a woman from Moab."
>
> "That's great Jim. Did you learn all this from me?"
>
> "No, from Teddy. He has watched this movie several times this week."

The film shows Boaz and Ruth getting married. A year later, Boaz is very upset because Ruth isn't feeling well. Naomi tells Boaz to go outside. As he is praying for Ruth, he hears them laughing. He goes back inside and Ruth tells him she is pregnant. A few months later, Naomi carries Obed, her newborn grandson, in a field. The film ends with Obed, who is the narrator, talking with David, his grandson. David walks away and Obed tells him he is forgetting his sling.

> "I love how this ends and shows that David is descended from Ruth," Avery says.
>
> As Jim and his family leave the theater, Chester says, "I really like this movie. How do you rate it Deb?"
>
> "I love it! The film shows a peacefulness in Israel that is almost magical. The entertainment is definitely a five and the accuracy is a four."

"Wait," Jim says, "we're forgetting Teddy. I've got to go back and get him!"

"What's he doing?" Deb asks.

"I saw him talking to Erica."

29

Mother-in-Law

WHAT DIFFERENCE DOES IT MAKE?

DEB BEGINS the Sunday school class by asking, "There is an important word that is omitted from both films we watched this week, did anyone notice this? This word gives us a clue how old Boaz is."

There is silence in the room and finally, Ian raises his hand. "In the original story, Boaz never calls Ruth by her name, he always calls her daughter."

"I also noticed that and almost laughed at the visual," Cindy says. "All I could think of is some seventy-year old man going into a club, walking up to some woman in her thirties and saying, 'Daughter, would you like to dance'?"

"I'd love to," Avery jokes. "But I don't know how to waltz."

People in the class start laughing. "He would sure score a lot of hits with that opening line," Joe smiles.

"It might work," Dave jokes. "Some girls like older men, but I sure haven't found any."

"So Dave?" Cindy teases. "What exactly are you looking for in a girl?"

"Someone who won't complain that I'm too tall. What are you looking for in a man?"

Before Cindy can answer, Deb says, "Moving right along, is there any other clue that Boaz is much older than Ruth?"

"Boaz compliments Ruth for not going after young men," Ronald says. "Smart girl!"

"I remember being at a restaurant and I looked over at the bar and saw several beautiful gals laughing." Jason smiles as he continues, "It put me in a good mood until the friend I was sitting with said to me, 'You know what Jason? To those girls, you and I are invisible.'"

"That's what I told Jim," Deb laughs.

"Despite what the films show, can we all agree that Boaz is much older than Ruth?" Deb asks. "Good," she says after no one disagrees.

"Both films mention a sandal," Deb says. "While the act of giving a sandal to the relative is not a law, there are two laws that do show up in this story. Does anyone know what they are?"

After a moment of silence, Deb explains. "There are laws involved here which movie viewers would never realize, one is the law of what happens on a Jubilee. The other law involves Levirate marriage. But since those are deeper subjects I have prepared handouts for you on them."

"There is also another handout which concerns the women mentioned in Matthew's genealogy. I think you will find it interesting. Next week is Samson. Have a great week everyone."

As they leave the room, Dave reminds Cindy she never answered his question. "I don't care about how tall a man is, as long as he doesn't block my view," Cindy responds.

"Then I suggest you sit next to that man Tuesday night at seven, instead of behind him," Dave says. "What say you?"

"I say yes."

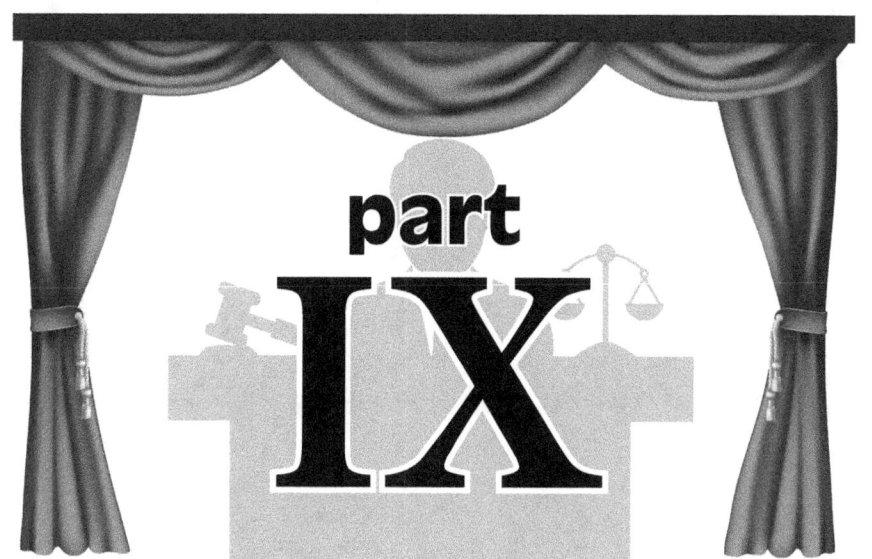

Having a Bad Hair Day

MOVIES ABOUT SAMSON

An Introduction

IN RY COODER'S SONG, "The Girls from Texas," a man learns the hard way there can be consequences from getting involved with the wrong woman. A man confesses to his girlfriend that he is married, and then she kills him. The judge dismisses the charges saying, "Ah, that's just the way the girls are down here in Texas."

Consider these quotes:

"I did not have sexual relations with that woman." Bill Clinton, January 26, 1998.

"I have sinned." Jimmy Swaggart, February 21, 1988.

"I have sinned." Al Bundy, *Married With Children*, 1995 Season Ten, Episode Four.

"I've looked on a lot of women with lust. I've committed adultery in my heart many times." Jimmy Carter, 1976 *Playboy* Interview.

This is nothing new. There is even a story in the Bible about a man letting his desire for a woman ruin his life. When reading this story, the average reader probably thinks the story of Samson is simply an ancient account of a woman using her beauty to get what she wants, costing the hero everything.

On first impression it is. Samson's story is great for Hollywood. Love, sex, and violence! What more is needed to fill a movie theater? This story has is it all. But there might be a little more than meets the eye.

30

Having a Bad Hair Day

As Told In
Samson and Delilah
1996 TELEVISION MINI SERIES

THIS TURNER PRODUCTION begins by showing that the Israelites, during the time of the judges, are being punished for their sins by God allowing them to be subjugated by the Philistines. The film shows Mara, played by Diana Rigg, being told she will no longer be barren and that she will have a son who will begin the liberation of his people. Years later, Samson, is introduced as a mischievous young man.

At the same time, the audience meets the Philistine king and his son, who is being trained by General Tariq, the king's advisor, played by Dennis Hopper. Delilah, played by Elizabeth Hurley, makes her entrance as she enters the royal courtyard where Tariq is training the prince.

"Does Delilah show up this early in the story?" Jim asks.

"No, she is not mentioned until the end."

Samson is walking with other young men and women in the countryside when Yoram, who is introduced as a young friend of Samson, starts narrating the events in the film. Naomi is a girl in that group that wants Samson to join others in a rebellion, but Samson does not want to get involved, and walks away from her to flirt with other girls.

> "He needs to get a student deferment," Ronald posts. "That way he can continue to chase women."

The people in the village are aware of Samson's strength and want him to join their rebellion. They talk to Samson's parents, wanting them to encourage Samson to fight with them, but the parents refuse, not wanting Samson to get killed.

> "They're enabling him to be a draft dodger," Dave says.

> "Are the Israelites planning to rebel against the Philistines?" Jim asks.

> "No," Deb answers. "If they were, they wouldn't eventually turn Samson over the Philistines."

Delilah is traveling with the Philistines in the country when she takes a walk away from their camp. Samson is in the area and he is watching her from a hilltop when a lion appears near her. Samson runs down the hill and kills the lion while Delilah watches from about twenty feet away. Tariq rides up with some men and it turns out they had also watched Samson kill the lion. Not only do all these people see this, but Naomi also sees Samson kill the lion from an adjacent hillside.

> "The film shows that Delilah, Naomi, Tariq and all his men watch Samson kill the lion," Jim says. "Is that true?"

> "No one sees Samson kill the lion, not even his parents who are traveling with him," Deb replies.

> "I planned to watch it too," Chester says to Deb, "but the ticket scalpers were asking too much."

Realizing Samson might pose a threat to them, the Philistines get two traitors, Jehiel and Amran, who are brothers, to point out Samson's house to the Philistine soldiers.

"Who are those guys?" Les yells.

"They are not mentioned in the story," Deb says.

The Philistine prince leads the soldiers into the house, and they capture Samson by throwing a net over him as he sleeps. His parents are awakened and follow the soldiers as they drag their son out of the house in the net. Villagers, including Yoram and Naomi, awaken and pour out into the street to see what is happening. Samson works his way out of the net and starts fighting his captors. During the fight, he finds a donkey skull and starts killing the Philistines with the jawbone of the skull. Samson also fights the prince, but the prince escapes. Samson then turns and yells at the villagers for not helping him fight the Philistines.

> "I remember when I was in high school I asked my coach a stupid question in front of the team," Dave says. "The coach responded by shouting, 'Slain by the jawbone of an ass.'"

> "This is all wrong," Deb says. "The jawbone doesn't appear until much later. The film is showing Samson being captured, but he actually gives himself up before he uses the jawbone. Plus, he never yells at the villagers."

Samson leaves the village and walks out into the wilderness where he sees the remains of the lion he killed, and he sees that the bees that have made a honeycomb in the bones. While he eats part of the honeycomb, a man rides up on a camel and takes him to a camp. At the camp Samson meets Amrok, an Israelite who now lives with the Philistines. He invites Samson to his home in Timnah, where they will eat with Amrok's adoptive father the next day.

> "Amrok is another fictional character," Deb says, "but I like him in this film."

When they arrive at the home, Samson meets Amrok's father, who welcomes him, and Amrok's sister, Rani, who falls in love with him. The love is mutual. Rani's father sends a message to the king asking for his blessing on a marriage between Samson and his Philistine daughter.

> "The father never asks the king's blessing," Deb says.

When Mara finds out about Samson and Rani, she gets upset and travels to Timnah to confront her son. She tells him she is ashamed of Samson and then slaps him on the face before leaving.

> "Maybe she's challenging him to a duel," Dave jokes.
>
> "No, she would have used a glove," Joe responds.
>
> "One of your old golf gloves? You must have fifty of them in your bag."
>
> "No, an oven mitt," Cindy says. "I forgot to tell you Dave, I love cooking."
>
> "These events are all changed," Deb says. "Samson actually asks his father to get the girl for him, and both his parents go with him to Timnah."

The next day is the wedding and the king sends men to the wedding, giving the appearance he approves of the marriage. Samson is very happy and feeling good, so he challenges the Philistines to solve this riddle, "Out of the eater, something to eat; out of the strong, something sweet." They ask him if they will win a prize if they solve the riddle and Samson promises them a prize of thirty linen garments.

> "This is changed too," Deb comments. "The thirty linen garments is a bet, not a prize."

As Samson walks away, Rani asks for the answer to the riddle and he whispers the answer to her while the Philistine guests watch.

> *As Ian is getting ready to get some popcorn he tells Avery, "The Philistines pressure the father to find out from the daughter the answer to the riddle instead of them pressuring the daughter, also a week passes before he gives up the answer."*

The leader of the Philistine guests tells Rani's father to get the answer from Rani or he will order the father killed and burn his property. Afraid for her father, Rani tells the Philistines the answer. The leader announces the answer to all the people at the wedding and Samson becomes enraged that he has been betrayed. He uproots a tree and starts beating and killing Philistines.

Chester says to Charley, imitating one of the Philistines, "Note to self, never invite a Danite to one of our parties."

"Samson doesn't kill the guests at the wedding," Deb says.

He takes the dead bodies out to a cliff and throws them down the ravine. The leader is still alive, so he gives the leader the garments and tells him to go back to Gaza and tell them Samson did this. As the leader reports to the king and tells him what happened, a guard yells out that the fields are on fire. They see Samson riding a horse, holding a torch and burning the fields outside the Philistine palace. To get revenge the king orders troops back to Timnah and they kill Rani and her father, and then burn his house.

"You know how Samson actually starts those fires don't you?" Deb asks.

"Not really."

"Samson uses three hundred foxes with torches tied to their tails to start the fires."

"There are no foxes in this movie, they must have been written out."

Ian returns to Avery, "There is a mob of foxes picketing the concession stand so I couldn't get popcorn."

"Is this a bunch of good looking girls?"

"No, these are real foxes. All of them have signs around their necks saying 'Out foxed.' Apparently they feel the film discriminates against foxes. WSOD News is covering the event and The Salty Dog is interviewing Charlotte who had to close the popcorn stand."

Samson returns home and the film shows events from Samson becoming a judge to his trip to Gaza. While at Gaza he is with a Philistine harlot when he sees the man who killed his wife. He jumps out of her bed to follow the man and kills him.

"Hey you forgot to pay the girl," Chester yells.

Philistine soldiers walk into the alley as he is standing over the body, and chase him through the city during the middle of the day. The chase scene shows Samson passing openings out of the city, however he goes to the locked city gates, tears them off, and escapes.

> "He doesn't see the man who kills his wife," Deb says. "Samson discovers soldiers are outside the house and sneaks out at midnight. The film is showing him leaving during the day and it does not show him carrying those gates to Hebron."

A soldier reports to Tariq that Samson escapes by tearing down the gates and he convinces the king that they must first defeat Samson, using Samson's lust for Philistine women against him. Delilah agrees to serve her country and be the "bait" to capture Samson, provided she is paid eleven hundred pieces of silver from everyone in the chamber. The Philistines accept those terms and Delilah starts looking for Samson. She finds Samson near a stream and introduces herself, which quickly leads to their love affair.

> "That's not a good deal," Ronald posts. "All the women I know would hold out for two thousand pieces of silver."

> "There is no mention of a plot to set Samson up," Deb says. "Samson meets her and when the Philistines find out about their relationship, they offer her the silver if she will help them capture him. She doesn't ask to be paid."

Delilah asks why Samson is so strong, and he tells her that if he were tied with seven new bowstrings he would lose his strength. She ties him with bowstrings, and later with ropes, but each time, while he is asleep she whispers, "The soldiers are coming." And each time, he wakes up and breaks the bonds. Delilah complains that Samson doesn't really love her because he won't tell her the truth, so Samson tells her the truth.

> "Men are so stupid," Cindy says.

> "I agree, a man should never tell a woman the truth," Dave says. "It can come back and bite him."

> "No, I'm saying Samson is stupid for not seeing through this girl."

> Up in the balcony Avery says, "I like how the film shows their relationship. It's great watching them fall in love."

> "Have you ever been in love?" Ian asks.

> "Maybe."

HAVING A BAD HAIR DAY

The next morning when Samson wakes up, Delilah tells Samson she had the power to destroy him the previous night, and shows him her knife. He lovingly says that she didn't use that power, but then, as she looks him straight in the eyes, she quickly uses the knife to cut off a lock of his hair.

"I told you, don't cut too much off the top!" Dave jokes. **"This haircut looks terrible!"**

Soldiers come into the tent, cut off more hair, tie him up and blind him.

"Now my hair must be a real mess! Give me a mirror! Oh wait, I don't need a mirror, I can't see!" Dave shouts.

"She doesn't cut his hair!" Les yells

"Delilah doesn't cut his hair," Deb agrees. "She lulls Samson to sleep and calls in a Philistine to cut his hair."

Back in Israel, Jehiel and Amran, the brothers who betrayed Samson, are planning a revolt against Gaza. They are out in the hills late at night and see a bright shooting star that crosses the sky, and they take that as a sign that they should start the revolution. Meanwhile in Gaza, Tariq sees the same shooting star.

"It's the space station," Chester yells.

The brothers form an army to march on Gaza, which is what Tariq wants.

"This is made up," Deb says. "These brothers are not in the story, and they don't raise an army."

"I wouldn't be in that army," Ronald posts. "My draft lottery number was really high! Higher than anyone's! Nobody has a higher draft number than I!"

Back in Gaza, Tariq visits Samson in prison and takes a physician to check Samson's eyes, but the physician tells Tariq he cannot restore Samson's vision, so Tariq orders him to give Samson something for the pain. Tariq offers Samson better treatment, but Samson refuses when he won't give the other prisoners better treatment. He tells Samson he will lead his army against the Israelites the next day, and will win. The next day the Philistines destroy the Israelites in the battle.

"Where does this come from?" Les yells from the back of the theater. "There's no battle in this story!"

Deb comments, "While the battle scene is made up, I really like Dennis Hopper and what his character adds to the story. I really enjoy watching him in this film."

Samson spends his days helping other prisoners push a millstone in a quarry. Later, when he is pushing the millstone alone, Tariq watches him. After Samson is taken away, Tariq attempts to push the stone, and when he can't do it, he realizes Samson's strength is returning.

"This is an addition," Deb says. "No one suspects his strength is returning."

It's festival time in Gaza and the whole town is having a celebration. Delilah requests that Samson be brought out so everyone can see him. Yoram has gotten a job in the prison where he can see Samson and bring him food. He escorts the guards who bring Samson to the temple and chain him to the pillars. Samson tells Yoram he loves him and then tells him to "Go."

"These conversations are all made up," Deb says, "but they don't take away from the story. I like how the finale is being set up."

In the meantime, Naomi has visited Delilah and they both visit Samson as he is being chained to the pillars. Samson tells Yoram and Naomi to leave at once because everyone is going to die. Tariq, who is watching, hears this and looks around at the temple. Once his friends have left, Samson destroys the building, killing the king, the prince, Tariq, Delilah, all the others in the temple, as well as himself. The final scene shows that his body has been recovered and is being returned to Israel.

As Erica and Charlotte are walking out the theater they see Jim, Deb, Chester, and Charley walking to their truck. Erica asks, "How did you like the film?"

"It was pretty good," Jim says. "We enjoyed it."

"I agree!" Deb says. "Hopper and Hurley are incredible in this film. I rate the entertainment at a five and the accuracy at a four."

31

Having a Bad Hair Day

As Told in
Samson and Delilah
1949

CECIL B. DEMILLE directs this movie and also narrates the introduction, describing a period of oppression that existed one thousand years before Christ, in the land of Dan, which is one of the tribes of Ancient Israel. DeMille tells the audience there is a man in this land named Samson who dreams of liberty for his people.

The film begins in a village where an old man is telling a group of children about Moses confronting the Pharaoh of Egypt, telling him to let his people go. The old man explains to the children the Pharaoh ruled Egypt the same way the saran, the title of the Philistine king, rules the Philistines.

"Plastic wrap can be pretty confining," Jim says.

Philistine soldiers walk by and when they hear what the old man is saying, they throw him to the ground. Among the children is a boy named Saul, who tells the soldiers that Samson would kill them if he caught them abusing the old man. The soldiers laugh and say that Samson saves his strength for the wenches.

"Isn't that Russ Tamblyn as Saul?" Jim asks.

"Yeah," Dave says sitting behind him. "He is a Jet from his first cigarette to his last dying day in West Side Story."

"Yeah, great film," Jim says.

"In the meantime, this is a big mistake," Deb says.

"In what way?" Cindy asks.

Deb turns around and says to them, "Saul is from the tribe of Benjamin, not the tribe of Dan. A boy from Benjamin would never have lived in that village."

"Maybe he is from the tribe of 'Danjamin,'" Chester says.

"There is no such tribe," Charley says. "But it could be the tribe of 'Benjadam.'"

"Are they related to the tribe of 'Givadam'?" Teddy asks as he walks by.

"I hear that's a very thoughtful tribe," Jim says.

"Cut it out boys, I'm laughing so hard I have to go to the restroom," Deb says and stands up to leave.

Samson, played by Victor Mature, is scolded by his mother for spending his time drinking and brawling with the Philistines instead of leading his people who chose him to be their judge. The mother is also upset that he is going to marry a Philistine girl named Semadar, instead of a Hebrew girl named Miriam, who lives in their village.

"Miriam is a fictitious character," Deb says.

"Wait!" Jim says. "Didn't she write a dictionary? How could a fictionary write a dictionary?"

In Timnah, Ahtur, played by Henry Wilcoxon, is the military governor of Dan, who wants to marry Semadar, and he is giving a gift to Semadar's father, hoping he will give her to him as his wife.

"You know who that is, don't you?" Joe asks Dave.

"No, who?"

"Henry Wilcoxon. He is in many movies, but my favorite role is the Bishop in Caddyshack."

"You mean the guy who has his best round of golf in a thunderstorm and then gets struck by lightning?"

"Yeah, that's him. He's been my inspiration ever since I saw that film."

"That's understandable, considering how much you play golf."

"Playing often hasn't helped my score though. I have been on a terrible streak lately, my scores really stink. But, at least I'm still a better golfer than Scheidt."

"Who isn't?"

The girl's father walks out to his courtyard just in time to see Samson climbing over a wall to see Semadar, who is played by Angela Lansbury. Semadar warns Samson he should leave because a hunting party, led by the Saran of Gaza, is arriving soon. As Samson and Semadar resume talking, Delilah who is Semadar's sister, played by Hedy Lamarr, watches them as she sits on the courtyard wall. She playfully tosses plum pits at them while eating the plums. Ahtur walks into the courtyard and is angry that Samson is there. He tells Samson to leave as the sounds of the dogs in the hunting party can be heard barking in the distance.

"It seems every movie introduces Delilah at the beginning," Jim says. "Are you sure she doesn't show up until the end?"

"See what I mean!" Deb says. "You're an example of people thinking the wrong thing because of how these movies change the story."

"So, she's not Semadar's sister?"

"No, we don't know who she is."

"Why, why, why Delilah? Why don't we know who you are?" Dave jokes as he parodies the Tom Jones song.

The saran, played by George Sanders, arrives and the hunting party leaves to find a lion. Delilah, using her father's horses, helps Samson beat the hunting party to the lion, where he kills the lion using his bare hands, while Delilah watches from a rock ledge.

"This part of the story is all wrong," Deb says.

"How?" Jim asks.

"Samson is actually traveling to Timnah when he kills the lion. No one sees him do it."

The hunting party arrives to find Samson and Delilah standing near the dead lion. The saran doesn't believe Samson could kill the lion without a weapon and demands proof that Samson can kill a lion barehanded, so he has his most intimidating soldier fight Samson. After Samson wins the fight with Garmiskar, a bruising hulk, the saran offers him a prize of his choice. He chooses to have Semadar be his wife, upsetting Ahtur and Delilah. Delilah suggests to the saran that Ahtur bring thirty of his companions to the wedding.

"All of this is made up," Deb says. "But I am enjoying this film."

During the wedding feast Samson tells a riddle to the guests and they agree to wager thirty garments that they can solve the riddle. Unable to solve the riddle, Ahtur forces Semadar to get Samson to explain the answer to the riddle, and he does. As the couple is preparing to say the wedding vows, Ahtur recites the answer to the riddle. Samson gets angry at Semadar and leaves the wedding to get the garments to pay the wager.

"This is condensed quite a bit," Deb says. "These events happen over a week, not one day."

He steals garments from other Philistines in the area and returns to pay his debt.

"Samson kills the thirty Philistines to get the linen garments, he doesn't just steal them as shown here."

After he returns and gives the guests the garments he finds out Ahtur has now married Semadar.

"The girl's father actually gives his daughter to Samson's best man, not Ahtur."

"Yeah," Dave says, "I think his name was 'Achoo.'"

HAVING A BAD HAIR DAY

Delilah tells Samson that Semadar helped Ahtur discover the answer to the riddle. When Semadar's father offers Delilah to Samson, he refuses, calling her a "forked tongue adder." A fight breaks out and Samson kills some of the guests, but Semadar gets killed by a spear thrown at Samson. Her father is also killed and their house gets burned down while Samson is in the fields burning Philistine crops.

Three foxes in the back of the theater yell, **"Outfoxed again!"**

"They're leaving out the foxes," Deb says.

"Come sit with us guys," *Chester yells to the foxes.*

As the foxes crawl over Deb's lap, one of them says, "Great seats!"

"You have to admit Deb," Jim replies. "That would be a hard scene to film. Three hundred foxes? Really?"

"But I love foxes, she says as she pets one. Couldn't they at least show one running alongside Samson's horse?"

"They would have to pay him," Chester says. "He's in the animal's union."

Delilah watches all the fires from a hilltop and vows to destroy Samson because he spurned her and called her a forked tongue adder.

Charlotte asks Rick, "What's am adder?"

"An ancient accountant," he answers, "a Certified Public Adder."

A year later Ahtur explains to the saran that he cannot capture Samson because the people of Dan protect him. The saran raises taxes to force the people to betray him, so when he hears about this, Samson gives himself up to the Philistines, who bind him in chains, and walk him behind a chariot heading toward Gaza.

"The people don't protect Samson," Deb says. "The men of Judah convince him to surrender."

"No one wants a loser who surrenders," Ronald posts.

Meanwhile, Delilah is with the saran, eating grapes that he hands her, as he is giving her a gift. A messenger arrives telling the saran that Samson has been captured and is being brought to Gaza. Delilah is happy and wants Samson publicly punished by being chained to a grist mill.

> "This is also made up, but it adds to the story," Deb says. "In a good way."

As Samson is being taken to Gaza, a dwarf wearing a turban holds a donkey's skull to his face and mocks him. Samson asks if the Philistines have honored their pledge to his people in exchange for his surrender, and Ahtur assures him they have. Samson starts praying as the dwarf continues to wave the skull in his face, and suddenly thunder is heard and the area gets dark. Samson breaks his chains, grabs the dwarf and throws him at the Philistines. He starts killing them with their own weapons, but then uses the donkey skull as a weapon and kills many of them, however the dwarf survives.

> "That skull belonged to an ancestor of mine," Chester says.

> "The dwarf is an addition," Deb says. "But he is funny. However, Samson finds the jawbone; he doesn't grab it from a dwarf. Also, he never asks the Philistines about a pledge."

A wounded soldier reports back to the saran, telling him how Samson escaped. Ahtur then shows up and admits Samson defeated them with the jawbone of an ass. As the leaders argue about how to defeat Samson, Delilah walks into the chamber and says she can deliver Samson to them, but everyone there must agree to pay her eleven hundred pieces of silver when she does. She also demands that Samson not be killed once he is captured and the saran agrees.

> "Once again, the film shows Delilah making the offer to betray Samson," Deb says. "They actually approach her. Plus, she makes no demands."

> "My ex-wife would have taken out an insurance policy on me and demanded I get killed," Dave says.

> "Forget her!" Cindy responds. "You need to move on."

> "I can't afford a moving van. She got everything."

A caravan travels in the wilderness as Samson and young Saul watch. That evening Samson sneaks into a tent while Delilah combs her hair. They talk, Samson falls in love with her, and the film shows her attempts to find the secret of his strength. Delilah pouts because Samson will not tell her the secret and then tells Samson she is ending the affair because he doesn't trust her. Not wanting to lose her, he tells her that his hair is the secret to his strength, and if it is cut he would lose his strength. She then asks Samson to come to Egypt with her so they could live there together.

"Delilah never says that," Deb says. "She wants the reward."

Miriam and Saul come to the oasis, and she tells Samson the Philistines killed his father, whipped his mother, and are killing first born children as well. Samson is enraged and wants to leave to get vengeance, despite Delilah asking him to leave for Egypt with her. He tells her he will meet her in Egypt.

"Again," Deb says, "none of this is in the story."

"I think it's in Second Cecilonians," Dave answers.

Delilah gives him some wine before he leaves, and Samson passes out because she had put a drug in the wine. As he lays passed out, she cuts his hair and sends for Ahtur.

"She doesn't cut his hair!" Les yells.

"Yeah!" Cindy shouts. **"She has him taken to the beauty salon!"**

"Love it!" Dave says to her.

The Philistines capture Samson and chain him. Delilah taunts him and leaves the tent while Ahtur tells her she will be paid for helping them capture him. He tells Samson this will be the last time he looks on her before his soldiers blind him. Delilah gets paid and later, the saran takes Delilah to the prison where they watch Samson, blinded and tormented, grinding wheat with a millstone, as guards and Philistines whip and mock him.

"Not only that, but he is still paying alimony!" Dave shouts.

"Dave! Move on," Cindy says.

"Delilah is never mentioned in the story after she betrays him," Deb comments.

Delilah walks down and stands in front of him, but when he passes by her she realizes he is blind. As time passes, Delilah's revenge turns into Delilah's remorse and she prays to the "God of Samson." By this time Samson's hair has grown back.

"Delilah doesn't show remorse or pray," Deb says.

The film describes events and conversations that lead up to the great festival to Dagon in the temple as all the citizens gather at the site to party, worship and be entertained. Miriam and Saul are in the crowd entering the temple because she wants to talk to the saran. Delilah also enters the temple as people yell out her name while she walks up and sits with the saran. As music sounds and dancers dance, Samson is the last person to enter the temple, bound and chained, as he is led to be tied to the pillars while the crowd taunts him. Saul runs out in the courtyard and tells Samson that he and Miriam are going to take him home.

"He just posted bond!" Joe yells.

"None of these people are mentioned as being at the temple," Deb says.

Samson tells Saul he cannot stay, but must leave so one day he can "Join them together and be their first king."

"Saul is never mentioned in the story," Deb says.

Miriam cries out to the saran, and he allows her to approach him. She begs the saran to free Samson, since he is now helpless, and allow her to return him to his people. The saran tells her that he will let Delilah decide if he will honor Miriam's request. Miriam begs Delilah to let Samson go free.

"Good luck with that!" Joe yells. **"You'll have better luck asking Dave's ex to give up her alimony."**

"They're not married Joe," Jim says over his shoulder.

"It doesn't matter. Ask Lee Marvin, who had to pay palimony."

"Notice, I didn't say a word?" Dave asks Cindy.

"That's better."

Delilah refuses her, saying, "I would rather see Samson dead than in your arms." She orders Miriam to be taken away.

Chester and Charley start singing the song "Delilah."

Ten dwarfs enter the floor of the temple and torment Samson, while the crowd laughs and shouts insults at him. Delilah leaves her seat to talk to Samson as Garmiskar approaches him with a whip. She tells Samson she will strike him with the whip instead of Garmiskar and he asks her to lead him to the pillars with the whip, which she does. Samson tells her to leave because everyone there is about to die, but she won't do that. He tells her he still loves her. She walks away, and when Samson calls her name, she doesn't answer, knowing that he will think she is gone, instead of being just a few feet away.

"While none of this is in the story it certainly is dramatic," Deb says. "I wish modern films could be so interesting."

Thinking she is gone, Samson prays that God will strengthen him just this once.

"Doesn't he discover he regains his strength back in the dungeon?" Ian asks.

There are four pillars at the stage of the temple, two on one side and two on the other. Samson is between the two pillars on the left side and starts pushing those pillars.

"That makes no sense, how can those two pillars on one side support the whole temple?" Ronald posts. "Terrible engineering! I would never hire that firm! They would really mess up the wall I am going to build around Wawasee!"

The temple collapses and all the main characters along with most of the people in the temple are killed.

"This film was made in 1949?" Jason marvels. "The special effects of the temple crashing are as good as many are today."

The final scene shows Miriam and Saul, still alive and mourning for Samson as Miriam tells Saul, "Men will tell his story for a thousand years."

"Well Saul must forget pretty quickly," Les yells as people are leaving the theater. ***"He never mentions Samson even once."***

"That was fun," Deb says as they get in the truck.

"Yeah," Jim says. *"DeMille made great films. What are your ratings?"*

"Entertainment is clearly a five. It's amazing a film that old can be so much fun, however I have to rate the accuracy at two."

32

Having a Bad Hair Day

As Told in
The Bible

2013 TELEVISION MINI SERIES

THIS EPISODE of the television series tells the story of Samson which begins a hundred years after the time of Joshua. The tribes have spread out in Canaan and are ruled by judges, although they are oppressed by the Philistines.

The opening scene shows the Philistines attacking a village and Samson fighting them. After the fray, Samson takes his mother into a house where she tells him he must fight the Philistines, reminding him of the messenger she saw before he was born. The messenger told her that Samson will begin to deliver Israel from the Philistines.

"I guess Samson is being raised by a single mother," Jim says.

"No, his father is very much part of the story," Deb says. "The series apparently leaves him out of the story. Another error here is that the mother never encourages Samson to fight the Philistines."

"I agree, my mom was worried I would get hurt playing basketball," Dave says. "She would never, ever, let me fight Philistines."

"Mine was worried about me playing golf," Joe says.

"How can you get hurt playing golf?"

"Have you seen how guys drive those carts? It's like they're all drunk! It's more dangerous than being on the interstate."

"Didn't Phil Scheidt crash a golf cart once?"

"Yeah, but he wasn't drunk, he was just incompetent."

Samson falls in love and marries a Philistine woman. Two Philistines talk during the wedding about how they don't want Israelites marrying their women, so to discourage these intermarriages they burn down the bride's father's house while she and her father are in it, killing them both.

"Where are the other twenty-eight guests?" Les yells.

"They divided into seven groups and are playing golf!" Joe shouts back.

"This is not even close!" Deb says. "The Philistines burn that house, but it has nothing to do with intermarriage. They are angry that Samson burns their fields, so they retaliate by killing the girl and her father. Also, Les is correct that there should be thirty guests at the wedding."

Samson becomes furious, starts killing Philistines, and then barges into a prison and breaks open the cell doors, freeing the prisoners.

"Where does that come from?" Les yells. **"Samson never frees prisoners!"**

"He has a 'Get out of Prison' coupon and doesn't want to waste it." Joe shouts back.

"I don't understand why the series ignores the father, the lion, and three hundred foxes but shows an imaginary prison escape," Deb says.

The Philistine leader tells the villagers that Samson must be turned over to him and that every day that goes by until then, one person in the village will be killed.

"*This never happens either,*" Deb says.

"*You think they're mean?*" Tiffany asks Ronald. "*You should try dealing with Republicans.*"

"*I will, as soon as I become one.*"

The villagers, including his mother, go out to him in the hills and ask him to surrender to the Philistines, so Samson holds out his hands to be tied, and his people deliver him to their enemy.

"*Good!*" Tiffany shouts. **"*I don't want those Philistines ruining a village.*"**

"*This does happen, but it happens in Judah, not in Dan, where his mother would be living,*" Deb says. "*Mom is not mentioned in this part of the story, so he doesn't ask her what she thinks.*"

Samson is chained to a stake in the town courtyard when the Philistine leader starts talking to him. He tells Samson he would happily kill all the Israelites. Hearing this, Samson breaks free, finds a jawbone, and uses it to kill the Philistines. After killing them, he runs through the town and meets a woman in a back street. Her name is Delilah.

"*He is bound with ropes,*" Deb says, "*and he doesn't meet Delilah until after he escapes from Gaza carrying the gate to the city, which is another part of the story that is not shown.*"

They begin a love affair, and when the Philistines learn about this, they bring Delilah to their leader. He wants to find out the secret of Samson's strength, so he offers Delilah a chest of silver coins if she can find out what the secret is and tell him.

"*The other films get this part wrong, but this series gets this part right,*" Deb says. "*They correctly show Delilah doesn't offer to give him up in exchange for silver.*"

Later, Delilah and Samson are in bed, and she asks him about his strength. He explains to her an angel appeared to his barren mother and said she will have a child, but he must never cut his hair or he will lose his strength.

> "That was easy," Joe yells, "why don't the Philistines just ask Samson about his strength when they have him tied up?"

> "Samson could never be trusted with trade secrets," Ronald posts.

> "The series is condensing weeks of her trying to find the answer into one evening," Deb says.

Samson rolls over, and once he is asleep, Delilah cuts his hair. The soldiers walk in immediately and tie him up. The leader pays Delilah while Samson watches, and then he blinds Samson.

> **"She doesn't cut his hair!"** Les yells.

> "Les is right, once again a film shows Delilah cutting his hair instead of a Philistine cutting it."

The Philistines drag him into their courtyard where he leans against pillars of a building. He tells the leader he will destroy them all, causing the crowd to laugh at him. Samson starts ramming the pillars and the building begins to shake. The leader yells for his soldiers to kill him, but when they attack him he kills them and continues ramming the pillars until the building collapses, killing everyone, including Delilah.

> "Again, the story is condensed," Deb says as they stand up to leave. "The series omits showing that Samson doesn't get his strength until his hair grows back."

> Rick says goodnight to them while he closes the theater. As Deb and Jim walk toward the truck, Jim asks, "What do you think of this part of the series?"

> "Considering how little time there is to tell this story, it's not too bad. But, there are unnecessary changes, like showing Delilah cutting Samson's hair. I just don't understand why all the films show that."

> "What are your ratings?"

> "It's entertaining, so that part is worth a three, but the accuracy only rates a two."

Having a Bad Hair Day

WHAT DIFFERENCE DOES IT MAKE?

DEB STARTS HER SUNDAY school lesson by describing the movies about Samson. "So what lessons are in this story?"

"Don't ever get married without a pre-nup," Dave says.

"He doesn't even marry her, Dave," Joe says. "He still loses everything."

"You're right, Joe. The lesson here is to never get involved with a woman."

"Really?" Cindy asks.

"I mean don't get involved with the wrong woman," Dave quickly adds.

"I think that message is universal to men and women," Deb says. "Many women have bad experiences with the opposite sex too."

"You just have to be careful when you get involved with anyone," Avery says.

"That seems like an obvious lesson," Jason says. "Do any of the errors in these movies hide this lesson?"

"Not really," Deb says. "Does everyone agree?"

"I do," Charlotte answers as the others agree.

"Before we close," Deb smiles, "I want to share a little nugget that none of the films show."

"Everyone knows that Samson kills the Philistines with a jawbone, but where does this happen?"

Everyone is silent.

"It was in the village of Lehi. Does anyone know what that name means in Hebrew?"

Ian raises his hand, "It means jaw."

"That's right Ian," Deb says. "Isn't that fascinating?"

"I never would have known that," Cindy says, as the others shake their heads in agreement.

"Today's handout looks at this story in a way we may not have considered," Deb says. "I think you will learn a new lesson that involves the number 'three.' I hope you enjoy it. See you in church in three minutes."

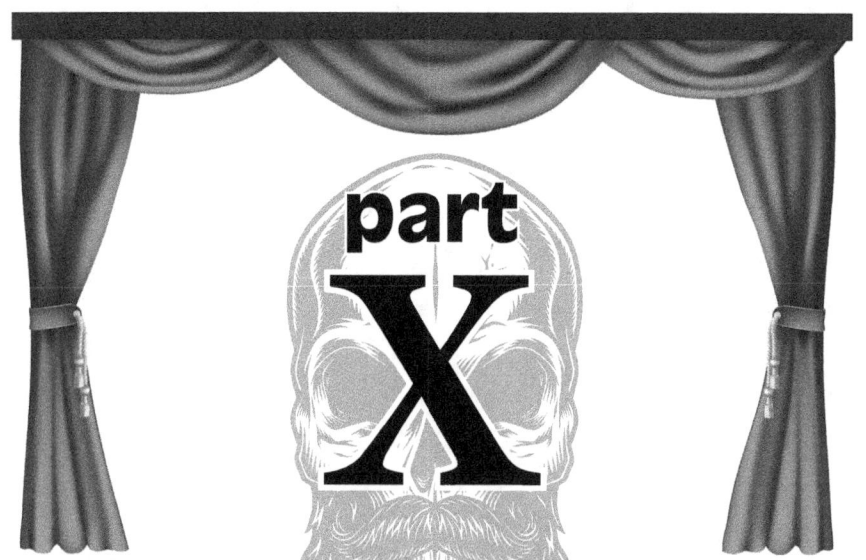

Skullduggery

Movies About David

An Introduction

"LIVE FROM CHICAGO, I'm The Salty Dog from WSOD, and this is the Leadership Selection Draft—better known as the LSD. As you know, professional sports drafts have become so popular, that the United Nations is adopting their own draft. Personnel departments from each of the great countries throughout history have sent representatives to Chicago for this soon-to-be annual event for selecting of leaders, doing away with the totally unreliable election process. Unlike win-loss records determining order of picks, our completely impartial commissioner, Nikita Khrushchev, has been freely elected by the participants and will select the order."

"The LSD is about to begin, so let's listen in as the commissioner calls the meeting to order."

"Welcome to the first annual Leadership Selection Draft," Khrushchev announces as he pounds his shoe on the podium. "The representatives are all in the building, so let's begin." He opens an envelope from the national accounting firm of Dewey, Cheatham and Howe, "And the first pick of LSD is . . ."

"The Babylonian Empire."

The Salty Dog, using his golf commentator voice, whispers. "The once powerful empire ruled the Middle East in the fifth century B.C."

"Second Pick, The Roman Empire Approximately First Century B.C."

"Third Pick, The Egyptian Empire Approximately Sixteenth Century B.C."

"Fourth Pick, The Greco-Macedonian Empire Approximately Third Century B.C."

"Fifth Pick, The Persian Empire Approximately Fourth Century B.C."

"Sixth Pick, The Israelite Kingdom Approximately Tenth Century B.C."

"The Babylonian Empire is on the clock." Khrushchev walks over and sits on a park bench located at the back of the stage and picks up a newspaper.

The camera switches to The Salty Dog.

"I would like to welcome our viewers and listeners from around the world. Now it's time to introduce our panel of draft experts who will provide insight on the selections."

"Benito Mussolini, Former Duce of Italy, is an expert on how to run a country efficiently."

The Salty Dog plays, "Takin' Care of Business" by Bachman-Turner Overdrive, as Benito walks on the set with his arms folded across his chest looking down his nose.

"Reminds me of Trump," Nikita thinks as he looks up from his paper and watches the television monitor.

"King Louis XVI, Former King of France, whose wife is an expert on how to keep the citizens of a country well-fed."

To Paul Anka's song, "Put Your Head on My Shoulder," Louis walks on the set as he jokingly looks at the audience with his mouth and eyes wide open as if in shock.

"And to complete our panel, his former Imperial and Royal Majesty Napoleon, Emperor of France, who is a last-minute substitution for Hannibal, whose elephant got stuck in traffic on the Dan Ryan. Napoleon, who won the dunking contest at the Pygmy Invitational Basketball skills event, is an expert on conquering Russia."

"He should be a midget wrestler," Nikita thinks.

The audience hears Randy Newman sing "Short People" as Napoleon, who is scratching his armpit, walks on the set and sits behind the table.

"What's under there anyway?" Nikita thinks, as he stops looking at the monitor and walks back to the podium.

"The commissioner is about to announces the first pick," The Salty Dog tells his audience.

"With the first pick, The Babylonian Empire selects, Nebuchadnezzar."

"That's a great pick," Benito says. "I love what this guy will do to beautify his country."

AN INTRODUCTION

"He will help that kingdom grow," Louis agrees, "but he does have some mental baggage. I hear he can be bipolar, but he will be good as long as he can keep his head on straight."

"With the second pick, Rome selects, Julius Caesar."

"I've studied this guy a lot," Benito smiles. "In fact, he is on the top of my board. He will definitely make the chariots run on time."

"He just needs to make sure his staff is loyal," Napoleon responds.

"With the third pick, Egypt selects, Ramses."

"He is not that high on my board," Napoleon frowns. "He has a very short memory, and I think he could be a disaster."

"Speaking of short," Benito jokes, pointing to Napoleon, "Hey Nap, can you even see over a steering wheel?"

"Seriously, I can't make heads or tails of this pick," Louis looks puzzled. "This guy could end up losing his whole army if he can't keep a level head."

"With the fourth pick, Greece selects, Alexander."

"That's a horrible pick," Benito shakes his fist. "How old is this kid anyway? Five?"

"I agree," Louis says. "He's way too young to ever accomplish anything. Kids that young tend to let power go to their head."

"We have a trade," The commissioner announces. "Israel is trading Gaza and its sixth pick in the draft, to move up to the fifth pick. With the fifth pick, Israel is selecting, Saul of Benjamin."

The Salty Dog looks at the panel and asks, "Did anyone see this coming?"

"I love this pick, this guy is way ahead of everyone in the draft when it comes to being a leader," Louis says.

"I have him number two on my board," Benito agrees. "I can't believe he slid this far down. He is a steal at number five."

"Saul has it all," Napoleon says. "Just look at that face. He has to be one of the most handsome men in the world, plus he has the height of a pro basketball player. Height is a great advantage, take my word for it! This has to be one of the most charismatic leaders ever born. He is a winner and he will make Israel great! They are lucky to get him. He was on my short list."

As the show ends, Benito asks Napoleon and Louis if they would like to bring Josephine and Marie to hang out with him and his wife for dinner after the show.

"Tune in tomorrow when other nations make their picks and get the man they want to be their leader," The Salty Dog says. "Let's close the show and listen to The Rolling Stones sing, 'You Can't Always Get What You Want.' Good night everyone. This is The Salty Dog returning to our WSOD studio."

So, what's the point? It's simply this. Israel wants a king. Not just any king. He must be tall and handsome and able to inspire people to follow him. So God gives them what they want. Throughout history, charismatic individuals have ascended to power. In the case of all these draft picks they either die early, or their administrations end badly.

Now let's join Ronald, as he and Tiffany have their second date to a movie.

34

Skullduggery

As Told In
The Bible

2013 TELEVISION MINI SERIES

THIS CONDENSED VERSION of the story of Saul and David begins in episode three showing that the Israelites want Samuel to find them a king. Samuel argues with the leaders, who do not want Samuel's sons to succeed him, and agrees to find them a king. Once he is alone, he prays that God will tell him who to choose and he sees a vision of Saul riding a horse.

"Where are the donkeys?" Chester asks. "Don't tell me they are not in the film."

"They went out looking for horses so you could have an ancestor," Charley says.

"This vision doesn't happen," Deb says. "Saul enters the city while he is looking for his father's donkeys and God points him out to Samuel, telling him that Saul is the man he told him about. He tells him about Saul, but he does not show him to Samuel in a vision."

Later, Saul walks through a cheering crowd and up to a platform where Samuel crowns and anoints him king of Israel, pouring oil on his forehead which runs down the side of his nose.

"**Watch out for his eyes!**" Joe shouts. "**That was close!**"

"I hate when I get anointed and oil gets in my eyes," Ronald says.

"So would I," Tiffany responds. "It would mess up my makeup."

"Well, you never had the chance to find out, did you, since you were never anointed?"

"Next time, Ronald."

"What? When you're almost eighty! Good luck with that."

"They must be crowning the wrong guy," Ian says. "Saul is the tallest and most handsome man in Israel."

"I agree," Avery says as she starts holding Ian's hand. "He's not bad looking, but he's not a head taller than all the other men."

"Samuel takes Saul out of the city and tells the servant to leave just the two of them alone before he anoints Saul," Deb says. "He is not anointed in front of a crowd."

"That's not how the British would crown a king," Jim comments. "Can you imagine how upset everyone would be if the next king of England is crowned, and they don't show the coronation on television?"

Episode four continues the story showing Saul is preparing for a battle with the Philistines. He is angry that Samuel is not there to make a sacrifice, so he makes the sacrifice himself before the battle by slicing a lamb's throat. Samuel shows up immediately and yells at Saul to leave the job of being a priest to him.

"Maybe Saul is a choir boy in church and feels he is capable of performing a sacrifice," Jim says.

"Not only that," Dave adds. "He possibly moonlights as a butcher and feels he is competent to butcher a lamb."

"Samuel doesn't say anything about leaving the job of being a priest to him," Deb says. "He actually tells Saul he will lose his throne for doing what he just did."

The series shows Saul winning the battle and not killing the livestock or the king. After that, Samuel tells Saul his kingdom will be torn from him.

"This is condensing the story quite a bit," Deb says, "since this does not happen after the first battle. But the series is doing a good job of making it clear why Saul loses the kingdom."

David is introduced, showing him killing a wolf with his sling as he protects his sheep. Samuel approaches him, and within seconds, anoints David the next king of Israel by pouring oil on his forehead.

"Watch out for his eyes!" Tiffany shouts.

"He almost got him that time," Ronald agrees.

"First, Saul is anointed in a crowd and then David is anointed alone," Deb says. "This is backwards. Saul anoints David in front of his father and brothers."

"They're all alone out there," Chester agrees. "No brothers, no father, not even the sheep, let alone the family mule."

"Mules don't matter," Charley jokes.

Meanwhile, Saul is going insane. David is brought to the king's court and plays music for Saul in order to comfort him. As Israel prepares to fight the Philistines, Goliath challenges the Israelites to fight him and David, hearing this, volunteers to kill Goliath. Saul gives him a shield, but David refuses it, instead he leans over and picks up a stone in the sand, and walks out to meet the giant.

"A shield!" Joe yells. **"That's it? I would insist on a Glock and five hand grenades!"**

"I would want an anti-aircraft gun, just like Kim has," Ronald posts. "The one he blasted his uncle with."

"Saul tries to give him more than a shield," Deb says. "They put armor on him and give him a sword, which he refuses. He doesn't pick up a stone in the sand, he goes over to brook and picks up five stones out of the water."

"Why five stones?"

"Goliath has four brothers, maybe he thought they might show up."

David walks up to the giant, and after they exchange a few words, the giant decides to kill him. The giant waves his sword back and forth, but David waves his sling and releases the stone which bounces off Goliath's head, killing him.

"The stone doesn't bounce off his head!" Les yells.

"He's right," Deb says. "It imbeds in his forehead."

"The film is showing David not moving after they talk to each other," she continues. "He actually runs toward Goliath just before he kills him."

"Despite the errors, I really like the guy who plays Goliath," Jim comments.

After killing Goliath, David fights the Philistines, first in his shepherd's clothing, next he is shown in armor, and finally he is shown as a grown man in armor. David is now tall, handsome, and charismatic.

"I wish the film starred Kirkwood as Saul instead of David," Deb comments. "His appearance would be perfect for the part of the troubled king."

David rises in power and popularity, to the extent Saul is now afraid of him. Saul offers his daughter, Michal, to David in return for killing one hundred Philistines. Accepting the assignment, David rides off in a chariot and quickly returns, giving Saul two hundred foreskins as proof that he kills the Philistines. Saul looks in the bag, flies come out and he is repulsed by the smell.

"Saul actually tells David to bring him one hundred foreskins," Deb says.

"So he doesn't actually tell David to kill the Philistines?" Jim asks. "Just bring him the foreskins?"

"Very funny," Joe says. "Maybe he just borrows them."

"We want those back with interest!" Jim mimics the Philistines.

As David walks away with Michal, Saul throws a spear near David sticking it in the door.

"You missed, Dude!" Chester jokes.

"Saul doesn't do this now," Deb says.

Saul and Jonathan die in battle and after a soldier reports their death to David, he tells his men to, "Get rid of him."

"David actually orders the messenger killed," Deb says. "The series does not make that clear."

After Saul dies, David and his men capture Jerusalem. As they are bringing the Ark of the Covenant into Jerusalem, David is dancing and at one point dances with Uriah's wife, saying, "You don't mind, Uriah?"

"What's your sign?" Ian jokes, imitating a guy trying to pick up a girl in a meat market.

"Virgo," Avery answers, as she plays along.

"What are you majoring in?"

"I'm not sure yet, but I hope to get an 'MRS.'"

"Have you joined a sorority?"

"No, have you?"

"No. I am already a Deke. But I would love to live in a sorority house."

"Stop it!" She elbows him.

Their joking is interrupted by Les yelling, **"Why does David have to ask who she is when he sees her on the roof?"**

"David sees her bathing at night and does not know who she is," Deb says. "That's why Les is yelling."

Later, David is in his palace during the day and sees Bathsheba bathing. **"It's at night!"** Les yells.

He orders her brought to him that night, and she gets pregnant as a result of what follows. Once this is discovered, David has Uriah deliver a message to Joab, setting him up to be killed in battle, which frees Bathsheba to marry David. Nathan confronts David about this after the baby is born and tells David, "He will take your son." David defiantly replies, "We shall see."

> **"Whoa Dude!"** Jim yells. **"What's with that mouth?"**

> *"David doesn't show that kind of attitude when Nathan confronts him,"* Deb replies.

David prays at the Ark for the life of his son, but his son dies anyway. Nathan comforts David telling him he will have another son, and the episode ends showing David playing with his son, Solomon.

> *As they stand up to leave the theater Deb says, "The series completely ignores David realizing he has done a horrible thing and acknowledging his guilt."*

> *Jim asks Deb how she rates the episode, "It's entertaining and fast paced, so I rate that part a four, especially because of the actors that play Goliath and David, but the most I can rate accuracy would be a three."*

35

Skullduggery

As Told In
"The Story of David"
1976 TELEVISION MINI SERIES

THIS TWO-PART television series tells the story of David's life. It stars Timothy Bottoms as young David and Keith Mitchell as the older version. Anthony Quayle plays King Saul and Jane Seymour is Bathsheba. David is shown having red hair in this film.

"This is a great cast!" Jim says.

"There is a strong possibility that David is a redhead," Deb says. "None of the other films show this."

The film begins with Saul leading a few men into the wilderness to see Samuel. The prophet is now speaking against Saul, and he wants to find out why. Samuel tells Saul it's because of his disobedience, and that he is going to lose his kingdom.

David is introduced bringing food to his older brothers who are fighting the Philistines under Saul's command, and he comments that no one is actually fighting the Philistines. By this time, Saul is now mentally ill and Abner, one of his officers, brings David to Saul to comfort him with his songs. Meanwhile, Goliath challenges Israel to send a man out to fight him.

Seeing this, David asks Saul if he can fight Goliath, which Saul allows him to do. David is successful and kills the giant.

"This film looks good so far," Jim says. "What do you think Deb?"

"The film leaves a few things out. It doesn't show David trying on the armor and refusing it because of its weight. It also omits David getting five stones from a brook, and it does not show David taking Goliath's head to Jerusalem after he kills the giant."

"Other than that?"

"It's all good."

The film follows David's story for the next hour and a half, showing his conflict with Saul, and ultimately becoming king of Israel.

"You've been very quiet Deb. Is it all good?"

"It's all good or very close."

The story continues with David seeing Bathsheba bathing and sending for her. When she enters the room, David comments that she voluntarily comes to his room, and she responds that she is his handmaiden. When David plays the harp for her, Bathsheba closes her eyes and starts moving her head, slowly, to the music.

"Do you come here often?" Ian jokes, mimicking David talking to Bathsheba.

"The lady doth not protest at all," Avery responds.

David removes her head cover and says, "I saw you on your rooftop when you bathed." Then he pulls down her clothing to reveal her shoulders.

She looks him in the eyes, "I have seen you often, Lord."

David unties her hair so it falls to her shoulders as she closes her eyes again and then looks at him, tilting her head to allow him to kiss her on the neck.

"You know he is watching and yet you continue to strip on your roof," Les yells. **"Have you ever heard of a shower curtain?"**

"The entire encounter is described in one verse," Deb says. *"There is no conversation in that verse."*

"What are you saying, Deb?" Cindy asks.

"It appears the film is saying that Bathsheba is partially to blame, instead of David being totally at fault. David is a great man, but he has serious issues."

"You mean he is not a sinless superhero?" Joe asks.

"Not by any stretch."

"I know what it's like to be approached by hot women," Ronald posts. *"Deb's wrong, David and I are hot."*

David carries her to his bed and she becomes pregnant. When David learns of this he is happy, but Bathsheba is worried she will be stoned for adultery, and pressures David to do something, so he comes up with a plan.

"You don't love me," Cindy mimics Bathsheba. *"You just want me to get stoned. It's your fault for not using protection."*

"There's nothing said about this in the story," Deb says. *"The film makes it look like she is pressuring David to take action."*

The plan works, Uriah dies, and David marries Bathsheba. Later she is shown in labor having a difficult delivery due to a breach birth. During this time, Nathan confronts David while he and his friends are waiting for news of the delivery. Nathan tells David a parable about a rich man taking the only possession of a poor man, his lamb, and accuses David of being that rich man. David genuinely repents, so Nathan tells him that God will not kill him, but he will be cursed, including having his baby dying during childbirth.

"The baby does not die at birth," Deb says. *"He dies a few days later."*

The second part of the curse comes to pass years later when Absalom, David's son, attempts to kill his father and take his throne. Absalom raises an army to fight David, but he loses the battle and attempts to escape on a horse.

"What's this?" Chester shouts. **"He actually tries to escape riding a mule. This is an outrage!"**

"Na na na na na," Charley taunts Chester.

"Deb, tell Charley it's a mule, and not to be mean to me."

"It's a mule, Charley. Now apologize to Chester."

"I'm sorry," Charley says turning away so Deb can't see him grinning.

Absalom rides through the woods and hits a low-lying limb, knocking him to the ground. He is captured and Joab kills him with a spear.

"What actually happens would be hard to film," Deb says. *"Joab finds Absalom hanging by his hair in the tree, and he drives a spear into him, wounding him. Ten of Joab's men finish him off with their swords."*

At the end of the film, David proclaims Solomon to be king and tells him, "Ride on my own horse to Gideon."

"It's a mule!" *Les yells at the screen."*

Les then walks down the aisle and talks to Chester who is crying and pets his head. "It's okay, Chester. Maybe we can find you a good lawyer and file a class action lawsuit."

"I have great lawyers," Ronald posts. *"They can get Chester millions! Millions!"*

Rick brings Chester a free tub of popcorn. "There, there," he says.

The film ends with David giving final advice to his son, Solomon.

As they leave the theater, Jim says, "I really enjoyed this film, how about you Deb?"

"It is really good. I love all the actors and how they stay real close to the story. They do omit Saul's encounter with the witch and David taking the census, but I guess they have time limits. Still, it's a great film. I give this film two fives."

"Except for horses replacing mules," Chester says.

Charley looks away and snickers.

36

Skullduggery

As Told In
David and Goliath
1960

ORSON WELLS plays the troubled Saul in this movie.

"So much for Saul being the tallest and most handsome man in Israel," Jim says.

"That's like saying Phil Scheidt is the best golfer and the hottest man in America," Joe laughs.

"Talk about fake news!" Ronald posts." I am a better golfer and definitely hotter than Phil."

"Orson is a great actor!" Deb says. "This should be fun."

A narrator starts the film by saying the Philistines have taken the Ark of the Covenant from the Israelites. Years later, the Philistines are preparing to go to war with Israel which is unarmed. Samuel makes his entrance into Saul's court and as he looks at Saul's sons, he asks, "Are these as they the sons of Saul, then?"

"What!" Dave yells.

"He said what?" *Joe shouts.*

"Don't tell me we have to listen to archaic English!" *Les screams.*

"Two and a half hours of thee and thou Les," *Jason yells from the booth.* ***"Get used to it! I just took another aspirin."***

Samuel recounts the history of Saul to the people and then privately tells him he will no longer be king and will be replaced by someone from Bethlehem. He tells Saul he has come to say goodbye.

"That doesn't happen," Deb says.

The film introduces David, appearing to be in his twenties, and having a girlfriend named "Eglah." She gets struck by lightning and killed early in the script.

"I thought David is a young teenager when his story begins," Jim says.

"He is," Deb answers. *"First the film shows an old and overweight Orson as a tall and handsome version of Saul, now it shows David as a well muscled adult who is taller than his father. Neither of these actors are right for their roles."*

"Does David have a girlfriend early in the story?" Jim asks.

"Only in Holy Wood," Deb responds. *"There actually is a woman named 'Eglah' who will be a future wife of David."*

As David talks to Eglah, Ian kisses Avery for the first time and asks, *"Wouldst thou wish me to speakest to thee such?"*

"Only if thou wishes to never see me again," she giggles as she kisses him back.

Abner is a military commander working for Saul. He is also conspiring to overthrow Saul with the help of Merab, Saul's oldest daughter. Moving along quickly, the movie introduces Asrod, a fictional king of the Philistines, and Goliath, played by Kronos.

"Goliath is never shown saying a word," Joe says. *"He just laughs like an idiot who has just been audited by the IRS, and no longer understands reality."*

"*Talk to me about reality!*" *Ronald posts.* "*My audits take eight years! Count them! Nobody has longer audits than I do!*"

Goliath does not have a shield bearer. Instead, he has an agent named "Cret."

"*Cret is annoying!*" *Charlotte says as she hurries back to the popcorn stand to wait on a customer.*

Cret arranges for Goliath to go on raids and kill Israelites as well as kill an emissary Saul sends to the Philistines.

"*He reminds me of a hit man in a gangster movie,*" *Jim says.* "*But this guy must have a sense of humor since all he does is laugh.*"

"*The real Goliath is not an idiot who can only laugh when spoken to,*" *Deb says.* "*He actually speaks quite well. He is not a deranged lunatic living in a cave.*"

Samuel comes to Jesse's house and anoints David. Later that evening "Sarah" is introduced as David's sister, and after that David leaves home to go out in the desert. While he is in the wilderness, someone speaks to him, it's not clear whether it's God or Samuel, but the voice tells him to travel three days and three nights to Jerusalem.

"*He must take a wrong turn somewhere,*" *Les, says to Charlotte as he buys some popcorn.* "*Bethlehem is only six miles from Jerusalem. He must go by way of Atlanta.*"

"*He should take a cab,*" *She jokes.*

"*Does David have a sister?*" *Jim asks.*

"*There is no mention of David having a sister named Sarah,*" *Deb says.*

"*Does his sister Sarah have any mules?*" *Chester asks.*

"*No mules either.*"

Once he reaches Jerusalem, David walks through a crowded marketplace. He sees a slave dealer selling two slaves with yokes on their necks. David buys the slaves and sets them free.

"***What?***" *Les yells.* "***Is he a rich shepherd boy?***"

As he continues to walk through the plaza he sees dancing girls and other things that trouble him. Walking further, he finds two men staked out on the ground who are dying of thirst and he gives them water. Guards try to stop him, but he hits one of them, knocking him to the ground. Then David stands on the steps of "The House of God" and makes a speech to the crowd, telling them that Saul is evil and they should rebel against him. When guards come to arrest him, priests come out and invite him into the Temple where they can protect him.

*"**Unbelievable!**" Les yells. "**This is absurd! David won't capture Jerusalem for decades.**"*

"He's right," Deb says. "There is no way David could walk around Jerusalem while it is still controlled by the Jebusites, not to mention that the Temple won't be built until after he dies."

"We studied this," Ian says to Avery. "David is very loyal to Saul; he would never try to get a crowd to rebel against him."

The crowd cheers as David walks into the temple with the priests.

"It will be many years before crowds will cheer for David," Deb says.

David meets Saul and tells him that while the treaty with the Philistines allows only the palace guards to have weapons, it does not limit the number of guards, so they can have all the weapons they want by just having more guards.

"That's brilliant!" Chester tells Charley.

"Chester, there is no treaty," Deb rubs Chester's head.

"That's stupid!" Chester tells Charley.

Saul orders David to stay in the palace and play music for him.

"What kind of music?" Cindy asks and turns to Dave saying, "I hope it's not that alternative music you play in your car."

"That's good stuff! Salty Dog plays European Alternative on his show, great groups like VNV Nation! Where have you been?"

David is next shown wearing a soldier's outfit, talking to his friend, Jonathan. Saul tells David that Samuel is dead, and that the Philistines are preparing to attack, with Goliath as their champion. Later that evening, Samuel's spirit talks to David, reassuring him that all will be well and that he will win and return the Ark of the Covenant to Israel. Michal, Saul's daughter, begs David not to go fight Goliath.

"Anything wrong here?" Jim asks.

"Samuel won't die for many years," Deb responds, "and when David fights Goliath, it's not to try to take back the Ark. Also, the only place Samuel's ghost shows up is when Saul visits the witch of En Dor."

"Does Michal even know David before he fights Goliath?"

"She might, but she is nowhere around him before the fight."

The movie shows the following events leading up to David's battle with Goliath. David travels on a white horse leading troops from Jerusalem to the battle scene and encounters Israelite refugees fleeing from invading Canaanites. Jonathan, Saul's son, is leading the army to attack the Canaanites, when David rides up and stops him from the attack, telling Jonathan that he will talk to Asrod and keep the Israelite army from being slaughtered.

"Really? David rides in on a white horse?" Les yells. **"Leading a company of troops?"**

"Why not?" Charley quietly asks Deb.

"Sweetie, David never rides a horse during this part of his life."

"Let alone, leading troops," Jim adds.

"Anyway, if he is going to ride something, it would be a mule," Chester tells Charley.

David rides up to the enemy king on his white horse. The king laughs and tells David he has heard of how wise David is. When the king asks David what he wants, David responds, "I ask thee, in the name of the Lord, to return to us the sacred ark, and not to pass with thy host on the land of Israel."

Ian and Avery start laughing and within seconds almost everyone in the theater is also laughing at what they just watched.

"David rides to Philistines on a white horse!" Joe yells. **"Why doesn't he just borrow a golf cart?"**

"David talks to the Philistine king!" Cindy laughs, "and the king has heard how wise he is?"

"I guess they don't have fake news!" Tiffany wipes tears from her cheeks.

"Please return the ark! Pretty please!" Dave shouts.

"Whatever you do, I beg you, don't pass with thy host on Israel!" Jason loads another reel on the projector. **"We don't allow hosts here."**

"If you do come to Israel!" Rick yells. **"The tickets are cheaper for the Tuesday flight!"**

Erica runs to the auditorium when she hears the laughter.

"What's going on Charlotte? Why is everyone laughing? I thought this is a Bible movie."

Charlotte, who has been watching the movie, also has tears pouring down her face from laughing so hard. She tells Erica what David says to the king and Erica starts laughing too as Teddy joins them, putting his arm around Erica.

"You want to help me clean the theater again tonight?"

"What a wonderful opportunity," Rick quietly says to Charlotte.

The king tells David that if he can defeat Goliath, Israel will not be destroyed. Next, before they fight, Goliath walks over a hill with four spear bearers. David rides up to meet him, still on his white horse, and dismounts. Goliath laughs and the horse runs away.

Charley, still laughing, says, "I would run away too, and go complain to my agent about putting me in this film."

"Even Goliath is laughing," Chester says.

Goliath chucks four spears at David but misses. Then Goliath takes his sword out and approaches David, who backs up.

"He doesn't back up!" Les yells.

David twirls his sling and launches a rock right into Goliath's nose and the stone bounces off.

"What?" Les yells. "The stone imbeds!"

This knocks the giant to the ground, and then David kills him with his sword. The Philistines think about this for a minute, and then attack. The battle scene is reminiscent of old westerns which show horses tripping forward, as a result of their front legs being tied to the ground as they run.

"The rock goes into his forehead; it doesn't bounce off his nose," Les tells Teddy, Erica and Charlotte who are standing next to him.

"When Goliath is killed, the Philistines panic and run away, they don't charge into battle," Deb comments.

David returns to Jerusalem where Abner, at Saul's direction, is going to kill David. But before he can throw a spear into David, Saul kills Abner with a bow and arrow.

"Joab actually kills Abner many years later," Ian says.

Saul embraces David and says, "Long live David." David responds by saying, "Long live Saul, king of Israel!" Saul gives his daughter to David and the film has a happy ending.

Leaving the theater, Charley says, "I'm glad I didn't have a role in the film. I might have gotten killed."

"How?" Chester asks.

"By falling down in that battle scene."

Chester turns to Charley, "I would have missed you, bud."

"How do you rate the film Deb?" Jim asks.

"It is entertaining, so I can give that a two and a half because it makes people laugh. However, I rate the accuracy at zero."

37

Skullduggery

As Told In
David

1997 TELEVISION MINI SERIES

THIS THREE-HOUR TNT production stars Leonard Nimoy as Samuel and Franco Nero as Nathan.

"This is a great cast!" Jim says.

The film begins with David narrating a flashback about Saul and Jonathan dying in battle and continues with David and his followers preparing to capture Jerusalem, which they do before the opening credits end. After the credits, the film looks back to the story of Saul's son, Jonathan and Abner taking care of mules in the wilderness. The mules disappear in a sandstorm and Saul shows up and tells Abner to stay behind, while Saul, a servant and his son search for the missing mules.

> *"These films don't show Saul as a very tall and extremely handsome man. That is important to understanding why Israel wants him as their king,"* Deb says. *"This film is not showing Saul's father, Kish, telling Saul to take a servant and search for the donkeys."*
>
> *"So, are they adding Jonathan?"* Jim asks.

"It looks that way."

"Do you see anything else?"

"Yes, I see Abner, who should not be in this part of the story."

When they arrive in a nearby town, they meet Samuel, and tell him they are looking for their lost mules. Samuel tells them not to worry, the mules have been found.

"See Chester?" Charley says, "It's not always mules that get left out. In this case the film substitutes mules for donkeys."

Samuel invites them to his house and tells Saul that the tribes of Israel have decided to ask God for a king.

"It's not quite like that," Deb says. "They actually ask Samuel to appoint a king over them."

Saul is humble but allows Samuel to anoint him king, pouring oil on Saul's forehead as Jonathan and the servant stand nearby.

***"Watch out for the eyes!"** Chester yells, as the oil runs down Saul's cheek close to his right eye and a little dripping into his left one.*

As Deb leaves to get hot dogs, she tells Jim, "Samuel actually instructs Saul to have his servant leave them," Deb says. "It is just Samuel and Saul in the woods."

Later, now that Saul is king, he raises an army to fight the Ammonites. Samuel tells him to wait for him, and he will join him in seven days. But Saul gets impatient when Samuel doesn't show up, so he sacrifices a calf. Samuel arrives and gets angry at Saul for not waiting. Saul is sorry and asks what he can do. Samuel tells Saul to raid the Amalekites and kill Agag, their king, as well as all the men, women, children, and animals in the camp. After the battle, Samuel rides into the camp and sees that Saul has disobeyed, sparing the cattle to feed his men, and not killing Agag.

As Deb returns from the concession stand she gives the hot dogs to Jim so he can feed Chester and Charley, and tells him, "That's not exactly what Saul says. Saul tells Samuel he spares the cattle and sheep so they can be sacrifices to God."

"This is changed?" Jim asks.

"Yes, it is. There's a difference between saving the animals for themselves as opposed to saving them for God. While saving them for God is a noble gesture, it's all about obedience, and Saul disobeys twice. The second disobedience results in him losing his kingdom."

After Samuel kills Agag, God tells Samuel to go to Bethlehem and find Jesse. He meets Jessie and goes to his house for dinner and to meet his sons. Samuel asks if there are any other sons and, when told the youngest son is out in the field, Samuel goes to him. He anoints David with oil and kisses him three times, the third time on the lips.

"This time the oil gets in the eyes," Chester says. "It's dripping off his eyelid."

"This is another film that reverses the anointing," Deb says. "Samuel actually anoints David in front of his family, but this film has him doing it alone, while Saul is actually anointed alone, but the film shows people are there watching."

Saul becomes tormented, so his son, hearing about David, brings him to the camp to play music for his father.

"It is a servant, not Jonathan that hears about David," Deb says.

The series introduces Goliath as a great warrior. He has killed Saul's best warriors in small fights, so Saul is going to face him alone. However, David volunteers to kill Goliath to keep Saul from going out on his own to meet the giant.

"No one fights Goliath," Deb says. "They are all too frightened."

David goes to a rocky hilltop, and Goliath comes over to him and berates him. As Goliath comes near, David backs up and falls down the hill. He stands up when he is on level ground and yells at Goliath, who is standing at the top of the hill. David slings a stone at him, severely wounding the warrior as it hits him and bounces off his forehead. Then David charges the fallen giant and cuts his head off.

"*The stone does not bounce off his head!*" Les yells.

"This is such a well-known story! How can the film get this so wrong?" Deb asks. "It doesn't show Goliath challenging the Israelite army for forty days. David is shown searching for Goliath, when he is actually between the armies taunting the Israelites. David doesn't back up, but runs straight to Goliath and kills him. All this occurs in front of both armies, not where they are alone and unseen. It also omits the Philistines running away in panic after David kills Goliath."

"So far, this has been a pretty good film. It's too bad it changes things so much in this part," Jim agrees.

"It also doesn't show what happens to Goliath's head," Deb says. "David takes it to Jerusalem."

Ten years later, David is still fighting Philistines. By this time, Saul wants to kill David. David has two opportunities to kill Saul when he is defenseless: one while Saul is sleeping and the other while Saul is relieving himself. The film consolidates the two opportunities, using elements of both stories, into one event while Saul is sleeping. After Saul wakes up and realizes David was in a position to kill him, Saul yells at Abner for not doing his job.

"Abner! I told you to set the alarm for five o'clock, Judean time!" Les yells.

"Actually, David yells at Abner for not protecting Saul," Deb says. "The film also consolidates Saul throwing a spear at David two times into one scene. However, I like the way David's marriage with Michal is shown during this period, it's very accurate."

Saul and Jonathan are facing a battle with the Philistines the next day. Saul is worried, so he takes his son with him to see the witch at En Dor, and pays her to conjure up a vision of Samuel in order to get advice about the next day's battle. Samuel is wakened and tells Saul that he and his son will die in that battle.

"That woman is beautiful but horrifying," Jim says.

"She reminds me of my ex-wife," Dave says. "Only she wasn't beautiful, she was just horrifying."

"Dave? Stop!" Cindy reminds him.

"You're right, sorry."

Deb tells everyone, "The film doesn't show Samuel telling Saul that he is being punished for not killing all the Amalekites, but I love how the witch is portrayed in this scene, she even scares me!"

The next morning, Saul leads the Israelites into battle and they are defeated by the Philistines. Knowing the battle is lost, Saul begs Jonathan to kill him, but an enemy soldier kills Jonathan in front of Saul, forcing Saul to kill himself by falling on his sword.

"The film changes a couple of things in this part of the film," Deb says. "It leaves out Saul's armor bearer, who Saul tells to kill him. The armor bearer refuses and kills himself after Saul falls on his sword."

"Doesn't David join the Philistines?" Jim asks.

"He does, but most people don't know that because none of the movies show that part of his life. However, the Philistines don't let him fight in this battle."

David becomes king and rules from Jerusalem. He asks a servant about a woman he sees in the house nearby and finds out she is Bathsheba, Uriah's wife. He tells the servant to bring her to the palace, and David has sex with her. Later, when David finds out she is pregnant, he calls for Uriah to come home from the war where Uriah is fighting, and encourages him to sleep with his wife.

Uriah won't do that, so David has him take a letter to Joab when he returns to the campaign. The letter instructs Joab to put Uriah in the hottest part of the battle, where he is most likely to be killed, which will solve David's problem.

"The letter doesn't say that," Deb says. "David tells Joab to have his troops abandon Uriah in battle, guaranteeing he will be killed. This is another example of a film not showing the extent of David's depravity at this point in his life."

Uriah and his patrol have a small fight while they are in the field, and after winning the skirmish, they undress at a lake and splash each other in the water. The enemy sneaks up and kills the unarmed soldiers in the lake.

"Come on man!" *Joe yells.* ***"Are they really so stupid they wouldn't post a guard?"***

Nathan tells David the child he has with Bathsheba will die because of what he has done to Uriah. David repents, saying, "I have sinned."

"It's clear he means it," Jim says. "I'm not sure everyone who gets caught means it as much as David does when they recite those words."

As Bathsheba is about to deliver the baby, David checks on her, and as he leaves, he tells a guard he does not want to be disturbed until the baby is born. He goes outside to fast and pray for mercy. However, the child dies during the delivery. Nathan comes to David a little later and when he finds him eating, he asks David why he is now eating.

"Because I'm hungry!" *Joe exclaims, holding up a hot dog.*

"The baby is actually living when Nathan tells David the child will die," Deb says. "David fasts for a week, but the child dies anyway. Once the child dies, it's the servants who asks him why he is eating, not Nathan."

Years later, Amnon, one of David's sons, falls in love with Tamar, his step-sister. He rapes her and Absalom, her brother, murders Amnon for what he does to her. This event leads to Absalom rebelling against David and eventually having enough supporters to force David to abandon Jerusalem. When Absalom occupies Jerusalem, he has three of David's concubines join him in a pool inside the palace and has sex with them.

"I thought we were going to play water volleyball," Jim laughs, imitating the concubine's conversation.

"This is completely changed," Deb says. "He has sex with all ten of David's concubines in a tent on the roof of the palace where it's obvious to the whole city what's happening."

"I think most men understand that one man cannot have sex with ten different women in a day," Jim laughs. "I would be one and done."

"Not me," Charley says.

"Nor me," Ronald texts.

"*I would be lucky to be one and done,*" Jim adds.

"*Jim,*" Dave says, "*here's a couple of pills that might help,*" as he hands Jim a couple antacid tablets as a joke.

Joab leads David's troops to fight Absalom's troops and defeats them. Seeing he is defeated, Absalom attempts to escape the battle riding away on a horse.

"This is outrageous!" Chester shouts.

Deb looks over to Chester and says, "*Sorry honey, once again the film substitutes a horse for a mule.*"

Chester looks up at the screen, and imitating Ronald Reagan, shouts, **"Well, there you go again."**

The movie concludes with David holding his son, Solomon, in the air while a vision of the temple is on the screen and the narrator says that Solomon's kingdom will last forever.

As they leave the theater, they all agree they enjoyed the film, although Deb points out, "They omit David's sin of having a census, which results in seventy thousand people dying of a plague. But, it's still a very good film. I rate the entertainment at five and the accuracy at a four."

Skullduggery

As Told in
David and Bathsheba
1951

THE FILM BEGINS with a battle scene. An adult version of David, played by Gregory Peck, and Uriah are fighting dozens of bad guys and winning. David receives only a small wound on his arm.

"*Back in the fifties, if a good guy gets hurt it is always in his arm,*" Jim says.

"*David is not out fighting with Uriah and the troops,*" Deb comments.

David and Uriah go back to the tent and drink wine to celebrate. Then David returns to Jerusalem where he is shown to be in an unhappy marriage to Michal, a nagging shrew. It's obvious there is no love between these two.

"*I'll take 'Iron Age Bitches' for six shekels, Salty,*" Jim responds as if he's on a WSOD quiz show.

"*Actually, Michal is never mentioned in this part of the story,*" Deb says.

Michal nags David and leaves his room. David, visibly unhappy, walks out on the balcony and sees Bathsheba, played by Susan Hayward, bathing next door.

> "Despite the fact David fathers children from as many as eighteen women, it is important to establish he is not a philanderer," Deb says sarcastically. "He is simply tempted because Michal makes his life hell."

> "I can relate," Dave says.

> "Dave!" Cindy says. "Let it go."

> "I remember when she gave you a hard time about playing golf," Joe comments to Dave, "and me as well!"

> "You too, Joe! You all need to forget about that woman."

David sends his trusted advisor to get Bathsheba.

> "He actually sends messengers," Deb says.

> "I thought he contacts her on that dating site," Dave says, "Jerusalem Wives Wanting a Good Time."

Bathsheba is in an arranged marriage and spends only six days with Uriah, her husband, in the seven months they are married, and to add to that, she doesn't love him. Later, the film shows Uriah prefers being in battle to being with his wife, but if she cheats on him, he fully supports stoning her.

> "Ok, we get it," Deb says. "They are both in unhappy marriages to horrible spouses, so we can't blame them if they want a little happiness."

> "I'll take 'Justifiable Homicides' for thirty shekels, Salty," Jim continues.

David and Uriah's wife have sex and continue the affair, which includes traveling through the countryside as well as riding around Jerusalem together. They arrive back in Jerusalem in time to see Israelites bring the Ark of the Covenant back from the Philistines. Nathan, played by Raymond Massey, does not allow the Ark to be taken into Jerusalem after Uzzah dies from touching it. That evening Bathsheba visits David and tells him she is pregnant, saying, "Our secret is no longer a secret."

"Well, you don't think people are going to see you riding in that chariot?" Les yells. **"Do you expect them to think he is your Uber driver?"**

"I'll take 'Famous Dead Rabbits' for four shekels."

David brings Uriah back to Jerusalem and suggests he go home to his wife for the night and then lectures him on how to be a good husband and attend to her needs.

"David would be an expert in this area, since he has so many wives," Deb says.

During their conversation, Uriah asks David that he be assigned to the front lines so he can serve his king to his utmost ability.

"I'll take 'Men Who Are So Stupid They Deserve to be Killed' for fifty shekels, Dog."

Several members of the audience start chanting "Kill him! Kill him!" as Chester and Charley stomp their hooves to the chant.

"This is another example of a film minimizing David's sin," Deb adds. "It's portraying Uriah as an abusive idiot who deserves what he gets. This is sad because he is actually a very noble person despite being a Gentile."

"He also might not be stupid," Jim responds. "He may very well suspect what's been going on."

Early in the morning, Michal comes to David and tells him she knows about his affair with Bathsheba, and that his plan has failed.

"It's all over the tabloids at the supermarkets," Erica whispers to Charlotte.

"I know. I saw a photo titled, 'Bathsheba's Bath,' taken by the paparazzi."

She tells David that Uriah did not go to his house last night.

"He was probably playing some war game on his Xbox and lost track of time," Joe says.

"It's the servants who tell this to David, not Michal," Deb says.

When David asks Uriah why he doesn't go home, he tells David he promised Joab he would not sleep with his wife while he comes home to Jerusalem if the battle is still going on.

"He never makes such a promise," Deb says. "He doesn't go to his wife because he feels it is the wrong thing to do."

Since the plan fails, David dictates a letter to Abishai, his assistant, which tells Joab to set up Uriah to be killed.

Rick jokes to the girls mimicking Abishai

Things to do today:

- *Clean David's throne.*
- *Clean the wives' thrones.*
- *Reorder toilet paper.*
- *Take part in murdering stupid soldier who deserves to be killed.*
- *Give David's other dirty laundry to the servants.*

"Don't forget buying Pampers," Charlotte adds.

"David actually writes the letter," Deb says. "He doesn't involve Abishai."

The plot is successful, and Uriah gets killed.
Immediately, Israel suffers a famine, apparently the result of David's sin.

Ian tells Avery, "Israel doesn't have a famine because of Bathsheba."

"Isn't there a famine during David's reign?" she asks.

"Yes, but it's later."

Nathan walks into David's palace and says, "Woe unto Israel and its people for its sin."

When David asks what sin, Nathan tells him he doesn't know. Nathan tells David that some people are ready to rebel and follow Absalom, who to this point is shown to be a snotty spoiled kid, but now he is inciting a rebellion against his father.

David and Bathsheba have their wedding and several months later, their baby is sick and dying. David fasts for seven days and goes to the baby just in time to see it die. Nathan, followed by a mob of people, enters the throne room and tells David the parable of the rich man taking the poor man's ewe.

> "I'll take 'Famous Ewes' for one shekel, Salty. 'Eww' is what girls used to say in college when Phil Scheidt asked them for a date."

> "The judges will allow that answer."

> "Nathan tells the parable before the baby dies, not after," Deb says,

With a crowd carrying torches in tow, Nathan confronts David for his skullduggery. Michal and David's favorite son, Absalom, who is quietly playing with a rock, are also there as Nathan demands that Bathsheba be stoned. David defends Bathsheba, but Nathan says her adultery causes the famine.

> "There is never any talk of stoning Bathsheba," Deb says as she returns with hot dogs for the animals. "Nor is there a famine at this time."

David now plans to escape from Jerusalem with Bathsheba.

> **"What?"** Les yells.

> Charley, with his mouth still full, leads a chant in the audience, **"Horsefeathers! Horsefeathers! Horsefeathers!"**

David quickly realizes this can't happen, so he plays The Twenty-Third Psalm for her on a harp while she waits to be stoned. He is bitter about what's going to happen and complains about a God that would kill a soldier for touching the Ark, saying this is not the God he worshiped as a youth.

> **"Total nonsense!"** Deb yells.

> **"Yeah!"** Tiffany shouts. **"I'm with you, Deb."**

Then David marches over to the tent where the ark is in the "Holy of Holies," a place where only the high priest is allowed to enter just once a year, he walks in and starts praying. He reaches out with both hands and grabs the side of the ark as he finishes his prayer.

"He can't go in there," Deb says, "let alone touch the ark."

Les sarcastically shouts, **"Put your hands on the Ark of the Covenant!"** Mimicking radio ministers who instruct their audience to "Put your hands on the radio."

"I'll take 'Bible Movies That Get It Wrong,' for one thousand shekels, Dog."

David has a flashback to his youth so the audience can see him fight Goliath.

Jim comments, "It's in Goliath's contract that he must appear in all movies, mini-series, or short films in which King David appears. Those Philistines have great entertainment lawyers."

David is out tending his father's sheep. Jesse sends a message for him to come back to their home because Samuel wants to see him. When he arrives home, his father, three of his brothers, and Samuel are waiting for him.

"So where are the other four brothers?" Deb asks.

"I think they are in the bedroom watching the quiz show on WSOD," Jim answers.

When Samuel meets David, who is played by Leo Pepsin, as a fourteen-year old boy, he pours oil on David's hair.

"At least he doesn't pour oil directly his face," Joe says.

"I'll take, 'Famous Prophets in the Bible' for two shekels, Salty,'" Chester jokes as he also imitates the quiz show.

David is in a tent cleaning a shield while King Saul and his officers talk about Goliath, who they can hear yelling from the field.

"I'll take 'Short Fat Ugly Kings' for three shekels," Chester continues.

"That's easy," Charley jokes. "It's Phil Scheidt."

"Phil's not short nor is he a king, but after careful consideration, the judges are giving you credit," Chester answers.

Saul is upset that nobody wants to fight Goliath. Then David, who is in the tent, volunteers to kill the giant. Saul allows him to fight Goliath because he realizes it's a win-win. If David wins, Goliath is defeated. If David is beaten, Samuel is discredited because he anointed David, and Saul won't have to put up with Samuel ranting at him.

"I'll take 'Famous Mismatches' for six shekels, Dog."

"It isn't like that," Deb says. "Saul never wants to discredit Samuel."

David walks out to the valley between the two armies and confronts Goliath. The giant fires three spears at David. The third spear pins David's robe to the ground. At the urging of Jonathan, David pulls himself free, approaches the giant, then backs up before he finally kills Goliath.

"I'll take 'Famous Jonathans' for ten shekels," Chester jokes.

"It's a bathroom?" Charley responds.

"I said 'Jonathans' not Johns," Chester fires back.

"Any comments Deb?" Jim asks.

"*The film leaves out what David says to Goliath and the cutting off his head. It also shows Goliath throwing spears at David, which doesn't happen. After telling Goliath what he is going to do to him, David runs toward him and launches a stone into his forehead, killing him. David never backs up.*"

When this flashback—at the *end of the movie*—ends, David hears the sound of falling rain, signaling that the drought is over. The rain extinguishes the mob's torches. so they all go home. A chorus sings The Twenty-Third Psalms as David walks to Bathsheba, so they also go home as the film ends.

"Let's go home too," Jim says. "What do you think, Deb?"

"*Gregory Peck is handsome, Susan Hayward is beautiful, Raymond Massey looks like a statue of Moses, so despite being an old film, I will rate the entertainment as a five, but the movie is loaded with errors, so I rate accuracy at one.*"

Skullduggery

As Told in
King David
1985

SAMUEL ENTERS the Israelite camp and barges into King Saul's tent as this film begins.

"The actor playing Saul is shorter than the other four characters in the scene," Deb says. "Saul is supposed to be the tallest man in Israel."

There is negotiation occurring about the ransom price the Amalekites must pay to save Agag, their king. Samuel is outraged, so he walks over and beheads Agag.

"Already?" Jim asks Deb, as he sees her rolling her eyes.

"Well it doesn't take long," Deb replies. "Samuel actually has Agag brought to him, and after talking with the enemy king, hacks him into pieces."

Saul asks Samuel for forgiveness but is told the kingdom will be given to a more-worthy man. Cue the title and credits.

Samuel is instructed to go to Jesse's home where God will choose a new king from Jesse's sons. Dad introduces him to David's three brothers.

Jim says, "This is the second movie that limits David to three brothers. What's with that?"

Samuel holds a rock in each hand as he meets each brother, but he looks at the rocks and shakes his head "no" when he sees each of the three sons. When Samuel asks if there is another son Jesse sends for David. When David is brought to Samuel, he holds the two rocks in his hand, and they magically cast laser beams in David's face, telling Samuel this is the right brother.

"What about the other four brothers?" Dave yells.

"They are playing video games," Joe shouts back.

When David is anointed, he asks why his brothers weren't chosen. "If I stand so well in God's sight, let him command me, face to face."

"What?" Les yells.

"That sounds like trash talk I used to hear playing basketball," Dave says.

"He sounds like a guy winning 'Israel's Got Talent' and the million shekels, then insulting Judge Simeon," Jim adds.

The film introduces Saul, who is waiting for Samuel to arrive before going into battle.

Saul is troubled that he is losing his kingdom, so Jonathan and Joab get David to sing to Saul, hopefully making him feel better. When Saul meets David, he comments about how he saw God face to face, referring to a dream where God wrestles with him until dawn.

"Wrong wrestling match!" Les yells **"The only person who wrestles with God is Jacob."**

The famous encounter between David and Goliath starts with the giant's armor bearer challenging the Israelites six times to come out and fight the giant, who is sleeping under a tree while the armor bearer talks.

"Goliath can talk you know," Deb says. "For all we know he might have gone to Oxford. In fact, his armor bearer talks like he might be an Oxford graduate. However, it's Goliath who actually challenges Israel *for forty days, as opposed to his armor bearer doing it six times as shown here."*

"I really like this guy," Jim says. "He wins the award for best armor bearer, very articulate!"

"I like him too," Ronald says, "he would make a great press secretary when I become mayor."

"Trust me, Ronald," Tiffany says. "You will never win that election!"

"I will, and I will make you First Lady of Wawasee!"

"You're cute when you get arrogant, even if you are seventy!"

The armor bearer yells, "There is no god in Israel." David, thinking otherwise, walks down the hill to face Goliath as he sings the Twenty-Third psalm in his head.

"The film leaves out quite a few things, such as David's conversation with Saul," Deb says.

"David, you're forgetting your five stones!" Les shouts.

"It also leaves out David's conversation with Goliath," Ian adds.

As in some other movies, Goliath throws a spear at David. David ends up fumbling around on the ground looking for another stone after Goliath uses his shield to deflect the first two stones David slings at him.

"You had five stones!" Les yells.

Joe mimics David looking on the ground for rocks. "No, not this one, no, that one won't work either."

Meanwhile Goliath is coming in for the kill, whipping his sword back and forth.

"It's too bad David can't just take out a pistol and shoot him!" Jim says.

Deb rolls her eyes. "Very dramatic, but Goliath doesn't even have time to draw his sword. After their conversation, David runs to him and kills him with his first stone before Goliath knows what hits him!"

David kills Goliath with his third stone which bounces off the giant's head.

"It doesn't bounce off his head!" Les yells.

"The stone imbeds in his forehead," Deb says.

After David cuts off his head, one of Saul's soldiers picks up the head and hands it to Saul.

"Can I get you anything else? Do you need a refill on your wine? Does the queen have room for dessert?" Dave bows to Cindy pretending to be a server at an elegant restaurant.

"David actually takes the head to Jerusalem," Deb says.

The film resumes ten years later and David, now played by Richard Gere, is a leader in Saul's army. After Saul gives David his daughter, Michal, to be his wife, the newly weds go into the wedding chamber, which is divided by a sheer curtain to consummate the marriage. They get undressed and as they get into bed, Saul and his wife are in the room watching them through the sheer curtain.

"See Honey? I told you he was circumcised," Joe yells, mimicking Saul.

"Really, they are in the room watching?" Les yells. **"Why don't they just invite everyone at the reception to drink wine with them and stand around the bed?"**

Jim laughs, "If your parents were watching us, Teddy never would have been born."

"Okay, seriously," Deb laughs. "This movie makes it appear Michal is the reward for David giving Goliath's head to Saul. While Saul promises his daughter to the man who kills Goliath, he never gives her to David at that time, possibly because he was too young. However, years later, he tells David the price for marrying his daughter is one hundred Philistine foreskins."

"I could have gotten him down to fifty," Ronald posts. "I can probably get Tiffany for twenty. If she wasn't so hot, maybe ten."

The afterglow of the couple is not what one would expect after the consummation. It is obvious Michal is not in love with David as she turns her head away from him when he starts to kiss her. This marriage is already in trouble.

"I hope you have a pre-nup!" Dave shouts.

"If we get together I'll sign one Dave, don't worry," Cindy says. *"You won't get fooled again."*

"Actually, in the story, they are happy at first, she even defies her father to save David," Deb says.

At the wedding feast, Saul makes it clear he wants to kill David, but Jonathan warns David and helps him escape. He goes to a monastery at Nob and Ahimelech, the high priest, gives him shelter. While he is there, Ahimelech reads a scroll that describes Jacob wrestling with a man all night and asking him his name. The response is "I AM that I AM."

"He doesn't give him his name!" Les yells.

"The high priest is misquoting Genesis," Deb says. *"Jacob asks for the name of the man he wrestles, but while he receives a blessing, the man does not give him his name. He is mixing Exodus and Genesis."*

When David is warned that Saul is coming to the monastery, he escapes. When Saul arrives, he finds that David is gone, so he kills all the priests for harboring David. Saul continues to chase David, culminating with the encounter in the cave where David goes alone into the cave and has an opportunity to kill Saul. Saul wakes up later and knows David was there, which is confirmed when David calls to Saul from a hilltop and shows the sword he took from him, and then throws it into the camp.

"He can probably get ten shekels for that sword," Ronald posts. *"He shouldn't just toss it away. Horrible businessman! Sad!"*

"This film also combines the two times that David has the opportunity to kill Saul," Deb says. *"The first time is in a cave and the second time is in Saul's camp."*

"Doesn't Saul take a potty break?" Jim asks.

"Yes, that's in the cave, and David cuts off a piece of his clothing in the process, but they don't show that."

"So, what happens in the camp?"

"David goes to the camp with Abishai instead of being alone and Saul does not wake up and know that David was there. David calls to Abner instead of Saul, showing the spear he takes from Saul as opposed to a sword. He does not throw the spear into the camp, instead he tells Saul to have one of the men come and get it."

"It sounds like everything is wrong. Is there anything else?"

"Yes, the film leaves out the jug of water that is next to Saul's head which David takes and shows Saul."

David joins the Philistines. However, in an Iron Age agreement, David promises the Philistines, the right to keep part of the land for peace.

"This is the only film that shows David joining the Philistines," Deb says. "Good job!"

"That land isn't Gaza by any chance is it?" Jim asks.

"That agreement doesn't happen. But it is interesting that this may be a 'land for peace' deal between the Palestinians and Israel like one that happened recently."

The events leading to Saul dying in battle are largely ignored. The film does not show the witch of En Dor or Samuel's ghost telling Saul what will happen to him in battle. However, the film shows Saul not letting Nathan make a sacrifice prior to the battle, which causes Saul's defeat.

"Loser!" Ronald posts.

"That doesn't cause the defeat," Deb says.

The battle scene is next.

"Saul's armor bearer is not shown," Deb says. "He is very loyal to Saul and falls on his sword when Saul is defeated."

"He's a stand-up guy," Jim says. "At least until he falls on his sword. This is like so many Hollywood battle scenes where the good guys lose, but they kill a bunch of bad guys before the hero finally gets killed."

After Saul is killed, David returns to Jerusalem, wearing very little clothing as he dances into the city with the Ark of the Covenant. Michal is no longer in love with David, having been married to another man while Saul was fighting David. After she rebukes him, David walks out on his balcony and sees a naked Bathsheba bathing and looking up at him.

"Hi David!" Les yells as he mimics what Bathsheba might say to David, **"I hear your wives don't understand you!"**

"Close your eyes ladies," Rick says to Erica and Charlotte.

"I hope Teddy isn't watching this nudity," Deb says.

"Once again," she continues, "we see another example of a film minimizing David's actions. First David loses Michal and then Bathsheba entices him."

"I know if I were to see Tiffany in a bathtub on a roof," Ronald posts, "I'd send for her immediately."

"Why are you looking at me that way Ronald?" Tiffany asks. "Oh no! Don't tell me you're thinking about you and me!"

"She's hot!" Ronald posts.

"It's been almost twenty-five years," Tiffany thinks.

David wants to build a temple, but Nathan won't let him because he has not killed all the heathens that still live in the land. David argues that would not be just.

"Mulewash!" Chester says. "David is told he can't build the temple because he is a man of war and has shed blood."

"That's very good, Chester," Deb pets his head.

David is talking to his son in the courtyard, when a man tells him Bathsheba, his niece, has come to visit him and is waiting for him in the palace. David meets her for the first time and discovers she has been married to

Uriah for five years, but the couple is not having sex, in fact he only touches her with a whip. Bathsheba is upset that Uriah is not giving her sex because that means she will never have children. However, David assures her she will have children. Bathsheba responds that as long as Uriah lives she will not have children.

> "This is all wrong," Deb says. "David sends for her at night, she doesn't show up in the day unannounced. And just like in David and Bathsheba, Uriah is shown to be an abusive moron with no interest in having sex."

> "Let me see if I get this right," Jim answers, "Bathsheba puts on a show for David, knowing he is a peeping Tom. She shows up at the palace and tells David she wants children and says she won't have any unless Uriah, the wife beater, is dead. I wonder if she wants David to kill her husband?"

There is no indication they have sex, as the next scene shows David sending a letter to Joab guaranteeing that Uriah will die in battle.

> "I never had sex with that woman," Joe quips.

Nathan confronts David about Bathsheba and tells him their child will die. The curse that Nathan lays on David leaves out the part that David's adversary would come from his own house. David prays that God can do anything to him, but his main prayer request is that he can keep Bathsheba.

> "I would pray for that too!" Ronald posts. "She's hot!"

> "Does David actually say his most important request is to keep Bathsheba?" Jim asks.

> "No," Deb replies. "David confesses he has sinned, but that's it. He doesn't ask for any clemency at this point. However, he will pray for the baby later."

Absalom murdering Amnon for raping his sister is condensed to showing Absalom slitting his throat at a party in front of David. Absalom's rebellion is next, concluding with the final battle between Absalom and Joab. Absalom loses and tries to escape in a chariot being chased by archers who kill one of his horses. He continues trying to escape on the remaining horse but gets caught in a tree and is killed by Joab.

> *Charley leans over to Chester, and pretending to be a reporter from WSOD holding a microphone asks, "Chester, any comments?"*
>
> *"Once again," Chester starts sobbing. "Absalom is riding a mule, not a horse. Why are we being disrespected this way? We have feelings too!"*
>
> *"It's okay, Honey," Deb comforts him. "We know you are perfectly capable of running under a tree and killing Jim."*

Joab is alone and uses a sword to kill Absalom as he is dangling from the tree.

> *"Wassap?" Dave jokes as he imitates Joab.*
>
> *"Just chillin," Joe responds, imitating Absalom. "You know, just hangin around."*
>
> *"Joab actually wounds him with a spear and several of his men finish Absalom off with their swords," Deb says.*

As David grieves over the loss of Absalom, Nathan criticizes David for grieving for his son.

> **"Look Nathan!"** *Joe shouts, mimicking David.* **"Go cook some hot dogs and leave me alone."**
>
> *"It is Joab who tells David the people are upset," Deb says. "Joab tells David many men died to protect his throne and it is insulting to them that he grieves for the man that causes their deaths. He warns the king his troops may rebel if he doesn't stop."*

David tells Nathan he will go to Absalom but Absalom will not return to him.

> **"That's what he says about the baby not about Absalom!"** *Les yells.*

The narrator says, "It came to pass, that David sinned no more."

> **"Really?"** *Les yells.* **"What about the sin he commits resulting in seventy thousand men dying in a plague?"**

At the end of the movie, David advises Solomon. "Be guided by the instincts of your own heart no matter what the prophets tell you for it is through the heart and the heart alone, that God speaks through man."

Ronald shouts for the first time, **"Okay then! Isaiah, Jeremiah, Ezekiel, Daniel...you're all fired! David says it's best to follow his heart and don't worry what the stupid prophets say. They're all fake news anyway!"*

Unfortunately, Solomon will obey this movie version of David.

As they drive home, Deb says, "This film is entertaining, so I can rate that part four. But the best I can give it is three for accuracy."

40

Skullduggery

WHAT DIFFERENCE DOES IT MAKE?

"I UNDERSTAND PEOPLE accused you of deleting e-mails," Ronald says to Tiffany as they walk into Sunday school.

"Ronald, I have to admit, I actually did deliberately delete some e-mails one time, but I deleted the wrong ones, I made a mistake. A patient wanted a few messages he sent to us erased, but I accidently deleted my personal e-mails, the ones where I joke about having my husband killed because he has an affair."

"So, did you?" Ronald jokes.

"Everyone knows he died years after the divorce in a boating accident Ronald. You have a macabre sense of humor."

"Oh well, I guess at this point he's dead anyway, so what difference does it make?"

"I like the way you think!"

"I am very practical, no one is as practical as I am."

They sit down and Deb starts the class by asking what people think of David.

"How can he be held up as such a great man?" Cindy asks. "He does a rotten thing to Uriah."

"In today's world," Dave says, "he would simply say, 'I made a mistake.'"

"I agree," Deb says, "people today don't want to admit they do wrong things, they pass that off by saying they make a mistake. There is an internet article by Scott Cochrane titled 'I Was Wrong' vs. 'I Made a Mistake,' where the writer points out five differences between the two statements. However, I believe David clearly feels bad that he sins. One of today's handouts talks a little about this."

"So where did you bury the body?" Ronald whispers to Tiffany.

Ignoring Ronald, Tiffany asks, "Why does David take Goliath's head to Jerusalem?"

"Yeah," Ronald says. "Why not just bury it with the rest of the body?"

"That's a great question," Deb answers. "I have a second handout on just that. It's a fascinating study."

The class discusses various errors in the films, the differences they make, and as the class comes to an end, Jason asks if there are any other handouts.

"I have three handouts which touch on Hebrew thinking," Deb says. "One deals with Saul's appearance which is shown wrong in all the films and the other two deal with New Testament parallels in the story of David. You will learn all about the 'Anti-Absalom.' Have a great week!"

part XI
Married with Wives

MOVIES ABOUT SOLOMON

An Introduction

SALTY DOG is starting his morning show.

"Guess what listeners, I checked out King Solomon's Internet dating profile and posted it on the WSOD's website. Here are some highlights."

King looking for a queen, does the slipper fit?

Age: 65

Status: Married seven hundred times and in three hundred committed relationships

Occupation: King of Israel

Hobbies: Building Temples and altars

Religion: Whatever you want it to be

About Me: I am on this site because I am looking for that one special girl. Race and religion are not an issue. But you must not be the jealous type or be someone who needs to see me more than once every thousand days. But, on those special days that we are together, we will take long walks in the desert, and I will share my wisdom with you. A little warning, you don't want to get into an argument with me because I am the smartest man on this, or any other planet, and you won't win. But if wisdom turns you on, you've come to the right man.

Two weeks later Solomon and three golf buddies, Joe, Les, and Dave are on the golf course.

"Tell us Sol," Les asks, "how did your first Internet date turn out?"

"Not so good," as he chunks a shot into the water.

"You showed us her profile photo, she looks pretty," Dave says.

Sol scowls. "She was thirty years old when that picture was taken."

"The old picture trick," Dave says.

"So, tell us what happened?" Joe asks.

"We agree to meet at the book store for a cup of coffee. Once there, I look out the window and see an attractive woman with short blonde hair, in her early seventies wearing a pants suit, walk across the parking lot. I ask myself, 'Is that her'?"

"As she walks in, someone steps in front of her, and I hear her yell, 'Get out of my way!'"

"I furiously call myself on my phone so I can pretend to take a call in order to get out of there, but my phone is dead."

"We sit down and the first thing I say to her is, 'You look a lot older than your picture.'"

"She gruffly replies, 'At this point, what difference does it make'?"

Joe asks, "By any chance is her name Tiffany?"

"Why yes it is," Solomon answers.

"Wow!" Les says. "Tiffany is cheating on Ronald!"

"So what happened?" Dave asks.

"I asked her to marry me, but she said no. She just wants to see what's out there before she commits to her current boyfriend."

The story of Solomon is the epitome of a tragedy. The richest and wisest man in the world ends up a failure because wealth and intelligence often lead to arrogance, which usually results in tragedy.

"It's not how you drive, it's how you arrive," is an expression often heard on the golf course. Some amateurs can hit a wonderful tee shots, but end up finishing badly. Well, the first hole of the golf course is where those players have something in common with Solomon, great start, but bad finish.

Now it's time to watch a film about Solomon which is about to begin. Splash has just finished cleaning the theater between shows, and asks Erica if she would like to attend Sunday school with him this weekend.

Erica answers yes and runs to tell Charlotte.

"We have a date!" Erika shrieks.

Charlotte then shrieks equally loud.

"These girls need to get to work," Rick thinks, as he watches Deb lead Chester into the auditorium.

Married With Wives

As Told In
Solomon

1997 TELEVISION MINI SERIES

THE MOVIE OPENS with Solomon, played by Ben Cross, taking time off from a hunting trip to have a chariot race against his brother, Adonijah. It does not end well with a severe injury to Adonijah. On their way home, they meet a man and his daughter, named Abishag, who has healing powers, so she attends to Adonijah and heals him.

After they return to Jerusalem, David, played by Max von Sydow, is old and can't keep warm in his bed, so he asks Solomon to bring Abishag to him to help him feel better. Abishag comes to David's bedroom and agrees to use her knowledge of drugs, and skill with the harp, to help the king recover.

"Abishag has only one job, and that is to snuggle with David to help him stay warm," Deb says. "She does not have healing skills."

Meanwhile, Adonijah and Joab, one of David's generals, are plotting to overthrow Solomon, who is to become king the next day while David is still alive. A day later, with the help of Joab and the army, all the stores are closed and the people are told to go out of the city so they can watch Adonijah be crowned. News of this reaches David, so he orders that Solomon be crowned, resulting in two coronation ceremonies on the same day. David orders Solomon to ride out on a donkey to the place where he will be anointed.

With that, Chester gets up and leaves the auditorium.

A little later Jim goes to check on Chester and then comes back to his seat.

"Deb, you have to see this, come with me. Charley, you stay here."

They go to the lobby and as they walk out the door, Jim and Deb see dozens of mules chanting in the street.

"Film mules not horses!"

"The whole stable's watching!"

"Whose mules? Our mules!"

"Say it Loud and say it clear, horses get out, mules are here!"

"Don't mess with mules or we'll make a mess!"

Walking up to the news truck, Deb and Jim hear the Salty Dog from WSOD saying to the camera, "American mules are furious. They feel that Hollywood discriminates against them in this and other films where mules are replaced by horses and donkeys. With me is Chester, the Spokesmule for M.A.D., which stands for, 'Mules Against Discrimination.' Chester, what do you have to say?"

"Our country will be judged by how it treats its mules. Once again, a mule is written out of the script in the television series, 'Solomon,' in which David instructs Solomon to ride out of Jerusalem on a donkey instead of a mule as told in the story. The nerve, once again some poor mule is put out of work."

Deb walks over and interrupts the interview, softly telling Chester, "You need to come back inside!"

Chester turns to Salty and the other reporters, "Oops! Sorry guys, I have to go. No more comments." *He then turns to the other mules,* "Bye kids, good work!"

As they return to the theater, another chant is heard, **"Yes mules can!"**

While Adonijah is getting ready to be anointed king, a man brings a message to him that Solomon is in a procession where he will be anointed king. The crowd deserts Adonijah and runs over to the procession led by Nathan and Solomon.

> "The timing is wrong," Deb says. "The series is showing Adonijah's coronation ceremony being interrupted because Solomon is going to be crowned as opposed to Solomon already having been crowned."

After David dies and Adonijah and Joab are killed, Solomon has a dream where he goes to paradise and asks God for wisdom. God promises him the "wisdom of a clear and discerning mind" if Solomon follows God's laws.

> "This is a beautiful scene, but it's not accurate," Deb says. "Solomon dreams that God comes to him instead of him going to paradise where he observes animals at rest. Solomon requests the ability to judge his people and discern between good and bad, as opposed to asking for wisdom or knowledge. And finally, God's response is that because he wants to 'discern justice' he is rewarded."

> "This is a wonderful vision of what Paradise must be like," Jim agrees. "I love the images of the animals."

> The audience agrees as everyone is contemplating the beauty of the afterlife until Charley changes the mood by shouting, **"I have a headache, Jim!"**

Ten years later, there is a skirmish with Egypt resulting in Solomon dividing the kingdom into twelve provinces. The Egyptians are massing their army to attack Israel, so Solomon leads his army out to meet them. However, before they fight, he confides in his general he is going to meet with the pharaoh and marry his daughter in order to avoid the war. The effort is successful, and he marries the girl.

> **"There is no war with Egypt!"** Les yells.

> "He's right, there is peace from the beginning of his kingdom until just before the end of it," Deb says.

> "Anything else?" Jim asks.

"The series changes a few things. First, Solomon makes the marriage agreement before he asks for wisdom. Furthermore, Solomon divides the kingdom after he makes the treaty, after he requests wisdom, and after he makes the decision to divide the baby as the series is showing."

Nathan visits an exhausted Solomon after the wedding night and asks how it feels to be married, giving the impression Solomon has never married.

"A Major disappointment!" Dave yells, remembering his own honeymoon.

"Not all marriages start out badly," Cindy tells Dave.

"The film is showing he divides the kingdom before he marries the Egyptian princess," Deb says. "The problem here is that two of the governors are already married to Solomon's daughters."

"Does he have them out of wedlock?" Jim asks.

"Maybe, but they would be nine years old," Deb answers sarcastically. "These events are shown to be ten years after he is given wisdom. So that's the oldest they could be."

Solomon asks Nathan why he never gets married.

"Why buy a cow, when milk is cheap?" Chester jokes.

Nathan responds that he chooses to concentrate on God's love.

"I guess he loses concentration because he has two sons!" Les yells.

"Does Nathan have sons?" Jim asks.

"There are two 'Nathans' during this time, one is the prophet and the other is a son of David. It is not clear which Nathan has two sons, but Samuel has sons, so it is possible that Nathan does too."

"Why do you think it is Nathan the prophet who has the sons?"

"Both of these sons become officials of Solomon. I don't think Solomon would put the sons of his step-brother in his administration after his experience with Adonijah. The last thing he would need to do is put two relatives in power."

Solomon takes a second wife, and later he gives the famous order for two women arguing that a baby is theirs to cut the baby in half in order to determine who the real mother is.

Deb whispers, "The film doesn't show the lying mother wanting the baby cut in half."

Solomon starts building the Temple, assisted by Hiram of Naphtali, who supervises the construction.

"It looks like the series consolidates King Hiram of Tyre and Hiram of Naphtali into one individual," Deb says.

Solomon asks who will supervise the workers when Hiram's workers depart and Hiram responds that he will. Solomon answers, "Men of Israel do not work well under foreign leadership."

"If Hiram is from Naphtali, he is an Israelite," Deb says. "Naphtali is an Israelite tribe."

When the film shows that the Temple is completed, there is a dedication ceremony where the priests bring the Ark of the Covenant into the Temple. As they cross the threshold, lightning strikes the altar outside the building, igniting a fire in the altar.

"That is very dramatic, but it doesn't happen," Dave says.

"The building is wrong too," Deb comments. "There are no windows and it shows stone blocks in the inner room, where all the walls are either cedar or covered in gold. The series also isn't showing one hundred and twenty thousand sheep being sacrificed."

"Are any sheep protesting that omission in the lobby?" Jim jokes.

"I saw hundreds in the street," Chester responds. "I think they are about to have a confrontation with the mules over who gets interviewed first."

Solomon rides a donkey out into the wilderness and receives a second message from God that if he serves other gods the Temple will be destroyed.

"The series leaves out an important part of the warning which is that Israel will be thrown out of the land if Solomon or his sons turn away from God," Deb comments.

Solomon meets the queen of Sheba as he is returning to Jerusalem. The next part of the series describes their love affair, during which they marry, and she becomes pregnant.

"This part is not in the Bible," Deb says.

Solomon tells her he wants their son to eventually become the king of Israel and Judah.

"Israel is still one country!" Ian points out.

The priests find out that Solomon wants his new son with the queen of Sheba to be heir to the throne. They tell Solomon he would be breaking the law by passing the throne to someone not born to Israelite parents and they would refuse to declare the child to be the heir. The queen leaves Israel as a result.

"Is that a law?" Jim asks.

"If the queen converts to Judaism, I don't think they would be breaking any laws. However, Solomon has already disobeyed God hundreds of times by marrying foreign women. Of course, none of this conversation is in the story."

"This love affair is all nonsense!" Les yells!

"None of this is in the story," Jason mutters in agreement.

Solomon is depressed because the queen leaves and expresses that depression to Jeroboam. He discusses vanity and the film quotes many of his writings.

"I remember how depressed I was when my third wife left me," Joe says. *"Jason shared some wisdom with me to make me feel better, saying 'It's okay, there are other fish in the sea.' I told him yes, but I already caught that one twice."*

Solomon rides out to the Temple of Ashtoreth and talks to one of his wives. She asks Solomon to make an offering but he refuses, saying he only worships the one true God of Israel. She asks again, holding out a bowl of some material, which Solomon takes and throws into the altar as Jeroboam watches.

"Does he actually do that?" Jim asks.

"He does way more than that," Deb responds. "He actually worships that god. By this time he is totally corrupt."

Jeroboam complains to the priests that Solomon's high taxes are turning the people away from him.

"Everyone must pay their fair share!" Jim jokes.

"I agree!" Tiffany says without smiling.

Ten years later, the film shows that Rehoboam, one of Solomon's sons, is a spoiled young man with no redeeming qualities. When Solomon dies, the northern tribes break away and follow Jeroboam, ending the film.

As they leave the theater, Jim says. "I really like this film."

"I do too" Deb says. "It is very close to the story, especially the way they show Solomon becoming corrupt. I feel the series deserves fours for both entertainment and accuracy."

42

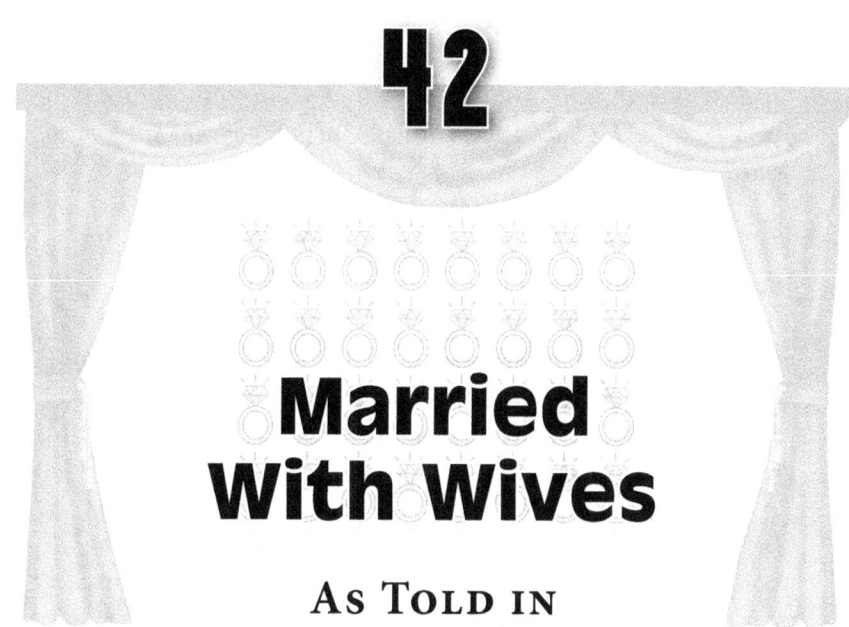

Married With Wives

As Told in
Solomon and Sheba
1959

THIS FILM BEGINS on the wilderness between Israel and Egypt just before daybreak, as the narrator tells the audience that the two enemy countries are in a cold war. Adonijah, played by George Sanders, along with his soldiers, are setting a trap to ambush Egyptians who are about to attack the Israelite camp, thinking the Israelites are asleep. Solomon, played by Yul Brynner, rides out to the Israelites who are on a hill outside the camp and tells his brother he wants to help in the fight. Solomon's brother is dismissive, but accepts the offer to help, regarding Solomon as a thinker, not a fighter.

After the Egyptians attack and ride through the camp, throwing spears into empty tents, the Israelites counter attack and the Egyptians that are not killed ride away. After the battle, a wounded soldier is found among the Egyptian dead and brought to Adonijah and Solomon, who discover he is a mercenary under the command of the Queen of Sheba who is allied with the Egyptians.

"So, the Egyptians ride through the camp throwing spears at tents?" Jim asks. "What if that is a supply tent, are they going to kill a bag of wheat?"

"That bag of wheat would be collateral damage," Dave says.

"That poor bag of wheat! I hope they give it a nice funeral," Joe comments. "I remember a guy in our foursome got struck by lightning on the third hole. After we finished the round and got back to the clubhouse, we called 911 to make sure they pick up the body so it could be properly buried."

"It's the least you could do," Dave agrees.

"The bad guys must buy their chariots at Honest Zarduk's Used Chariots," Jim says, "since a couple of them collapse for no reason as they are driven through the Israelite camp."

A messenger comes from Jerusalem and tells Adonijah and Solomon that King David is dying. Solomon is concerned for his father and rides back to Jerusalem, while Adonijah, already claiming the throne, rides out to find the queen of Sheba. He and a few of his soldiers overtake the queen, played by Gina Lollobrigida, as she is driving a chariot, leading her soldiers in a retreat from the fight. Adonijah asks her to form an alliance with him, but she is not interested, hitting Adonijah's face with her whip before she rides away on her chariot.

"Deb, you're not saying a word," Jim says.

"I am speechless. First, there are no battles between Israel and Egypt at this time. Second, the queen of Sheba doesn't appear until Solomon has ruled for many years. Third, when she does appear, she is bringing gifts to Solomon, not leading her soldiers to help the Egyptians who attack the Israelites."

"Wow, anything else?"

"Yeah, even if she does, she is not going to dress up and look like a fashion model as she drives her chariot at full speed across the desert. She's wearing a tight yellow outfit! Really?"

"I agree," Cindy says. "It appears to be winter since there are no green plants, she should not wear yellow at that time of the year."

"I always give my yellow pantsuits to charity at the end of September," Tiffany agrees.

"I must say though, this is a great cast," Deb says. "Gina looks great, despite wearing an out of season yellow outfit."

Solomon arrives in Jerusalem, walking through praying crowds to get to his father as he lays dying on a bed in the palace, and talks to him. King David sends orders to Adonijah to come home and tells Solomon to summon the leaders of the twelve tribes. The servants carry him into the throne room and help him get seated while the twelve leaders and others stand before him. He asks where Adonijah is. Then he delivers his message, starting by thanking Ahab for giving him his daughter Abishag as a pledge of his loyalty to serve him. He tells Ahab that Abishag is like a daughter to him.

Jim jokes, "Is that 'Ahab the Arab'?"

"I bet it is," Dave responds. "Ray Stevens sings he is the sheik of the burning sand."

"Speaking of sand," Joe says. "Phil got in eighteen sand traps Saturday. He screwed up every one on his way to a score of one hundred and twenty."

"There is no mention of Ahab until centuries later when he is described as a king of the northern tribes," Deb comments. "Also, Abishag is not there because of any loyalty pledge."

Adonijah and Joab walk into the proceedings just in time to hear David proclaim that Solomon will be the heir. Adonijah gets furious, draws his sword and proclaims he should be king. David rebukes Adonijah, who then storms out with Joab just before David anoints Solomon king of Israel.

"Deb, you're squeezing my hand so hard it hurts. What's wrong?"

"This keeps getting worse, Jim! David doesn't anoint Solomon, he has Nathan do it. It isn't done in Jerusalem, it's done miles away. Plus, there is no confrontation between any of these people."

"Anything else?"

"Yes, Adonijah doesn't get angry, he gets terrified and begs Solomon not to kill him."

Then she whispers to Jim, "Don't tell Chester the film isn't showing Solomon riding out of Jerusalem on a mule."

"I heard that," Chester says, "why is Hollywood so mean to mules?"

"I forgot about his big ears," Deb whispers.

David is on his deathbed and asks Solomon to promise to build the Temple and then he dies. Solomon goes to an altar on a hilltop and prays for help in judging his people. A voice responds that his prayer will be answered and that because he does not ask for riches he will be given riches if "thou will walk in my ways."

"More archaic English! You think God actually talks like that!" Les yells.

"Does the film change anything here?" Jim asks.

"Yes, the promise of riches is unconditional, also, Solomon does not go to an altar, God comes to him in a dream."

Adonijah and Joab are at Adonijah's house throwing spears at a target when Solomon shows up. Solomon tells Adonijah he has elected to stay at his house when he could serve Israel by leading its army.

"Is this true?" Jim asks.

"Adonijah doesn't elect to stay in his house. Solomon tells him to stay home if he wants to stay alive. He would never offer to turn his army over to him."

Solomon builds the Temple and the movie describes Israel being at peace when Solomon walks into the eight-story Temple and prays in front of the congregation.

"The Temple isn't eight stories high!" Les yells. **"And it doesn't have wings!"**

"*Solomon's dedication is not inside the Temple with a couple hundred people attending,*" Deb says. "*It's in front of thousands of people outside the Temple.*"

Meanwhile in Sheba, while the queen is playing with a parrot, an advisor tells her that she should go to Egypt and meet with other rulers who are afraid of Solomon because Israel is getting stronger. The queen attends the meeting where the kings are planning an attack on Israel, and the pharaoh asks "Sheba" who she will send to attack Solomon's country.

"**That's not her name!**" Les yells. "**That's the name of her country.**"

She responds that she will go to Jerusalem and meet Solomon and determine how to destroy him by exploiting his male weakness for women.

"**Hogwash!**" Les yells stumbling into his seat.

"*Dad!*" Rick steps over and puts his hand on his shoulder. "*Have you been drinking again?*"

"*I guess I had a couple before the movie. I'll stop.*"

The queen travels to Jerusalem, bringing her entourage and gifts for Solomon.

"*It's amazing! All these white European people living in Africa!*" Ian says.

"*Maybe they flew up from Cape Town,*" Avery jokes.

"*Actually, it's possible that her kingdom is on the Arabian Peninsula instead of in Africa.*"

Abishag, who is secretly in love with Solomon, takes a message to Sheba and they have a conversation. During the conversation, she tells Sheba that the unity of Israel is of the utmost importance in maintaining their country.

"*Is that a light bulb appearing above Sheba's head?*" Jim jokes.

Statues of gods and goddesses are placed around the queen's tent, which the queen points out to Abishag before she returns to Jerusalem. After that, Adonijah visits the queen, asking her to help him overthrow his brother.

"*Adonijah is killed long before she comes to Jerusalem,*" Jason mumbles.

The queen sits next to Solomon as he is administering justice when two women claiming to be the mother of a baby argue over who is the real mother.

> "The timing is wrong," Deb says. "This event occurs long before the queen visits."

Solomon falls in love. So much so that he walks through his harem and decides not to take any of the twenty-five beautiful women back to his bed chamber. Instead, he starts spending all of his time with the queen.

> "It would take a housing project to hold all those women," Deb says. "He has hundreds of wives."

In an attempt to gain power, Adonijah sends Joab and another assassin to kill Solomon and the queen. They fail when Solomon kills one assassin and captures Joab. As a result, Solomon banishes Adonijah and Joab from the country.

> "Sanders is in the movie way longer than Adonijah is in the story," Deb says. "Adonijah and Joab are killed right after David dies."

Despite the warnings of the priests, Solomon attends an orgy at the queen's camp where handsome men and beautiful women dance while preparing to have sex. As Solomon watches, Sheba dances out to him in a very revealing outfit.

> "Ian, will you stop staring at her?" Avery says.

> "Ian! Look at me!"

> "I'm, sorry, I was just noticing the beautiful scenery."

> "I'm sure you were!" she laughs.

> "Solomon never attends a pagan orgy," Deb says.

> "I did," Dave says. "It was called the senior prom."

Solomon is seduced and joins the party, ultimately having sex with the queen as part of a worship service to a pagan god.

Lighting strikes the pagan statue causing Solomon and Sheba to emerge from a cave. Lightening then strikes the Temple. Again and again it strikes until the Temple is destroyed. Abishag is in the Temple and she dies as it collapses around her.

"The Temple isn't destroyed for over four hundred years!" Les yells.

Not only is the Temple destroyed, the Israelite tribes abandon Solomon so the kingdom is also destroyed. Israel even suffers a drought because of what Solomon does.

"It's global warming!" *Dave shouts.*

"Deb, are you alright?" Jim asks.

"First the Temple is destroyed hundreds of years before it happens, then the tribes abandon Solomon, instead of abandoning his son Rehoboam after Solomon dies, and now there is a drought. This is all completely wrong!"

This sets up the final battle where Egypt sends its army, under the leadership of Adonijah, to invade Israel. Solomon is able to gather a few troops and engage in battle, but they are badly outnumbered. Seeing they are losing, Solomon orders a retreat, someone blows a ram's horn, and what's left of Solomon's soldiers, flee.

"This is hysterical," Jim says. *"The Egyptians are also retreating."*

That night, after suffering defeat, Solomon is inspired to defeat the Egyptians by having his soldiers burnish their shields in order to reflect the next morning's sunlight into the Egyptian army and blind them as they attack.

"He's going to 'razzle dazzel' them," Jim says. *"He will dazzle them with his brilliance."*

"This whole battle scene never happens," Deb responds.

This plan works, and all the Egyptian chariots and horsemen run off a valley cliff that is between the two armies. When they show all the dead soldiers and busted chariots at the bottom of the valley, there is not a dead horse to be seen.

"Not one dead horse! If those had been mules, the bottom would be littered with them," Chester yells.

Solomon returns to Jerusalem and saves the queen from Adonijah and Joab, who get killed in the fight with Solomon and his men. Solomon is now repentant and the queen, who is now converted, returns to her homeland, ending the movie.

"Final comments Deb?" Jim asks.

"This is a classic 1950's movie that is very different from what's told in the original story. The actors are fun to watch, and the film is very entertaining so I rate the entertainment at four. It would be five except for that stupid battle scene where bad guys throw spears into empty tents."

"I think the biggest error is showing that Solomon ends up coming to his senses. He doesn't do that! The whole point of the story is that the richest and wisest man in history becomes a total failure because he stops following God, so I rate the accuracy at zero."

43

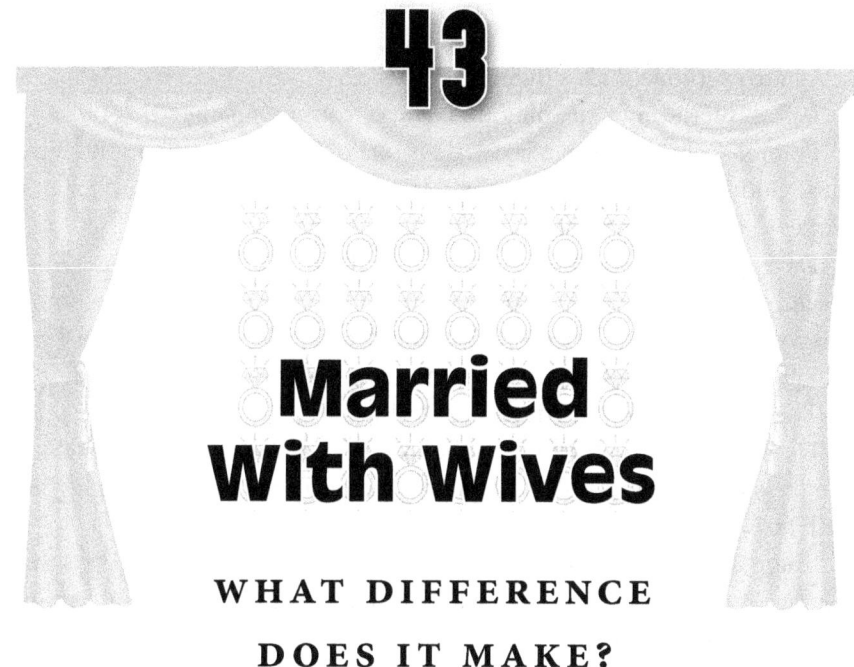

Married With Wives

WHAT DIFFERENCE DOES IT MAKE?

TEDDY MEETS ERIKA outside the church and as they walk into Deb's class, she says, "You had a great game Friday!"

"Thanks, I saw you making some really cool moves on the sideline. I heard you made the volleyball team, you're quite an athlete yourself."

"It's funny how that happened. A year ago my grandpa, who used to play volleyball, gave me a volleyball. When Memaw told him I never played volleyball, Granddad told her, 'She will.' Granddad spent hours working with me, and now I love the sport."

"I love volleyball too!" Teddy looks at her. "I'll teach you how to play beach volleyball and we can play together in a sand tournament!"

"I can't wait!"

They walk into class, and Deb notices how Erika is looking at her son just before she starts the class.

"Does anyone know any women today named 'Jezebel'?"

No one in the class does.

"How many people know any men named 'Judas'?"

Again, everyone shakes their head no.

"Isn't it interesting that Solomon is a very common name?"

"I'm not surprised," Dave says. "He is one of the wisest men in the Bible. Plus, God blessed him with incredible wealth. Clearly people honor that name because of his wisdom."

"Dave, you just responded the way I would have a few weeks ago. But I recently watched a video on YouTube by Mark Biltz titled 'King Solomon.' It is a real eye opener. Solomon is one of the most flawed men in the Bible, and he dies a very corrupt man. I won't go into it now, but I have a handout on Solomon that will surprise many of you."

The class discusses the films on Solomon, and Deb concludes by telling the class about why Abishag attempts to keep David warm by snuggling with him.

"There is an interesting article in Wikipedia titled 'Abishag' that says that having Abishag snuggle with David is an attempt to excite him and demonstrate he is not impotent, which would allow David to continue to rule Israel. It quotes the Interpreter's Bible which says if David was impotent he could no longer be king. The article compares Adonijah's request to marry Abishag, to Absalom sleeping with David's concubines as a way for him to proclaim himself the new king."

"I guess some things never change," Jason says as they all stand up. "It's all about sex and power."

After class ends Deb notices that Teddy and Erica seem to be hitting it off.

"I like her," she says to herself and smiles.

part XII
Prophecy World

MOVIES ABOUT DANIEL

An Introduction

IT'S ERICA'S FIRST DATE with Splash as they join Ian and Avery on a trip to the theme park, Prophecy World, which is located just a few miles north of Notre Dame University.

"Wow! This place is packed," Ian says as they stop and buy some Michigan fudge. "Where should we go first?"

"We need to be selective." Splash says. "We will wait at least an hour on each attraction, so we cannot see everything and still be home by eleven, which is Erica's curfew."

"There are some awesome things here," Avery says. "Trib Times, is the main attraction I want to see."

"Star Signs and Dan's Den are at the top of my list," Splash adds.

"Not to mention the ride through Moses Mountain," Erica says.

"You like roller coasters?" Splash asks.

When Erica says she does, Ian remarks, "Most girls are worried about their hair getting messed up. That's great Erica!"

"I also want to go on Red Sea Rapids, the dispensational water slide."

"You're going to get soaked girl," Avery comments.

"All of us will," she responds. "I'm not going to let anyone chicken out."

As they approach the Trib Times attraction, Ian points out this will be the first time this attraction is open to the public. After almost a two-hour wait, they are surprised when they get seated to find out this is an animated feature taking place in the old west town of Post, Arizona, where trouble is brewing in a bar.

Inside the bar are six cartoon characters with the heads of ducks, wearing old west clothing, including cowboy hats, sitting at a table playing poker. This is the infamous and widely hated, "Post Trib" gang. Everyone in town knows they are either from hell or will eventually go there.

A bartender with the head of a raccoon is cleaning glasses when a cartoon goose with a card reading the word "Press" on his felt hat enters the bar. The music stops and all eyes are on the reporter as he passes through the swinging doors and introduces himself.

"Hi, my name is Eugene Hurst. I am a reporter for a newspaper back east in Indiana here on assignment to write a story about the feud in this town."

One of the ducks asks the reporter, "What paper do you work for Pilgrim?"

"It's the Middlebury Tribune, located in Middlebury, Indiana. We refer to it as the 'Mid Trib.'"

Immediately, all six ducks whip out guns, and empty them into the reporter, leaving nothing but a coat and hat covering a pile of goose feathers.

"The only good mid trib guy is a dead mid trib guy," Cecil, the leader of the ducks says.

"AWWWOOOO!"

After the plaintive cry of the wolf is heard, the undertaker, with the head of a wolf, wearing a trench coat and tall stove pipe hat, enters the bar with a broom and dust pan and cleans up the feathers, while Jesse, the town drunk with the head of a cat staggers into the bar.

"The Pre-Trib gang heard the shooting and is on the way from across the street thinking you've run out of ammo."

The Pre-Trib gang, made up of six angry owls, walk side by side across the dirt street with guns drawn. In the background the sound of whistling is heard as each duck leaves the bar, but they get killed before they can reach the street. That is every duck except Cecil who mows the owls down with a Gatling gun from inside the bar window.

"Not so wise now, are you guys?"

"AWWWOOOO!" The undertaker cries as he comes into the bar just after the bartender shoots Cecil in the back.

"I guess that settles this argument," the bartender tells the undertaker. "No one wins!"

AN INTRODUCTION

"Wow! That was intense!" Ian says as they head to the next attraction. "Where do you guys stand?"

"I'm a duck!" Splash says.

"I'm an owl!" Avery says.

"I know better than to comment," Erica says. "Where do we go next?"

"Let's check out Star Times."

Right after they are seated in the auditorium, the lights dim and the image of four red moons appear on the screen and the ceiling becomes a planetarium. The host comes on the stage and explains that signs in the heavens can be messages from God that something important is about to happen. He draws attention to the ceiling and points out the constellation Virgo, and shows what planets and stars make up what has become to be known as the "Revelation Twelve Sign" in that constellation, which occurred near the time of the birth of Christ.

After that, he explains what causes a blood moon, pointing out there are important events that have occurred in history which happened after the occurrence of four consecutive blood moons that occurred on Jewish Holy days. The feature ends with an image of a United States map during the August 21 American Eclipse and concludes showing the second path of another American eclipse that will occur seven years later, intersecting the first path in Southern Illinois.

"That was incredible!" Avery says as the walk over to Dan's Den. "I can't wait to see what's next."

The lobby has a moving tram that they climb into. As Ian and his friends get into a buggy and ride into a dark room the first things they see are animals behind glass partitions while a voice from a speaker in the buggy explains the prophetic significance of various animals that appear in the Book of Daniel.

The ride takes them into another room where art and photographs from the past are shown along with the year associated with each of those images. Starting with the year 500 and up to current times, each image relates to a failed prediction of Christ's return.

The next room has images of Jerusalem at the time of Christ's birth. The recorded message explains that it is most likely the people of that time were expecting the Messiah to appear as a result of reading Daniel's prophecies and the appearance of the Revelation Twelve Sign which occurred during that time. In this case, the voice explains, the prediction came true.

As Ian and his friends leave the attraction, it is now dark so they find a place to eat before going home.

"This has been fun," Avery says. "I'm looking forward to seeing the films on Daniel this week."

Getting Erica home before eleven, Splash gently takes her hand and tells her good night.

Prophecy World

As Told In
The Book of Daniel
2013

ROBERT MIANO plays the older version of Daniel in this film. He was also Mordecai in *The Book of Esther*, both films released in 2013 by Pure Flix Entertainment. *The Book of Daniel* starts near Babylon in 538 B.C. when Daniel is in the wilderness praying for his people who have been in exile for seventy years. The prayer explains why the people went into exile, mentioning the warnings the prophets gave to the previous generation. As he is kneeling in prayer, a sword appears from off camera and the tip is held against his throat.

King Cyrus is holding the sword, and asks Daniel why he has come to his camp. Daniel tells Cyrus he has come to him to tell him the "tale of four kings, one great, one foolish, one who has been deceived, and one who is destined to be regarded as wise." King Cyrus welcomes Daniel and invites him into his tent for dinner, where he and his subordinate, Croesus, listen to Daniel's tales.

> "These don't look like ancient Persian rulers to me," Joe says. "They have short hair and remind me of some of the old men I see on the golf course."

"*Croesus could use a new golf hat,*" Deb comments. "*It's old and out of style. It looks like something Phil might wear.*"

"*Speaking of style,*" Ronald says, "*Tiffany, just how many pants suits do you own?*"

"*Not nearly as many long ties as you own Ronald.*"

Daniel starts by telling the story of Nebuchadnezzar and how in the third year of Nebuchadnezzar's reign he besieges Jerusalem and captures it, taking ten thousand of the highest-class Jews back to Babylon as captives. The movie flashes back to the time Daniel is a young man, the time of the first king.

"*The dating is wrong,*" Deb says to Jim. "*It is actually in the third year of the reign of Jehoiakim, the king of Judah.*"

Daniel and other gifted young Jews are brought into the king's court to serve him and be instructed in the ways of their new country. Years later, the young Jews are trusted advisors when Nebuchadnezzar has a dream, wakes up, and summons his other advisors to interpret his dream without telling them what he dreams. He tells them that if they cannot tell him the dream and its meaning by sunrise, they will be executed. A few hours later the advisors, along with Daniel and his friends are brought before Nebuchadnezzar and Daniel tells the king about his dream of a giant statue and the interpretation of the dream. Daniel is rewarded and promoted to rule over Babylon and his friends are made administrators.

"*What do you think Deb?*" Jim asks. "*Is this film accurate so far?*"

"*The film is pretty close, but it makes a mistake about how soon the king needs an answer concerning the dream. This may be nitpicking, but the period of time has to be longer than a few hours for an answer because Daniel is told he will be killed after some advisors had already been killed. There is no mention of a sunrise deadline in the story.*"

"*Neb already started killing these guys?*"

"*In the story, he does, but in this film no advisors have been killed yet. When Daniel interprets the dream, Nebuchadnezzar falls on his face in front of Daniel, which is not shown. It's a shame about these errors when everything so far has been really good."*

That scene fades out and the new scene fades in showing a ninety-foot high statue of king Nebuchadnezzar that is made of gold.

"Whose face is on that statue? It sure isn't Neb," Avery asks. *"The king is going to be furious."*

"Do you remember Mike who used to work at the gym?" Ian responds. *"Someone made stickers that are the size of postage stamps with Mike's smiling face on them. The stickers kept showing up on exercise machines in the gym."*

"Where on the machines?"

"You know how those machines show instructions diagramming a gender-neutral body using the equipment? Someone put a stamp where the face should be. Every night the manager would remove the six stamps, but the next day six new stamps would appear on different machines. It's hysterical. Mike swears he's not doing it."

"So you think..."

"Yeah, that might be an ancient Persian version of Mike's face on the statue."

The people of Babylon are ordered to bow down to the statue when a horn sounds, but Daniel's friends refuse to do so. When the king asks them if this is true, they tell him they cannot worship the statue so he orders them thrown into a furnace. As the king watches them standing still in the furnace, a fourth person appears with them in the flames, and none of them get burned. They come out of the fire and are brought before the king, and he acknowledges that God has saved them.

"What about the guards?" Les shouts.

"What's Les yelling about?" Avery asks.

"The film omits the heat from the furnace killing the guards while they are throwing the Jews into the furnace," Ian replies. *"It also shows that*

the three men and the angel in the fire are standing still as opposed to walking through the fire."

Everything goes well until Nebuchadnezzar's next dream featuring a large tree which a messenger from heaven orders to be cut down. Daniel tells the king that the tree represents him and he will lose his kingdom unless he repents. After he repents, his kingdom will be restored to him. A year later the king is bragging about his accomplishments when a voice is heard telling him he will lose his mind and wander the land until he acknowledges that God is greater than he is.

> "I think Neb needs to take Benadryl before he goes to sleep so he will have fewer dreams," Jim says. "Do you see any issues here Deb?"

> "The length of the madness, 'seven times' is omitted from this scene," she replies. "But even more important is how the warning Daniel gives to Nebuchadnezzar is changed."

> "How is the warning changed?"

> "The film is showing Daniel telling Neb to 'seek the Lord while he may be found.' He doesn't say that. He tells him not to sin and be merciful to the poor."

> "Those both sound like good Bible quotes, what difference does it make?"

> "It makes it sound like Daniel wants to convert the king. There is no effort to convert any of these foreign kings during this period."

> **"Put your hands on the Ark of the Covenant!"** Dave jokes.

The last part of the story about Neb begins by showing the king's feet as he wanders through the wilderness. The camera zooms out showing he is wearing primitive clothing and eating weeds, while the sounds of wild animals near him can be heard. He spends seven years in the wilderness until he repents, and is restored to his throne. The scene fades out as Daniel tells Cyrus that other kings will rise after Nebuchadnezzar dies.

> "Did you notice his toenails? They look manicured after seven years. What's going on?" Dave asks. "Don't they grow?"

"Maybe the wild goats trim them," Cindy answers.

"Someone's been cutting his hair too," Jim adds.

"Maybe 'Pets Are Them' has a grooming center out there," Chester says.

"That's where Deb takes us," Charley responds.

In the tent, Cyrus tells Daniel that he was told in a dream to destroy the dams that control the river that flows through Babylon, which would lower the river level, allowing his troops to enter the city. Daniel now begins the story of the second king, Belshazzar, king of Babylon, a "foolish and wicked man."

The story starts with the king having a feast, and he is not happy with the cups at the party, so he orders that the gold cups from Jerusalem be brought to the feast in order that he and the guests can drink from them. Belshazzar raises one of the cups and proclaims a toast to the Babylonian gods when a woman screams and points to a wall.

The wind starts blowing and a barely visible hand begins writing Greek letters on the wall from left to right, giving a message to the people at the party. The king tells the guests that he will reward anyone who can interpret the message, but nobody there can understand the message. Daniel is brought to the hall and tells the king the message which says that Babylon will be overthrown that night and Belshazzar will be dead by morning.

> Up in the balcony, Ian is asking Avery if she would like to have a pizza after the movie, when he suddenly says, "Did you see that?"
>
> "See what?" She asks.
>
> "The film is doing a very good job with this part of the story, but it would be better if it would show the handwriting done correctly. Hebrew is written from right to left as opposed to words being written from left to right as shown here."
>
> "You're writing a paper on this aren't you? Do you think the message is written in Hebrew?"
>
> "Yes, I do. When I researched what language those words are written in I could not find a conclusive answer. I did find an article online in the Jewish Encyclopedia suggesting that Hebrew had changed during

the captivity with the result that even the Jews in the court could not translate the words. If that is true, the message would be written in Hebrew, and be written from right to left."

"You're so smart!"

"I know, but you left out good looking."

"I know I did."

Avery kisses him and smiles, "Yes, you are very handsome too. A pizza sounds great, but I have to be back at the dorm by midnight."

Later that night, an army captures Babylon and the leader kills Belshazzar. Daniel is there and the leader turns to Daniel, points a sword at him, and asks him if he knows who is standing before him. It is Darius, the third king.

"Daniel keeps having swords pointed at him," Joe comments.

Darius decides he can trust Daniel and makes him part of his administration to rule Babylon. Eventually Daniel rises very high in power, generating jealousy among the other administrators, who want Daniel killed, so they meet and devise a plan to do away with Daniel.

They suggest that the king issue an edict that no one can pray to anyone but the king for thirty days, which would expose the potential rebels who would continue to pray. If anyone is caught praying to anyone but the king, they would be thrown to the lions.

Daniel continues to pray, is arrested, and brought before Darius, who is angry that Daniel has been put under arrest. The evil advisors remind him of the law he signed and that he is forced to have Daniel put in the lion's den, despite the fact that he loves Daniel. Daniel tells the king he must obey his own command, and he walks into the stone pit and hears the lions growling.

During that night, the king fasts and the conspirators celebrate, while Daniel prays in the presence of the lions. The next morning, Darius returns to the den and finds that Daniel is still alive. While Darius is overjoyed to see Daniel alive, the three conspirators quietly try to sneak away, but Darius orders them thrown to the lions, whose appetites have returned. Darius then issues a decree that everyone in his kingdom must fear and revere the God of Daniel.

> *Jim is just returning from the concession stand with a drink, when Deb tells him, "The film leaves out Darius saying Daniel's God will deliver him, and it also deletes the part of the story that says the conspirator's wives and children are also tossed to the lions."*
>
> "That omission is understandable. I wouldn't want to watch that."
>
> "I'd watch if they show wise cracking mules fed to the lions," Charley says.
>
> "If some lion messes with me, I'll whip his ass," Chester responds, quoting part of Jimmy Carter's famous response to the possibility of Ted Kennedy running for president.
>
> "Why would you beat up Kennedy's mule?" Jim smiles at Chester.
>
> "Speaking of whipping asses, you might end up on the wrong side of an encounter with lions," Charley tells Chester.

The flashbacks end, and now it is time for the story of the fourth king. Cyrus asks who the fourth king is and Daniel reads from the scroll of Isaiah, which names Cyrus a century and a half before he is born, as the king who will decree that the Jews can return to Jerusalem. Cyrus believes Daniel and issues that decree, which allows Jerusalem and its Temple to be rebuilt and that any Jews who want to return to Judea will be allowed to do so. At the end of the film Daniel does not return to Jerusalem, but stays in Babylon.

> "I really like this film," Deb says. "The final scene where Daniel reads to Cyrus the prophecy about him freeing the Jews to return to Jerusalem is one of my favorite scenes in all the movies we have watched."
>
> "I agree," Jim responds, "Lance Henriksen as Cyrus is excellent as is Kevin McCorkle as Croesus. That scene is worth the price of the entire movie."
>
> "This film deserves fives for both entertainment and accuracy, although Croesus still needs a new golf hat," Deb says, as she gets into the truck.

45

Prophecy World

As Told In
The Bible

2013 TELEVISION MINI SERIES

THIS VERSION of the story of Daniel starts in the middle of the fifth episode of season one in the series. He is among the captives walking five hundred miles to Babylon. The series shows that Daniel has visionary powers and is forced to work in Nebuchadnezzar's court when he reaches Babylon.

"This is wrong," Deb says, *"he is in the court because he gives better advice than the king's advisors."*

In the king's court, while advisors huddle in groups, Nebuchadnezzar is angry that none of them can tell him the dream he had that night. He says to everyone, "Can you not even describe my dream?" Daniel approaches him and describes the dream of the statute to the king, telling him the statue has a head of gold and it gets struck by a giant stone that destroys the statue.

"Daniel is not there!" Les yells.

Meanwhile, in the third row, Deb says, "He's right Jim. Daniel is not there initially. The film is also leaving out the silver, bronze, iron and clay, which are materials in the statue. It is only mentioning the head of gold."

The king is still angry and asks for the interpretation of the dream. Daniel tells him he is the head of gold and the statue represents other empires that will follow his. The king asks about the stone that destroys the statue and Daniel tells him the stone represents the kingdom of God that will rule the world. The king asks, "What's your name?" and Daniel introduces himself. The king tells Daniel he will serve him from now on.

"The king knows Daniel!" Les yells. **"He doesn't ask who he is! Daniel has served him for years!"**

"He's terrible with names!" Dave jokes.

"Les is right," Deb whispers. "He's already an advisor. The king previously interviewed him as well as three other Jews and determined they are ten times better than his Babylonian advisors and made them advisors as well."

"I'm sorry, I remember your face, but I can't recall your name," Chester jokes to Charley.

"We've been sharing a stable for ten years!" Charley jokes back.

A tall gold statue can be seen as people leave Babylon, going out of the city to worship the statue. Daniel is begging his three friends not to do what they are planning on doing.

"Are they going to kneel during the national Anthem?" Rick jokes to the girls in the back of the theater.

Daniel is with Nebuchadnezzar in the viewing stand as all the people gather in the plain to bow down to the statue when the horns sound.

"Daniel's in a box seat with Nebuchadnezzar?" Les yells. **"Really?"**

"Great tickets! He got them online for $20," Jason yells down to Les.

The horns sound and everyone except Daniel's three friends bow down. The king orders the three of them to be put in an alcove with firewood and oil is thrown on them. The king takes a torch and lights the fire while Daniel watches the men scream in agony as the flames surround them. The fire continues, the men stop screaming and the king turns to Daniel and asks, "Why do they not burn?" The men walk out of the fire, and Daniel joins them as they walk away from the king.

> *"There is no way these guys are screaming!" Now it's Rick yelling as he stands next to his dad.*
>
> *"Feel better son?" Les asks.*
>
> *"That felt good, really good, Dad!"*
>
> *Back in the third row, Jim says, "If you tell someone you are going to burn them and then put an ice cube on them they will feel heat. Maybe that's why they are screaming, they just think they are being burned."*

The narrator says that the miracle unites the Jewish people and the main books of the Bible are written down while they are in exile.

> *"If he is saying this was the original time these books were written, I disagree," Deb says. "But I realize some scholars think otherwise."*

He continues by saying that in Babylon, the only man who can set them free, is now insane. Daniel visits Nebuchadnezzar in a dungeon where he is chained to walls, behaving like a wild animal. Daniel chides the wild man and tells him that he could have set the Jews free, but now he is as trapped as they are. As Daniel walks out of the cell, while the insane king kneels down on the floor to eat, Daniel says, "A new king is coming."

> *Deb is getting irritated, "He's not in prison," she groans. "He is roaming around in the woods, eating grass, growing long hair and fingernails, and acting like a wild animal."*

A massive army rides toward Babylon after Nebuchadnezzar dies, being led by Cyrus, the king of Persia. The narrator says "the Babylonians know they don't have a chance, and they let Cyrus in without a fight." As Cyrus leads his army into the city, Daniel tells his three friends that Cyrus will free them "if the prophecy is right." Daniel befriends Cyrus and continues to interpret dreams.

> *Chester and Charley start singing "I had a Dream Last Night."*

"Darius captures Babylon!" Les yells.

"This is wrong," Deb says. "It is not showing Darius and replacing him with Cyrus."

In the back of the theater, Splash explains to Erica and Charlotte that Babylon is captured at night when the river level drops, allowing invaders to take the city. He then asks Erica if she enjoyed the game the previous night.

"You were really good," she responds. "Three touchdowns in the first half!"

"The team did all the work, I had the easy part."

Daniel becomes a close advisor to Cyrus and Cyrus is questioning Daniel about a dream. Daniel tells him it is not a dream and says, "There is a prophet here in Babylon, Isaiah, who says, 'Here is a king whose right hand I take hold of to subdue nations before him. He is Cyrus.' He names you sire. It means God is with you."

"Isaiah has been dead for over a century!" Les yells.

"Yeah!" Rick yells too.

In the room are other advisors to the king who become jealous of Daniel and plot to have Daniel removed. They bring an edict for Cyrus to stamp which bans prayer for one month, telling the king it will expose people who are disloyal to him, so he seals the edict. Daniel continues praying, asking for protection when the conspirators see him praying and report his praying to Cyrus.

"This part is mostly true and well done, except that it's not Cyrus, it's Darius!" Deb says, "and Daniel does not ask for protection."

Daniel is sentenced to death and is taken to the lion's den and resists his captors as they push him inside. He is afraid and backs up to the door in sheer terror as the lions approach him. A lion leaps at him and the scene now changes to the palace, in the middle of the night, where the king cannot sleep.

"There is nothing to indicate Daniel resists or is afraid," Deb says, "although I would be terrified."

Cyrus is rapidly pacing toward the lion's den hoping he is not too late to save Daniel.

"It's Darius!" Les yells from the back.

Cyrus arrives at the door to the den and orders it to be opened. He looks in and sees that Daniel is unhurt. Cyrus is happy to see his friend is unhurt, and rewards Daniel by giving an order which permits the Jews to return to Jerusalem. As he turns to walk away, he orders the chief conspirator to be fed to the lions.

"Hey, just one conspirator?" Chester jokes, mimicking a lion. "We gotta eat down here, that's just an appetizer."

"More errors," Deb says. "This scene does not make it clear that Darius tries to keep from obeying his own order, and then reassures Daniel that his God will protect him. Plus, the king waits until morning before checking on Daniel, he doesn't get up in the middle of the night and go to the den."

"You're on a roll Deb. Anything else?"

"Yes, it also shows the king throwing only one advisor to the lions for trying to kill Daniel instead of all the advisors and their families. Finally, it's Darius at the lion's den, not Cyrus. Darius does not free the Jews to return to Babylon, Cyrus does that years later."

The closing scene shows Jews leaving Babylon while Daniel and his friends remain. They go outside and watch the procession to the sound of women doing a ululation.

"That sound is annoying," Jim says.

"Not when I do it," Chester says, as he starts imitating the women.

Immediately people in the audience start booing, throwing popcorn, and begging Chester to stop.

Daniel tells his friends he is still worried about the future of his people and describes a dream of a terrible beast which will conquer the world, but ultimately, a great new leader, "like the Son of Man," will rise and be given power to rule the world, ending the episode.

"What are your ratings Deb?" Jim asks as they walk through the lobby while Teddy says goodnight to Erica.

"I feel the series keeps your attention, so I give it three for entertainment, if it didn't have the ululation I would give it a four. I rate the accuracy at two especially since it confuses Darius with Cyrus."

"Teddy, we have to go soon," he reminds his son.

Prophecy World

WHAT DIFFERENCE DOES IT MAKE?

THE FOLLOWING SUNDAY Deb is leading her class. "What is the primary message in the story of Daniel?"

Joe raises his hand "The book is primarily information that God reveals to Daniel about what will happen in the future. Daniel's good, I need to take him to the casino."

"You're right Joe, but what is the importance of that information?"

Dave raises his hand. "So we can see what's going to happen in the future?"

"Are there any other messages we see?" Deb asks.

"One important message is that God protects his people," Ian answers, "even when they are in captivity, and that God can even cause that captivity for their benefit."

"Sort of like when he protects us while we have to pay high taxes," Ronald says. "Of course, I have good accountants to help me out with that."

"What about alimony?" Dave asks.

"I have good accountants help me out with that too," Ronald says.

"Some of you were able to see the films on Daniel. Did anyone see any mistakes?"

Teddy answers, "I think we all saw a bunch of them."

Several people shake their heads in agreement and point out various errors.

"Did any of these errors affect the central themes of Daniel?"

"Not really," Teddy replies. Again, everyone agrees.

Just before the class ends, Jason joins the conversation. "Many people think prophecy is all about the future, but I think it's all about the present."

"I agree," Deb says. "There are two schools of thought about prophecy. One school of thought believes prophecy is foretelling, meaning it is intended to tell the reader what will happen in the future. The other school is forth telling, which means prophecy is given to help the reader understand what is happening when it happens. I have a handout today that deals with Daniel and provides an example of modern forth telling."

"In the meantime, take a look at YouTube this week and search for videos that make predictions. You will find predictions that Yellowstone is about to blow up, predictions of the rapture occurring on some specific date in the next few weeks, and predictions that planet Nibiru is about to collide with earth."

"There have been many videos that were obviously prepared by intelligent people who spent a great deal of time analyzing Daniels timelines, only to be proven wrong when they offer up a precise date that ultimately fails."

"Sad!" Ronald says.

"This is why I refer to such activity as 'non-profitcy,'" Deb says. "This endless sequence of setting dates does not profit anyone. In fact, it does just the opposite; it gets hopes up and then rips them apart. So, until next Sunday keep looking and stop counting."

"Next week we look at a favorite woman of mine named Esther," Deb says as she and others are leaving for the sanctuary.

part XIII
Hide and Seek

MOVIES ABOUT ESTHER

An Introduction

GOLF IS SUCH A WONDERFUL SPORT. Joe knows there is nothing that can compare to swinging a club, feeling the club head strike the ball, and seeing the ball sailing high in the distance toward the target. In order to achieve this experience there are a few things Joe must remember while setting up and swinging his club at a golf ball. Here are eighteen of them.

1. Imagine you are gripping your club softly like you would hold a parakeet.
2. Turn your shoulders first.
3. Shift your weight through to the left side during your swing.
4. Follow through.
5. Release your hips when you start your downswing.
6. Imagine having towels under both your armpits as you swing.
7. Get your right shoulder below your left shoulder.
8. Get your left shoulder back to address at impact.
9. Imagine you are going to shake hands with the target at the end of your swing.
10. No flipping your wrists.
11. Have your back face the target as long as possible on your downswing.

12. On iron shots bump your hips to left before you swing.
13. Posture is important, don't lean over too much.
14. Ensure that your right arm stays against your body on take-away.
15. Left shoulder should be pointing at ball at top of the backswing.
16 Execute shot with smooth tempo.
17. Swing slow, don't bend your arm (To the tune of "Swing Low Sweet Chariot")
18. "Shank," don't ever let that word enter your brain.

There is a hidden message in these golf tips that relate the author's golf game to the feeling Esther and Mordecai must have in the book of Esther. Before reading the next page, read the golf instructions carefully and try to find the coded message.

Here is the way to discover the message. Take the first letter of each tip and you will read, "It's friggin' hopeless." Just as it is impossible for the author to play good golf like Joe, saving the Jews appears impossible after the king signs Haman's edict in the story of Esther.

Dave and Cindy are also discussing something that seems impossible while they walk to the theater.

"Do you think Ronald has a chance with Tiffany?" Dave asks.

"I don't see how. They are polar opposites in so many ways, plus he keeps questioning her about the way her former husband died, and then he jokes about where she hid the body, it's creepy."

"I know. I can't imagine what those two see in each other, but they are obviously in love. They are constantly holding hands and kissing."

47

Hide and Seek

As Told in
The Book of Esther

2013

THE YEAR IS 482 BC in Persia when Hadassah, a young girl of about twelve, is called by her uncle to hear about a dream he has. After he tells her that he does not understand the entire dream, he warns her that she should never tell anyone she is a Jew, and that from now on she will be called Esther. He also tells her she must never call him "uncle," but instead she should call him "teacher," and that God gave him this dream for a reason, so it may have something to do with hiding her identity.

"*I like the way this begins,*" Deb says. "*It is fictional but it is consistent with the story.*"

When Esther becomes a young woman, her uncle is preparing to go to the King's feast. She tells her uncle she wishes she could be the queen because she wants to be married. Her uncle tells her she will be married when he finds a suitable husband for her. She asks if she has anything to say in the choice, and he tells her she first must learn obedience.

> "This conversation is not in the story," Deb says, "and neither is there any indication that Esther needs to learn obedience."

There are about a dozen people at the banquet, including Haman and a eunuch. Their conversation makes it clear that Haman hates Mordecai and the Jews and that they don't like each other, even though they must work together as advisors to the king.

> **"There are leaders of over a hundred provinces at that feast!"** Les shouts. **"Where are the rest of them?"**

> **"They're out by the pool smoking cigars!"** Joe shouts back. **"The king hates that smell!"**

> "Mordecai is not mentioned this early in the story," Deb says, "for that matter neither is Haman, but I like how the film shows Haman's hatred for the Jews."

The king welcomes the guests to the anniversary of his ascension to the throne and expresses his wife's greetings as well, even though Vashti is not present. When the queen does not show up, Xerxes sends orders for her to come and dance for the king's guests. An officer goes to her chambers and gives her the command from the king, but she refuses to obey his order. When Xerxes is told of her refusal he issues a decree that Vashti is to be removed from the palace and their marriage is now null and void.

> "Good luck with that when she hires an attorney," Dave says. "With his income, she will get a fortune in alimony."

> "He probably has a pre-nup," Ronald says.

> "It didn't help me, I even have to pay for her tickets to the horse races."

> "You had the wrong lawyer," Tiffany says. "When I did divorce work, I would have had her paying you when it was all over."

> "Let's change the subject," Cindy says. "Deb, how do you like this part?"

> "So far so good in this part, the film does a good job here."

Now that Persia does not have a queen, Haman sees an opportunity to elevate his position in the court by trying to get the king to marry his daughter Zara, who in her parent's opinion, is ugly.

> "Does Haman have a daughter?" Jim asks.
>
> "There is no mention of a daughter," Deb responds. "In fact, that name doesn't even show up in the Bible."
>
> "Why would the film show this girl as ugly?" Cindy asks, "She's very pretty."
>
> "If the film shows a girl that is actually ugly, it might offend anyone in the audience that looks like her," Joe responds. "Just think how that would turn out when a wife in the audience turns to her husband and asks, 'Do I look like her?' I fell into that trap with my fourth wife and had to go out and look for number five."

Meanwhile Esther is praying at the dinner table in her uncle's house as they prepare for the Sabbath dinner.

> **"Nobody prays in the book of Esther!"** Les shouts.

After a search for a queen among Persia's allies does not find a suitable woman to be queen, a eunuch under Haman's orders recommends that a queen be found that is a daughter of one of the king's advisors. When he recommends that Zara be considered, Mordecai stands up and recommends Esther, a girl to whom he has been a guardian, also should be considered. Other councilors stand up and say they have candidates as well, so the king decides to have Persian girls brought to the palace so he can choose a future queen.

> "This part is not true," Deb says. "There is no search among Persia's allies nor does anyone suggest that the next queen should be a daughter of an advisor."

The next day Mordecai tells Esther she must enter the competition to be queen. Esther is not excited to marry a man who banishes his first wife, but she agrees to do as Mordecai asks. She then prays about her decision, because if Haman's daughter wins, the Jews will be in danger because of Haman's hatred for the Jews.

> **"Nobody prays in the book of Esther!"** Les shouts again.

Meanwhile, Ronald is busy posting: "I want the television rights to this competition. It will be huge, I'll call it the 'Miss Virgin Persia contest!' Nobody can put on a pageant like I do!"

"This is not a voluntary competition," Deb says. "Virgins are gathered from all over the kingdom."

Esther prays and tells the Lord that if he will call her by name, she will obey.

Immediately Esther hears a soft voice say, "Hadassah," which assures her that if she obeys him, he promises her she shall not be harmed.

Les has run out of patience as he stands and throws his bag of popcorn at the screen. **"How many times do I have to tell you, there's no praying in the Book of Esther?"**

"Don't you think she might have?" Jim quietly asks Deb.

"Yes, it's possible. But the theme of this book is that God is hidden throughout the story, so prayer is not mentioned."

"Why would God hide himself?" Jim asks.

"I have a handout for next Sunday's class regarding that," Deb responds. "There is another thing in this scene, showing God answering her prayer, which is even worse than showing her praying. This diminishes Esther's courage by showing that God promises her she won't be hurt. This is nonsense, she will end up risking her life."

In another part of town, Haman's wife has prepared their daughter for the competition. When the pretty girl comes into the room, Haman complains bitterly that he doesn't have a daughter as pretty as he is handsome, threatening her that if she does not win, he will kick her out of the family.

"Haman, you're no prize yourself," *Tiffany yells.*

In the palace, the girls are brought before the king, one at a time, and he shakes his head no as each girl comes before his throne. It's Zara's turn, and her mother has wrapped her so her face can't be seen, but before the king can decide on her, he sees Esther behind her, and the king narrows the competition to the two of them and has them brought into the palace. The king ultimately decides that Esther will be queen.

"Each of dozens of women spends a night with the king," Deb says. "They aren't just paraded before the king in one evening."

"That's great!" Cindy says, "How would you like to be number one hundred and twenty-seven?"

Haman plots to kill the Jews by examining their scrolls for information that will prove they are disloyal to the king. His search is rewarded when he finds a passage that says that God is king of the entire world. He uses that scroll to prove the Jews are disloyal and deserve to be killed. Haman prepares an edict that sets a date for their execution and the king issues the edict.

"Haman doesn't just set a date!" Les yells. **"He casts lots, which is why it's called Purim."**

"Is he right?" Jim asks.

"Yes," Deb answers, "this is a huge omission."

Mordecai sends word to Esther of this edict, which says that on the thirteenth of this month, all the Jews will be put to death.

"The date for the execution is almost a year before it will be carried out," Deb says.

Mordecai asks that Esther approach the king and beg mercy for the Jews. Esther responds that she cannot approach the king uninvited without getting killed, but she decides to do so anyway. When she walks into the throne room where the king and Haman are meeting she is welcomed by the king.

"Haman is not mentioned meeting with the king in this part of the story," Ian tells Avery, "and the film omits the king holding out his golden scepter to Esther."

She gives them an invitation to a banquet she will prepare for them the next day where she will make a request to the king. The next evening, when Haman and the king are at her banquet, she makes her request, which is to spare the lives of her and her people.

"The film condenses two banquets into one," Deb says.

The next day, the king summons all his noblemen to review his decision to exterminate the Jews. In the proceedings, each man presents his position. During this review, Haman asks Mordecai if the king issues an order that contradicts a commandment from God, who he would obey. When Mordecai says he would obey God, people in the room call him a traitor. But Esther reasons with him and he admits a man should follow his conscience. The king rules that there is no treason in Mordecai or his people and that they may live.

> *"The king cannot rescind his edict!"* Les yells.

> *"I don't think he is even allowed to take mulligans!"* Joe shouts.

> "Les is right," Deb says. "He allows the Jews to be armed and defend themselves."

> "I allow myself two mulligan's a hole in golf, and unlimited replacement wives in marriage," Ronald posts.

> "What are you typing?" Tiffany asks.

> "I'm telling my followers how much I love you."

Then the king condemns Haman for the bad advice he gives him and sentences him to death. Haman's eunuch tells the king that Haman made gallows to kill Mordecai, so the king orders it be used on Haman, which is the final scene in the film.

> "Haman isn't killed because he gives bad advice," Deb says. "It's because the king thinks he is assaulting his wife."

> "Well Deb," Jim asks, "how do you rate this version?"

> "I like some things in this film, especially the actor that plays Mordecai, so I rate the entertainment at four, but the film leaves out some significant things such as the size of the banquet and the Jews being allowed to defend themselves. The gallows are not nearly high enough to hang Haman's ten sons, a part the film also leaves out. It's hard to make up my mind between two and three on accuracy, so I will give accuracy two and a half."

48

Hide and Seek

As Told in
Esther
1999

THIS FILM BEGINS by giving a brief understanding of the time this story takes place: after Cyrus frees the Jews to return to Jerusalem. There are some Jews that do not return from the Persian Empire, and some remain in the capital city of Susa where they can live in peace.

Mordecai, played by F. Murray Abraham, talks to Ezra near the marketplace when Haman rides nearby, and Ezra says he will not bow to the Amalekite because every Jew on earth knows they are not safe as long as one Amalekite still lives. When Haman rides by, he sees that Mordecai does not bow to him.

> "The introduction does a great job of describing the time this story takes place," Deb says. "It's also correctly describing the relationship between the Amalekites and the Jews. This film starts really well!"

Hadassah is introduced as Mordecai's cousin who is teaching languages to children, when Mordecai comes back to his house where she has lived since he adopted her. She is unmarried and patiently waiting for her cousin to choose the right man for her.

> "The last film also shows Esther waiting for Mordecai to choose a husband for her," Deb comments. "I don't know where this idea is coming from, because it's not in the story."

> "Maybe they were onto something," Tiffany comments. "I know my parents would have done a better job of selecting a husband than I did."

Nehemiah is also in Susa, washing goblets and treasures that are being used at King Ahasuerus' banquet, where about half a dozen men and a few servants are enjoying wine. Haman asks if Queen Vashti can be brought to the banquet, so the king sends a servant to get her, but she refuses to appear before the drunken men. An advisor suggests to the drunken king that a royal decree expelling Vashti should be written, so her expulsion cannot be revoked.

> "Where are the other hundreds of guests that are at this banquet?" Dave asks.

> "They must be in the bar," Joe answers, "smoking cigars and watching the soccer playoffs."

> "This is a huge banquet as opposed to what's shown here," Deb comments, "but the film is making a good point."

> "What's that?" Jim asks.

> "Once a law is given it cannot be revoked. This will be very important to remember later in the story."

A replacement for the queen is needed, so virgins from all over the empire are kidnapped and brought to Susa to be among those chosen to become the new queen. Hadassah is one of those girls, and as they take her away, Mordecai tells her to change her name to the Babylonian name Esther saying, "You know what that means," and to hide her identity as a Jew. When she arrives at the palace, she and the other girls are told by

Hegai, the king's eunuch, that they will be trained and prepared to be presented to the king.

"This part is way more accurate than the previous film," Ian says.

"What does the name Esther mean?" Avery asks, referring to Mordecai's comment.

"It means star, it is related to the Babylonian goddess, Ishtar."

"You're so smart. I'm amazed you know all this."

"Not only that, but Mordecai's name is also related to a Babylonian god named Marduk."

"I'm dazzled by your brilliance Ian!" she jokes.

"Be careful Avery," Teddy says as he walks by. "He might think you're serious."

"I see you are now going steady with Erica," Ian says. "Great choice!"

"She's so beautiful!" Avery adds. "You guys look great together. Is it true neither one of you has dated before?"

"True, I'm glad she was my first date."

Mordecai knows an official in the palace and obtains a job as an assistant so he can be near Esther as she and the other girls are trained in the palace where the girls find life pleasant. When Esther comes to the king she explains to him that her name means, "hidden" in the tongue of her people.

"Didn't you say it means 'star'?" Avery asks.

"It does, but the Hebrew root means hidden. So her Babylonian name referring to a Babylonian god hides her identity as a Jew. This is a neat combination of a word having two appropriate meanings."

"You should teach our Old Testament class!"

"Maybe, but then we couldn't date."

Shortly after Esther is chosen and becomes queen, Mordecai hears two men plotting against the king and sends word to Esther, who warns the king. He asked who warned her and she answers that a Jew named Mordecai warned her of this. He has the men executed and orders the events to be written down in the records.

Haman gets promoted to be chamberlain when the current chamberlain dies. Meanwhile the king is ignoring Esther, who is not summoned for weeks to his bedchamber.

> "He must have run out of his pills," Dave jokes.

> "I never use those," Ronald tells Tiffany. "Never have, never will."

> "You won't need them until after we get married," she responds.

However, Haman is not ignoring Mordecai, who still refuses to bow to him. He plots to kill not only Mordecai, but all the Jews in the empire. Haman and his advisors cast lots and determine the execution date will be on the thirteenth day of the month of Adar, and they send the decree to all the provinces.

> "This film continues to be very accurate," Deb says.

Mordecai sends a message to Esther and asks her to plead to the king to save her people. When Esther gets this message, she is upset because she knows if she goes to the king unannounced she will be killed. But Mordecai, sends a second message saying that she must plead with the king.

Esther has Mordecai brought inside the courtyard where she tells him to have all the Jews fast for three days, and after that she will go to the king. In addition to fasting, Ezra, Mordecai and Esther will all pray to God for deliverance during this time.

> **"There is no prayer in this story!"** Les shouts.

> "Hollywood must feel a movie about a Bible story should include prayer," Deb says.

> "Yeah," Jim responds. "It's like writing a book about Bible movies without quoting the Bible."

> "That's something only Phil Scheidt would do," Dave says.

The king and his advisors are in intense discussion about problems in the kingdom when Esther walks into the room. The advisors stand aside as she walks toward the king with her head bowed. The king looks over at her, totally surprised by her appearance. He stands up, visibly upset and walks to her, but then his appearance softens, and he holds out his scepter, telling her not to be afraid.

"This is slightly off," Deb says. "The king welcomes her immediately."

When he asks what she wants, she asks that he and Haman come to a banquet that afternoon that she has prepared for them. That afternoon at the banquet, the king asks Esther for her petition, and she requests they both come to another banquet the next day, and at that time she will make her request.

"Both meals are in the original story," Deb says. "This film is getting a lot of things right!"

As Haman walks home, he encounters Mordecai, who still won't bow. Once home, he complains to his family and his son suggests he build a gallows fifty cubits high and hang Mordecai on it.

"Why don't you just hang him in the closet with a pine scent deodorizer?" Cindy yells.

"Maybe they should hang him on a tree with their wind chimes and hummingbird feeder!" Tiffany shouts.

"He might make a great chandelier in the dining room!" Cindy yells again.

"He might look even better in the kitchen!" some woman yells.

"Who is that?" Cindy asks.

"I don't know, but she makes a good point."

"What's with women and decorating?" Jim asks.

"It's just in our nature," Deb responds. "But I should point out it is actually Haman's wife, Zeresh, and Haman's friends that tell him to hang Mordecai," Deb says, "not his son."

That night, while the gallows is being built at Haman's home, the king is lying awake and says he cannot sleep. A scribe is brought in to read to help the king fall asleep and reads about Mordecai saving the king's life. The king calls for Haman to come so he can ask him what should be done to reward the man who the king wishes to honor.

Haman, thinking he will receive the honors, tells the king the man should be put on a horse and paraded around Susa, resulting in Haman leading Mordecai around Susa, passing the gallows he has built, which are about fifteen feet high. Haman returns to his home afterward and his wife tells him this is not the end of his troubles.

> "There is another small error here," Deb says. "The gallows is about seventy five feet high."

> "There is a lumber shortage and Home Supplies World is closed," Jim answers.

A knock on the door signals that he is summoned to a banquet with Esther and the king. As he leaves his wife and sons, he assures them he is still the king's right hand man. When he arrives at the banquet, he compliments Esther on the food. The king asks Esther what her petition is and she tells the king she wants her life and the lives of the Jews to be spared. She reveals she is a Jew and that she and her people will die as a result of Haman's edict. The king is furious and orders Haman hanged on the gallows Haman had built for Mordecai.

Mordecai is elevated to Haman's position and given his property. Esther asks the king to revoke the edict, but he cannot, so Mordecai, in his new position, issues an edict that will allow the Jews in the empire to arm and defend themselves on Adar thirteen.

> "Unlike the previous film," Deb says, "the film shows the king cannot revoke his edict. This is very accurate."

The evening before that day, Ezra prays that God will assist the Jews in defending themselves the next day.

> Les is immediately on his feet. **"What is wrong with these films? There's no praying in Esther. The story doesn't even mention God!"**

> "The film keeps showing prayer," Deb says, "once again, this is wrong."

There are battles, with people dying on both sides, the king reports to Esther, but he finishes by telling her, "Rejoice my queen, you saved your people." Esther issues a decree that the Jews will commemorate the 14th and

15th day of Adar, as days of celebration, and call it the Feast of Purim. The final scene depicts Ezra and Nehemiah leaving Susa to resettle in Jerusalem as they return to rebuild the Temple.

> *As Jim and Deb stand up to leave the theater, Jim asks, "How do you like this film, Deb?"*

> *"Like the other movie, it shows prayer, which is never mentioned in the story and it leaves out what happens to Haman's sons, but it is still a great film. I love it! I give it a five for entertainment, but I can only give it a four for accuracy. I would give it a five if the film did not keep showing prayer, because I believe it's important that it not be shown."*

Hide and Seek

As Told in
Esther and the King
1960

A S THIS MOVIE BEGINS, King Ahasuerus, played by Richard Egan, is the king of Persia twenty-five hundred years ago, who is leading thousands of his troops home after a fresh victory in Egypt. One of those soldiers is Simon of Judea who saves the king's life in battle, and when the army stops to rest, the king gives him his golden sword as a reward. The king also tells Simon he will make him part of his palace guard when they return to Shushan.

> *"That's nonsense!" Les yells. "There is no campaign in Egypt and no character named Simon."*

> *"Oh yeah?" Joe yells back holding his unlit cigar. "Haven't you heard the expression, 'Simon says?' How do you know it doesn't come from the book of Esther?"*

Simon thanks the king and tells him he can't wait to show the sword to the woman he will marry. The king also gives Simon a string of pearls to give to his bride as a gift from him. When Simon returns to his village, he sees a man hanging by his neck from a building.

In the village, Esther, played by Joan Collins, tells a villager to take the body down, but the villager refuses, saying Haman, the king's chief minister wants the body to remain on display as an example to those who don't pay their taxes.

A group of state revenue officers in the audience start cheering and applauding.

"I hope someone got a picture of that," one of them says.

"I did," a woman answers, "I'll put it on our website in the section under penalties."

Simon and Esther embrace when he greets her, but Esther is unhappy about how the villagers have been treated. When Simon gives her the pearls, she throws them down, saying they have bloodstains on them because of the injustice of the king.

"You should sell them on eBay," Dave shouts.

A messenger arrives at the gate to the city at night announcing that the king's army approaches. Guards push large wheels which open the gates, and the messenger rides his horse on a dirt trail into the city announcing the king is returning.

"Really?" Jim asks, "They don't pave the entrance to the finest city in Persia?"

"They can't," Dave says. "OPEC has an oil embargo in effect, and they don't have any asphalt."

"I prefer dust roads," Charley says. "Those hard streets would hurt my hooves."

Vashti, the queen wakes up to the announcement, lipstick and eye makeup intact, and tells Haman, who is in bed with her, that the king is arriving, but Haman assures her the king won't be there until the next day. Relieved, she lays back down with her lover. Their conversation the following morning provides insight into their character. Vashti is sleeping with many men and Haman is plotting to overthrow the king.

"It's a good thing for them the servants keep their mouths shut and not rat them out," Jim says.

"We're eight minutes into this film," Deb says, "and we already see an imaginary battle, an imaginary soldier being engaged to Esther, Haman already being a prime minister who hangs people, and Vashti having an imaginary affair with Haman."

"Is any of this correct?"

"Nothing so far."

When the king enters the city to cheering crowds, he walks up the steps to Haman and asks where Lord Mordecai is. Haman tells the king he is the one person who did not show up. The king walks into the palace where Mordecai meets him and welcomes him home. When the king tells Mordecai that Simon saved his life and he rewarded him, Mordecai tells the king he is also rewarding Simon by giving him his niece in marriage.

"The king has no idea who Mordecai is at the beginning of the story," Deb comments.

The king comes into Vashti's room and accuses her of adultery, telling her that soldiers have told him she has been unfaithful. He demands to know their names, but she denies she has cheated on him. The king doesn't believe her, telling her that she is dead to him as he pushes her to the floor, banning her from the upcoming feast.

"She isn't banned from the feast for being a slut!" Les yells.

"That's right," Deb says. "She is summoned to the feast and refuses to attend."

"She's disloyal," Ronald posts. "I would trash that slut on my website."

The king is having a feast, featuring fine food, wine and dancing girls. Meanwhile, Vashti is bored staying in her apartment, so she tells a servant girl she is going to the feast and to help her get prepared.

"It's just the opposite!" Les shouts. "She refuses to go!"

During the feast, the king has Haman and Mordecai follow him to another room where they discuss a future war with Greece. The king says he will cut off Alexander in his youth and annihilate his army. After a brief confrontation between Mordecai and Haman, involving the Jews in Persia, the king describes his war plan and instructs Mordecai to "inscribe this and place it in the vaults as our secret strategy against Greece." The king tells Mordecai, "Remember they must be kept secret at all costs." Then the camera zooms in on Haman contemplating what the king just said.

"Look out!" Joe yells. "Haman is getting an idea!"

"Let's see, the king tells the good guy to hide tablets that describe strategy, not once, but twice. The bad guy hears this and gets an evil look in his eyes," Jim laughs. "Do you think these tablets might surface later in the film?"

They get up and return to the banquet just in time to see Vashti make her entrance to the party performing an exotic dance for all the guests. During the dance, she throws part of her veils to the people watching, leaving on very little of her clothing, and almost nothing to their imagination. She finishes the dance topless with the result that the king banishes her from Persia.

"She should do another dance and get tips from the guests," Dave comments. "At least she wouldn't leave broke."

"She gets banished because she refuses to come to the feast," Les yells. "Not because she strips for the guests!"

Vashti's banishment never takes place because Haman has one of his followers, a stupid and crude looking henchman, go to her bedroom and put a pillow over her face. While Haman plots with a general about assassinating the king, Keresh, one of the king's concubines, who is also a frequent bedmate of Haman, walks into the room and Haman introduces her to the general as the next queen of Persia.

The king will need a new queen, so Persian soldiers kidnap beautiful screaming women from all over the empire so that one of them can become the new queen.

"Why are these girls screaming?" Rick yells. "They are going to have a chance to live in the palace and possibly become the queen."

"Maybe they know the king looks like Phil Scheidt," Joe answers.

Soldiers kidnap Esther right in the middle of her marriage ceremony to Simon. Simon fights the general of these soldiers and seeing he is losing, he escapes into a dense field.

> "So, no one knows Esther is a Jew!" Les yells. "She is kidnapped from a Jewish settlement during a Jewish wedding!"

> "The ceremony is in a restaurant that serves great chicken soup!" Jason yells back. "All the fashionable Persian weddings are there! Their ham is delicious! The Presbyterians love that restaurant."

Esther is now in the palace. Haman picks three beautiful girls in the group, including Esther, to be kidnapped by new soldiers and given to the troops. The soldiers are doing this when the king sees them and kills them. He notices how beautiful Esther is as he looks at the girls and then he walks away.

> "This is pretty far out," Deb says. "There is no way Haman does this!"

Esther walks through the palace looking for a way to escape back to her people when she sees Mordecai. After she tells him what happened, Mordecai tells her she must stay in the palace, forget about Simon, and try to become queen. Esther agrees and joins the girls, including Keresh, as they get prepared to meet the king. During the preparation, Hegai, the eunuch is so impressed with Esther that he gives her a gold cloak to wear.

> "Hegai does like Esther," Deb says. "The film is right about this."

Haman talks to Keresh though a curtain and finds out Esther is Keresh's main competition. Haman points Esther out to his henchman as she is wearing the cloak and tells him to remember her well.

> "It starts out showing the girls being kidnapped," Tiffany says, "and now it's a competition?"

> "You would win that hand down," Ronald answers.

> "Easily, but I'm happy now just to hang out with you."

The audition begins. The king is sitting by a pool as the girls come before him one by one, but he waves each of them away. Most of the girls have approached the king, so it is now Keresh's turn, and as she leaves the room, she steals the cloak from Esther and walks down the hall. The henchman sees the cloak and thinking it is Esther, drags her behind a curtain and kills her. When Esther goes before the king and he recognizes her as one of the girls he saved, she is picked to be his queen.

"The selection process is not a one night event," Deb says. "Each girl spends a night with the king."

Esther and Mordecai meet in a garden and talk about her feelings for the king. She now likes the king, and questions whether she was ever in love with Simon.

"Simon is like Nikita Khrushchev!" Les yells. **"He's become a non-person."**

Simon is hiding out in the city of the dead, where Mordecai goes to visit him. Once there, Mordecai gives Simon some supplies and tells him that Esther has affection for the king and she will become queen. Simon takes the news badly.

"Cheer up Simon," Chester jokes, "try this dating site I found."

"He did," Charley replies, "and he found her on it."

Simon arrives at Shushan and enters the palace, holding up the gold sword every time he is challenged.

"How do they know he didn't buy that at a flea market?" Chester jokes.

Simon makes his way to Esther's bedroom and tells her he is coming to take her away.

"He's coming to take me away, ha ha!" Chester and Charley start singing.

Esther rejects Simon, and begs him to leave, but Simon pulls out his sword and tells her he will kill the king. Not knowing what to do, Esther takes out a mallet and hits a gong, bringing soldiers running to her room.

"I guess he put on a lousy act," Dave jokes, referring to the 'Gong Show.'"

Simon manages to escape the palace, but several chariots chase him as he flees on another chariot.

"Look at all that dirt kicked up. I wouldn't want to be in the last chariot," Rick tells Charlotte as they watch the last half on the movie.

"I hope it's an air-conditioned chariot." Then, seeing Erica walk over, Charlotte says, "Avery told me you and Splash are going steady, that's wonderful!"

"Erica," Rick says, "you've never even dated, why go steady this early?"

"I don't want him to find someone else."

"You're the prettiest girl in the school, he would never look elsewhere. If he did I would fire him."

The wedding day arrives and the king marries Esther. At the end of the ceremony Haman cites a long-neglected law of King Cyrus, which states that anybody who would not worship Mithras shall be killed. Haman says he can order the Jews killed and enrich the king by ten thousand talents of silver.

"The ten thousand talents part is correct," Deb says, "but the rest of this is nonsense. There is never any mention of worshipping Mithras."

Esther speaks to the king and then Haman quotes another law that says that any woman who interrupts the king, will be put to death, but the king holds his scepter out to Esther, saving her from execution. The king overrides the edict of Cyrus and issues a new law that will allow the Jews to worship God as they choose. He then banishes Haman to a remote outpost.

"He can't revoke that order," Deb says. "Once a king issues an order it cannot be revoked."

"Even if it's Richard Egan?" Jim jokes.

"This is really messed up. Esther is not sitting next to the king, she has not seen him for thirty days. She risks her life by going to him uninvited before he holds out the golden scepter."

Haman is not defeated yet. He has made copies of the war plan tablets to incriminate Mordecai for treason. He and the general cast lots to determine the day they will do this to Mordecai. A red piece of dice lands that represents the month of Adar, which Haman says is that month, so they decide to carry out their plan that night.

"Those are loaded dice," Joe yells.

"The lots are tossed on Nisan," Les yells, *"Adar is eleven months later."*

The general leads soldiers to a Jewish Temple and plants the counterfeit tablets in a cabinet and then takes them back out in front of the soldiers while the Jews that are present. The general takes them back to the palace, and Haman presents the fabricated evidence to the king who orders that Mordecai be put in prison and hanged unless he is proven innocent. Esther speaks out and tells the king she is a Jew, and the king asks Esther to renounce her faith.

"That won't work!" Joe yells, *"Two guys wearing short sleeve white shirts came to her house yesterday to share good news and she still would not renounce her faith!"*

"First of all, there are no war plans on tablets," Deb says. *"Mordecai is never accused of a plot and the king never asks Esther to renounce being a Jew, which wouldn't save her anyway!"*

"Don't kill us, we're Pentecostals, watch us eat ham from the deli!" Dave jokes.

Esther won't renounce her faith, but begs the king to go to Persepolis to inspect what's happened to the money stored there. She says what he finds there will be proof that Haman is the actual traitor. He agrees to go and suspends the death penalty for Mordecai and the Jews until he returns.

"I'll wait until next week Honey!" Jim jokes. *"This weekend is a big soccer match with that Irish team. I don't want to miss it!"*

"Over there," Joe says, *"They call it football."*

Haman sends the general and his troops out to the City of the Dead to ambush the king as he goes to Persepolis. But Simon, still holding the golden sword, is hiding there and he injures the general who is walking through the deserted ruins. The king and his escort ride by and get attacked by the general's soldiers. Simon ends up fighting the king but stops when the king finds out Simon and Esther were going to be married.

"You never invited me to the wedding," Dave jokes. "How would I know?"

They hear groaning from a dark room and find the general still alive. He asks that the king end his pain, and the king agrees if he will tell the truth. The general tells the king what Haman did, and then the king ends the general's pain, and tells Simon to ride back to Shushan to arm all the Jews so they can protect themselves.

"This is actually pretty close," Deb says. "The Jews are allowed to arm themselves."

In Shushan, Haman is instructing troops to kill the Jews, and he gives specific instructions to one officer to lead Mordecai to the gallows. Haman tells his henchman to go get the queen, but she manages to escape.

Simon climbs over a wall and sees one of his fellow soldiers from the Egyptian campaign, and together they start collecting weapons for the Jews. Meanwhile Mordecai is in prison, reciting psalms and praying as he awaits execution.

"This is all wrong," Ian says.

"How is it wrong?" Avery asks.

"Mordecai is never in prison, he is outside the gate, and he is never described as praying."

The next morning, Haman watches the Jews approach their Temple and proceed inside, with Esther, wearing a shawl so she won't be recognized, coming in last. Once everyone is inside, they start arming the Jews. A battle scene follows and during this time a hangman's noose is put on Mordecai as he stands on the gallows. Simon fights soldiers at the gallows and saves Mordecai, but is mortally wounded in the process. Haman, realizing his soldiers are beaten, attempts to escape on a chariot.

"Those gallows are only fifteen feet high," Ronald posts. "They are supposed to be seventy-five. I would fire that contractor. Nobody builds better gallows than I do!"

The king arrives and stops Haman from escaping and orders him to be hanged on the gallows he had erected for Haman. Simon's friends take him into the Temple and he dies there as Esther sits by him. Mordecai, sitting next to Esther says the Jews should remember this day as Purim, and then Simon says his last words, "Let it be remembered with holidays of gladness."

The film begins with Persian soldiers returning from a battle and it also ends with them returning from a battle. The difference is they lose this battle with Alexander, but the king survives and returns home to Esther, ending the film.

> "Let's go home and make cheeseburgers," Jim says as they leave.

> "This film is a little cheesy," Deb says. "However, it's fun to watch Joan Collins when she was so young. What a beautiful woman she was and still is after five decades. She is the perfect actress to play Esther; it's too bad the film is so inaccurate."

> "What are your ratings?"

> "I rate the entertainment at four and the accuracy at zero."

Hide and Seek

As Told in
One Night with the King
2006

THIS MOVIE OPENS with a flashback of God telling Saul to exterminate all of the Amalekites. Agag, the king of the Amalekites, and his queen are dragged before Saul after the battle. That night, the prophet Samuel shows up at Saul's tent to confront Saul about not killing Agag. During this conversation, a soldier comes into the tent and tells them the queen has escaped. Saul comments that one woman escaping is not important, but Samuel angrily tells him that she is pregnant. While Agag is killed, the queen, with her seed of vengeance growing in her, survives.

> "Although Agag's queen is fictional, I love how this begins," Deb says. "It shows what sets up certain events in the book of Esther and also gives an explanation of how Haman can be a descendent of Agag."

Five hundred years later, Esther is living in Susa, the capital of the Persian Empire, with her uncle, Mordecai. A caravan from Jerusalem arrives, and Esther reminds her uncle that Cyrus freed the Jews to return to Judea years before, and they should leave Persia. Mordecai, who lives comfortably, is not ready to leave. At this point in the story, Esther is known to her neighbors as "Hadassah," and that Mordecai has raised her since she became an orphan when she was a child.

Haman is introduced as an Agagite, who carries a token the Amalekite queen made centuries before. He understands he is her descendant and vows to exact vengeance on the Jews for what they did to his people.

> *"Did you notice the shape of that token?" Ian asks Avery.*
>
> *"It seems pretty weird."*
>
> *"If you look closely you will see it is a swastika with a serpent winding through the image."*
>
> *"Why is that important?"*
>
> *"It shows the evil nature of the original Amalekites continues right up to current times, including Nazi Germany."*

While Haman rides by, Esther is telling a story about David and Goliath to some children in the street. Jesse, the grandson of Mordecai's housekeeper, sneaks up on Esther from behind to surprise her as she tells the story. It is obvious he has a crush her.

King Xerxes is having a feast, and Mordecai, being a scribe, has to attend because there are rumors of an upcoming war with Greece, and he needs to be kept current on what's happening. The feast is attended by hundreds of people in a great hall, but Queen Vashti is holding her own feast in protest of the upcoming war with Greece, refusing to attend her husband's feast.

> *Chester comes back from the popcorn stand where Charlotte was feeding him. "There are thirty camels outside protesting the upcoming war, shouting, 'Make Peace with Greece!'"*
>
> *"Why didn't you join them?" Charley asks.*
>
> *"They were spitting too much!"*
>
> *"This is the only one of these four films that shows that Vashti is having her own feast," Deb says, "but her protesting a war with Greece is not in the story."*

That night Esther wants to sneak into the palace so she can see the feast and she is joined by Jesse. They watch from a balcony as the crowd of guests shouts they want to see the queen, so the king sends for her. Vashti refuses to leave her own feast, so the king's advisors tell him he must find a new queen, and he tells his guest the "land has no more queen." Seeing what is about to happen, Esther and Jesse decide to leave for Jerusalem the next day.

> "Remember, we need to arrive at the airport four hours before the flight," Dave jokes.

> "The idea that Esther is going to escape to Jerusalem is fiction," Deb says, "however the imagery of the feast in this film is spectacular. It's the only film that captures just how many people were there."

> "If we get married, we'll have twice that many guests at our wedding," Ronald says.

> "Four times as many," Tiffany says, "but Ronald, you're going to pay for the wedding."

> "I forgot, you lost a lot of money in that nonprofit business you started. Don't worry, those bankruptcies I took saved me millions, I'll pay for it"

The king issues an edict that all the beautiful young maidens in the kingdom will be brought to Susa to be considered to be the next queen, as well as young men to serve the girls while they are in the palace. These young men, which include Jesse, will be turned into eunuchs. Esther is worried she might be taken and Mordecai says there is little chance that this will happen, but if she is, she must hide her identity, so he tells her to adopt the name Esther. She walks out the door and doesn't get ten steps before she is captured and taken to the palace.

> "There is no mention of Jesse in the story," Deb says, "nor is there any mention of young men being captured to become eunuchs for the girls."

> **"They'll take my mulehood out of my cold dead hooves,"** Chester yells.

A dozen girls, including Esther, walk into the palace together and meet Hegai, the royal eunuch, who will prepare them to go before the king. Over the next few months, while the officials in the court consider going to war with Greece, Esther and the other girls live a pampered life as they prepare to come before the king. Haman uses this time to set up the Jews as Greek sympathizers and starts a campaign against them in remote areas of the empire.

> "The film is placing a lot of emphasis on a war with Greece," Ian says.
>
> "Didn't the Persians go to war against Alexander?" Avery asks.
>
> "They did, but there is no mention of Greece in the story about Esther. However, this film does a great job of showing how long Esther is in the palace, which the other films don't do."
>
> "What was the war about?"
>
> "The naming rights to a brandy cocktail. The Persians wanted to call it a Brandy Shah instead of a Brandy Alexander."

Esther becomes a favorite of Hegai, and knowing she can read, he has her go to the king's room and read reports to him as he is behind a sheer veil. She starts reading a report but then begins reciting the story of Jacob meeting Rachel. The king is intrigued by her story, and he comes from behind the veil, talks to her and tells her she will read to him again.

> "This is more fiction," Deb says, "but I like what the movie is doing here. It's a beautiful scene, however there is no evidence Esther meets the king before she spends her night with him."

The king starts interviewing candidates. The first girl is so laden down with jewelry she falls off the horse that servants place her on to be brought to the king.

> "That's a funny addition," Deb says.

The second candidate walks into the king's tent, and after five seconds starts throwing up.

> **"One of Phil's blind dates in college had a similar reaction,"** Joe yells.
>
> **"That girl was my mom,"** Avery yells. **"I know for a fact she threw up after the date!"**

> "Don't be mean, Joe," Cindy comments. "I bet Phil had a lot of dates when he was in school."
>
> "I'm sure he did, but never more than once with the same girl."

It's Esther's turn, and Hegai walks her to the king's room. When she enters the room the king tells her there is a scroll there for her to read, saying that he is weary of the procession of candidates. The initial conversation does not go well when the king recognizes Esther is the girl who reads to him, but, by the end of their conversation he makes the decision to choose her. He asks her about her past, but she only tells him it takes the glory of God to conceal a matter and the honor of kings to search it out. They have a king's wedding and Esther is named queen.

> "This is a great addition!" Deb says. "While this Bible quote is not in Esther, it emphasizes the hidden things that are in the story. I love this!"

Later, a crowd gathers at night and Haman enters the hall where they wait for him to speak. He appears and gives a powerful speech against the Jews.

> "This part reminds me of films I see showing Hitler speaking to German crowds," Jim says.
>
> "As it should," Deb answers. "Hitler loathed the Jews. He had the spirit of the Amalekites."

Later, Mordecai discovers that the food taster for the king bought poison and he tells Esther to warn the king. The king is a day's ride away, so she tells the prince, who is his cousin. Meanwhile, Hegai tells Haman of the plot and Haman kills the conspirators, and then tells the prince, in front of Esther, that they plotted alone.

> "The prince is not part of the story," Deb says. "While he may exist, he is not mentioned."

Another crowd gathers, and Haman makes an even more powerful rant against God and the Jews with a voice and mannerisms not unlike Adolph Hitler. He speaks against Greece for its democracy and against the prince for being sympathetic to them and being a traitor. Esther is in the crowd, hidden by a robe, and after hearing this speech, returns to the palace and discovers scrolls that show that it was Haman who killed her parents.

> "This is a good addition," Deb says. "It offers an explanation why Esther is an orphan and ties Haman to a fictitious persecution."

Esther meets with Mordecai in a secret place in the garden where lovers sometimes meet and tells him what she found in the scrolls. As Xerxes returns home, he sees her leave through the gate and thinks she might be having an affair, and is very cold to her when he walks into the palace. When he asks if she had been alone that day, the prince walks in before she can answer her husband's question.

> "Again, the film is offering fictional information to answer an unasked question," Deb says. "No one knows why the king ignores Esther before she appears to him unannounced. This is also a good addition."

Haman sets up the prince, who wants to overthrow the king. He double-crosses the prince, and is promoted to the prince's position inheriting the prince's house, wealth, prestige and power, after the prince is executed. As the king discusses war plans against Greece, Haman uses his new position to lobby the king to exterminate the Jews and confiscate their wealth to finance the war with Greece.

> "The film is offering a reason why Haman gets promoted," Deb says. "While it's fictional, it is another good addition that does not compromise the book."

The king agrees to Haman's request and letters are sent to all the provinces of the empire that the Jews are to be exterminated on Adar 13, which will be in six weeks. Mordecai has Jesse take a message to the queen, asking her to intercede for the Jews because the Jews now feel hopeless. Esther tells Jesse that if she approaches the king uninvited it means death for her. After Jesse leaves, Esther prays to God for help, while Mordecai mourns outside the citadel, wearing sackcloth.

> **"There is no praying in the book of Esther!"** Les yells.

> "This timing is also wrong," Deb says. "They cast for lots on the first month of the year and the day the Jews are to be killed is in the twelfth month. The film shrinks twelve months down to six weeks."

Haman goes through the street and everyone—except Mordecai—bows to him. A servant is going to kill Mordecai, but Haman stops him, asking Mordecai why he won't kneel. After Mordecai tells him he will bow only to the king and to God, Haman asks who he is and Mordecai tells him his full name, which Haman recognizes as being Jewish. Haman strikes Mordecai but doesn't have him killed.

> Up in the balcony, Ian tells Avery, "Mordecai doesn't mention God. In fact, this film continually quotes from the Bible and refers to Bible stories such as David and Goliath, but none of those references are in the story."
>
> "God's not mentioned in the Book of Esther?"
>
> "Not at all. That's an important part of the mystery of this book."

That night, Haman's wife suggests a public execution for Mordecai to honor the king, who will be leaving in three days, so Haman orders that gallows be built. At the same time, the king can't sleep and has the chronicles brought to him. The next morning, the king asks Haman what should be done to honor a man who has done a great service for the king, and Haman, thinking he will be honored, tells the king to dress this man in a royal robe and lead him on a horse around the city.

Haman is not happy when he finds out he will have to honor Mordecai. As he walks down the hall, he complains to Esther about what he must do, but when Esther is not sympathetic, he becomes suspicious of her identity. Although he is furious, he obeys the king and leads Mordecai through the city on the king's horse, shouting his praise.

> "This is an addition that is wrong," Deb says. "There is never any indication that Haman suspects Esther's identity."

That night, a shadowy figure comes into Esther's bedchamber while she is falling asleep. She realizes someone is there and starts to call the guards, but Jesse stops her and tells her that Mordecai has another message for her. He tells her that the king will be leaving the next day and that Haman will then be in charge, so she must beseech the king before he leaves, and he tells her she too will perish, and that maybe she has come to the palace for such a time as this.

"This whole storyline about an upcoming war with Greece and the king having to leave is just not true," Deb says.

She instructs Jesse to tell Mordecai to have the Jews fast and pray, and that she will do the same. She will go to the king the next morning, and she tells Jesse, "If I perish, I perish."

"Esther doesn't tell her people to pray!" Les shouts.

"This is a huge error all these movies make," Deb says. "There is no mention of God or prayer anywhere in the book of Esther. Les is right, Esther doesn't tell her people to pray. The film also shrinks three days, which is the actual time she will fast, down to one night. The period of three days is important."

"Why's that?" Cindy asks.

"You'll find out Sunday."

It's raining the next day, and Hegai will not provide a litter for Esther, because he does not want her to die, so she runs through the rain to the palace, where Xerxes is making a speech to hundreds of his people, telling them that he is putting Haman in charge because he is leaving within the hour.

"You'll never make it!" Joe yells, "That plane leaves in one hour."

"The king never puts Haman in charge while he leaves," Deb says.

With wet clothes, and even wetter hair, Esther opens the doors and enters the hall, walking through the astounded people in the court. She walks over a hundred feet up the aisle as Haman says she comes uninvited, and Mordecai, who is in the audience, watches her approach the king. Haman, mentioning protocol, calls for the guards. As she climbs the steps toward the king, a guard approaches from the side, takes out his sword, raises it high in the air and swings it down toward Esther's neck, but is not able to finish the decapitation because the king grabs his arm just before the sword can kill her.

"I hate it when someone grabs my arm in the middle of my golf swing," Joe yells.

Xerxes holds out the scepter, saving her life.

> "I love this scene!" Deb says. "It really captures what she must feel at that moment, although there is nothing in the story about how many people were with the king when she comes in unannounced."
>
> "It takes courage to walk in like that," Cindy says.
>
> "Let alone with her hair a wet mess," Tiffany adds.

That night, the king and Haman walk to a banquet Esther has prepared for them. As they are finishing their dinner, the king asks Esther what is her petition. She responds that she would like to finish the story she told him about Jacob and Rachel, and she tells him their story does not end with their wedding, but continues as the story of Israel, and that she is a Jew of the tribe of Benjamin, a son of Jacob. She then begs for her life and the lives of her people.

> "The last part of this is true," Deb says, "but she never mentions Jacob or Rachel."

Haman accuses her of lying, and then of attempting to thwart the king's plans to march off to war. Xerxes is skeptical, but he allows her to continue. Esther holds the stone on her necklace to a candle and the light reflects stars of David all over the room, but she doesn't realize only she can see the stars. Haman says this is mockery and the king leaves the room.

> "Haman is terrified; he never accuses her of lying," Deb says. "However, the stone showing the Stars of David is a neat addition."

Haman mocks her, asking her if she thought he would beg for his life, and then sarcastically starts asking her to forgive him, reaching out and grabbing her throat. Xerxes comes back into the room and stops Haman, and when he finds out Haman has prepared a gallows for Mordecai, he orders his guards to hang Haman on it. He then admits to Esther he saw the stars.

> "The film changes some other things here too," Deb says. "It shows only one banquet instead of two, and Haman certainly doesn't grab Esther by her throat, he trips and falls on her causing the king to think he is assaulting her."

The king gives Haman's position and wealth to Mordecai, and at the end of the film he issues an edict allowing the Jews to defend themselves on the day appointed for their destruction. Mordecai then commemorates this day as Purim, and sends out the order signed by "Mordecai, Prince of Persia, a Jew."

"What a great ending!" Joe stands up to leave, "I love this film."

"I really love the imagery in this film," Jim agrees. "The magnificent feasts, the visuals of the citadel, especially at night, are stunning."

"I agree," Deb says. "John Rhys-Davies and Omar Sharif are great in this film. I really like this film too, despite some errors. One of the things I like is how the writers come up with plausible explanations for some unanswered questions about this story, for example, what happened to Esther's parents?"

Dave who is walking out with them adds, "There are other unasked questions that it also answers such as why doesn't the king see Esther for thirty days? How could Haman be a descendent of the Agag if all the Amalekites were killed? Why is Haman promoted? I like how the film comes up with explanations that don't contradict the story. It's a very good film."

"Goodnight Dave, we'll see you Sunday," Deb says as she gets in the truck.

"Wait Deb," Dave says, "What are your ratings?"

"The entertainment is definitely a five, and that's only because I don't have a higher number to give, and I rate accuracy at a solid four."

Hide and Seek

WHAT DIFFERENCE DOES IT MAKE?

D EB BEGINS Sunday school class. "As some of you know, the feast of Purim is based on events in the book of Esther and the festival commemorates how Esther saves the Jews from extermination. Does anyone know there are two modern events that relate to this book?"

No one raises their hand.

"In 1946, ten Nazi leaders are hanged and one of them shouts, 'Purim Fest 1946,' as he walks up to the gallows. A second, more recent event is that the Prime Minister of Israel, Benjamin Netanyahu, pleads with Congress against the Iranian Nuclear Deal on Purim. It is interesting that Mordecai and Esther are both from the tribe of Benjamin, and that the name of the Prime Minister is 'Benjamin.'"

"But what is the most important thing to remember while reading the book of Esther?" Deb asks.

Ian raises his hand, "Ian?"

"This book is about hidden things, such as Esther hiding her identity and even God hiding himself."

A woman disagrees, saying, "I don't believe God hides things or himself."

Deb responds, "I believe he does, and guess what?"

"I don't have to guess," Dave says. "You have a handout on this."

"That's right Dave; I also have handouts on why some people hate the Jews, the structure of the gallows, and a Christian perspective on how Purim can be compared to Passover. But that last handout will be given out after our final class on the films about Jesus, since it directly relates to his death and resurrection. But the others should give you plenty to read until we meet next week. Enjoy the rest of your weekend."

part XIV

Please Don't Let Me Be Misunderstood

The Animals 1965

Movies About Jesus

An Introduction

A GRAND JURY is convening in Jerusalem approximately two thousand years ago. The prosecuting attorney announces, "This grand jury is now in session. We are here to determine if action needs to be taken against a certain man for a horrible crime."

A juror, referring to the Tom Wolfe quote in *The Bonfire of the Vanities*, jokes, "Are we here to indict a ham sandwich?"

"No," the prosecutor responds. "We are here to determine if an individual named Jesus of Nazareth should be charged with a crime. I will present evidence and testimony that he is guilty of the crime of wearing his hair long, like a girl."

The prosecutor shows a book to the jurors. "Before calling witnesses, I will introduce written evidence that the accused has long hair. I will read from a book published by Henry Holt and Company in 2013 that is written by Bill O'Reilly and Martin Duggard. On page 103 the authors write, 'Jesus of Nazareth has long hair.'"

The prosecutor slams the book on his table. "That should be sufficient evidence by itself! But we will also see there is further evidence to be considered." The prosecutor then presents his first witness, Michelangelo.

The prosecuting attorney asks, "Michelangelo is it true you have painted images showing Jesus having long hair?"

"Yes, I have."

"Why do you show him having long hair?"

"A lot of my friends have long hair, so why wouldn't he?"

"So, you don't know if he has long hair?"

"How could I? WSOD interrupted broadcasting in 70 A.D. Television news wasn't available when I was painting."

"The witness is excused."

The prosecuting attorney calls his next witness. "Matthew, you write about the accused. Does he have long hair?"

"I can't answer that question."

"Why not?"

"First of all, it is a stupid question and second, I never thought about it."

The prosecutor brings Mark, Luke and John to the stand and asks them the same question and receives the same answers.

It is obvious the prosecutor is perplexed and frustrated, when a member of the grand jury raises his hand.

"Do you have a question?"

"Yes sir, my name is Brad Scott. I think I can help you understand why the four witnesses answer your question the way they do."

"Mister Scott, this would be highly unusual. Are you qualified to offer an opinion regarding this matter?"

"Yes sir, I am the author of several books about topics in the Old and New Testament, including a book on Hebrew thinking which is titled, *Let This Mind Be in You*. In that book, I point out that Hebrew thinking concentrates on function as opposed to form. To the Hebrew mind the appearance of the accused is not important, so they are not concerned about whether he has long hair. In their mind, you ask a stupid question because it is what he says and does that is important, not what he looks like."

"Thank you for your insight, Mister Scott."

Scott continues, "May I suggest you bring Paul to the witness stand and ask him some questions that I have written down for you."

"This also would be highly unusual, but I will do that," the prosecutor responds.

Paul steps up on the stand.

"Paul, is it true that you wrote to the Corinthians that it is shameful for a man to have long hair?"

"Yes sir, I did."

"Would you make such a statement if Jesus has long hair?"

"No, of course not. If I were to make such a statement, I would be trashed on the Internet by thousands of his followers."

The jury members look at each other and shake their heads in agreement. The jury foreman stands up and speaks to the prosecutor. "Sir, I speak on behalf of this jury, we believe this case should be dismissed."

The prosecutor smiles and says, "I agree, there is no way Jesus wears his hair long like a girly man. Thank you for your service. Why don't all of you take the afternoon off, buy some popcorn, and watch a movie."

52

Please Don't Let me be Misunderstood

As Told in
The Jesus Film
1979

THIS FILM BEGINS with images of Adam and Eve happily living in the Garden of Eden as a voice narrates what is happening. Satan, in the form of a snake, tempts Eve, causing the couple to eat the forbidden fruit, and become separated from God.

"A snake! Why is he always a snake?" Les yells.

"Satan doesn't want anyone pulling his leg!" Jason yells.

The narrator continues, reciting quotations of prophets concerning the Messiah, including details about his birth and what he will do and preach. An image of a man walking on a barren rocky hill is shown while the narrator says that Jesus might be the one that the prophets talk about. The narrator says the events that follow will be based on what is written in the scriptures, although later, in the opening credits, it says they are based on the Gospel of Luke.

"Long Hair! Why does he have long hair?" Les yells.

"This was made in the seventies!" *Jason responds,* ***"Everyone had long hair!"***

Mary and Elizabeth speak to each other when they are both pregnant. Shortly after that, a Roman official is declaring there will be a census. While much of the dialogue consists of direct quotes, other dialogue is presented to smooth out the presentation of the film, for example, this government official declaring there will be a census.

A baby is born and when angels tell shepherds in the hills of his birth, they visit the baby in the stable. A week later the baby is circumcised and named Jesus.

"The film should make it clear he is circumcised on the eighth day," Deb says. "There is significance to that day."

Years later, John is baptizing Judeans at the river when Jesus approaches him, stands before John, and immerses himself in the water. The only individual that touches Jesus is a dove that lands on his shoulder and remains there while a voice from heaven is heard.

"Wait, I thought John baptizes him," Dave says. "It looks like he is baptizing himself."

"This is the first example of a self-service wash in the New Testament," Cindy responds.

After the baptism, Jesus goes into the desert where a snake tempts him.

"A snake! Why is he always a snake?" *Les yells.*

"The film needs someone who speaks with a forked tongue!" *Jason shouts.*

Jesus returns to Nazareth and goes into the synagogue where he is called on to read a portion of the prophet Isaiah. He quotes Isaiah, and while he stands in front of the worshippers, he tells them this passage has come true today. The crowd gets angry at this proclamation and takes him over to a cliff, where they intend to throw him to his death.

"The film messes this scene up by deleting an important part," Deb says. "The Jews don't get angry because he announces he is the Messiah. What infuriates them is what he says after they question him."

"What does he say?" Jim asks.

"He angers them by saying that during a three-year drought and famine, the revered prophet Elijah went to stay with a Gentile woman rather than a good Jewish family who is in need. That is what infuriates them."

Later in the film, he is in a large room with dozens of followers. One asks him why he talks in parables, and he explains that the knowledge of the kingdom of God has been given to his disciples, but he speaks to the crowds in parables so they will not understand the message.

"I like this because most people assume there are only twelve disciples," Deb says, "but there could have been as many as seventy."

The film shows the major events in his ministry, his crucifixion, and his resurrection. The film ends showing Christ giving his followers the great commission to teach all nations and that he will be with them always as the film shows his ascension.

As they leave the theater, Deb says, "While almost all of this film is from Luke, the great commission is from Matthew. That's a good addition to the film."

"Mom, do you like the film?" Teddy asks.

"Yes, this is a very accurate film since most of what is shown is taken directly from the Bible. There's very little to argue about. I can give entertainment a four and accuracy a five."

53

Please Don't Let me be Misunderstood

As Told in
The Passion of the Christ
2004

IT'S NIGHTTIME in the garden of Gethsemane when Jesus finishes his prayer, walks back to his disciples and finds them asleep, in this film that focuses on the last twelve hours of the Christ's earthly incarnation. Three of the disciples awaken and ask him what they should do and he tells them to stay with him and watch.

"*Long Hair! Why does he have long hair?*" *Les yells.*

"*The barbers are on strike in California!*" *Jason answers.*

With his friends watching, Jesus prays to his Father to deliver him from what is about to happen in the next few hours. When Jesus is alone again, a man with pasty white skin, wearing a black robe appears and speaks to him, telling him no man can carry the burden he has to carry. A worm crawls out of the man's nose, leaving no doubt that this is none other than Satan.

"*Some saline solution up the nose will clear that!*" *Joe yells.*

"*Satan doesn't appear and discourage him,*" Deb says. "*An angel appears and strengthens him.*"

As Satan observes the agony Christ is enduring while he prays, a snake slithers out of Satan's robe at his feet and winds its way over Jesus' hand. Jesus stands up, and then stomps on the snake.

"**Hey, they help control the rat population!**" *Dave yells.*

"**A snake! Why is he always a snake?**" *Les yells.*

"**Satan doesn't want to be a square peg fitting into a round hole!**" *Jason yells.*

Torches in the distance signify the Temple guards are coming to get Jesus. When they take Jesus back into Jerusalem, he is beaten before he is brought before the Sanhedrin.

"*There's no evidence of this beating,*" Deb says.

Judas, feeling repentant, attempts to have the priests release Jesus, but they refuse, and he throws the money at them. He goes out into the street and sits down against a building when children come to him. The boys offer to help him when they see he is bleeding, but Judas tells them to go away, at which time their faces distort and their appearance becomes demonic.

"*From this point forward, our babysitting fees will double in Jerusalem,*" Charlotte tells Erica.

At sunrise, eleven young boys chase Judas through the countryside. Satan appears with them, and then he and the boys disappear, leaving Judas alone with a dead animal that has a rope around its neck. Judas will use that rope to hang himself.

"*The film is showing Judas being tormented by demons,*" Deb says. "*This doesn't happen in the story.*"

The Jews bring Jesus to Pilate and he asks them why they have punished him before the trial. Since he is from Galilee, Pilate tells them to have Herod judge him. Herod questions Jesus and asks him to perform a miracle. When Jesus remains silent, he decides Jesus is crazy and tells the priests to get him out of there. Herod then mocks him as he is taken out and back to Pilate. By this time Jesus has been horribly beaten for hours.

> "Herod is actually anxious to meet Jesus because of all he had done," Deb says. She then shakes her head after watching all the graphic violence in this film and says, "The film is showing Jesus being brutally beaten continually from the time he is taken from the garden which is not in the story."

Pilate does not want to condemn Jesus, so when the Jews return with Christ, he gives them the choice of freeing Christ or freeing Barabbas. The Jews choose Barabbas, which in Pilate's mind frees him from guilt. When Barabbas is freed, Pilate asks the crowd what he should do with Jesus. The crowd shouts that he should be crucified.

"No!" Pilate shouts, he will have him chastised and then set free. Jesus is scourged as the crowd, including Satan, watches. Satan walks through the crowd, but this time he is holding a baby that has an old man's face, who looks at Jesus, smiling.

> "The rate is triple for babysitting that kid," Charlotte says.

> "I have no doubt Jesus suffered terribly during the scourging," Deb says, "but this continued fixation on graphic portrayals of the Romans and Jews torturing Christ is turning my stomach."

A flashback to the time the woman being accused of adultery is shown. After the flashback, Mary, the woman he saved, watches as the soldiers torment Jesus.

> "I like the way the film has these flashbacks," Deb says. "It not only gives some relief from the sadistic violence, it adds much to the background of the story."

Jesus is crucified and most of the events that happen while he is on the cross are described, ending with an earthquake when he dies. At that point, Satan is now defeated, screaming in the abyss. Jesus' body is lowered from the cross and taken to a tomb. Just before the film ends the rock covering the tomb rolls away, the cloth covering the body collapses, and Jesus, now alive, walks out of the tomb into the morning sunlight.

"Jesus was already out of the tomb before daylight," Deb says, *"but for the most part the film is pretty accurate except the constant violence."*

"Deb, you look pale," Jim says as they leave.

"This film was too violent and intense for my stomach. Let's get home before I get sick."

Once home, while Deb is throwing up, Jim asks her from outside the bathroom door, "How do you rate this film, Honey?"

"Three for accuracy," she gags, then after heaving again into the toilet she manages to weakly say, *"but zero for entertainment."*

"Hey Dad!" Teddy yells, **"Chester and Charley are throwing up in the stable!"**

54

Please Don't Let me be Misunderstood

As Told in
Jesus Christ Superstar
1973

AN OLD BUS drives across a Middle Eastern desert toward ancient ruins. Once there, a group of young actors pile out of the bus, unloading various props for a play, which includes a wooden cross. They put on their costumes for what promises to be a musical. An actor puts on a white robe to the symphonic overture, spreads out his arms, and is introduced to the audience as "Jesus Christ, Superstar."

> *"Long Hair! Why does he have long hair?"* Les yells.

> *"This is the time of the hippies, Les!"* Jason yells.

The musical begins on top of a mountain where Judas is sitting. He stands up and walks down the mountain, singing the opening song about Jesus, as scenes of Christ talking to his disciples and walking through crowds fade in and out.

Mary is comforting Jesus before they make their final trip to Jerusalem. In the second song, Judas speaks ill of Jesus for letting her stroke his hair.

The next song takes place late in the evening when a priest goes to Caiaphas in the Temple where they discuss what they should do about Jesus.

Mary sings "Everything's Alright" as she anoints Jesus with oil, while Judas complains money is being wasted that could be spent on the poor.

"*This is my favorite song in the show!*" Dave says.

"*I love it too,*" Cindy responds.

Jesus enters Jerusalem to the sound of the word, "Superstar," while priests repeatedly sing "He is dangerous." However, the crowd is waving palm fronds and singing "Hosanna" while Jesus sings that word along with them.

"*Uh oh,*" Deb says, "*I don't think Jesus says that word as he enters Jerusalem.*"

A troupe of dancers materialize near ruins in the desert and sing their praise to Jesus, telling him he will get power and glory while Judas watches. Jesus sings back to them that they don't understand why he is here.

Pilate sings about meeting Jesus in the next song and is upset because he will be blamed for killing him. "Jerusalem," a song about merchandise in the Temple and its depravity is performed next, leading to Jesus overturning displays of merchandise, clothing, and postcards, as he drives people from the Temple.

Afterward, in the wilderness, people with all kinds of disabilities ask Jesus to touch them and heal them. He is overwhelmed by their number and finally sings for them to leave him alone. Jesus goes back to their camp where Mary comforts him and, as he falls asleep, she sings "I Don't Know How to Love Him."

"*This song is my favorite Dave,*" Cindy says.

"*I agree,*" he responds, "*but you should never sing this because you sure know how to love me.*"

Judas is in the desert when several tanks come over a hill roaring toward him. He goes to the priests, who are standing on modern scaffolding, and offers to betray Jesus, accepting the bag of coins they offer him. A chorus sings, "So long, Judas," as modern fighter jets fly over him.

"This part is so cool!" Ian says. "I love seeing modern fighter jets and tanks in ancient Judea. Although I guess some things never change."

"It's too bad they don't have WSOD on the air with the Salty Dog, he would fit right in," Avery responds.

"I heard he is covering a grand jury hearing in Jerusalem."

In the garden of Gethsemane, the disciples approach Jesus in the afternoon, singing they always thought they'd be apostles, as they set up an outdoor picnic dinner under the trees, which will be the Last Supper.

"This song is hauntingly beautiful," Cindy says.

"I agree with you about this song," Deb says, "but there are errors here. Does anyone spot any?"

"I know one," Dave says. "That supper is not in a garden, it's in an upper room."

"The film shows each disciple drinking from his own wine glass," Tiffany says. "That's not right either."

"I should make people share wine glasses in my restaurants," Ronald says. "It would save on dishwasher labor."

"One thing is being shown correctly, they are actually using unleavened bread," Dave says. "It's hard to tell if the other films do."

Jesus sings that one will deny him and one will betray him in the next song, and as Judas leaves the disciples, they continue singing about becoming apostles. Jesus walks after Judas, and Judas sings that he does not understand why Jesus let things get so out of hand. Then Judas runs off to see the priests.

"This is another one of my favorite songs in this musical," Dave says.

While disciples sleep, Jesus sings that he wants the cup to be taken away as he walks through the garden, wondering if he will truly make a difference. Images of paintings of Christ on the cross appear as he sings that he will die. Judas kisses Jesus, who is captured while he sings to his disciples not to fight.

As Jesus is led back into Jerusalem, members of the crowd sing questions to him including, "What would you say were your big mistakes?" Jesus faces Caiaphas, who asks him if he is the Son of God, and he sings that he is. While Jesus is being taken to Pilate, Peter denies him three times.

When Jesus appears at Roman headquarters, guards are holding automatic weapons as Pilate walks down the stairs and asks Jesus who he is. Pilate claims Jesus is not in his jurisdiction, and sends him to Herod, who is overjoyed to meet Jesus face to face.

> **"I can't believe this!"** Deb yells for the first time, **"This is the only film that gets this part right!"**
>
> "Gets what right?" Jim asks.
>
> "It's showing Herod is overjoyed to meet Jesus."

Herod sings to Jesus, "Prove to me that you're divine, change my water into wine."

> Ian says, "This Herod is okay, but you've got to admit, Alice Cooper was amazing in the live TV version in 2018."

When Jesus will not perform a miracle, Herod sends him back to Pilate. Meanwhile, Mary and Peter sing, "I think you've made your point now," as they see a vision of him in the wilderness.

Judas, seeing how Jesus suffers, sings to Caiaphas that he did not know how this would turn out. Caiaphas sings back to him that he was paid "pretty good wages for one little kiss" and for him to go away. Judas sings his version of "I Don't Know How to Love Him" as he leaves to kill himself, and then sings he does not know why he was chosen to commit this bloody crime. As he hangs from a tree, voices sing, "So long, Judas."

Again, Jesus is before Pilate, as Caiaphas sings that they have no right to put Jesus to death, so they need the Romans to kill him. As the crowd sings, "Crucify him." Pilate sings back to them, "He's done no wrong, not the slightest thing."

> "Once again, this film is getting it right," Deb says. "Some other films don't show this."

Pilate orders Jesus flogged to keep the vultures in the crowd happy, and Jesus is whipped thirty-nine times.

> "This film is showing him getting whipped thirty-nine times," Deb says. "This deserves another thumbs up. Although the Romans were not limited to thirty-nine lashes."

Pilate tries to save Jesus, but the mob forces Pilate to crucify him. He reluctantly orders Jesus crucified, calling him "an innocent puppet." The words, "Who are you what have you sacrificed" are heard as the title song, "Jesus Christ Superstar" is heard. While this song is performed, images of Jesus carrying the cross and being crucified begin to appear on the screen. Elements of his last hours and his final words are heard before he dies.

This ends the performance. The actors get in the bus and ride away, leaving the cross on top of the hill outlined by the setting sun.

> *As Jim and Deb stand up to leave the theater, Deb says, "I love this film, but it leaves out the resurrection, which is the central focus of Christianity."*
>
> *As they walk out, Jim says, "It's interesting that the two most entertaining movies we watched, this and the Joseph movie, despite being musicals, are among the most accurate films we have seen."*
>
> *"You're right Jim," Chester says. "I rate this film a five for both accuracy and entertainment."*
>
> *"I couldn't agree more!" Charley says.*

55

Please Don't Let me be Misunderstood

As Told in
Jesus of Nazareth
1977 TELEVISION MINI SERIES

JOSEPH, who is unmarried with several sons, is teaching the boys how to do carpentry as this four-part miniseries begins. Anna, Mary's mother, comes to visit him and talks briefly about his upcoming wedding to Mary. The next day Joseph and Mary have a betrothal service. Mary is asleep and wakes up at night to a soft light coming in her window. She walks over toward the window and receives a message that her mother, Anna, cannot hear as she wakes up and watches Mary. Mary accepts the message and responds, "May it be done unto me according to your word." Anna asks Mary who she was talking to, and Mary tells Anna that her cousin Elizabeth is going to have a son in three months, and that he was conceived on the nineteenth day of Tishri.

> "This information dates Christ's birth in the spring," Deb says. "I personally believe the nativity is in the fall."

Mary and Joseph travel to Bethlehem, the three wise men and their entourage also travel there, following a star so bright, its light can be seen during the day.

> *"It is very unlikely there is a bright star that brings the wise men," Deb says. "The star is most likely a planet or conjunction of planets that are in a constellation that is seen at night. There actually is such an event in 3 B.C. involving the constellation Virgo."*

After Jesus is born, Joseph takes the baby to be circumcised. An old man named Simeon is sitting outside, and when he hears Jesus cry, he goes to him and gives thanks that he sees this baby. After Joseph registers for the census, he, Mary and the baby return to the cave and find the three wise men waiting for them. After the wise men present gifts to the baby, they warn Joseph that Herod knows about the baby and they need to escape to Egypt.

> **"I'll take 'Famous Flights to Egypt' for $200,"** *Chester yells.*

> **"Moses leading the Israelites!"** *Charley shouts.*

> **"Wrong, that was from Egypt!"**

> *"Who actually warns Joseph to flee to Egypt?" Avery asks.*

> *"An angel," Ian responds.*

> *"It is very unlikely the wise men visit Jesus in the stable," Deb says. "Herod orders that babies up to two years old be killed, which means that order could have gone out more than a year after Jesus was born and he would no longer be in a stable."*

Part two of the miniseries begins with Joseph dying, as he tells Mary to have his sons handle his business. Later, John preaches at the river and is baptizing people when the next person in line to be baptized is Jesus.

> **"Long Hair! Why does he have long hair?"** *Les yells.*

> **"The barbers are also on strike in Galilee!"** *Jason yells back.*

Jesus bows to his knees in the river, and John pours water on him while a dove circles overhead. John says to the crowd that he hears God tell him that this is "My beloved son in whom I am well pleased."

"John doesn't say those words, a voice from heaven does," Les shouts.

Jesus walks into the synagogue at Nazareth as a rabbi tells the people there will now be "a reading from the prophet Isaiah," and asks, "Who's our reader?" One of the men in the Temple comes forward to take the scroll, but Jesus walks up to the rabbi and takes hold of the scroll before the other man has a chance to receive it.

"Hey, get in line!" *Joe yells.*

"It doesn't happen that way," Deb says. "He is already in the synagogue. He stands up to read when they hand him the scroll, and then he opens it and reads."

After reading the scroll, Jesus announces that in their hearing these scriptures are fulfilled. This statement makes the men in the synagogue furious and they call him a blasphemer. The commotion gets worse when Jesus says, "Blessed is he who is not ashamed of me." This angers them even more as the mob now wants to stone him. When he walks out of the synagogue they are yelling at him and a few of them are actually throwing rocks, but he escapes unhurt.

"He doesn't make that statement to them!" *Les yells.*

"This is all wrong," Deb says. "They don't get angry at his announcement, it's when he tells them about Elijah visiting the gentile widow and healing a gentile leper that they get furious."

"Yeah!" *Les yells.* ***"We don't mind you calling yourself God, but don't be nice to the dirty Gentiles!"***

After Jesus meets Simon, he speaks to the people at Simon's house, telling them parables. During this time, Matthew walks into the house and is told by Simon to leave as other people call Simon names. Jesus is quietly sitting down and starts talking to Matthew, asking him if he can come to Matthew's house for dinner.

"That's not how they meet," Deb says. "Jesus sees him at his office and tells Matthew to follow him."

A crippled man on a stretcher is lowered through the roof of Simon's home as he yells that they are ruining his house. The cripple tells Jesus he has been cursed because of his and his parent's sins. Jesus tells the man his sins are forgiven. When he is challenged about this, he tells the man to walk and he stands up and walks.

"The paralyzed man doesn't talk about his sins," Deb says.

While Jesus is in Capernaum, Herod visits John in prison and asks him what he wants from him, because he is desperate as crowds outside demand that he free John. When he returns to his wife, Herodias tells Herod she was wrong and that Herod should send John away. Herod laughs at this suggestion because he thinks she would have John killed once he is let go.

"Nonsense," Deb says. "Neither of those conversations happen."

It's Herod's birthday. Everyone is having a good time while John is down in the dungeon screaming about their sins. Herod hears that screaming in his head and is terribly disturbed. Seeing this, Herodias talks to Salome and tells her daughter to approach Herod. When he asks Salome to dance, she asks him what he will give her. He responds that he will give her whatever she wants, up to half his kingdom. She dances, and Herod is forced to give her John's head on a platter.

As John is buried, some of his followers talk about engaging Rome in open rebellion. One of those followers mentions about another way to defeat Rome using a different kind of leader named Jesus. That man is Judas Iscariot, the first of several characters introduced in this part of the series.

"There is no mention of Judas being a disciple of John," Deb says.

A crowd gathers as Jesus starts to speak. In that crowd is Joseph of Arimathea and other Pharisees. A wealthy young man comes to Jesus and asks what he must do to inherit eternal life. He is told, "Go and sell all you have and give it to the poor and you shall have treasure in heaven, then come and follow me." After the young man declines that invitation, Joseph invites Jesus to dinner.

"The film leaves out the first thing Jesus says to him which is to keep the commandments," Deb says.

Judas volunteers his services to Jesus as a scholar and a translator. Jesus invites him to join them, ending part two of the series.

Jesus accepts Joseph's invitation and has dinner with him and other Pharisees. During the dinner they discuss the law and in the middle of their conversation, Mary runs into the room shouting and then washes Jesus' feet with her tears. When a Pharisee tells Jesus what kind of woman she is, Jesus rebukes him and says to the woman, "Daughter, your sins, and I know they are many, are forgiven you because of the greatness of your love."

"Another misquote," Deb says. "He simply says to her, 'Your sins are forgiven.'"

Jesus sends out his disciples to teach, and instructs them that whatever city does not receive them, after they shake the dust of that city from their sandals, that city will have it worse than Sodom.

"The film only shows twelve disciples going out," Deb says. "He actually sends out seventy."

"The other fifty-eight had their flights canceled because of overbooking," Dave jokes.

Amos, and some zealots that followed John, attack Herod in the market place and are captured and killed when the attack is unsuccessful.

"Amos and the rebellion are fictional," Deb says.

Before Jesus goes to Jerusalem, he delivers the beatitudes to a large crowd on a hillside and then prays the Lord's Prayer.

"He doesn't recite those to that crowd!" Les yells.

"Les is right," Deb says. "The sermon on the mount is a private conversation with his disciples, as opposed to the sermon on the plain, which is given to a crowd. He also doesn't pray in front of the crowd."

A great many people are walking to Jerusalem as Passover is approaching. While Jesus is walking, a rider comes to him and delivers a message from Martha, the brother of Lazarus. She asks Jesus to come to their house because Lazarus is near death. Jesus sends a message back that he will be there.

Martha meets him when he arrives and she tells him that if he had been there, her brother would still be alive. But she says to him that he can still help. Jesus tells her to take him to the grave, and once there, tells them to take away the stone. He walks to the tomb entrance and prays. He thanks God saying that he is the resurrection, then he looks up and shouts, "Lazarus, come forth!"

Lazarus walks out of the tomb.

> "The film leaves out the fact that Jesus deliberately waits three days before going to the tomb," Deb says. "When he says he is the resurrection, he doesn't say that to God, he says it to Martha."

Judas goes to Jerusalem and meets Zerah, an official in the Temple, and tries to convince him to help Jesus become king of Israel. Right after that, Jesus arrives in Jerusalem riding on a donkey while cheering crowds wave palm fronds. Zerah watches this entry from a porch overlooking the city.

Jesus enters the Temple and overturns the tables of the moneychangers. Zerah comes out to meet Jesus, and asks if he wants to destroy this Temple. Jesus responds, "Destroy this Temple and in three days I will make it rise again."

> "That's taken completely out of context," Dave says. "The Jews are asking for a sign that Jesus is the Messiah."

> "Watching this scene gives no clue he is referring to his body," Cindy agrees.

Barabbas, a revolutionary zealot, approaches Jesus and tries to get him to lead them in a revolt. When Jesus tells Barabbas he should love his enemies, Barabbas departs the pool where they are talking, since he does not receive the message he wants to hear.

> **"Where does this come from?"** Les yells. **"Jesus and Barabbas never have a conversation!"**

> **"Everyone knows all they do is text!"** Jason responds.

> **"But never while driving!"** Dave yells.

> **"And besides,"** Les yells, **"Barabbas is in prison for murder and insurrection!"**

A woman runs through the city being chased by men who want to stone her for adultery, and they trap her near a wall. The priests tell the mob to take her to the master, so they take her to Jesus who is sitting down writing in the dirt with his finger. When the priests ask what should be done to her, Jesus replies, "He among you who is without sin, let him cast the first stone."

Members of the mob drop their stones and walk away.

"This is completely wrong!" Les yells.

"Is Les drunk?" Jim asks. "What is he yelling about?"

"The mob doesn't drop their stones because of what Jesus said, it's because of what he's writing, possibly the names of those who have been with the woman. And yes, Les is probably drunk."

Deb continues, "Another error is that he is writing in the sand before they bring the woman to him."

"Maybe he is making sand temples," Jim jokes.

Chester and Charley start singing, "Love Letters in the Sand."

Jesus spends a great amount of time teaching in the Temple as the days lead up to Passover. During one of the sessions, a Roman centurion asks him to heal his servant. Jesus asks him if he would like him to come to his house, but the Roman answers that if Jesus says the word, his servant will be healed. Jesus tells his followers, "I have seldom found such faith among the people of Israel."

"The actual quote is, 'not found in all of Israel,'" Deb says. "He doesn't use the word 'seldom.'"

Jesus tells him to go home. His faith has healed his servant. As the officer walks away, a few minutes later his friends come and excitedly tell him the servant is healed. The officer is surprised and says, "What?" Then he looks back at Jesus.

"What?" *Chester, Charley, Dave, Joe, and Jim all yell at the same time.*

"He just said he believes Christ!" *Rick yells. "Why is he surprised?"*

After Jesus heals a blind man, there is a confrontation with the Pharisees, who claim the man was just pretending to be blind in order to get money. Jesus preaches against them, calling them hypocrites, making them furious at him. As Jesus leaves the Temple, a riot breaks out as a result of all the discord that Jesus starts by speaking against the priests. Barabbas takes advantage of the commotion and kills a Roman soldier, trying to instigate a rebellion.

> *"The film is making Barabbas a central character,"* Deb says, *"but he's not, plus there is no mention of him killing a Roman soldier."*

That afternoon, outside the city, Jesus and his followers are resting in a grove of trees when Nicodemus comes to warn them they are in danger and to stay away from public places. Nicodemus tells Jesus that he and some other leaders recognize that he must be a teacher from God and asks him to help them see the truth. Jesus responds that he must be born again to see the kingdom of God which confuses Nicodemus, so Jesus explains the Holy Spirit to him, trying to help Nicodemus understand the message he is teaching. This ends the third episode.

> *"Nicodemus comes to Jesus at night, not during daylight,"* Dave says.

> *"Maybe there is a power outage and the lights aren't working,"* Jim jokes.

The final episode begins with priests arguing about whether Jesus is a legitimate prophet or possibly the true Messiah, with those who propose this being shouted down. Caiaphas says the most important thing is to consider that Jesus proclaims himself to be the Son of God, a horrible blasphemy. He asks Nicodemus and Joseph if they believe Jesus is the Son of God and they remain silent.

> *"This conversation is not in the Bible,"* Deb says.

The council decides to take Jesus and question him, but no one knows where to find him. Zerah, thinking of Judas, says he knows a way to find him.

The night Passover begins, Jesus is having his last meal with his disciples, and he tears apart soft bread with air pockets in it, and shares it with his disciples.

> **"That looks like leavened bread!"** Les shouts. **"They would be eating unleavened bread."**

Then he shares wine and delivers a final message to them. Afterwards, Jesus and his followers leave the house to go out in the night to Gethsemane.

> "What about Judas?" Deb asks. "The film isn't including him in this scene. How can he be left out?"
>
> "Maybe he went to the wrong restaurant," Jim jokes.

Judas shows up in the garden of Gethsemane, walks over to Jesus and kisses him, while Zerah watches from the bushes along with the Temple guards. The guards arrest Jesus, waking Peter and the disciples who rush to help him. Peter calls Judas a traitor. The guards take Jesus away to be tried by the Sanhedrin.

> "The film doesn't show Peter cutting off a guard's ear," Deb says.
>
> "You just said an earful," Joe responds.

Judas is very upset, so he runs to the Temple and demands to see Zerah. When Zerah comes out, he tells Judas that Jesus is on trial, and then thanks him for his help, giving him a bag of coins before walking back inside.

> "The film is presenting Judas as a man attempting to help Jesus," Deb says. "That is not true. Satan enters Judas and while being possessed, Judas hates Jesus."

Jesus is taken before the priests, including Joseph and Nicodemus, as well as other priests that sympathize with Jesus, and they argue about whether Jesus is a false prophet. Caiaphas then asks Jesus' "Are you the Messiah, the Son of God?" When Jesus says he is, Caiaphas tears his robe, and Zerah orders that Jesus be taken to Pilate in order to have him crucified.

> Deb comments, "Everyone in that room wants Jesus killed!"

As Jesus is taken away, Peter denies knowing him three times. When dawn approaches, Peter hears the rooster crow.

> "The film doesn't show Jesus telling Peter this will happen," Dave says.

Pilate sends word to bring the delegation to meet him in the great hall, where the priests accuse Jesus of religious crimes as well as sedition by claiming to be the king of the Jews. Pilate questions Jesus briefly and decides he is nothing but a dreamer and orders him flogged as a sign of Roman justice, which will wake him up. Soldiers take Jesus to the courtyard where they whip him. Then the soldiers mock Jesus by putting a robe and a crown of thorns on him and then bowing down to him.

Pilate decides to let the people decide whether Jesus gets crucified by presenting Jesus and Barabbas to them, letting the crowd choose which one should be freed. Friends of Barabbas encourage the crowd to yell for Barabbas, silencing anyone who yells for Jesus, resulting in Pilate sentencing Jesus to be crucified. Pilate then walks back inside the building.

> **"Pilate considers him innocent!"** Les yells. **"He isn't even shown washing his hands!"**
>
> **"There are no paper towels, only those stupid blow dryers,"** Jason shouts.
>
> **"If he had to use one of those, he would have to wipe his hands on his toga afterwards to get them dry!"** Joe shouts.
>
> "Les is right," Deb says. "Pilate does not want to have Jesus crucified. The series actually hides that. In addition to that, there is no evidence that anyone in that mob wants to save Jesus."
>
> "I think the timing of the whipping is also wrong," Dave says as he hears Deb talk to Jim.
>
> "In what way?" Cindy asks.
>
> "The series shows, scourging, Barabbas, and then crucifixion, when it is actually, Barabbas, scourging and then crucifixion."

Jesus is nailed to the cross, and the series shows what happens until he dies. Later, women walk to the tomb, waking up the guards who are sleeping, and ask permission to go to the tomb so they can anoint the body.

> "They get around pretty good for men who are so frightened they are like dead men," Deb says of the Roman guards. "The film is also showing the women arriving during daylight, however when Mary first comes to the tomb, she is alone, and it is still dark."

The guards allow this, and as they all walk toward the tomb they pass two men who tell them Jesus is not there.

> *"They don't see the two men until after they reach the tomb,"* Dave says.

The soldiers arrive first and see the tomb open and that the body is gone. A soldier throws the burial cloth to the ground and as they walk away, the women enter the tomb.

> **"Hey, be careful with that!"** *Jason yells from the projection booth, "That's going to be a holy relic. Now it will have to be dry cleaned."*

The disciples are in a house when Mary delivers the news about the tomb and that she has seen the risen Jesus. With the exception of Peter, they don't believe her.

Zerah, priests, and Roman soldiers come to the tomb and Zerah says that he was afraid the disciples would steal the body. The guards tell him this is impossible because the guards and the priests were there all night. Zerah goes into the tomb and when he sees the burial cloth lying on the slab he says, "Now it begins. It all begins."

> *"I like this part,"* Deb says. *"While it is fictional, it powerfully conveys a great deal of truth."*

As the series ends, Jesus is in a room with his disciples, explaining to them all that has happened. He tells them he is about to leave again, and that they must travel out and make disciples of all nations. Peter asks him not to leave, but Jesus tells them, "Don't be afraid, I am with you every day till the end of time."

> *Deb and Jim are quiet as they get in the truck before Jim asks her what she thinks of this version.*

> *"There are some really good things, despite the long hair, but the series still omits some things and changes others. I certainly enjoyed the great cast in this film. I just wish they didn't have so many errors. This is a good movie that could have been a great movie."*

> *"So, let's hear the ratings,"* Chester says.

> *"The entertainment is definitely a five, but I can only give accuracy a four."*

56

Please Don't Let me be Misunderstood

As told in

The Greatest Story Ever Told

1965

THREE MEN, called magi, ride across the wilderness on camels, accompanied by an entourage of guards and servants. They are traveling to Jerusalem in order to speak to Herod the Great. When Herod finds out they are looking for a baby that will be the future king of Israel, Herod asks his advisors about this future king. They tell him the king will be born in Bethlehem. Telling the wise men this, he allows them to continue their search, telling them to report back to him where the child is, so he too, can go worship the boy.

As they travel toward Bethlehem, snow can be seen on the hillsides.

> "Most scholars believe the birth occurs in the fall or the spring," Deb says. "It's very unlikely the birth is in the winter."

As they ride toward this bright star, shepherds in the field also see the star and take their sheep down to a Bethlehem cave, where the newborn baby is laying in a manger.

"This is another myth," Deb says. "There is no mention of shepherds seeing a star. I'll have a handout about this on Sunday."

The shepherds watch the wise men present their presents to the newborn king, and also notice that mounted riders are on the top of a hill, observing the area. As the wise men are leaving, Joseph sees one remaining rider on the hilltop and tells Mary they must flee.

"Joseph is told in a dream to flee," Deb says. "He doesn't see a rider on a hilltop."

Years later, travelers in Egypt tell Joseph of Herod's death, so he returns with his family to Nazareth.

"An angel tells Joseph in a dream it is safe to return, not some travelers," Deb says.

In the wilderness, the voice of Charlton Heston, in the role of John the Baptist, cries out for repentance as he preaches and baptizes people in the Jordan River.

"Heston is perfect as John the Baptist," Jim says.

A man in a white robe appears, and John, being startled asks, "Who are you?"

"He's your cousin!" Les yells.

Chester and Charley start singing "Who Are You," a seventies song by The Who.

Jesus, played by Max Von Sydow, walks up to John and says to him, "Baptize me, John." John determines that Jesus is the Messiah when he finds out he is from Bethlehem. John baptizes him while all the people on shore, wearing identical white robes, watch what's happening.

"Whoever has the white robe concession in Judea must be making a fortune," Ronald says.

John's voice can be heard for miles from the valley below as Jesus walks up to the surrounding barren hills in the wilderness for his period of temptation. Hours later Jesus is still climbing and now it is dark, but John can still be heard preaching from below.

> "Whoever has the loud speaker concession also must be making a fortune," Tiffany comments.

> "I like the way you think, Tiffany."

> "A twenty-minute sermon on Sunday morning is five minutes too long for me," Jim says. "This guy has been at it for twelve hours. There must be a lot of people sleeping by the River Jordan."

At the top of the mountain, Jesus enters a cave which is occupied by Satan, who appears as an old man. After Jesus refuses the food that Satan offers him, they go out on the ledge outside the cave and look out over the wilderness. Satan offers Jesus the kingdoms of the world if he would pay homage to him, but Jesus refuses that offer and rebukes Satan every time he speaks.

> "Satan comes to Jesus, not the other way around," Deb says. "And he doesn't do that until Jesus has fasted for forty days. The film is showing it on the first day of the fast."

> "This version has Jesus in the express lane," Joe answers. "He has less than ten temptations."

> "The film also doesn't show Jesus ordering Satan to depart," Deb continues.

Later, Jesus is back at the river while John is preaching and baptizing. Riders arrive and their leader tells John, "You are ordered to stop in the name of the Grand Sanhedrin." John refuses, and calls them hypocrites as they ride off. Jesus walks over to John and tells him he is going back to Galilee.

> "None of that happens," Deb says.

As Jesus leaves the river, Judas, Andrew, John and Peter ask Jesus if they can join him. Jesus tells them to come with him and he will make them fishers of men.

> **"You can call me Simon, you can call me Simon Peter, but you doesn't have to call me Peter!"** Les yells, mimicking a beer commercial from the seventies.

> "Les is right, he is not referred to as Peter when he meets Jesus," Deb says. "Also, he doesn't become a disciple this early."

On their journey to Galilee, they stop and talk under a bridge as Roman troops ride over the bridge. While Jesus teaches his disciples, some people walk across the bridge above them, as other people walk across the creek behind them, not taking the bridge.

> "What's that all about?" Joe asks. "Why don't those guys use the bridge?"
>
> "It's a one-way bridge," Dave answers.
>
> "Maybe they are afraid of heights," Joe says. "That bridge must be is at least six feet high."
>
> "If I was there, I would set up a toll booth," Ronald adds.
>
> "I bet it would be a great toll booth!" Tiffany jokes. "But who would pay for it Ronald?"
>
> "The Palestinians," he answers.

As Jesus speaks, a man stops on the bridge and kneels over to hear what Jesus is saying. He joins them and tells Jesus his name is James, who becomes his fifth disciple.

As they continue their journey to Galilee, Jesus and the five disciples are welcomed into a beautiful home owned by Lazarus. Jesus talks to the home owner and asks if he would give up all he owns and follow him. Lazarus asks who would do such a thing. In response, Jesus looks at his five disciples, and they stand up to leave.

> "This is more fiction," Deb says. "This encounter with Lazarus is never mentioned, but I like how the film sets up the friendship between Jesus and Lazarus."

John is dragged to Herod, where a shouting match breaks out, culminating in John telling Herod he will burn in hell and calls his queen an adulteress. Herod tells John he will be put to death and there will be no pardon for him, to which John replies there will be no pardon for Herod either. John is then taken to prison.

"This is completely wrong," Deb says. "The main reason Herod has John arrested is because John speaks out against him for taking his brother's wife to be his queen. The film makes it appear this is the first time John talks about Herodias."

It's nighttime in the wilderness when Jesus finds out that John has been arrested. In the following weeks and months, his ministry continues to grow while he preaches and gathers more disciples. News of this comes to Herod, who has John brought to him so he can ask about Jesus. John answers Herod's questions, but his answers give Herod the impression that Jesus is gathering an army.

"This conversation doesn't happen," Deb says.

Jesus is asked to come to Capernaum. He arrives there at the same time Nicodemus and other priests sent by Caiaphas, arrive for the purpose of observing his activities. Almost all of the people in Capernaum are wearing off-white robes. The notable exception is a woman wearing a low cut bright red dress, who is being chased by a crowd of men.

"Packaging is a very important part of advertising," Ronald posts. "She sells her product well!"

The woman is dragged to Jesus and shoved to the dirt in front of him. When Jesus asks what she has done to be treated this way, a man in the mob says she was caught in the act of adultery.

"If she wasn't wearing that outfit she might not have been caught!" Joe yells.

"The Pharisees bring her to him, not a mob," Deb says.

Jesus kneels down and asks her if this is true. When she is silent, he stands up and says she is guilty of adultery.

"How can he say that? She exercised her Fifth Amendment right against self-incrimination!" Dave shouts. "She never says a word!"

"Also," Cindy adds, "Jesus never says she is guilty of adultery."

A man speaks out saying, "The law calls for her to be stoned." Jesus picks up a rock, faces the mob saying, "Let him among you who is without sin cast the first stone."

> "Well, Hollywood, there you go again," Dave jokes to Cindy, sounding like Ronald Reagan. "You don't show him writing in the dirt."

> "What do you mean?" she asks.

> Deb turns around to answer Cindy, "These movies don't make it clear that Jesus writes something in the dirt that makes all the priests walk away, possibly the full text of the law and the names of the men who had sex with her, which would result in them being stoned along with her under the law."

No one in the crowd takes the stone, so he throws it to the ground and asks the girl her name. She responds that she is Mary of Magdalene.

"The woman is not named," Les yells.

As Jesus continues his ministry, the priests send word back to Herod about the miracles he performs and that the people are calling him a king. Herod visits John in his cell and asks about Jesus. John tells him that Jesus is the one prophesied to be born in Bethlehem. Herod tells John that his father killed all those babies, but John tells Herod that Jesus, as a baby, escaped to Egypt.

"You lie!" Herod says and then tells John he came to say farewell because John is going to die this night.

> "This is another error," Deb says. "Herod has no idea John will be beheaded until Salome makes her request. Herod knows John is a just and holy man and protects him."

A girl dances for Herod while he goes into his throne room and sits down. John's last word, "Repent!" is heard, followed by the sound of a beheading. Herod then orders the Nazarene to be arrested.

> "Herod does not order Jesus to be arrested after John is beheaded," Deb says.

Jesus is standing on the top of a mountain among his sitting disciples, preaching the beatitudes to a large crowd. After that he prays the Lord's Prayer, pausing at each verse for the crowd to recite each verse he speaks.

> *"Well Hollywood, there you go again," Dave jokes to Cindy again. "He does not teach the beatitudes to the crowd. He is speaking privately to his disciples and they are all sitting down."*

> *"Once again," Deb says, "another film shows him praying the Lord's Prayer. He's not praying! He's giving them an outline of how to pray."*

Jesus and his followers are sitting by a brook when he asks, "Who do you say that I am, Judas?"

> *"He doesn't ask Judas or Thomas that question," Deb says.*

Judas responds, "You are a great leader, the greatest teacher of all."
"And you, Thomas?" Jesus asks.
"You are Jesus of Nazareth, that's all I know," Thomas answers.

> **"Wow!"** Les yells, **"You've sure learned a lot!"**

Peter then says that he is the Messiah.

Jesus is warned about Herod, so he leaves and goes to Nazareth. The people there have heard about him so they ask him to show them a sign. The people say to Jesus, as he stands by a water trough, "If you are the Messiah, say so plainly." Jesus quotes Isaiah and says that prophecy is about him. Then one man says, "That's blasphemy!"

> **"You just asked him to say so plainly!"** Les yells. **"What more do you want?"**

Someone says, "Bring old Aram." They get old Aram, who is blind and say to Jesus, "Make him see." When Jesus refuses to heel old Aram, the people get mad and start saying, "Stone him!" As Jesus walks away from them, someone throws a rock and hits him in the back.

> *"This whole scene is so wrong!" Deb says. "First of all, the encounter at Nazareth is at the beginning of his Ministry not days before he makes his final trip to Jerusalem. He quotes Isaiah to them in a synagogue, not at a water trough. They don't challenge him to perform a miracle, let alone would he refuse to perform one by healing old Aram, who,*

by the way, doesn't exist. And he doesn't stay at Nazareth after this incident, or go back to his mother's house."

"Slow down Honey!" Jim says.

"I probably should concede this event is recorded later in another gospel, but it's generally accepted this event starts his ministry."

Lazarus, who is sick, comes to Nazareth and warns Jesus they are coming to arrest him. As Jesus leaves, he sees old Aram sitting by the water trough, leans over, and touches his eyes, healing him.

"Herod does not order him arrested anytime during his ministry," Deb says, "but I like how they show Lazarus being ill at this time."

By the river, just after sunset, Judas asks Jesus a question. Jesus answers him by leading the disciples in a responsive prayer in which he recites the Lord's Prayer, with the disciples chanting each verse after he speaks it.

"There is no description of him ever leading a responsive prayer," Deb says.

Word comes to Jesus that Lazarus is dead and he tells the disciples they will go to Bethany. When asked, "If Lazarus is dead, what need is there to go now?" Jesus responds, "My Father's work is there."

"The film doesn't show him saying Lazarus is asleep," Deb says.

They arrive in Bethany as guests are still mourning Lazarus. Martha approaches Jesus and sadly asks why Jesus did not come while Lazarus was still alive, while Mary, her sister who is a few feet away, joins them.

"Mary is in her house when Martha talks to Jesus," Ian says.

Jesus walks alone to the tomb while everyone watches, including old Aram, who stands with his hand on a boy's shoulder. Reaching the tomb, Jesus prays to his Father, "Come from the four winds, O breath, and breathe upon this man that he may live."

"Where does that come from?" Dave asks.

"That's from the Old Testament," Deb says. "But there's no mention of Jesus referring to the winds when he raises Lazarus. He will later refer to them as coming during the resurrection."

Jesus walks to the tomb and opens the door, softly saying, "Lazarus."

"He does not open the tomb!" Les yells.

"Maybe he's checking to see if he has the right tomb," Jason responds.

He then shouts for Lazarus to come forth. After more than a minute of vocalise, Lazarus walks out from the tomb.

"Sorry to keep you waiting," Joe yells. **"Am I late?"**

"He actually tells them to roll away the stone, and Martha tells him he should not have them do this because of the stench," Deb says. "Then he prays and after that, shouts for Lazarus to come forth, and Lazarus emerges from the tomb."

To the sound of the "'Hallelujah Chorus," three men who witness this event, including old Aram, the healed cripple, and Van Heflin playing the role of a witness, walk the short distance to Jerusalem and announce this miracle in front of the city gate to the soldiers looking down from the wall.

"This is a beautiful scene, especially with this music," Deb says. "It's too bad this part is fiction."

"I'd give them a pass this time," Jim says. "It is a beautiful scene."

The scene is so powerful everyone in the audience is completely quiet and still. That is, everyone except Charley.

"I have a headache, Jim!"

Word of this miracle comes to Caiaphas in the Temple while Jesus is getting his feet washed as the next part of the film continues. Caiaphas is not in a welcoming mood when he hears the crowd cheering Jesus and orders him arrested. Meanwhile Jesus walks into the Temple, turns over tables, and calls it a "den of thieves." He then says, "It is written in the scriptures, 'I desire mercy, not sacrifice,'" as he starts releasing animals from their cages.

"He doesn't say that when he enters the Temple," Deb says. "He is not saying they should not sacrifice animals. Those laws are still in effect until he is sacrificed."

Once in the Temple, Jesus speaks to the people, but Roman guards come into the courtyard and drive the people out. That night, the disciples prepare tables for supper while Judas leaves them and walks toward the Temple, being watched by Satan as he passes. Judas offers to give Jesus to them if they promise not to hurt him.

"That's not in the story," Deb says. "He never asks for such a promise."

Jesus goes to Gethsemane and prays. While he is praying, Judas is receiving silver coins and then leads the guards out to capture Jesus. Before they arrive, Jesus walks back to his disciples and finds them asleep as a line of torches approach in the dark with Judas leading the soldiers coming to arrest Jesus. Judas almost steps on Peter's feet as he walks over to kiss Jesus.

"How can Peter still sleep after dozens of soldiers march into the clearing?" Chester asks.

"It's all that bread he ate as well as all the wine he chugged," Charley responds.

Peter wakes up and yells at Judas taking out his sword, but Jesus tells him to put it away, allowing the guards to take him from his disciples.

"Did you notice what they leave out?" Deb asks.

"The ear?" Jim responds.

"Yeah, the film isn't showing Peter cutting off the soldier's ear."

Jesus goes before the Sanhedrin. The first witness is old Aram who testifies Jesus restored his sight.

"Old Aram isn't there!" Les yells.

Deb looks at Jim. "No one testifies in favor of Jesus that night."

Jesus remains quiet but finally speaks when they ask him about committing blasphemy. He tells them to question those that have heard him about the things he said. Nicodemus interrupts and asks why he was not informed of this tribunal. In response, Caiaphas turns and asks Jesus if he is the Son of God, to which Jesus responds "I am." Nicodemus sadly sits down.

> *"There's no evidence Nicodemus is there, let alone he speaks out," Deb says.*

Caiaphas takes Jesus to Pilate, who asks him which god is his father. Jesus responds, "The Lord our God is one" which leads to a short theological discussion.

> **"He never says that to Pilate!"** *Les yells.*

Pilate finds no fault in Jesus and orders him taken to Herod, who asks Jesus to perform a miracle, but Jesus remains silent. When Jesus won't respond to Herod, He is given a crown of thorns and taken back to Pilate who gives the crowd assembled the choice of a prisoner who should receive amnesty. People shout for Barabbas, so Pilate orders Jesus crucified and has his hands washed as Jesus is led away.

> *"This movie really distorts Pilate's character," Deb says. "He knows Jesus is an innocent man and does not want him crucified."*

Jesus carries his cross through Jerusalem and in another part of the city Judas prepares to commit suicide. At the point Jesus can no longer carry the cross, a man steps out and helps him carry it through the gates and up the hill.

> *"The man doesn't volunteer," Deb says.*

In the Temple courtyard, Judas walks up the steps to a flaming altar, stands before the flames with his arms stretched out, and falls face first into the flames.

> *Joe, Dave, Ronald and Jim stand up holding scoring placards with numbers between one and three, judging the quality of the dive.*

> *"Judas hangs himself," Deb says. "He doesn't burn himself like a monk protesting against the South Vietnamese government."*

"So, he doesn't run amonk," Dave laughs.

Jesus is lifted up on the cross, and the last hours of his earthly life are shown. Darkness covers the land when he asks God why he has forsaken him. He then cries out, "I thirst." A sponge is held to his lips, but he turns away and says, "It is finished." He says, "Father into thy hands I commend my spirit," and then he dies on the cross.

> "He does not refuse the vinegar," Deb says.

Loud thunder is heard, followed by pounding rain, and the centurion says, "Truly, this man was the son of God."

> "Is that John Wayne?" Chester asks.

> "Yes, he rode my grandfather once while leading cavalry," Charley responds.

> "Undoubtedly this is the smallest role he ever has in a film," Dave says.

Caiaphas asks Pilate to place a guard around the tomb, because he is afraid the body will be stolen by the disciples and people will proclaim the Messiah has risen. Roman soldiers seal the tomb, rolling a stone across the entrance.

To the music of the Hallelujah Chorus, dawn lights up the area, a Roman soldier awakens and sees the rock has been moved exposing an empty tomb. Mary, remembering the prophecy about the three-day period, tells the disciples she is going to the tomb. When she arrives at the tomb, an angel played by Pat Boone tells her he is not there and asks why she seeks the living among the dead.

> "This is a small error," Deb says. "Mary does not go to the tomb thinking Jesus may have risen."

Caiaphas, hearing about the empty tomb, says, "Incredible, in any case the whole thing will be forgotten within a week."

In the final scene, Christ talks to his disciples and then ascends to heaven as the film ends.

> *Outside the theater, Jim, Deb, Chester and Charley talk to Ian, Avery, Charlotte, Erica and Teddy before the kids walk to the diner to get hamburgers.*

"I heard there were a lot of famous actors in that movie," Avery says, "but I don't recognize any of them."

"There were," Jim answers. "The actors include Max Von Sydow, Charlton Heston, Jose Ferrer, Dorthey McGuire, Claude Rains, Martin Landau, Telly Savalas, David McCallum, Sidney Poitier, Carrol Baker, Angela Lansbury, Victor Bueno, Sal Mineo, Richard Conte, Roddy McDowell and Shelly Winters, as well as Pat Boone and John Wayne. All of them were very famous."

"I don't recognize any of those names," Erica says.

"Just like I don't understand Phil's jokes," Avery says. "Who is Nikita Khrushchev?"

"One name is familiar to me," Teddy says. "Richard Conte was a gangster in 'The Godfather.'"

"You know what individuals are missing in the film?" Deb asks everyone.

"No," Erica answers.

"Angels," Deb answers. "Except Satan and the angel at the tomb, angelic beings don't show up in this film. Angels are not shown telling the shepherds to go to Bethlehem. Instead of an angel telling Joseph that Herod is dead, travelers give Joseph the message. An angel is not shown ministering to Jesus after forty days in the wilderness, nor does an angel appear to him at Gethsemane just before he is arrested."

"Why do they omit all the angels?" Charlotte asks.

"Their union is on strike," Jim jokes. "But they do want to appear in a baseball movie. However, their shop steward tells them that have to wait two thousand years."

Jim and Deb load the animals in the truck and, as they drive home, Jim asks Deb for her ratings.

"This is a great film with great actors, so I rate the entertainment at five, but the most I can give accuracy is three."

57

Please Don't Let me be Misunderstood

As told in
King of Kings
1961

DECADES BEFORE the birth of Christ, the Romans take over Judea and install Herod as a puppet ruler in the region. Years later, Joseph and his pregnant wife, Mary, travel to Bethlehem because of a decree that people must return to their home town to be taxed. When they arrive they cannot find a place to stay until an innkeeper provides a stall in the stable for Mary, played by thirty-eight year old Siobhan McKenna, to deliver her baby.

"A thirty-eight year old woman is playing the Virgin Mary?" Deb comments. "Really?"

"She was waiting for the right man," Tiffany says. "It took me fifty years to meet my Ronald," as she kisses him on the cheek.

While shepherds are sitting with Joseph, three wise men bring gifts for the baby.

"**The wise men don't bring gifts that night!**" Les yells.

"Those aren't gifts!" Jason shouts. "These guys are multi-level marketers selling baby products. The actual wise men show up much later!"

"The Magi arriving at the manger is a common myth," Deb says. "They visit them up to two years later."

"Deb, have you noticed that Jason is making way more comments than he has in the past?"

"Yeah Jim, I have. He seems to be having a great time lately, I wonder what's going on in his life?"

Herod hears about the birth of a possible new ruler and orders Lucius, a Roman officer, to kill all the newborn males in Bethlehem. The Roman refuses, but Herod reminds him that Caesar told him he is to obey Herod's orders. Joseph awakes from a dream and tells Mary they must escape to Egypt, so they leave just before Roman soldiers arrive and kill the babies.

"This film shows Joseph's dream correctly," Deb says. "Several films don't."

Herod later dies making it possible for Joseph and his family to return home safely. Years later, Lucius is confirming the census and stops by Joseph's home and discovers that Jesus was born in Bethlehem twelve years earlier. Lucius then realizes that the boy escaped being killed. He considers this, but orders a soldier to go to the next house, telling Joseph to get the boy registered. Twenty years later the next events are shown.

"*If twenty years pass since he was twelve then that would make him thirty-two when he starts his ministry,*" Les shouts. "*He is thirty when he begins his ministry.*"

"Hey Les," Joe yells. "*You don't understand the new math!*"

John the Baptist, played by Robert Ryan, is baptizing people at the Jordan River, when the next person in line to be baptized is Jesus, played by Jeffrey Hunter.

"*Long Hair! Why does he have long hair?*" Les yells.

"*Because he loves longhair music!*" Jason replies.

Jesus walks up to John, kneels down in the water, getting his robe wet just above the knees and looks up at John, who is holding a cup of water in his right hand. John recognizes Jesus, and puts his left hand on the top of his cousin's head. Jesus stands up and the two men stare into each other's eyes until Jesus turns and wades away.

"Hey John, you forgot to baptize him," Les yells.

"He never even poured the water on him!" Dave yells.

"John was thirsty and drank the water," Joe joins in.

"It's a new form of baptism," Jason shouts from the projection booth. *"It's called 'knee immersion.'"*

"That's a knee slapper, Jason!" Rick shouts.

"Hunter just had his hair done," Cindy tells Dave. *"I can understand why he wouldn't want it to get it wet."*

Pilate arrives in Jerusalem and meets with Lucius, telling him to place golden reliefs of the emperor on the walls of the Temple. John preaches against this outside of Herod's residence while Herod is entertaining Roman guests with wine and food. The guests, including Pilate, go out on a porch and a verbal exchange follows, resulting in Lucius bringing John inside the palace. Once inside, John accuses Herod's wife of having sex with the captains of Assyria and the young men of Egypt, which results in Herod ordering Lucius to put John in the dungeon.

"What's wrong with middle-aged men of Egypt?" Ronald posts.

"Just like WSOD, she covers the Middle East from Assyria to Egypt," Tiffany comments. *"What a loony tune!"*

"The film does a pretty good job with this part," Deb says. *"However, there is no mention of Herodias being a slut."*

Sick people are being healed and blind men are receiving sight as Jesus begins his ministry. Barabbas and Judas, hearing about these miracles, seek out Jesus to see if he will help them with their rebellion against the Romans.

"There is no rebellion against Rome mentioned anywhere in the Gospels," Deb says.

When they get close to Jesus, a woman runs down the street being chased by a crowd of people who want to stone her. When Jesus sees what's happening, he steps between her and the crowd and asks what she has done. A man tells Jesus the woman has been caught in adultery and must be stoned. Jesus picks up a rock and approaches the mob and says to them, "Whoever is without sin should cast the first stone." A man starts to throw a stone, but Barabbas stops him. Everyone else in the crowd drops their rocks and walks away.

> "Not only does the film not show Jesus writing in the dirt," Deb says, "but it shows Judas and Barabbas are friends who just happen to be in the crowd. This is really a stretch."

Jesus goes to visit John in prison. Lucius is in Herod's dungeon eating a meal when Jesus walks into the prison, and they briefly talk. Lucius realizes their paths have crossed before, including the time he was supposed to have killed Jesus as a baby. Remembering this, he allows Jesus to visit John.

> "Why does Lucius leave the party and go to the dungeon to eat?" Cindy asks.

> "Herod's wife is a terrible cook," Chester says without turning around.

John is chained in a cell when he sees the shadow of a man on the wall. He turns around and sees Jesus through the bars of the window high above him. With great effort, he climbs the steep incline of the wall to the window, reaches out his hand to Jesus, and as they grasp each other's hand, he asks Jesus for his blessing. They look at each other, then losing his grip, John rolls back down the incline to the floor of the cell. The scene fades out.

> **"He forgot to bless him!"** Jason yells. **"And shouldn't the Almighty be able to keep his grip on poor John?"**

> **"Not only that!"** Les yells. **"He never goes to Herod's prison in the first place!"**

> "Jesus does not go to a prison," Deb says. "He actually has John's disciples take a message to John."

Jesus continues his ministry, performing many miracles and adding disciples, including Judas. Lucius reports the miracles to Pilate, who questions if Lucius is mocking him and throws the report into a pool. By this time, Lucius is beginning to wonder if the miracles are actually happening. He visits John, who thanks him for treating him well and then asks one more favor: go to Jesus and ask him, "Was it your coming that was foretold or are we to expect another?"

"John sends disciples," Les yells. *"Not some Roman officer!"*

"He should Google that question!" Jason shouts. *"Not rely on hearsay."*

Pilate hears that Jesus is going to deliver a sermon, so he sends Lucius to hear what Jesus says in order to determine if he makes any seditious statements. A huge crowd gathers to hear the Sermon on the Mount with people from all over the territory flocking to this site, including Pilate's wife and Barabbas.

> *"I'm surprised Les isn't yelling,"* Deb says. *"Christ says the beatitudes privately to his disciples on top of the mountain after he goes up there to get away from the crowds."*

Jesus is sitting alone under a tree, when a disciple comes and tells him the crowd is all gathered and waiting to hear him speak. From the valley below, people see Jesus appear on the top of the mountain, spread out his hands and begin to recite the beatitudes.

> Suddenly Joe yells, *"Hey Splash, call 911, Les just stood up, grabbed his chest and passed out!"*

"Jason, stop the film!" Rick yells.

> *The film stops and the lights come on as paramedics rush into the auditorium and attend to Les. But they soon realize he just had a terrible attack of acid reflex.*

"Is he okay?" Deb asks Teddy.

> *"He's fine Mom. They poured some antacid into him and he's back at his seat, just softly shaking his head and saying, 'no.'"*

After Jesus finishes the sermon, he walks into the crowd and takes questions. Unlike modern press conferences, questions are asked one at a time, and Jesus answers them individually, giving many of the lessons contained in the gospels.

"I like this scene," Deb says. "It covers a lot of material without sounding preachy."

When a member of the crowd asks Jesus to teach them to pray, Jesus responds by praying the Lord's Prayer in front of the crowd.

"Hey Les," Jason yells. **"Don't watch this!"**

"Once again, a film is showing Jesus praying in front of a crowd," Deb says. "He wouldn't do that."

Jesus enters Jerusalem on a donkey and people wave palm branches as the city prepares for Passover. Meanwhile, Barabbas is handing out swords. Once Jesus goes into the Temple, Barabbas climbs a ladder and shouts, "Long live Judea!" Armed insurgents rush into the street and start fighting Roman soldiers, pushing them into their fortress.

"Push them back, push them back, way back!" *Charlotte and Erica do a cheerleading routine as Splash blows a whistle.*

The rebellion fails and Barabbas is captured.

"There is no rebellion," Deb says.

Judas joins Jesus and the other disciples when Jesus tells Judas that he must quickly do what he is going to do. Judas leaves, and Jesus tells the others to join him in his final meal where he gives them bread and wine. After the meal, Jesus takes his disciples to the Mount of Olives, where he is betrayed by Judas who leads soldiers there to capture him.

After the Jews find Jesus guilty, he is taken to Pilate who will act as a judge to determine if Jesus should be killed, flogged, or set free. When he asks Jesus what he has to say in his defense, Jesus remains silent. Pilate then says, "In view of the continued and obstinate silence of the accused the court appoints Lucius Catanus, advocate of the defense."

In the back of the theater laughter breaks out.

"They're going to give him a lawyer!" Les yells.

"This could become a TV series," Jason laughs. **"Jerusalem Legal!"**

Pilate sends Jesus to Herod, but Herod sends him back to Pilate, who then orders Jesus to be scourged in order to make him confess.

> *"That Lucius is a terrible lawyer! The defendant is being coerced to confess."* Les yells. *"Anyway, the whipping is to placate the Jews!"*

> "I agree," Deb says. "Pilate argues on behalf of Jesus, knowing he is innocent. The scourging is to satisfy the crowd in hope that that he would not have to crucify Jesus."

After Jesus is scourged and taken away to be crucified, Lucius escorts soldiers to the dungeon where the two thieves are waiting their fate. Barabbas is freed and joins Judas to watch the crucifixion. Jesus is nailed to the cross and when Mary comes to him, he says to her, "Woman, behold your son."

> *"He's referring to John when he says that!"* Les shouts, *"Not himself!"*

> "Talk about taking something out of context," Deb says. "He tells his mother that John, who is standing next to her, will fulfill the role of her son after Jesus is gone."

Hours later, Jesus says his final words, "Father, into your hands I commend my soul."

> "I have looked at over fifty translations," Ian says, "and not a single one uses the word 'soul.'"

Lucius then says, "He is truly the Christ."

> "Another error," Ian adds. "The centurion doesn't use the word, 'Christ.'"

Jesus is put into the tomb, and at sunrise Mary, who is sleeping by the tomb, wakes up and sees the tomb is uncovered.

> *"Mary walks to the tomb before daylight!"* Les yells.

> *"Maybe she sleepwalks like Joe!"* Jason shouts back.

> *"It's a good thing she didn't walk into that popcorn machine!"* Dave yells.

She peers in and sees that his body is missing. Days pass, during which Christ is seen by various people and then seen a final time by the shore of the Sea of Galilee. He commands his disciples to go out into the world, ending the movie.

As Rick is closing the theater, he sees Deb and her family walking to the truck.

"What are your thoughts on this film, Deb?"

"I think it is a typical film from that era, so I rate the entertainment at three, but it is so full of mistakes that I rate the accuracy at one. If it did not have those battle scenes I would give it a two."

58

Please Don't Let me be Misunderstood

As Told in
Son of God
2014

AS RICK ARRIVES to open the theater, he notices the town's one ambulance parked in front. It's Paul, the paramedic.

"What's up?" Rick asks.

"Just being prepared in case there's another heart attack report tonight."

"Oh, like we thought about Les."

"Or any additional issues. I saw this made-for-TV movie, and it's sure to cause some elevated heart rates and high blood pressure."

"That bad, huh?"

"I'm just wanting to be prepared."

This motion picture is a consolidation of the final episodes of the television miniseries, *The Bible,* which includes stories of Jesus. Excerpts from earlier parts of the series are shown as the narrator tells the audience that Jesus was with all the characters featured in earlier episodes such as Noah, Moses, and David. It begins with John on Patmos beginning a narrative of the life of Jesus.

Wise men follow a star and join shepherds in Bethlehem immediately after Jesus is born.

> *"Two! Two! Two errors in One!"* Charlotte, Erica, Avery, and Teddy chant in the entrance to the auditorium.

> *"They're probably right,"* Deb says. *"It is most likely the celestial sign the wise men see was not a single bright object, but was actually an alignment of stars and planets. It is also unlikely they visited Jesus on the night of his birth."*

Jesus is now an adult, making his first appearance walking over barren hills down to the shore of the Sea of Galilee where Simon is bringing his boat in after an unsuccessful night of fishing.

> *"Long hair! Why does he have long hair?"* Charlotte, Erica, Avery, and Teddy again chant in the entrance to the auditorium.

> *"You beat me to it kids!"* Les shouts.

> *"Okay,"* Rick says. *"Three of you need to get to work."*

As Jesus wades into the water, he asks Simon to help him get into the boat. When asked what he is doing, Jesus tells him they are going fishing and says, "Peter, just give me an hour and I will give you a whole new life." They go out and catch baskets of fish on every cast. Jesus tells Peter to join him and he will make him fishers of men.

> *"That's not his name yet!"* Les shouts. *"Simon's name is not Peter when they meet. Jesus changes Simon's name later."*

Other men join Jesus as he begins his ministry, and they follow him as he walks into a village where a rabbi is talking about the law to some villagers. Seeing Jesus, the villagers all get excited and leave the perplexed rabbi, following the new rabbi to an open space in the village where he tells them the parable of the mustard seed. During the teaching, a crippled man is brought to Jesus. He tells the man his sins are forgiven. The rabbi, who has followed the crowd, challenges Jesus about him forgiving the man's sins. Jesus responds to the rabbi by telling the man to get up and walk, which the man does.

As Jesus walks through the city, followed by the rabbi, they both see Matthew collecting taxes. The rabbi tells Jesus he should have no contact with the tax collector, but he responds by telling the parable of the Pharisee and the tax collector. He approaches Matthew and invites him to join his followers.

> "That's not how Jesus recruits Matthew," Deb says. "He doesn't tell him a parable, he simply says, 'Follow me.'"

Jesus teaches his followers, reciting the Beatitudes as they walk through the hills. When they stop and rest, Mary asks him, "How should we pray?" Jesus answers, "Like this," and prays the Lord's Prayer as everyone bows their head.

> "This is another presentation that repeats this mistake," Deb says. "He isn't praying when he recites the "Lord's Prayer," he is providing them with an outline of how to pray. Notice he says, 'In this manner,' not, 'In these words.' He just finished telling them not to pray using vain repetitions. He's not going to turn around in the next verse and give them a repetitive prayer to pray."

A woman is dragged into the village square, after being found guilty of adultery. The rabbi tells Jesus the law requires her to be stoned and asks Jesus what he believes. Jesus picks up a stone and walks over to the crowd saying, "I'll give my stone to the first man who tells me that he has never sinned." Rocks drop on the ground, except the one the rabbi holds, and the crowd walks away from the woman.

> "This is another film that doesn't show Jesus writing in the dirt," Deb says. "If you don't understand that it is this action that causes them to drop the stones, then you cannot understand the story."

As the film continues, the disciples sail across the lake and a storm comes up. High waves and lightning have the disciples fearing for their lives. However, they soon see Jesus walking on the waves toward them in the night. Jesus holds his arm out toward the boat and says, "Peter, don't be afraid, come." Two steps into his walk on water, Peter sinks like a stone, but Jesus pulls him up out of the water.

"While I like the imagery, this scene is wrong," Deb says. *"Peter asks Jesus to command him to come to him."*

Jesus is walking through a town when Martha approaches him, telling him that her brother is dead. He responds, "Show me the tomb." Once he is at the tomb, workers pull rocks away from the place where Lazarus is buried. As Jesus enters the tomb, Martha says, "He's been dead four days."

"He never walks into the tomb!" Les shouts.

"He stands outside the tomb and yells, 'Lazarus, come forth,'" Jason yells from the projection booth.

"There was a single stone against the tomb, not a pile of rocks!" Dave calls out.

Inside the tomb, Jesus walks behind the dead body and quietly says, "Lazarus, I am the resurrection and the life. Anyone who believes in me, even if he dies, he will still have life." Jesus leans over Lazarus and breaths on his head. Lazarus opens his eyes and walks out of the tomb.

"He doesn't say those words in the tomb to Lazarus; he says them to Martha before he goes to the tomb!" Les shouts.

In Nazareth, Mary is kneading dough, when her son comes to town and goes to the synagogue. Mary rushes there, arriving in time to hear him recite Isaiah and announce to them he is the Messiah. The rabbi yells at him, saying that his healing is the work of demons.

"Mary is not going to be kneading dough on the Sabbath!" Les yells.

"Jesus reads from Isaiah in Nazareth at the beginning of his ministry," Deb says, *"not a few days before they crucify him."*

Jesus goes to Jerusalem, a city on a barren hill where there are no trees to be seen, riding on a donkey, while the crowd waves palm fronds in the air.

"Where do they get the palm branches?" Joe yells. **"There is not a tree in sight!"**

"*They buy them online!*" *Dave yells back.*

"*The film doesn't even show an olive grove!*" *Deb says.* "*Clearly, there were trees and vegetation there.*"

Jesus walks into the Temple, and seeing the commercial activity that is taking place, turns over the moneychanger's tables. When he cries out that they have turned a house of prayer into a den of thieves, Nicodemus comes out of the crowd and yells at Jesus, "Who are you to tell us this?"

"*What?*" *Les screams.* "**Nicodemus would never have challenged Jesus like that!**"

"*He's nothing but nice to Jesus when he meets him secretly at night!*" *Jason yells back.*

Nicodemus walks up to Jesus and says, "We teach law not you." Jesus tells Nicodemus that he and the priests are hypocrites. Later, inside the Temple, Nicodemus asks Jesus if they should pay taxes to the Romans.

"*No, you idiot!*" *Dave yells.* "***You pay them to the IRS!***"

"***You can even use a credit card!***" *Joe shouts.*

As Jesus leaves the Temple, he sees a little girl, and leans over to her saying, "Do you see all the great buildings? Not one stone of this place, not one stone, will be left standing."

"*He doesn't stop and say that to some little girl,*" *Deb says.* "*He says that to his disciples in response to what they are saying about the Temple.*"

Caiaphas hears about this comment and is alarmed that Jesus says he will destroy the Temple. Judas meets with Caiaphas, who asks Judas to bring Jesus to him so they can talk quietly. Judas, thinking Jesus will not be hurt, agrees to do so and asks what he will receive in return. Malchus, the Temple guard, hands him a bag of coins. In the meantime, Nicodemus goes to Jesus and talks to him privately, apparently having changed his mind about Jesus.

That night, disciples climb stairs to a room where they will have supper with Jesus, who says a prayer before everyone starts eating. As a disciple tears bread apart, there are obvious holes in the middle of the bread.

"That looks like leavened bread," Ian says.

"Why do you say that?" Avery asks.

"Leavening agents cause air pockets to form in the dough, causing it to rise, leaving holes. This would be a huge mistake!"

That night, Jesus is brought before Caiaphas and the other priests and charged with blasphemy. They find him guilty, even though Nicodemus argues against the verdict. Malchus announces to the crowd that Jesus has been found guilty of blasphemy and threatening to tear down the Temple. Then they put Jesus in jail.

"I'm in the jailhouse now," Chester starts singing.

"Don't worry!" Joe yells. "Judas has a twenty-four hour bail bond service just around the corner!'"

"Jesus was never put in jail!" Les screams.

Pilate visits Jesus' cell, questions him, and goes back to Caiaphas, telling him that Jesus is guilty of being deluded but nothing else.

"Pilate says he finds no fault in this man!" Les shouts. "Being deluded would be a fault!"

"We can't sacrifice this lamb!" Joe yells. "It's deluded! It thinks it's an elephant!"

"Is it the elephant in the room?" Rick shouts.

"Les is right," Deb says. "Pilate's actual statement means that Jesus is the equivalent of an unblemished lamb. This pronouncement completes the inspection of the lamb, a process which the film doesn't address."

When Caiaphas insists that Jesus be executed, Pilate tells him he will allow the people to decide if Jesus or Barabbas should be put to death. Then he orders his guards to give Jesus forty lashes to teach him some respect.

After Jesus is scourged, Pilate allows people into a plaza where the crowd can now choose to save either Jesus or Barabbas, however the priests select which people go in, insuring that Barabbas is saved.

"This is backward," Deb says. "The people choose to free Barabbas and then Christ is scourged."

The crowd yells to free Barabbas and crucify Jesus, so Pilate orders Jesus to be crucified.

"Wait, Pilate!" Ian yells. "**Always wash your hands before crucifying.**"

Jesus and the two thieves are lead off to their execution. As Jesus struggles to carry his cross, Caiaphas asks what will be the inscription on the cross. Pilate answers, "Put in Aramaic, Latin and Greek, 'Jesus of Nazareth, the king of the Jews.'"

"I'll take 'Ancient Signs' for $500," Chester shouts.

"**For five hundred dollars, what languages were on the sign on the cross?**" Charley yells back.

"**Greek, Latin and Hebrew.**"

It's still morning when Jesus struggles up the hill carrying his cross while priests are slitting the throats of lambs.

"**They don't do that yet!**" Les yells. "**The first lamb is slain at three o'clock—the exact same time Christ dies!**"

Just before an earthquake shakes the land, Christ dies after taking his last breath. The veil in Temple collapses to the floor like a shower curtain slipping down a wet tile wall.

"**The veil is torn!**" Deb yells. "**It doesn't fall to the floor!**"

"**Good call, Deb!**" Les shouts back.

The centurion sticks a spear in Jesus.

"**He does that before he dies!**" Dave shouts.

Jesus' body is put in the tomb. Three days later, in bright sunlight, Mary visits the tomb and finds the boulder moved and the body missing.

"**She goes out there while it is still dark!**" Les shouts.

Jesus appears and tells Mary to tell the others that he is alive. She relays the message and Peter goes out to the tomb and returns to the other disciples, telling them Jesus is back. Jesus then appears to the disciples and tells Thomas not to doubt. Forty days later, to the sound of thunder, Jesus vanishes on a hilltop.

The film ends with John finishing his narrative. As he walks outside he sees Jesus, waiting for him.

> *"I love how the ending shows Jesus waiting for John," Deb says. "I can give this film a four for entertainment but only a two for accuracy."*

59

Please Don't Let me be Misunderstood

As Told in
Killing Jesus
2015 TELEVISION MOVIE

*I*T'S FRIDAY AFTERNOON and football practice is just over at Lilly High School. Splash runs up to Coach Bravos and asks if he can take his helmet to the theater for something he plans to do that night.

"No problem," Coach says. "I'll be there too!"

Herod is having a terrible nightmare. He wakes up in a rage after the prophet Isaiah tells him in that dream a child has been born in Israel who will be a far greater king than him and that he will destroy Herod and his seed.

His son, Antipas, hearing his father, rushes to his chamber where Herod tells him to wake the Sanhedrin and for them to meet with him immediately. A priest tells Herod the dream was a result of sorcery and that Herod should go to the Temple to have the sorcery neutralized, so Herod follows his advice and worships in the Temple. The Temple leadership is pleased that there can now be more unity in the land, as a result of his attendance in the Temple.

"I don't remember reading that in the Bible," Avery says.

"You didn't," Ian says, "it's not there."

A procession of wealthy men on camels enters the courtyard in Herod's palace while Herod watches them dismount and be greeted by his son. The men, who are from beyond Parthia, have their servants bring gifts to Herod and ask to speak to him.

That night, as Herod entertains them, one of the men tells Herod that an alignment of the stars has brought them there. When Herod asks if they foretell a great event, the man tells him that Israel's Messiah, prophesied by Isaiah, has been born. Herod tells them to find the child and when they do, tell him where the child is, so he can venerate him.

"This is really good," Deb says. "Most films show them following a bright star."

The procession leaves Herod's fortress, and when they reach Bethlehem, the visitors give gifts to the young child, who appears to be about two, while many people in the village watch them meet the family.

"The film gets this right too!" Deb says. "Almost all films show the wise men visiting the stable when Jesus is born."

That night, Joseph tells Mary that they need to leave because their child's life is in danger as a result of the attention he receives. Mary doesn't want to leave, saying, "But our home!"

"Doesn't an angel warn Joseph in a dream?" Jim asks.

"He does," Deb answers. "Another error is that Bethlehem is not their home, Joseph has a home in Nazareth."

Zechariah, a Temple priest who is visiting the family along with his wife Elizabeth, Mary's cousin, sees Joseph preparing to leave Bethlehem while it is still dark and asks him where they are going. Joseph tells him they are getting away from Herod, as he prepares to flee to Egypt. Zechariah tells his wife they will also leave with Joseph and Mary. Early in the morning, Joseph, Mary, the baby, Zacharias and Elizabeth leave Bethlehem, which can be seen in the distance behind them.

"Hey Zechariah! Aren't you forgetting something?" Les shouts.

"What's he forgetting?" Jason yells back.

"They're forgetting to take John the Baptist, their two-year old son."

"I was old enough to be on my own at two," Chester yells, *"he'll be fine."*

In Egypt, ten years later, Joseph meets a trader from Jerusalem. During their conversation, Joseph tells the trader that he heard years ago that Herod had died and asks the trader who is ruling the area. The trader tells Joseph that Rome has a governor ruling Judea, and Herod's sons remain as tetrarchs. Joseph puts his arm around his son and says to Jesus that maybe it's time to go home.

"I thought an angel tells Joseph that Herod is dead making it safe to return, so he returns immediately," Cindy says. *"Not ten years later."*

"Maybe they are a couple who are always late," Dave answers.

"I know a dog like that," Chester says. *"He was late getting to his master and little Tommy died in a well."*

Twenty years later, Pilate and his wife Claudia are arriving at Jerusalem in a gilded cart escorted by Roman soldiers as he tells her about the conditions of the province where he is starting his new assignment as governor. Meanwhile, in Nazareth, Jesus walks home to greet Elizabeth who is visiting his family.

The film stops and is replaced by words projected onto the blank screen. Teddy, wearing his football helmet, walks on the stage, faces the audience, raises his arms as if signaling a touchdown, instructs the audience, "At the count of three, one two three!"

The entire audience screams the words written on the screen, **"Long hair, why does he have long hair!"**

"Good job, Splash!" *Coach Bravos shouts to Teddy as he is leaving the stage.*

That night at dinner, Elizabeth tells them that her son, John, is unpopular in the Temple, so he preaches in the wilderness. One of Jesus' brothers comments that Jesus argues with the scribes and the Pharisees in the synagogue, so Elizabeth responds that he and John would find kinship.

"If Jesus is being argumentative, why would the priests give him a scroll to read just before he announces his Ministry?" Avery asks.

"They wouldn't," Ian answers. "This is not accurate. But the film does introduce a brother, which is a good thing."

In the wilderness, the voice of John the Baptist can be heard at dawn. As Jesus walks over a hill, he sees a large crowd gathered to hear John preach and watch him baptize people in the Jordan River. Jesus walks through the crowd to the riverbank and when John turns and sees Jesus, he announces to the crowd that the "Lamb of God" is there with them. Jesus gets a confused look on his face and asks John, "How could you know me?"

"We're cousins!" Les shouts.

"Hey Les!" Jason shouts. "**You forget, his parents abandoned him when he was two!**"

"**He must have had the terrible twos!**" Rick shouts.

"Yeah," Dave yells. "**Every time Elizabeth corrected him, he yelled at her, 'Repent!'**"

"Obviously, John would never have talked to his mother like that," Deb says. "But just as obviously, John's parents would never have left him alone to visit Mary and Joseph."

"Even if Jesus returns to Nazareth at the age of twelve, how could John not know who his cousin is?" Deb asks. "He has been back in Judea twenty years."

Chester looks at Charley, "Charley I need some help with a math problem."

"I'm on it," Charley says.

"Jesus goes to Egypt at the age of two, so that's two years, right?"

Charley stomps his right hoof, clomp, clomp, "Yes, that's two years."

"Next, he spends ten years in Egypt, right?"

Charley nods his head, "Yes."

"How many years is that?"

Charley stomps his hoof ten more times. "Twelve," he answers.

"The next scene is twenty years later, before he is baptized and starts his ministry," Chester says. "How old would Jesus be now?"

Charley stomps his hoof twenty times.

Someone in the back of the audience yells, **"Will you stop that?"**

"He would be thirty-two."

Deb interrupts, "The film is simply getting it wrong Chester. Jesus starts his ministry close to his thirtieth birthday."

After the crowd leaves, Jesus and John talk privately. John tells Jesus that voices in the desert told him that his cousin is the Messiah, and Jesus responds that he is just a carpenter. After a very short conversation, Jesus realizes he might actually be the Messiah.

"He knew who he was when he was twelve!" *Les shouts.*

He tells John that he will also go into the desert and listen to the voice of God, then he asks John to baptize him. After John baptizes him, Jesus walks to a desert mountaintop.

"So, the film is telling us that Jesus goes into the desert to listen to the voice of God!" Deb says. "That's wrong, a main purpose of him going into the desert is to reject the voice of Satan, who will tempt him."

Jesus goes up to the top of a mountain, looks up and prays, then briskly walks back down the mountain.

"It's too bad there's no snow!" Joe yells. **"He could ski down the mountain!"**

"That's it?" Les screams. **"He's just up there twenty-eight seconds?"**

"Hey Les," Jason shouts. **"There are snakes 'DEMONstrating' in the street about Satan being written out of this scene!"**

"Jesus spends forty days in the wilderness," Deb says. "At the end of that time he is near death."

After leaving the mountain, Jesus walks to the Sea of Galilee and talks to a fisherman named Simon. His boat is in bad shape, so Jesus uses his skill as a carpenter to help him repair the boat and then they go fishing. Out on the lake, the water is perfectly calm and the net is in the water with the floats forming a half circle about four feet from the boat. As Jesus looks at the scenery, Simon wiggles his fingers in the water.

"Do you expect the fish to jump in the net?" Dave yells. He then turns to Cindy, "You're supposed to throw the net out over the water, not just hope fish jump out of the water into the net."

"Maybe they need a fishing guide," she comments.

Jesus prays and the net becomes filled with fish.

Back in town, Jesus starts preaching in the street, telling a few people who gather that the kingdom of God is within them, but those who listen quickly walk away. One of the disciples says, "A bountiful catch, maybe nothing more."

"The term 'Kingdom of God' can have multiple meanings," Deb says. "But the film misuses the term badly. It is not something that comes from inside a person, as it implies, it's something that comes to a person, or that a person enters."

At a campfire in the wilderness, Jesus talks to Nicodemus about being born again. He tells Nicodemus, "I'm here to speak of a light coming into the world. And those who live by the truth can enter this light."

"Another error!" Deb says. "Their conversation begins with discussing the Holy Spirit and then Jesus declares he is the light that has come into the world. The film implies there is a separate light other than Jesus."

Two men come to the campfire and tell Jesus that John is now Herod's prisoner. Jesus gets angry and says he feels like he wants to get a sword and fight this injustice.

"Mule feathers!" Chester yells. **"He never says he wants to fight!"**

"That's right Chester," Deb says. "He says just the opposite."

While John is still in prison, Jesus and his followers enter the Temple where he tells the people in the courtyard, "Not one stone will remain upon the other, and that it all will be thrown down." He continues his message by calling the priests vipers, and adding, "Destroy this Temple and in three days I will raise it up again. Destroy this marketplace," as well.

"Someone needs to sweep up these mulefeathers!" Chester yells.

"I've got a broom and a long-handled dustpan!" Teddy shouts.

"While Jesus does say those words, the context and even the meaning are shown wrong!" Deb says. "First, he does not say these things while John is in prison. But even worse, when he says, 'Destroy this Temple and in three days I will raise it up again,' the film makes it appear he is making a revolutionary statement to a crowd. That's not true, he is referring to his body, not that building, plus he says that in a private conversation with the disciples. The film appears to repeat the same lie that false witnesses will tell the Pharisees before he is crucified."

After leaving the Temple, Jesus is on top of a cliff overlooking a pond where he preaches the beatitudes to a crowd and then prays the Lord's Prayer in front of all the people gathered there. The crowd then shouts, "Amen."

Cindy says to Dave, "Our minister says Christ tells us not to pray in public."

He answers, "No Cindy, he tells us not to pray in Publix."

"Cindy is right," Deb says. "Jesus tells his disciples to not pray in public. Not only that, but the beatitudes are given privately to his disciples on top of a mountain where they have gone to get away from the crowd below. If you read the passage, you will see they are all sitting down, which the actor does not do. When is the last time you ever watched a healthy minister sit down outdoors to deliver a sermon to a crowd?"

"I did hear about a minister who was sitting in the woods at scout camp," Jim says, "but I don't think he was delivering a sermon."

The Sanhedrin is meeting and the next item on their agenda concerns a woman who is brought to them for committing adultery. They decide to stone her and drag her outside the city gate. Jesus and his disciples are walking toward the city when he sees what is happening, so he hurriedly walks toward the men who are taking her to a pit to be stoned.

Jesus jumps into the shallow pit and stands next to her. A priest pronounces her guilt and under the law of Moses she is to be stoned, and then asks Jesus if he denies "the law revealed on Mount Sinai?" Jesus does not answer the question. The priest then asks Jesus his opinion on what is about to happen.

Jesus responds, "Any among you who is without sin, let him be the first to cast a stone at her."

Everyone drops their rocks, however a priest tells Jesus, "We are the law. We will see you accused, judged, and punished for this."

> "First of all, the Pharisees bring her to Jesus. He doesn't come to her," Deb says. "Once again, another film doesn't show him writing in the dirt. This story is all about hypocrisy, it's not about doing away with the law."
>
> Jim laughs, "If he was writing the names of the men who had sex with that woman, you can be sure Bill Clinton's name is not on that list."
>
> "I never had sexual relations with that woman!" Dave jokes.

Jesus is staying at the home of Lazarus before Passover. While they are eating, John and James ask if they can sit next to him when he is on his throne and tossing evil people into eternal flames.

> **"There goes crooked Hillary!"** Ronald yells. "Oh sorry Tiffany, I forgot how much you love her."
>
> "Almost as much as you love Donald Trump!"
>
> "I guess it's time to point out another error," Deb says. "Their mother—not them—asks if they can sit next to Jesus. Plus, there is nothing mentioned about condemning people to hell."

Jesus tells his disciples in the kingdom of God there are no thrones, no crowns, no rule of nations.

> **"Well, it's clear that John has not had his Revelation yet!"** Les yells.
>
> "Clearly, God will sit on a throne," Deb says.

"So who will rule the nations with a rod of iron?" *Joe yells.*

"That's good, Joe," Dave says. "It looks like you've been learning. By the way, have you quit smoking?"

"Yes, it's been two weeks now. By the way, I see you and Cindy are a real item. Congratulations, she's a good catch."

"Plus, I can see now!" Cindy says. "Except when Chester stretches."

"Do my hooves and ears block your view?" Chester asks.

"You go right ahead and stretch Chester, I'll peek around."

Jesus rides into Jerusalem on a donkey and is greeted to shouts of "Hosanna" and people waving palm branches before him. As Jesus walks into the Temple, he says to the priests walking with him, "I'm told of a great rabbi who was asked to recite the Torah while standing on one leg. He said, 'Do not unto others as you would not have them do unto you. This is the true wisdom of the Torah. The rest is all commentary.'"

"That guy Moses is a great commentator!" *Dave yells.*

"Doesn't he write the famous ten comments?" *Cindy laughs.*

On the next day, he returns to Jerusalem, walks into the Temple, and overturns the tables of the money changers, shouting, "Down with the money lenders!"

"Jesus turns over the tables the first day he comes to Jerusalem, not the second," Deb says, "and he never shouts, 'Down with the money lenders.'"

Jesus grabs a man and tosses him aside so he can release birds the man is selling.

"I never knew he was a wrestler!" *Joe yells.* **"Maybe he should lift him over his head and body slam the guy!"**

He throws coins to the crowd. When Temple guards come down to restore order, Jesus tells the guards to stop, and they do.

"Those guards are incompetent!" Ronald posts. "They might as well have surrendered! Losers!"

Having stopped the guards. Jesus leaves the Temple, telling Caiaphas he has done what he came to do.

That evening, the Last Supper begins with Jesus washing the disciple's feet. When Peter objects to that, Jesus tells them, "I wash your feet to show that no master is greater than his servant."

> "This is a terrible distortion," Deb says. "Jesus just got done telling them he is their Lord and teacher."

After the supper, Judas is leading the guards to Gethsemane where he identifies Jesus with a kiss. The guards surround Jesus, but Peter slashes the ear off of one of them, Malchus, before Jesus tells Peter and his other followers to escape.

> **"Are you forgetting something?"** Les yells.
>
> **"The film doesn't show Jesus healing the guard,"** Jason answers.
>
> "It's not in the actor's contract," Dave jokes. "The guy is still walking around without an ear."

It's sunny in the desert where Judas wakes up the next morning and sees a young man bringing goats on the path to Jerusalem. Judas gives him the thirty pieces of silver to buy the young man's rope so he can hang himself with it, telling him he will have enough money to buy a nice horse.

> "He actually throws the coins to the priests in the Temple," Deb says.

Pilate orders Jesus to be scourged. After the whipping, Caiaphas tells Pilate to put him to death, in order to prevent the deaths of many more people. Pilate reluctantly agrees, and Jesus is ordered to be crucified.

> "The film leaves out Pilate giving the crowd a chance to free Jesus or Barabbas," Deb says.

Jesus carries the crossbeam through the city toward Golgotha, and Malchus, a Temple official, mocks him all the way. They have a brief exchange which includes Jesus telling Malchus that he loves him.

> "While that conversation could have happened, it doesn't take place," Deb says. "However, I do like that addition."

Jesus is nailed to the cross and the two thieves who are being crucified with him are off to his right!

> *"They don't have room to put him in the middle!"* Dave shouts.

> *"Isn't that Malchus in the middle?"* Joe shouts.

> "He is crucified between two thieves," Ian says. "This is a huge error!"

> "Do you think Mary might be in front of the wrong cross?" Avery jokes.

The young man who sold the rope to Judas does buy a nice white horse with the coins. As he walks home, he sees the body of Judas hanging from a tree. He shakes his head in pity and keeps walking past the tree.

> *"He gave you a good price for the rope!"* Joe yells. *"Can't you at least take his body down?"*

> *"It's not in the sales agreement!"* Ronald shouts.

At Golgotha, Jesus speaks his last words, "It is finished." Then a Roman sticks a spear into Jesus' side, finalizing his death. It is still bright daylight when Nicodemus tells Mary he has brought a shroud to wrap around Jesus for his burial.

> "The film leaves out several things that Jesus says in his final hours," Deb says. "It also omits the crowd that comes to watch the crucifixion."

> "They take him off the cross late in the day," Dave adds. "They get him in the tomb just before sunset."

Three days after the crucifixion, Mary and others go into the tomb and discover the missing body. Instead of weeping, she smiles and laughs, apparently knowing Jesus has risen.

> *"Mary is very upset the body is not there!"* Les yells. *"She doesn't start laughing!"*

In the final scene, Peter is alone on the Sea of Galilee fishing. He puts out the net, prays, and fish mysteriously appear, bubbling on the surface of the water inside the net. Peter prays again that he will become a fisher of men, and shouts to the others on shore that Jesus is back.

"I guess I don't have to ask what you think of this film," Jim says to Deb as the lights come on in the theater.

"It is entertaining, so I give that part a three, but it is very inaccurate, so the most I can give accuracy is a one. I am very depressed, let's go home and get cheered up by watching the evening news."

60

Please Don't Let me be Misunderstood

WHAT DIFFERENCE DOES IT MAKE?

"EIGHT FILMS!" Deb says as she starts the Sunday school lesson, "That's how many films we watched about Jesus in the past couple of weeks. While we are in the theater watching these movies, we see quite a few contradictions with what the Bible says. Do any of these contradictions make a difference? Let me start. Does anyone notice that in *The Jesus Film*, the circumcision is described as being 'a week later'?"

"Yeah, they should say it occurs on the eighth day," Ian answers. "This is an important day in the Bible."

"Do you have a handout on this?" Dave asks.

"Yes, but it is a very short one," Deb answers.

Ian raises his hand, "When Jesus announces his ministry by reading Isaiah, the films show the Jews getting mad because he claims to be the Messiah, but that's not the reason they get mad. They get mad because Jesus tells them they do not have an exclusive relationship with God."

"The presentation of the 'Lord's Prayer' is shown wrong in every film," Dave says. "We are not supposed to pray in public or recite a prayer litany. We are to pray in a manner he gives us."

"These films all give the wrong impression about why the people don't stone that woman caught in adultery," Avery says. "The films give the impression that people are now free to break the law."

"Let's talk about snakes," Cindy says. "I can't tell you how many times I hear people say they won't believe in any religion that teaches Satan is a talking snake. This depiction makes believers look like idiots. It does make a difference."

I would like to comment on the Mel Gibson film, The Passion of the Christ," Ian says. Many of the extra biblical scenes are from "*The Dolorous Passion of our Lord Jesus Christ* by Anne Catherine Emmerich. According to *The Catholic Encyclopedia* she exhibited 'strange powers.' There certainly are some strange things in this film."

"Those are all good points," Deb says, "and give us a lot to think about. I have several other handouts today including, when Jesus is born, where Jesus is born, what is Jesus wearing right after he is born, who the shepherds are, hidden messages in the parables and the last handout deals with what day Jesus enters Jerusalem before Passover. I also have a leftover handout from the movies on Esther that dovetails with the final handout. I hope you enjoy them. Since this is the last class for awhile, I will not see some of you until fall, but I will see several of you next Saturday at Dave and Cindy's wedding. Have a great summer and thanks to all of you for going to the movies with us!"

This is the End
The Doors 1967

AN EPILOGUE

ONCE IAN AND AVERY finish registering for their sophomore classes, they walk downtown to the candy store for some coffee.

"Hi Cindy. We are really looking forward to your wedding Saturday!" Avery says when Cindy comes to take their order.

"Hopefully it won't rain," she replies. "I would hate to see Chester and Charley get soaked when we ride away in the carriage they will be pulling."

"Even if it does rain, I'm sure everything will be beautiful."

"I understand class registration is today, have you two decided on majors?"

"My dad's a CPA and Mom is an attorney," Avery responds. "I am going to major in accounting and hopefully pass the CPA exam and then go on for an MBA. After that, I want to go to law school and become a tax attorney."

"It sounds like you will have several years in post graduate work."

"That she will," Ian responds. "In my case, I plan to go to seminary after graduation and become a television evangelist. Salty over at WSOD is hiring Les to do a Sunday morning Bible study television show, and I will be helping him with it until I finish my undergraduate work."

"What will you do with all that money you are going to make?" Cindy jokes.

"Maybe, I'll buy a nice diamond for a special girl," Ian responds.

"Hey look who's coming in!" Avery says.

"Hi guys," Splash smiles as he, Erica and Charlotte walk into Cindy's store dressed for beach volleyball. "We were just practicing for a tournament that is coming up soon."

"Have you guys decided on schools?" Avery asks.

"We made our choices," Erica answers. "I will be going to DePauw in Greencastle and Splash is headed to Indiana."

"How far is IU from Greencastle?"

"It's less than an hour, so I'll be able to see all the home games. After football season is over, we should be able to get together most weekends."

"Charlotte," Avery says. "I hear Rick gave you a promotion."

"Yeah, he sure did. Rick is going to sponsor Joe for the Senior's golf tournaments this summer. He's going to be Joe's caddy. They will be going all over the country for tournaments, so Rick is making me the assistant manager to run the theater while he's gone. When summers over, I am really looking forward to my senior year at Lilly, but I'll miss cheering for Splash."

"In the meantime, I guess we'll all see each other this weekend at the wedding," Ian says. "It should be fun."

On the other side of town, Ronald and Tiffany are planning their own wedding.

"Tiffany," Ronald says as he hugs her, "I want this to be the finest wedding in the history of the world, even better than anything that the royal family has done. In order to do that, we are going to go to England. I have arranged to have the ceremony take place at St. George's Chapel in Windsor Castle on Valentine's Day."

"How many guests can we have Ronald?"

"We are going to have 800 guests, four hundred for each of us. I'm budgeting fifty million dollars for this event, and guess what? I'm going to set aside one million dollars for you to have cosmetic surgery, plus a half million for the pantsuit of your choice. Nobody knows how to put on a wedding better than I do!"

They kiss and leave the office. Ronald has an appointment to meet with his lawyers and Tiffany has a houseguest coming to spend a couple of days with her. About an hour after she gets home Abigail, a friend who is a private investigator Tiffany has known since college, comes in to give her the news.

After they hug, Tiffany asks, "What did you find out?"

"Nobody has less money than Ronald Rink has, he is completely broke."

Tears well up in Tiffany's eyes, "Well I guess all I can say is, at this point, what difference does it make? I love him, so I'll still marry him."

Dave and Cindy's wedding is stunning, and when the seven-foot groom leans over to kiss his four-foot-eleven bride, he actually has tears of joy coming down his cheeks. Even Ronald is crying. As Dave and Cindy greet the guests, Dave is surprised to see the familiar face of his ex-wife Caryn, and she is accompanied by Jason.

"What a pleasant surprise Caryn, I didn't know you were coming!"

"You Betcha, I wouldn't have missed this for the world. I'm so happy for you."

After Dave introduces his ex-wife to Cindy, Caryn surprises Dave again.

"I thought you might enjoy this day even more after I tell you that Jason and I are engaged to be married this fall. So, you will no longer have to worry about paying me alimony!"

"Oh, that didn't bother me."

"I think it did. You see, I have attended most of these Bible films sitting in the projection booth with Jason. I heard your comments. By the way your comment about Victor Mature as Samson still paying alimony was hysterical! I was afraid you'd hear me laughing."

"So, where's the wedding?"

"Well Dave, as you know, I have always been a maverick, so I decided to have it on a fishing boat off the West Coast of Alaska within sight of Russia."

"We'll also go fishing," Jason interjects a joke. "Just for the halibut."

"Well I am really happy and I hope the two of you will be happy."

All the guests gather outside the church as Jim arrives in a carriage pulled by Chester and Charley, along with four other horses.

Deb climbs on with Jim, and the wedding party gets into the carriage.

After applause, there is silence as Jim prepares to get the animals going. Suddenly Charley blurts out, **"I don't have a headache, Jim!"**

Everyone cheers.

Thinking about last night, Jim and Deb look each other in the eyes and smile before Deb shouts, **"Giddy up!"**

*This book is dedicated to the memory
of my wife Nancy,
who passed away in 2019,
and my son Justin,
who passed away in 2017.*

Why I Wrote Holy Wood

AS WE WERE ENJOYING a glass of wine a couple years ago, my wife Nancy asked me if I am afraid to die. I was able to provide an answer based on what happened to me on October 29th, 2015. My answer was... I remember my last memory before the head-on collision was being a mile from the scene of the crash.

I was in a daze as I looked around the inside of the car. I knew something had happened, but I didn't know what. I noticed blood on the inside of the door and realized I had been in an accident. Then the extreme pain in my chest hit me. I remembered hearing that heart attacks hurt, so my next thought was I am having a heart attack and that I was going to be dead in a few seconds. What really bothered me was that I was going to be alone when I died. Because of that feeling I was incredibly grateful that when Nancy died in 2019, I awakened at three in the morning and held her as she passed away. She did not die alone.

When I realized I was not going to die immediately, I also realized I better get out of the car in case it catches on fire. Despite the excruciating pain, I crawled out of the car on my back. The first face I saw was that of an off-duty paramedic who was in the car behind me. He stayed with me until the ambulance came and also called Nancy. That evening, a sheriff's deputy came to my hospital room and the first thing he said to me was, "I assumed you were dead."

A few months later, a minister and his wife stayed with us. Richard's wife, Beth said to me, "There's a reason you survived that accident. The fact that a paramedic was in the car behind you and the very fact you survived makes me believe God has plans for you."

Back in the early nineties I wrote a book of about eighty-thousand words which was nothing like Holy Wood. When I started to write that book, I asked God that if this is not what he wants me to do, to let what I say fall on deaf ears. That is exactly what happened. Nobody read or was the least bit interested in what I had to say. It was clear to me that God did not want me to write a book. I deleted the manuscript from my computer and shredded the hard copy.

For several years I organized a Friday evening Bible study. During one of these studies a woman said to me that I should write a book. Normally, when someone says that, they are just trying to get you to stop talking, but I think she was serious. I replied that God made it very clear that is not what he wants me to do.

In 1999 I was trying to decide whether to end a failed marriage. I asked God to show me a sign whether he wanted me to continue bearing a cross, or to go out in the wilderness like the Children of Israel did when they left Egypt. I received no sign. A few years ago I was listening to Ronald Dart deliver a sermon in which he described a similar experience. He was trying to make a decision and asked for God to help him make the decision by giving him a sign. No sign was forthcoming. But, the decision that Ronald made was blessed, and he attributed that blessing to his prayer to God about what to do. Likewise, I was blessed for fifteen years with an incredible relationship that was the exact opposite of the terrible years I had before.

Considering what Beth said to me, the only thing I could come up with is that maybe now, God wants me to write a book. So in 2016 I prayed about it and asked for a sign. I not only asked, but I insisted that God give me a sign. I said to God, that I could not rely on him to bless my decision because he had made it very clear he didn't want me writing a book. This time I needed a sign!

I collect music. I was a late night music programmer for ten years in the 80's and 90's. I have about fifteen hundred songs in my library on three flash drives which I have in my car. After thirty minutes in my car praying, I was still about a ten minute drive to work as I finished my prayer, so I turned my music on. I certainly did not ask for the song title to be a sign, but I did think it would be interesting to see what title popped up on the screen.

I had a flash drive in the receptacle that I rarely listened to, so when the title of the song came up, I honestly did not remember having that song in my collection. In fact, I later looked to see if I had bought that song, and indeed I had. The song was performed by Edward Sharp & The Magnetic Zeros, titled, "Give Me A Sign."

When I stopped laughing, I called my friend Richard and said no title came up saying, "Write A Book." So, it appears God was telling me to give him a sign. This book is that sign.

Pentecost was approaching. I had recently learned that the number 3000 is associated with that feast. When Moses came down the mountain, it was most likely on Pentecost, and about three thousand perished. Sixteen hundred years later, three thousand were saved when the Holy Spirit was given on Pentecost. Nancy told her minister about this and he mentioned it in his next sermon. I also told Richard, and he said he had never connected those two events.

After three months I had written about sixteen thousand words and I felt like I was in over my head, and that I was wasting my time. I was walking Teddy through the neighborhood when I met this delightful couple named John and Lynn Reinhardt. We talked for a few minutes and upon saying our good-byes, I asked John what he did before he retired. He informed me that he was not retired and that he is a book designer with experience in the publishing industry since the 70's, adding that he has been involved in the publication of over three thousand books.

"How's this for a sign, Phil?" I could almost hear God asking.

I told John what I was doing and then asked if it had already been done. He replied that it had not, but he thought it was a great idea. A few days later he e-mailed me, telling me he wanted to help me get the book done and get it done right. He would connect me with an editor and provide services to me, adding that he was not going to charge me for these services.

John set me up with my first editor, Deb. She warned me she would not be able to finish the job if she could get a full time job, which she did. She referred me to a second editor named Jim. Between these two people I learned a great deal about writing.

From 2016 until 2018 I wrote five versions of this book, and many bad things occurred during that period. Both my editor and designer had health issues which delayed the book. My CPA business drastically declined, a leak in a pipe caused $10,000 in damage to our laundry room, I was in a golf cart accident that resulted in my left leg being partially paralyzed. It took eighteen months of physical therapy to recover from the accident. In one three day period during March of 2017 Nancy's daughter-in-law ended her marriage to her son, I was diagnosed with bladder cancer and my son died. Nancy said to me many times, "Stop writing that book, we're being attacked!"

During this period, writing was my catharsis. I would awaken at four and write until 7:30 before going to work. I would proof the book and be surprised at some of the humor I had written despite all the bad things going on. I finished writing the book and had it edited in late 2018. But then I was in a state of deep grief for several months because of losing Nancy. During that time I never looked at the book, but after that period of grief I concluded the design work with John in December.

If you are reading this, then God wanted me to write a book.

Handouts

Part I
Talking Snakes

SNAKE IN THE GRASS

There are two important concepts that are used throughout this book that need to be grasped in order to understand what is said in certain passages of the Bible. Both concepts deal with the difference between Hebrew thinking and Greek (Western) thinking. Brad Scott has written about these differences and others in his book, *Let This Mind Be In You.*

The first concept deals with function over form which is briefly discussed, using the example of describing a pencil. This example is from a video by Scott called "Esau and the Tares."

The second concept, linear thinking verses circular thinking, will be discussed in a later handout.

Searching the internet for images of Eve and the serpent will result entirely of the serpent having the body of a snake. With all due respect to the movie, *The Private Lives of Adam and Eve,* the serpent looks nothing like Mickey Rooney in a snake costume.

According to Appendix 19 of *The Companion Bible,* the word serpent is the Hebrew word *n|toachash* which means "a shining one." Satan is clearly identified in the Bible as "that old serpent," but he is also described as being able to transform himself into an angel of light. Putting this together, we can see that the individual that seduces Eve is a shining angel with great beauty. He is described as being wise as well as beautiful, plus he wears jewelry. It's hard to imagine a snake wearing jewelry. "That ring you gave me keeps falling off!"

There are many places in the Bible where this concept appears. Alexander's empire is pictured as a leopard which relates to the speed with which it conquers the known world. Christ is pictured both as a lamb and as a lion. It is highly unlikely his appearance is similar to the character played by Bert Lahr in *The Wizard of Oz*. These and many other passages describe the *function* of an individual, as opposed to his appearance. In the case of Christ being described as a lion, Christ is shown to be a ruler. As a lamb, he is shown to be a sacrifice that is gentle and harmless. In the case of Satan, he is pictured as a serpent in order to show he is a deceiver.

Art and motion pictures that depict Satan as a snake miss the whole message of the passage. Satan is shown to be a shadowy being when, in fact, his appearance is glorious. This is a lesson for today. There are very charismatic ministers telling their congregations things that are not true, but because of how attractive they are or how well they speak, they are believed. The same thing can be said of political leaders. So the very first lesson in the Old Testament is that you cannot believe what you see and hear, no matter how appealing it may look or sound if it contradicts God's teaching.

WHERE'S MY SWEATER?

Since Adam is alone, God brings animals to him to see if a suitable helper can be found for him. Since it is not possible to have a meaningful argument with a dog, cat, or monkey, there is no one suitable for Adam as a helper. This is not a joke. Adam actually needs someone that would have different ideas than he has in order to challenge him to be better. A minister once said the term "helpmate" is not equivalent to a servant. It means "a helper" that can sometimes be helpful by having a different, possibly opposing, view.

"Are you going to wear that old brown sweater with the hole in the armpit?" The author's wife, Nancy, asked her husband before he played golf. When he told Nancy the sweater is mentioned in this chapter, Nancy responded by saying, "It is old enough to have been in the Garden of Eden."

Paintings and movies also make a huge mistake by showing Eve alone with Satan. Both of them encounter the serpent, and Eve does all the talking while Adam—standing right next to her—remains. Her role in the family is to help Adam, not to replace him. Clearly, Adam has turned over control of the family to Eve. If he meets his responsibility as the head of the family, he would order the angel to shut up and leave since he has the authority to do so.

Later, when God confronts them for their disobedience, Eve admits she was deceived, but what does Adam do? He blames Eve, and then blames God for giving her to him in the first place.

Adam's failure to lead the family, and then blame Eve and God for his transgression, demonstrates that Adam is totally worthless. Once this is understood, one of the curses can also be understood, which is that Eve will be ruled by her husband. It becomes obvious why the first sin God mentions to Adam is that he obeyed his wife.

God firmly establishes that Adam is to lead the family. The very first thing that happens after the curses are given is that Adam, assuming his role as head of the family, names the woman "Eve." This is appropriate, when considering the first thing God has Adam do when he is created is to name the animals, which demonstrates his authority over them. Now Adam finally gives the woman a name instead of just saying, "Hey you."

Part II
Cloudy With a Chance of Rain

DATE SETTING

There are very specific time periods described in the flood narrative. Harold Camping taught on his radio show that Jesus would return on May 21, 2011, and rapture the church to heaven. He supported this prediction by saying the Genesis flood begins on the seventeenth day of the second month, a date which coincides with May 21, of that year. The spiritual year begins in spring and the civil year begins in the fall, so Mister Camping has to be using the spiritual year for his calculation.

There are two significant dates that occur in the civil calendar. The ark rests on Nissan 17 which is the same day that Jesus is resurrected. The waters dried up on Tishri 1 which is the first day of the Feast of Trumpets, also known as Yom Terah, the first day of the New Year. The fact that very significant dates from both the New Testament and the Old Testament occur on the civil calendar and no significant dates occur on the spiritual calendar suggests that Mister Camping was using the wrong calendar.

Part III
She Ain't Married, She's My Sister

"RAMA LAMA DING DONG"
THE EDSELS 1957

The films described in the chapters dealing with Abraham all conclude with the possible sacrifice of Isaac. In Genesis, a ram is provided as a substitute sacrifice, which is confusing, so much so that the television series, *The Bible,* erroneously shows a lamb being the substitute. The Christian understanding that a lamb represents Christ is enough in itself to necessitate the use of a lamb, but when Isaac specifically mentions that they do not have a lamb and Abraham answers that God will provide a lamb, a ram shows up. This becomes confusing to Christians.

God has to be delivering a message since he can easily arrange for a lamb to come walking by, but he not only provides a ram, it's one caught in a thicket. There is significance to both the ram and the thicket, but this handout only addresses the substitution of a ram for a lamb.

When asked about this substitution, Richard Ritenbaugh, the pastor of Church of the Great God, points out that a ram is generally a ruler. Brad Scott of Wildbranch Ministries also notes that his research shows that the

Hebrew root word for ram is the same word as the root word for God. Putting these two responses together, the death of a ram in place of Isaac could mean that the leaders of the world at that time, including their gods, are perishing to pave the way for the Messiah to eventually be born.

There are possibly two different sacrifices involved. On the one hand, the sacrifice leads to the end of the current status of the relationship between God and man. God is sacrificing himself in order that he can start a relationship with Abraham's descendents. On the other hand, it pictures the future sacrifice of Christ which will usher in the time that God will have a relationship with all the people in the world.

THREE DAY EVENT

There is a phrase used in this story that is seen over and over throughout the Bible: "the third day." Throughout the Bible, hidden things are revealed on the third day. The earliest example of this is in creation week where plants are not created on the third day, but that is the day when God reveals them. The pattern of the third day is even seen in the physical world where every month in late evening the new moon is revealed on the third day of the lunar cycle. In the Bible, Joseph reveals himself to his brothers, God reveals himself to Israel, Esther reveals her Jewish identity to the Persian king, and Christ is raised on the third day.

The story about Abraham being willing to sacrifice Isaac, shows the first explicit use of revelation occurring on the third day. The trip to the mountains of Moriah takes three days and he sees the mountain on the third day from "afar off." Researching the expression, afar off, shows that expression can refer to *distance* or *time*. So when the expressions third day and afar off are used in the same verse, there is something very important in the distance of time and space that is being revealed to Abraham and it's not just the top of a mountain.

It is very possible that God is revealing to Abraham a vision of the Lamb of God being sacrificed on that mountain. This is not a huge leap of faith. In fact, without understanding these expressions, Abraham's statement about God providing a lamb makes no sense unless you believe that Abraham is lying to Isaac as some commentators suggest.

PART III: SHE AIN'T MARRIED, SHE'S MY SISTER

"IT'S DÉJÀ VU ALL OVER AGAIN" YOGI BERRA

There are recurring events throughout the Bible and readers should recognize "This must be important." Brad Scott, of Wildbranch Ministries, noted at a conference that if something is important, it won't be said just once in some obscure part of the Bible, it will be everywhere.

In Scott's book, *Let This Mind Be In You*, he differentiates Greek thinking and Hebrew thinking. In chapter one of this book, a previous handout mentions Scott's book and how it shows that Hebrew thinking relates to function while Greek thinking relates to form. He later points out that Hebrew thinking is cyclical while western thinking is linear. The best way to summarize this is that there is repetition in the Bible, which in many cases is cyclical.

There is a pattern that significant events in God's plan repeat themselves on the same day in the Hebrew calendar. Consider that God gives the law on Pentecost and sixteen hundred years later gives the Holy Spirit on Pentecost. Another of many examples is that the Jewish temple is destroyed twice, each time on the ninth of Av.

This concept can help readers understand Acts 2:16, which seems confusing. Peter seems to be saying this is the "Day of the Lord." But this can't be, because the Day of the Lord has not happened yet. That is linear thinking, which says that if something happens once it cannot happen again. Hebrew thinking is that an event can happen more than once and still be the same event. The event that Peter is describing is a type or pattern of the future Day of the Lord.

Once it is understood that there is repetition in the Bible, and that many times the repetition occurs on Holy Days, a whole new understanding of the Bible emerges.

In the story of Abraham, including the account of Lot at Sodom, there are two events that almost certainly happened at Passover, both involving death. The first event, the death of the people at Sodom, probably happened during the Passover season. Notice that Lot offers the angels unleavened bread. The first reason he might be doing this is to recognize that they are holy and without sin. But, the second reason is that this bread could have been prepared just before the "Days of Unleavened Bread, "which immediately follow Passover.

Scholars might say, "Phil, you're crazy. That feast will not be observed for centuries."

That is true, but isn't it possible that God could have inspired Lot to have that kind of bread in his house on that particular day? Isn't it also possible that the patriarchs knew about the feasts? To quote Dennis Miller as he so eloquently says, "This is just my opinion, I could be wrong."

The second event that probably occurred during the Passover season is the sacrifice of Isaac. Again, there is no proof, but understanding that important events recur during Holy Days, leads to this conclusion. When comparing the events, it reinforces this idea. In the first event at Sodom, people die for their sins, in the second event on Mount Mariah a Ram dies for sins, and finally, Christ dies for the world's sins. There is definitely a pattern here, and it would make sense that they all occur on Passover.

LEAP OF FAITH

There is no question that Abraham has great faith, but does he start out that way? It appears that Abraham's faith, on a scale of one to ten, with ten being the highest, starts out at about six. This is a good score since everyone else is probably at zero. But as Abraham and Sarah try to have a son using a surrogate, they show a lack of faith. This lack of faith creates problems that continue to this day, in that Abraham's descendents are divided.

Consider that God speaks to Abraham five times prior to his encounter with Abimelech, but once again he hides Sarah's identity as his wife. He still is not showing faith that God will protect him. Despite lacking faith, God talks to Abraham again, and tells him the importance of Isaac. After *six* encounters with God, will Abraham finally believe that God is with him and will protect him?

God apparently wants to know the answer to that question which results in the command to sacrifice Isaac. It is extremely important to understand that there is no way God will let Abraham kill that child. God is not going to commit murder. The question is, will Abraham be willing to obey God or will he unwillingly obey God? The difference reflects faith.

PART III: SHE AIN'T MARRIED, SHE'S MY SISTER

All the films show that Abraham is very upset at this command. Most, if not all commentaries on this issue also assume that Abraham is reluctant, but they offer the opinion that he knows God will resurrect Isaac after he plunges his knife into the boy. In a sermon tape, Ronald Dart talks about how beautifully George C. Scott captures the anguish that Abraham feels as he comprehends what he must do.

But in the story, Abraham does not express any anguish or reluctance to obey God. It is possible and even probable that Abraham is willingly obeying God, knowing that Isaac will not die. He tells the two witnesses that he and Isaac will return to them. He is ready to use that knife knowing that God will not let that him harm Isaac.

Notice this is the seventh and final time he blesses Abraham. Since Abraham believes and obeys, there is no need for God to speak to him again until an eighth time, which will come when he is resurrected into God's kingdom.

Part IV
Please Pass the Salt

"DON'T YOU (FORGET ABOUT ME)" SIMPLE MINDS 1985

Christ warns his disciples to, "Remember Lot's wife!" Various commentaries attribute reasons why Lot's wife looks back. A common explanation is that she does not want to leave her possessions or lifestyle. While this can certainly be true, there is another more important explanation that can be shown by examining certain verses.

The most important piece of information needed to understand not only why Lot and his wife have to almost be dragged out of Sodom, and why Lot's wife turns around, is to know the size of Lot's family. When Abraham receives assurance that the city would not be destroyed if ten righteous people live there, and he stops at ten, instead of negotiating to four, this provides evidence that there are ten members of Lot's family in the city. If this is true, then Abraham probably assumes that all ten members are righteous.

The narrative shows that Lot has at least two married daughters and two sons-in-law. It is possible that when the angel says "your sons," he is not asking if Lot has sons there, he is most likely asking if the sons he has are in Sodom. In that case the plural use of the word son in the narrative gives evidence that Lot has at least two sons. Lot, Mrs. Lot, two virgin daughters, two sons-in-law, two married daughters and two sons. That would bring the number of people in the family to ten.

There are other arguments for ten people in the family, although those theories do not include any sons. There are also reasonable arguments that there are only four members in that family and that the "sons-in-law" are not actually married to the daughters. Even if that is true, Mrs. Lot would look back because she is concerned for them and her daughters, who stand to lose their future husbands.

While it may be true that Mrs. Lot looks back because of possessions and lifestyle, common sense dictates that she is looking back because there are members of her family still in Sodom or maybe she looks back to see if they are following them. Possibly she is terrified by what may be happening to them as she hears the sounds of destruction. How many mothers would do the same thing and look back? Guess what moms; you are not to look back!

"I'M PROUD TO BE A SODOMITE"

If asked, "What is the sin of Sodom?" the universal response would be homosexual behavior. There is no question that homosexual behavior is condemned as a sin in the Bible. However, Ezekiel says the reasons are pride, fullness of food, abundance of idleness, and not helping the poor. Immediately after those reasons, being haughty and committing abominations is mentioned. If sins could be ranked from worst to least, that would mean homosexual behavior is number six. If they are listed in order, then pride would be the worst.

Pride is clearly one of the sins God hates most. Maybe that is the reason humility results in forgiveness of such a broad range of sins. Throughout the Bible, angels have displayed an appearance that is so magnificent that the reaction of humans is to immediately bow down to them. What is the reaction of the citizens of Sodom? They immediately want to rape them. It is very possible that if those would-be rapists immediately bow down to the heavenly messengers and ask to be forgiven, that they would not perish. But their pride is so unbounded they have no chance of redemption and reconciliation, so there is no alternative but to wipe them out.

PART IV : PLEASE PASS THE SALT

Christ says that the time of his return will be preceded by the world being like it was in the times that God poured out punishment before the flood and punishment on those cities of the plain during the Abraham's time. If people look out on the world today, do they see pride, fullness of food, abundance of idleness and not helping the poor? And finally, have any of those sins become a virtue in today's society?

Part V
Cheaper by the Dozen

I WILL HATE THAT STRAWBERRY FIELD FOREVER

A YouTube video featuring Brad Scott of Wildbranch Ministries, "Esau and the Tares," teaches more information in three hours than can possibly be adsorbed in that time, so the video needs to be watched more than once. One of the themes is the explanation of what it means to be in the field. It explains that God is in a house, and he wants his followers to be in it with him and not in the field, because the field represents the world. Esau is called a man of the field as opposed to Jacob who lives in tents, so Jacob represents a man living with God in a house and Esau represents a man living in the world.

This is extremely important because there are two seeds at work in the world. There is God's seed which comes from Jacob and Satan's seed which comes from Esau. These two individuals are against each other at the time they are in their mother's womb and their seed will be against each other until the Last Day.

Currently, one seed might be attacking the other seed. Esau's seed, which might be ISIS and similar organizations, want to destroy Jacob's seed, which are the Jews and Christians. This battle has been raging for decades if not centuries or millennia.

Ministers are sometimes asked if God hates Esau. A common response is that he doesn't hate Esau, he simply loves Jacob more. Once the concept of the two seeds is understood it is much easier to understand what is meant when the Bible says that God hates Esau. It means God hates Esau.

Part VI
Family Feud

THREE'S A CROWD

There are some interesting parallels in the story of Joseph interpreting the dreams of the cup bearer and the baker and the last twenty four hours leading up to and including Christ's crucifixion. Tony Robinson points these out in a video called "Messianic Samson." Here are some questions and answers that demonstrate what Robinson points out.

> *What does a cup bearer do?* He pours wine into the Pharaoh's cup.
> *What does a baker do?* He makes bread for the Pharaoh. Wine and bread. Does that sound familiar?
> *What are the key elements of the last supper?* Most people understand they are wine and bread.
> *How many men are with Joseph in prison?* Two.
> *How many men are with Christ being crucified?* Most people agree that there are two.
> *What happens to the baker?* He gets hung on a tree.
> *What happens to Christ?* He gets hung on a tree.
> *What are the fates of the other men in each case?* In the case of the two men in prison, one is saved and the other is not. In the case of the two men being crucified, one is saved and the other is not.
> *What does Joseph say to the cup bearer?* "Remember me."
> *What does the repentant thief say to Christ?* "Remember me."

These are just a few of many Messianic moments that can be found in the Old Testament.

BROTHERLY LOVE

Researching the ages of Joseph and Benjamin opens a big theological can of worms. It turns out the Bible is silent about their age difference, but researching this issue shows there many articles about the ages of the boys. For example, Conservapedia.com/Benjamin puts him at ten years old when Joseph is sold into slavery, but there are other different opinions. Assuming Benjamin is actually about ten, it is highly unlikely he conspired with his brothers as shown in the musical.

Part VII
Surf's Up

LET MY PEOPLE SHOOT FIREWORKS ON THE FOURTH OF JULY

The most important lesson that is hidden by all of the productions of the story of the Exodus is the reason that God raises Moses to lead the Israelites out of Egypt. These movies present the idea that God is simply freeing them from slavery. Nowhere in any of these movies is there a message that the purpose of freeing Israel from Egypt is so they could be the first nation on Earth to serve and worship God in the way that he wants to be served and worshipped. People are freed when this happens, but it is a different kind of freedom.

If the purpose of freeing Israel is so they can all be free men, then why, following the second giving of Ten Commandments, does God tell Israel how masters are to treat their bondservants? These are not just hired help; they are the equivalent of slaves that are owned by their masters for six years.

There are detailed instructions on what happens if a servant decides to become a servant to his master for the rest of his life as opposed to becoming free. These rules are so important they are given before rules about violence, animal control, responsibility for property, morality, justice, and even the Sabbath. These rules not only apply to Israel, but they also provide a picture of how, in the future, Christians will surrender their freedom to Christ.

Everybody who has ever lived has three choices of whom they can serve. They can serve themselves, they can serve another human, or they can serve God. The whole purpose of God bringing the captives out of Egypt is so they would no longer serve another human, but would serve God, and in doing so, reflect God's light to the world.

HARD-HEARTED PHARAOH

The late Ronald Dart of Christian Education Ministries clears up a question that has puzzled many people for thousands of years. How does God harden and soften the heart of Pharaoh? The answer is that the plagues soften his heart and stopping those plagues hardens his heart. This is human nature. When bad things happen, such as a divorce, people will turn to God, this is an example of the softening of the heart. Once those things pass and things are better, then human nature tends to harden the heart and people turn away from God. So each time the plagues stop, Pharaoh's heart gets hard.

SEVEN SISTERS

It is most likely that Moses is in Midian for some period of time before he has the encounter with the shepherd girls and the bad shepherds at the well. The story starts with him dwelling in Midian and sitting by a well. The fact he is dwelling there indicates the encounter does not happen on his arrival as shown in the movies. This encounter involves seven daughters of a powerful priest who ministers over Midian. His seven daughters are shepherds over his flock and while they are at a well, providing water to their flock, other shepherds come and try to drive them away. Moses saves the daughters from the bad shepherds and then waters their flock.

Before reading further, a question must be asked, "Is there anything about this story that might suggest there is something more going on here than a heroic figure saving girls from bad guys and marrying one of the girls?"

Consider that there are four individuals or groups of individuals in this account that might have a New Testament meaning. There is Moses, the seven daughters, the evil shepherds and the flock. The story also takes place at a well and at the end of the encounter, Moses waters the flock.

Doesn't it seem unusual that such a powerful man would have his seven daughters taking care of his flock? The fact that they are taking care of their father's flock instead of attending to their husbands, would imply they are not married and are virgins. It would seem that a daughter of such a powerful man who owns a flock, would have no trouble finding a husband, let alone all seven of these daughters.

Is it possible the seven daughters represent something more than giggling teeny boppers? In the night sky there is a cluster of stars in the constellation of Taurus. The seven brightest stars form a shape that is similar to the big dipper and is called the Pleiades, which has at least two other names: "The Seven Sisters" and "The Seven Virgins." Mark Biltz, of El Shaddai Ministries, points out in a YouTube video, "Signs in the Heavens," that this cluster represents the Church to some Christians. Being aware of this might support the idea there is a hidden meaning in this encounter.

Is there a story in the New Testament about Christ at a well? Sure. Who does he encounter? A Gentile. Who will ultimately make up his church? Primarily Gentiles. This is just speculation, but it might be possible the seven sisters represent the church pictured in Revelation, which has yet to be born.

Many Christians believe Christ appears in the Old Testament. If that is true, is it possible his church also makes an appearance in the Old Testament? If you look at the other elements, a pattern emerges. There are bad shepherds, who might represent false ministers, and their flocks might represent congregations that do not follow God's laws. Moses watering the flock might be a type of Christ and that flock might represent the members of his church.

WESTWARD HO

All three of these presentations omit what causes the Red Sea to part, as well as what time of day it divides. While Moses is still on the west side of the Red Sea, an east wind starts at evening, and blows all night, parting the sea. They cannot start to cross until the parting reaches the west shore from the east. The Israelites cross on land made dry by the wind with a wall of water on both sides, and they are shown to be on the opposite shore the next morning. This means that they have to cross at night, walking directly into a wind that is powerful enough to part the sea. This undoubtedly is a great struggle, walking into a powerful wind in darkness, with the end not in sight.

The fact that the wind is out of the east is significant because there are patterns in the Bible about the wind from the east bringing trouble. At the time of Joseph, the Pharaoh's dreams include an east wind that dries up the crops and brings famine. The plague of locusts the Egyptians suffer during the time of Moses also comes from an east wind. The wind from the east allows Egyptians to partially cross the Red Sea and they die as a result. This wind also has to cause a great struggle to those Israelites who are walking into it through the Red Sea. This struggle though, ultimately results in salvation.

The east wind is bringing a different kind of trouble from the east in our time. Terrorism is a scourge to Western Europe and the United States that is coming from the East. There has been a wave of immigrants from the Middle East which, not only brings potential terrorists into Europe but might eventually weaken the European Union itself under the strain of weakest economies having to absorb and assimilate this wave of refugees. Is the pattern of the east wind continuing in our time?

Bill Cloud has more on this subject in a YouTube message, "Do Not Fear the Locusts of Isis."

IT'S HIS PARTY

Is there more than one reason the Israelites go to Mount Sinai? Clearly, they go there to receive the Ten Commandments, but is there someone there that they are supposed to meet at a specific time? Is this some form of an appointment?

Only a small number of Christians understand that the slaves are going to a "feast to the Lord," and even fewer understand that this feast will be held each year on the same day in the ancient calendar. All these films omit why the slaves need to be freed, which is to take a three-day journey to have a feast. This is another example of revelation on the third day, in this case the feast of Passover will be revealed to them.

When the slaves make the golden calf, Aaron proclaims that the next day would be a "feast to the Lord." The word that is used for Lord is *Elohim*, the same word that is translated as God in many places in the Bible. The feast the next day is not to worship the golden calf; it is to worship God, but using a calf as his image.

Is this the same feast where the slaves are to be freed to attend? No, there are differences between these two feasts, so they are not the same feast. Mount Sinai is more than a three-day journey from Egypt, and there are no animal sacrifices involved at Mount Sinai.

There are seven feasts during the Hebrew calendar. It appears these are two of them. The first feast includes Passover, which features animal sacrifice. The second feast is the day known as Pentecost. Jewish tradition says that Pentecost is the day on the Hebrew calendar that Moses brings the Ten Commandments down from the mountain.

It is extremely interesting to compare the event at Mount Sinai to the New Testament event that occurs on Pentecost. In the Old Testament, the law is given on Pentecost and "about three thousand" people are *killed*. In the New Testament, the Holy Spirit is given on Pentecost and "about three thousand" are *saved*. Is this just a coincidence? Maybe, but there might be a message here saying everyone is guilty under the law and deserves the death penalty, but everyone can be saved from that penalty by the Holy Spirit.

The key to understanding why these events occur on the same day is understanding that the word feast does not mean a dinner party. It means an appointed time. There is a great deal of material available on the Internet about appointed times and how significant they are to Christians. The bottom line is that all seven of these feasts concern Christ's first and second coming. Mark Biltz, of El Shaddai Ministries, has a four DVD set, "Feasts of the Lord," explaining these feasts and their connections to Christ.

ALTERNATIVE FACTS

After watching these films and reading Exodus, there are five questions that must be answered.

1. How does the pharaoh's daughter explain the appearance of a baby when she was not pregnant?
2. Why doesn't the pharaoh order the baby to be killed, since this might be the baby that would free the slaves?
3. Why does Moses wait until he is forty years old to visit the slaves?
4. If Moses is like a son to pharaoh, why would he worry if someone sees him kill the Egyptian?
5. Why would the pharaoh order Moses killed without at least hearing his side of the story?

Information in Exodus, Acts, and Hebrews can provide additional insight into Moses' life in Egypt. This shows it is possible to present different events from what is shown in the movies that are consistent with Scripture and answer the questions above. These events can be presented in a proposed storyline, which if accurate shows how wrong the films present this story.

Moses is a beautiful baby, so it is probable that he becomes a handsome man, "mighty in words and deeds." However, by the time God tells Moses to return to Egypt, he protests he is not an eloquent speaker. He is described as the meekest man on earth. Clearly, if all of this is accurate, Moses changes from a mighty man in words and deeds to a meek man who possibly stutters. This transformation is critical. God must feel Moses is not ready to be given the responsibility of leading the Israelites out of Egypt until he becomes meek and humble.

The most important thing to remember is that the Israelite babies are not ordered killed because a potential leader might be among them; they are killed because there are too many Hebrews. The proposed storyline would assume that Pharaoh's daughter tells her father that she finds this baby and wants to keep it. Seeing what a beautiful baby it is, and loving his daughter, he would allow her to adopt it, undoubtedly thinking, "One Hebrew baby would not make a difference." It would be similar to her bringing home a puppy. Pharaoh would not be worried about a prophecy of a Hebrew leader being born because there is no such prophecy.

Growing up in the palace as the Pharaoh's daughter's son, Moses would be well-educated and probably have authority in the court of the Pharaoh.

However, when Moses comes of age, he refuses to be called the son of the Pharaoh's daughter. This is critical information because in Exodus he goes out to the Hebrews when he is grown and in Hebrews he makes this refusal when he comes of age. These could be at different ages in his life.

So, how old is Moses when he comes of age? It is known that Moses leaves Egypt at the age of forty. So, is that the time he comes of age? It is possible, but there is evidence that the age of thirty could be when he comes of age. There are five examples of thirty being the age Israelites are given responsibility. There is also New Testament evidence that thirty is coming of age, namely, that Christ begins his ministry when he is about thirty years old.

Why would Moses refuse? A possibility is that Moses knows he is a Hebrew and is disgusted that the Pharaoh killed those Hebrew boys, which he knows are his people.

Assuming that Moses is thirty when he refuses to be called the son of Pharaoh, then he lives in the palace for ten more years before he goes out to see the Hebrews. It could be during this time that he decides that he will lead the Hebrews out of slavery. His journey out to look at his brethren reflects that he knows it is time to start the process.

When he looks around to see if he is being watched before killing the Egyptian, it demonstrates that he is not close to Pharaoh. If he has the relationship shown in the Hollywood productions, he could easily explain his actions to a "fatherly pharaoh." Instead, he fears for his life—and rightly so. As soon as Pharaoh hears of this killing, he orders Moses killed. If the relationship is close, Pharaoh would at least give Moses an opportunity to tell his side of the story. This model concludes with Moses, still a mighty man in words and deeds, escaping from Egypt, not to return until forty years later, transformed into a different man.

While the proposed model may not be accurate, for example he might become of age when he reaches twenty or possibly forty, it would appear to be more consistent with the Bible than the presentations made by the two movies and the mini-series. This model explains how Moses can be a well-educated part of the household but still immediately be sentenced to death, in absentia, by his adoptive grandfather. It explains how he could become faithful to God while living up to ten years in Egypt.

During this time his refusal to be called the son of Pharaoh would be an insult to the Egyptians and probably make him unpopular, resulting in a very easy decision by Pharaoh to have him executed. It also explains his motivation to visit the slaves, his secrecy in the act, and his fear for his life. It makes clear that there is a critical transformation that takes place before God would allow Moses to lead his people out of Egypt. None of the films show this transformation.

Part VIII
Mother-in-Law

FAMILY LAW

There are two laws that have significance in this story. The first law involves Levirate marriage. In Judaism, this type of marriage requires the brother of a deceased man to provide a child to the widow if the man dies without having a child by her. The second law regards what happens every fifty years. Both of these films deal with this law as it is practiced in ancient Israel, but they don't make it clear that this law is the motivation for Ruth to approach Boaz.

In ancient Israel, every fifty years is a Jubilee, when property is returned to the original owner or his family. This law might influence Naomi to return to Israel if a jubilee year is approaching. "That's not fair!" Someone might say. "You mean someone could sell the land and a year later someone else could claim the land for free if it is Jubilee year?" That is true, however the seller would only charge the equivalent of one year's rent for the land. If he charges the full value of the land, he would be stealing.

When reading the Bible, a question should be asked, "Is this story taking place during a Jubilee?" It may have. If so, when the friend of Naomi tells her in the film, *The Book of Ruth*, that she would get a good price for the land, it is actually not true. All she would get is the equivalent of a few months rent for the land.

There appears to be two issues in this story. The first issue is that Boaz will continue the line of Elimelech, and the second issue is the land would return to Elimelech's kin. The Jubilee laws deal with the redemption of the land and that issue is directly mentioned in the fourth chapter of Ruth.

HANDOUTS

FOUR QUEENS AND A KING

John J. Parsons writes in an Internet article, "The Chesed of Ruth," that there are only four women beside Mary mentioned in Matthew's genealogy.

> Tamar (She has sex with her father-in-law)
> Rahab (A prostitute)
> Ruth (A Moabitess)
> The wife of Uriah (an adulterous)

Isn't it interesting that all these women have flaws?

Notice that all Christians have the role of a woman as part of the "bride of Christ."

Consider this. The blood of imperfection is mixed into the blood of perfection and results in perfection. This is a direct contradiction to everything in nature where imperfection contaminates perfection.

Part IX
Having a Bad Hair Day

THREE LITTLE PIGS FIND THREE MILE ISLAND ON THE THIRD DAY

When reading this story there are some things that jump off the page when remembering other stories in the Bible:

1. A barren woman giving birth
2. A wedding feast
3. The number three thousand appearing twice
4. Something hidden not being revealed in three days
5. Something hidden being revealed three days later
6. Foreign women
7. Blindness

This is similar to completing a jigsaw puzzle without having the benefit of seeing the picture of the finished puzzle. There seems to be a picture, but what is it? Each of these words or expressions have a significant meaning when they appear in other parts of the Bible, so why do all these elements show up in this story?

The Bible has several stories of barren women giving birth. A wedding feast is used to picture Christ and the Church, three thousand is the number of people lost when the law is given and the number of people saved when the Holy Spirit is given, both on the same day of the Hebrew calendar. The Bible teaches that God hides things. It also teaches that God reveals hidden things on the third day. The false church in Revelation is presented as a foreign woman. And finally, God partially blinds part of Israel to Christ. What really proves there is something else going on is the continued use of the number three.

A video series by Tony Robinson, "Messianic Samson," shows that there are Messianic messages throughout the Old Testament especially in the story of Samson.

Robinson points out that not only is the number three thousand significant, but any number starting in three can be significant. He admits that one or two appearances of the number three can be a coincidence, but the story of Samson is full of numbers in multiples of three. There are thirty guests at the wedding party and thirty sets of clothing. There are three hundred foxes used to start a fire as well as three thousand men of Judah handing Samson over to the Philistines and three thousand dying at the destruction of the temple. Does that sound familiar?

There are other events that are significant. One event concerns the prophecy about the descendents of Abraham possessing the gates of their enemies. This prophecy is clearly about a group of people, but what does Samson do when he leaves Gaza? He steals the gate and carries it many miles to Hebron. This is no ordinary gate designed to keep a dog out of the kitchen, it weighs hundreds of pounds and Samson carries it many miles uphill. Why would he do that? One reason might be that he knows about this prophecy.

Yes, these elements are part of a jigsaw puzzle. But the finished picture is not of a single event or even a single individual. This story contains elements of the Bible from Genesis to Revelation and the picture, if there could be one, would be of a Bible sitting on a dusty shelf.

Part X
Skullduggery

"ONE LITTLE MURDER AND I'M JACK THE RIPPER." BILLY CRYSTAL "THROW MOMMA FROM THE TRAIN" 1987

While some movies, such as *Goodfellows* and *The Godfather*, have wise guys who show a certain amount of ethical behavior, Bible movies often make their heroes godly saints, minimizing or completely omitting their human flaws. In two of these films about David, the movies actually try to blame Uriah for David's act of skullduggery. In one, Uriah is a wife beater and the other a blithering idiot. While the films do show David being sorry, they give the impression this is an isolated incident.

David cannot only be underhanded, he does things way worse than anything most average persons would ever even think of doing. All of the movies leave out the census that result in seventy thousand men being killed by a plague God sends as a result of David committing a sin. David's circumcision of an extra one hundred Philistines shows he can be unnecessarily violent. Having so many children that Jerusalem looks like a puppy mill shows he is not a devoted husband to one wife. David has many flaws, but yet he is described in the Bible as a man after God's own heart.

The author's wife questions this description after a Sunday school study about him. "He does terrible things!" She's right, David can be terrible, and it is so important to understand that. It's only then that people can fully appreciate the song, "Amazing Grace," which includes the words, "a wretch like me."

David is not some television minister saying "I have sinned" after getting caught. He doesn't say he made a mistake, he is truly sorry for what he does. Does he sin again? Yes. Does God forgive him again? Yes, just as he continues to forgive people today who are honestly sorry for doing things wrong.

EVERYBODY OUT FOR VOLLEYBALL!

After killing Goliath, David takes his head to Jerusalem. He isn't looking for a soccer field or a volleyball court in hopes of picking up a game. The story is silent about the motive and none of the movies show this event. As obnoxious as this term has become, this omission is "huge!"

At the time David kills Goliath, Jerusalem is in enemy territory that is controlled by the Jebusites. These people are enemies of Israel and would not welcome David carrying that head in a ticker tape parade down Main Street. They probably would kill him the minute he comes to town. So if David is not going to play hoops with Goliath's head why does he take it to Jerusalem? Most likely, this episode is a play on the word Skullduggery. David digs a hole and buries the skull in it.

Christ is crucified at a place called Golgotha which means the place of the skull. There is no clear explanation given how this area gets its name. One possible reason, it is where Adam's skull is buried.

It is fascinating that the English translation of this Aramaic word closely resembles two English words put together, "Goliath" and "Gath." Could this mean the skull belongs to Goliath of Gath? There are articles available on the Internet that teach that David takes the head to Golgotha and buries it in the same place the cross will be put a thousand years later. These articles tie this act to the prophecy given to Eve that the serpent's head would be bruised. Only this time it is Goliath's skull that is finally crushed under the weight of the cross, Goliath being a type of Satan.

PART X : SKULLDUGGERY

AND THE WINNER OF THE MISTER ISRAEL CONTEST: SAUL!

You can almost hear Burt Parks singing, "There he is, Mister Israel." As discussed in earlier chapters, in Hebrew thinking function is more important than appearance, and the Bible presents things in a circular manner as opposed to a linear manner. Both of these concepts are evident in these stories about David.

Regarding function being more important than form, this is made clear by the selection of Saul, a tall and handsome man, to be their first king. While his appearance is what everyone wants, that appearance conceals fatal flaws. Western thinking makes appearance more important than character. Saul's failures bring to mind the Rolling Stones song, "You Can't Always Get What You Want." Israel does not get what it wants when it gets what it thinks it wants.

"ROUND AND ROUND" PERRY COMO 1957

As stated in the previous handout, the Bible presents things in a circular manner. There are interesting parallels between the Old and New Testament, hidden in plain sight, including a couple of parallels in the story of David. Since the Hebraic mind thinks in a circular pattern it should be no surprise that there would be parallels of some events despite the fact they occur a thousand years apart.

The first parallel is David leaving ten concubines to take care of the house while he leaves Jerusalem. Is a similar event going to show up in the New Testament? Yes, and that event is described in a parable of the ten virgins. These accounts have a lot in common. In each case they involve ten women. In each case they involve a king who leaves them. In each case they are or should be waiting for the king to return. All ten concubines have an intimate physical relationship with the king, while all ten virgins have a spiritual relationship with the king. None of the concubines resist Absalom so none show faith that David will return, and all of them lose their relationship with the king when he does return. Five of the virgins also lose their relationship with King Jesus when he returns. Those five receive the same punishment as the concubines because they too, lack faith. This is an obvious lesson to Christians who wait for the king to return.

The second story is the death of Absalom. Could Christ be described as the "Anti-Absalom?" Absurd? Well, maybe not. Both of these stories revolve around the relationship of a father and a son. In one story the son is not faithful, but in the other story, he is. In one story, the son rides out of Jerusalem on a mule, while in the other story the Son rides into Jerusalem on a donkey. (Sorry, Chester.)

In both stories, the sons end up hanging from a tree. In one case it is by the head and in the other case by the hands and feet. Both sons have a spear struck into them. In one case the wound leads to death, but in the other case the wound causes death. In one story, the father feels unimaginable grief and wishes he could die in the son's place. In the other case the Son suffers unimaginable pain and dies for humanity.

Oh, and this. David has twelve sons while he is in Jerusalem, however one dies. Christ has twelve disciples while he is in Jerusalem, however, one dies.

Part XI
Married With Wives

"I'M RELLY RICH!" DONALD TRUMP

Is the age of Solomon a period of prosperity for Israel? It obviously is for Solomon, but what about the citizens of Israel? It must not be because the first thing that happens after Solomon's death is that the people complain to Rehoboam that Solomon, his father, put a heavy yoke on them, but if he would reduce the heavy taxes, they would serve him. He certainly does not inherit Solomon's wisdom so he does the exact opposite by raising taxes.

When Israel comes out of Egypt, God instructs them that when they get a king, that king should write a copy of the Torah and read it every seven years. By doing this, the kings will not have an excuse for not following the instructions in the law which include not making a covenant with or intermarrying the inhabitants of that land, but rather they are to destroy any pagan altars there. Also, anyone who worships other gods must be stoned. In addition to these instructions there are specific commands for these kings, which include not acquiring a large number of horses, having multiple wives, or accumulating gold and silver.

So what does Solomon do? He makes a deal with Hiram. He builds four thousand stalls for his horses, he marries seven hundred women and acquires six hundred and sixty-six talents of gold each year. (Isn't that an interesting number?) Assuming a talent is sixty-seven pounds this amounts to 713,952 ounces. At $1,200 an ounce the amount would be $856,742,400 in modern terms. That's close to a billion dollars per year.

Does Solomon destroy altars to foreign gods? No, he builds them, not only for his wives, but he builds one that he uses to worship the Moabite god, Chemosh. It gets worse. He builds it on the Mount of Olives. This occurs even though God talks to Solomon twice, the second time warning him to keep his commandments. Does he ever slap himself on the face in front of a mirror and say, "What am I doing?" No, there is no sign he ever repents of these actions.

David is not allowed to build the temple, that task is left to Solomon. How soon does Solomon start building the temple? He waits four years. It then takes seven years to complete. The building is not a huge building like Herod's temple; it is ninety feet long and thirty feet wide. So what takes so long? Is it possible he is slowed down by building his own house which takes thirteen years to build, as well as a second personal house and a house he builds for his wife, the Pharaoh's daughter. It's obvious he is not focusing all his energy on building God's temple.

What about Solomon's stewardship of Israel? Notice that he builds cities just to store his chariots and cavalry. When you look at what Solomon spends, other than on the temple, it's all on him and his army. There is nothing mentioned about spending money to help the people of Israel. Even worse, he gives twenty cities to his foreign friend Hiram, which are not his to give away.

There are two things that stand out about Solomon's character when he dedicates the temple. The first thing Solomon asks is that God keeps his promise to David so Solomon can stay on the throne. The second thing is that he keeps repeating the phrase, "The Temple, which I have built."

These comments demonstrate Solomon is thinking more about himself than about God.

Is Solomon focused on God or himself? In Ecclesiastes, Solomon says there is nothing better than to eat, drink and be merry. This egocentric behavior and attitude may be the reason Christ quotes Solomon in a parable in Luke and in just a few verses later he refers to Solomon by name.

Mark Biltz, of El Shaddai Ministries, points out these and other issues in a YouTube video "King Solomon."

Timothy Leary once said, "Intelligence is the ultimate aphrodisiac." While this may or may not explain Solomon's accumulation of wives, it goes a long way in explaining how wisdom and wealth can sometimes lead to corruption and destruction.

Part XII
Prophecy World

TEN CARD STUD

The films about Daniel's prophecies do not spend much time explaining their meanings. This is understandable since there is a great difference of opinion as to what they mean. For example, some groups believe the fourth kingdom in Nebuchadnezzar's dream of a statue represents Greece, while other groups believe it is Rome.

Among prophecy writers, there is a widespread belief that there will be a world government consisting of ten rulers in place when Christ returns. Nebuchadnezzar's dream of a statue representing world governments through the ages until the end of time is one of two proofs of this doctrine. The conclusion of this dream shows a stone, representing Christ, hitting the statue's feet. The statue disintegrates and the stone, which also represents the Kingdom of God, takes over the Earth.

Daniel tells the king that in the time of the statue's toes, Christ would return. This is one of the two major prophecies that are the basis for the theory that there would be a ten nation government in power at the end of the age. The other prophecy is John's vision of a beast in the book of Revelation. In that vision ten horns represent ten kings who will have power just before Christ returns.

However, a different conclusion about the interpretation of these prophecies can be reached. The author believes that each of these prophecies is dealing with time and not with the number of rulers in an end time government and that the ten kings are not joint rulers. In Daniel's prophecy it clearly says that Christ's kingdom will be established in the time of the ten kings which the toes of the statue represent. Notice that the toes and the feet are the same material so they must represent a single government, so the question is, do the toes lead this final government? While this is possible, the answer must be no when you consider the other prophecy in Revelation which all writers agree is a parallel prophecy to Nebuchadnezzar's dream.

In John's vision the ten kings receive power for one hour, along with the beast. All articles or books the author has read assume that the ten kings rule the beast, but it doesn't say that. Again, this message is about time. Notice the use of the term "one hour," which is a period of time.

The first reference to the ten kings is in Nebuchadnezzar's dream which tells of a specific time that Christ will return. It will be during the existence of these ten kings. The second reference to the ten kings tells how long they will have power, using the term "one hour," a length of time. This must indicate there will be a very short period that they will have power *"with the beast."* The word with is emphasized because they are not *the* beast, they are other entities who receive authority along with the beast. There is no evidence they rule the beast.

Putting these two prophecies together leads to this simple conclusion. When ten kings or nations join a strong government that represents the beast, there will be a short time before Christ returns.

It is possible the final prophetic "one hour" actually started when ten countries joined the European Union on May 1, 2004, a time when they received power with the beast, all on the same day.

There is disagreement about the identity of the beast. Some people believe the beast is a continual reincarnation of the Roman Empire that is presently incarnated as the European Union. But there are others that believe it is modern day Islamic countries or that is simply some other form of a world government. It is important to remember that the Jews at the time of Christ had a total misunderstanding of who he would be and what he would do. That was an important reason he was not recognized as the Messiah.

However, if the author is correct, this is one of the greatest fulfillments of Bible prophecy in two thousand years. The author was shocked when ten countries joined the EU on the same day. What was even more shocking is what the author could not find after spending hours searching the web to see if there are any other articles that agree with his theory and he couldn't find any.

Consider this. There must have been hundreds of articles in the last dozen years written about these prophecies. Isn't it amazing that there wouldn't have been at least one article pointing to this date as being significant, or at the very least, one article telling people not to get excited about this date? In hours of searching different terms, not one article could be found which tied May 1, 2004, to the "one hour" Bible prophecy. While the author believes a great moment in Bible prophecy happened in 2004, he must quote Dennis Miller who has said so many times, "That's just my opinion, I could be wrong."

Part XIII
Hide and Seek

HIDE AND NOT SEEK

In the first chapter of this book, the concept of function being more important than form is introduced. In the third chapter, the concept that Western thinking is linear and Hebrew thinking is cyclical or circular is introduced. The pattern of the third day, an example of circular revelation, shows up in the Book of Esther.

A third concept is that God hides many things, often in plain sight. God is not mentioned in the book of Esther. Despite that, all of the movies about Esther mention God over and over again and show the act of prayer many times. Every one of those scenes is in error because there is no mention of God or of anyone praying in this story.

In the original story there are no prayers of supplication when the edict to destroy them is given. People wear sackcloth, but they don't pray and when they are saved they don't offer a prayer of thanksgiving. Is it possible this story is demonstrating that God saves His people despite the fact that they may have become secular? (First century historian, Josephus, in *Book Eleven* Chapter 6 recounts the story of Esther. In his account both Mordecai and Esther pray. The author believes Josephus as well as the Hollywood films are wrong.)

Over and over again in the Old Testament, God says he will hide his face from his people. Is that what is happening in this book? Maybe it is. Maybe these people have been scattered so far that they have assimilated into Persian culture. But, even though the Jews don't see him or even seek him, he sees them and he acts. For example, placing a Jewish girl on the throne of Persia, or causing the king to not be able to sleep which results in him remembering that Mordecai saves his life, probably result from God's intervention.

There are two things happening in this story. God saves his people and he remains hidden. Is it possible the reason he remains hidden is that his people no longer have their faith? Maybe the message in this book is that God works to save his people even though there is no outward evidence that he is doing so. Is it also possible, as the modern nation of Israel also becomes secular, that God still plans to work with them?

I HATE THOSE GUYS

One Night With the King does a very good job explaining why Haman hates the Jews, but it is incomplete. While the movie cannot go deeply into this lesson, it should mention that the hatred of the Agagites for Israel can be traced back not only to the Agagites, but all the way back to Esau.

Agag is the king of the Amalekites. Amelek, the first Amalekite is the grandson of Esau. Esau and Jacob fight in Rebekah's womb. Jacob is definitely flawed, but he is renamed Israel later in life after he overcomes his flaws. Esau is never renamed, and it is clear that Esau hates Israel, and this hatred continues not only to the time of Esther, but to modern times as well.

While reading the story of Esther, it must be understood that there are two seeds at work and they are against each other all the way back to Adam. There is man's seed and there is God's seed. There is a pattern that the firstborn is man's seed and the second born is God's seed. Jacob—later named Israel—is God's seed. Cain, Ishmael, and Esau, which include Amelek and Haman, are all man's seed. Just as Cain killed Abel, this battle between two different seeds continues to this very day. The portrayal of the Agagite, Haman, as a type of Hitler, is very appropriate, considering Hitler's hatred for the Jews.

It is very important to understand that the seed while physical, is also spiritual. There can be physical descendents of Esau who are spiritually part of Israel, and there are also physical descendents of Jacob who are spiritual descendents of Esau. Palestinian Christians and anti-Semitic Europeans are classic examples of each spiritual seed. One of the central themes of

Esther is that man's seed wants to kill God's seed and almost succ-seeds in this story. (Don't boo. It's a great pun!)

I CAN SEE CLEARLY NOW (JOHNNY NASH, 1972)

Does it matter whether the gallows are fifteen feet or seventy-five feet high? It does, especially if the hanging is actually impalement. There is strong evidence that impalement is what often happens when ancient Persia executes criminals. In fact, several Bible translations use the word impale as opposed to hang. Haman probably wants everyone in the city to see Mordecai's impaled body seven stories up, like an angel on top of the Rockefeller Christmas tree, so the citizens could see what happens if you don't bow to Haman. In his hatred, he actually makes it possible for all of his sons to be impaled on the same pole months later, like a giant shish-ka-bob.

Most Christians and Jews know about Lot's wife, but actually there is another wife in the Bible who also suffers punishment. Her name is Zeresh, Haman's wife. It is her idea to "Have a pole set up" to impale Mordecai, which reaches seventy-five feet in the air. Haman likes the idea and sets this pole up next to his house. So the next day, when Haman is impaled on that pole, Zeresh is treated to the sight of her husband becoming an ostentatious lawn ornament, albeit the highest one in Shushan. Almost a year later, she will walk out her front door and see the macabre scene of the ten bodies of her sons impaled, one on top of the other, on the same pole she encouraged Haman to raise. No doubt her neighbors are not thrilled about their property values.

Part XIV
Please Don't Let me be Misunderstood

"EIGHT DAYS A WEEK"

It is interesting that the Beatles sing this song. The pattern of creation has seven days. The pattern of a six day work period followed by a seventh day Sabbath is all through the Bible. So what's with Pentecost? Why is it not on a seventh day instead of a fiftieth day?

The answer is that there is more to God's plan than is shown in the seven day week at creation. The plan includes an eighth day following the week revealed at creation. The eighth day signifies a new beginning, so it is not surprising that Peter refers to eight people being on the ark. Circumcision follows a seven-day week, so it can picture man being changed after that period, once again a new beginning.

HAPPY BIRTHDAY TO YOU!

Two of the movies deal with the time the Messiah is born. One movie, *Jesus of Nazareth,* gives a specific date of Tishri 19 for John's birth, which would mean the Messiah is born six months later in the spring. A second version,

The *Greatest Story Ever Told,* implies a winter birth by showing patches of snow on the ground as the wise men journey to Bethlehem.

Researching the birthday of Jesus will reveal scholarly articles that prove he is born on December 25. Other scholarly articles prove he is born in March. Still others prove he is born in the fall. So, what's wrong with the Fourth of July? Why did it get left out?

If an event takes place in the middle of the first month of a year and another event takes place in the middle of the seventh month of a year, how long is the period between those two events? It is six months. What part of a year is six months? Is it one half of a year?

The next question is, "How long a period is it from the beginning of Jesus' ministry to the end of his ministry?" The overwhelming consensus about the length of the ministry is three and a half years. Richard Ritenbaugh, a minister of the Church of the Great God, says the Book of John shows evidence there are four Passovers during the ministry, which would allow for a three and one half year period ministry.

Assume that Passover is the time Jesus is crucified, then what would be the date three years before that event? It would be the first of four Passovers. Okay, back to the math. If Passover is on the fourteenth day of the first month of the year, then three and a half years before that date is the middle of the seventh month of the previous year.

There is no doubt that Passover is an important day to the Jews. Is there another day that is important to the Jews in the middle of the seventh month? Yes there is, it's the first day of the Feast of Tabernacles, also called Sukkot, which falls on the fifteenth day of Tishri.

Luke says that Jesus begins his ministry when he is about thirty years old. Luke also says he begins the ministry by getting run out of town after reading a passage in Isaiah. Would the passage Jesus reads provide a clue as to the day Jesus reads that passage?

There are passages from the Old Testament, specifically the five books of Moses, that are read on a weekly basis throughout the year. Those verses are referred to as the "Weekly Torah Portion." There are other verses from other parts of the Old Testament that are also read on those days. Since the date in the Hebrew Bible these passages are read is known, can that information determine what date Jesus reads from Isaiah?

When asked what day the Isaiah passage would be read, Brad Scott of Wildbranch Ministries, an expert in Hebrew thinking and language, provides this response: "Rabbinical commentary states that in many circles [sects] the Haftarah portion for Kiy Tavo (Deut. 27:1-29), they read all of chapter 60 and many sects concluded with the first two verses of chapter 61 of Isaiah, which Yeshua is quoting in Luke 4 which usually falls around Yom Teruah."

Yom Teruah, also called, Rosh Hashanah or The Feast of Trumpets, marks the first day of the Hebrew civil year, which is the also the first day of the seventh month in the religious year. While the fact that Jesus reads Isaiah 61 is not proof this day is Yom Teruah, it provides significant evidence that he is doing just that.

To summarize, if there is a three and one half year period from the beginning of the ministry to Passover, that puts the beginning in the fall since Passover is in the spring. If Isaiah 61 is read on Tishri one, which is in the fall, this adds further evidence that the ministry begins in the fall, since that date is going to be late September or early October.

Since Luke says Jesus begins his ministry when he is about thirty years old, and it can be assumed his birthday is in the fall, is it possible that since he is crucified on Passover, and the church begins on Pentecost, another important day in the Hebrew calendar called Shavuot, that his birth would also be on an important day in the Hebrew calendar? There are four days to choose from, Yom Teruah, Yom Kippur, Sukkot, and Shemini Atzeret: the last Great Day.

Each of these days can be very close to the time Jesus begins his ministry, falling on or within twenty-two days. Since the Feast of Tabernacles has people leaving their homes to live in a temporary dwelling, it seems obvious that this day could picture the Messiah leaving His permanent home in heaven to live on earth in a temporary body beginning on that day.

There is another way to arrive on a fall birth that can be seen in a fifteen-minute YouTube video by Mark Biltz, "The Birth of the Messiah Revealed in Scripture." Biltz arrives at a birth date by determining when the course of Abijah mentioned in Luke occurs. He assumes a static date based on the courses beginning on the same date each year. There are twenty-four courses and Biltz says that they each occur twice during the year, and are supplemented by additional courses for the week feasts occur.

In a scholarly article by Kenneth Frank Doig, "New Testament Chronology," the beginning date of the first course is not static, but shifts throughout the year, making the dating much more difficult, but he actually arrives at a December-25 birth date.

So, who cares? Most people don't. However, if Biltz is correct, then Jesus is born on a feast day. If significant events in the life of the Messiah have already happened on feast days, then is it safe to assume that events that have not yet happened, such as his return, will also happen on feast days? If so, it might help people not be in darkness and be overtaken when these events happen.

NO ROOM AT THE HOLIDAY INN

When Jesus is born, angels announce the birth to shepherds, who according to common tradition, are at the bottom of the social structure at that time. The movies don't get into their status, and in most of the films, they are not even shown, however there is interesting information available about the identity of these shepherds.

According to an article by Dr. Charles Dyer, "Shepherds: More Than Field Hands," the shepherds were priests of the temple, and the sheep they are watching are sheep that are destined to be sacrificed in the temple. The priest's duties include keeping the sheep free from injuries or being blemished.

If you listen to "Linus" reading Luke 2, in *Charlie Brown Christmas,* the only directions the shepherds are told to find the baby is that he will be in a manger. In fact, it is a sign, not a direction. Now, if a manger is a stable, that might narrow the search area, but it is not a stable, as some people believe, it is a wooden box or trough. The shepherds are only told the baby is laying in a trough in Bethlehem, yet they know exactly where to find him. If Dr. Dyer is correct, it would be easy to understand how the shepherds would know exactly where manger would be.

When Linus reads "swaddling clothes" he should be saying swaddling *cloths*. There is an article available online that explain what is meant by this term. An online article by Sh'ma Israel—Hear, O Israel—explains that the baby is wrapped in strips of linen that are made from worn out garments used by the priests. These strips are used to keep lambs warm in the winter as well as wicks in the temple. Elizabeth gives these linen strips to her cousin Mary before the baby is born. The article goes on to explain that the baby is born in the temple sheepfold in a lambing cave in Migdal-Edar.

Was the hotel full, so they had to stay in a stable? Not according to online *Christianity Today*'s article, "No Room in the What?" by Ben Witherington III. He explains that Mary and Joseph were attempting to stay with relatives, but there is no room in their home. The Greek word mistranslated inn, is *kataluma*, which means "upper room" and is the same word to describe where the Last Supper was held. In most Jewish homes, the family lived in the upper room while animals were kept on the first floor.

The movies all show the baby born in a stable, but according to these articles it is probably not a stable where travelers keep their animals, but a place where priests protect the lambs during the winter.

MY WIFE DOESN'T UNDERSTAND ME

Many people believe that Jesus uses parables to teach a lesson so that the lesson will be easily understood. Unfortunately, not only is this not true, it is the exact opposite of that. He uses parables to hide the meaning of some of his messages. The parable of Lazarus and the rich man is a classic example. On the surface there is a lesson that the rich should share with the poor, but is that the only meaning of this parable? Remember, listeners would not be able to understand the meaning of parables unless Christ explains their meaning. Is sharing with the poor a hidden meaning that needs to be explained? Were people at that time, including the Pharisees, so stupid they would not understand that message?

Since Jesus is not here to explain the meaning of this parable, there is only one thing to do to understand what this parable means, and that is to look at how words and expressions in the parable are used elsewhere where the meaning is obvious or explained. If this is a parable, the characters must first be identified, so let's start with the rich man. Is he really an evil person? Here is the first clue. The rich man is clothed in fine linen. The term, "fine linen," describes righteousness.

This gives evidence that the rich man might not be a bad person; in fact he might be righteous. The author has looked at dozens of commentaries on this parable and found only one commentator that recognized there is nothing evil about the rich man. Now consider that the rich man says, "Father Abraham." Clearly he is a Jew since Islam won't be around for hundreds of years. Is it possible the rich man represents righteous Jews? Wow! That would shock 99 percent of Christians.

What about Lazarus? Who could he represent? There is one clue to consider and that is Lazarus is the only individual named in all the parables. The reason that may be a clue is that when an individual is named by another individual it can mean the individual doing the naming has dominion over the individual being named. Remember, Adam is told to name the animals as well as he eventually names Eve. So, who could possibly have dominion over Lazarus? Well, in this case, it might be Christ.

Who are the dogs? The reference to crumbs falling from the table in the parable also shows up when Jesus ignores the Gentile woman who asks Jesus to heal her daughter. By the way, Jesus calls the Gentiles dogs in this account.

There are other parts of the parable to consider. Notice that the rich man asks Lazarus to dip the tip of his finger in water and touch it to the rich man's tongue. Why would a single drop of water comfort the rich man? Why wouldn't he ask for a case of Fiji Water to put the flames out? Why just a drop of water to his tongue?

Answering this question with a question tells the answer. Where does the Holy Spirit first show up? It's on the apostle's tongues. There a similar analogy in the Old Testament where a priest dips his finger in blood? Is it possible that water is now replacing blood for the remission of sins?

If the rich man represents righteous Jews, then maybe Lazarus represents the Gentiles to whom Christ is now going to go. The water clearly represents the Holy Spirit, food clearly represents the Word of God. So putting this together, the Jews had a close relationship with God, but the Gentiles did not. This represents the food the rich man receives. Now the Gentiles will have that relationship while the Jews, becoming blind, will lose it. The torment the rich man has is that being righteous, he is aware of his sinful nature, but does not have the Holy Spirit or a redeemer to save him.

PART XIV : PLEASE DON'T LET ME BE MISUNDERSTOOD

WARNING!

The following handouts presuppose a Wednesday crucifixion, a doctrine with which will anger some people. Rather than burning the author at the stake, please read with an open mind.

ALTERNATIVE FACTS PART DEUX

In chapter three the pattern of the third day is discussed. This pattern, which is contradicted in *One Night with the King* and ignored in the other presentations, is present in the book of Esther. In the notes to chapter seven there is an alternative timeline of events in the life of Moses. This handout will present a possible sequence of events leading to the death of Haman that the author has not seen presented.

All the articles the author has read assume the fast begins on the thirteenth and Haman dies on the fifteenth. There is a serious problem with this timeline. If there is a three-day fast after the decree is issued, it is impossible for Esther and the Jews to fast for three full days. Unless they had incredible Internet service in Shushan, some of the Jews would have already eaten during the thirteenth. The following is an alternative timeline that deals with this issue and has interesting New Testament parallels.

On Nissan 13, the decree to kill the Jews is issued. It is uncertain when Esther agrees to go to the king, but what if Esther agrees on Nissan 14 and she asks that the Jews fast for three days along with her and her attendants. To avoid confusion, the fifteenth is the date she starts to fast.

If she does, an interesting chronology can be constructed. For the sake of the following chronology, assume Esther asks that the fast begin on a Wednesday evening right at sunset which begins the first day. Remember the Hebrew day starts at sunset. Nissan 15, the first day begins on Wednesday at sunset and ends on Thursday at sunset. Nissan 16, the second day begins on Thursday at sunset and ends on Friday at sunset. Nissan 17, the third day begins Friday at sunset and ends Saturday at sunset.

On or after sunset on Friday, Esther approaches the king at the beginning of the third day and invites the king and Haman to the first banquet which occurs that evening. Later Friday evening, after the first banquet,

Haman sees Mordecai not bowing and goes home to meet with his family and friends. The gallows—or pole—is erected late Friday evening.

Red flags immediately go up! Isn't Esther fasting on the third day? Is it possible she does not eat during the two banquets she prepares? There is no passage in the story that says she eats the banquet she prepares, so it is possible she is still fasting.

"These are great pork chops you made us honey, aren't you going to join us?"
"No thanks your Majesty, I'm dieting."

Early Saturday morning, when the king is unable to sleep, the chronicles are read to him and he learns Mordecai saved his life without being rewarded. Later Saturday morning, possibly at Sunrise, Haman approaches the king and is told to honor Mordecai, which is done that morning. Late Saturday afternoon, at the second banquet, which is still Nissan 17, Esther reveals her identity and Haman is killed, possibly at sunset. Esther revealing her identity on the third day follows the pattern of revelation on the third day which is seen throughout the Bible.

Compare this to New Testament events where Christ is crucified on Nissan 14 and everything appears hopeless, but he is victoriously resurrected on Nissan 17. On the third day Haman is raised up on a pole to death and Christ is raised up in a tomb to life. It is even possible that on the exact last second of the third day, Saturday at sunset, Haman closes his eyes in death, and Christ, also on a future Saturday at sunset, opens his eyes in the tomb to life.

PALM SATURDAY

The last note in this book concerns a scene in the movie, *King of Kings*. When Jesus is brought before Pilate, there is no indication that Pilate feels Jesus has done anything wrong. However, this film indicates just the opposite; Pilate acts as a prosecuting attorney, and sends Jesus to be whipped in order to get him to confess.

This may not seem important, but it is. Many Christians are not aware of the period known as "The inspection of the Lamb." This period starts on the tenth day of Nisan when a lamb is brought into the house and ends on the fourteenth day of Nisan when the lamb is sacrificed. This "inspection" dates back to the time of Moses when he tells the Israelites to inspect it

PART XIV : PLEASE DON'T LET ME BE MISUNDERSTOOD

before it is sacrificed to make sure there is no blemish or deformity in the animal.

When Jesus enters Jerusalem the four-day inspection period begins on Nisan 10 when he is challenged by officials at the Temple. On Nisan 14, Pilate ends the inspection period, saying he finds no fault in Jesus, and turns him over to be crucified.

The entry into Jerusalem is observed by many Christians on Palm Sunday. The next event these Christians observe is Good Friday, the day they believe Jesus is crucified, followed by the resurrection, three days later on Sunday morning.

If there is a four-day inspection that begins on the tenth when he first enters Jerusalem, which is a parallel to the lamb being brought into the house, then there is a problem. If Palm Sunday is the tenth, that would make Monday the eleventh, Tuesday would be the twelfth, Wednesday would be the thirteenth, and Thursday would be the fourteenth. So if Palm Sunday is the day he enters Jerusalem, then the four day inspection would end with the crucifixion on Thursday, not Friday.

The next question about the accepted timing of events is how you get three days and three nights from a period that is at most, part of a day a night, a day, another night and part of a final day. To solve this dilemma, it is useful to listen to an online message by Ron Dart, "Three Days and Three Nights." He proposes there are three days and three nights that begin on a Wednesday evening just before sunset. This is not some obscure doctrine. The appendixes to *The Companion Bible*, written over a hundred years ago by Dr. E.W. Bullinger, support this theory.

The strongest argument against a Wednesday crucifixion is Luke's account of what happened on the road to Emmaus. The disciples say on a Sunday afternoon that it is the third day since all the events concerning Jesus have occurred. While this is a valid argument, it does have at least one rebuttal, which is that all the events can include the sealing of the tomb on Friday. This is clearly a situation where there is overwhelming evidence on one side and one passage from one writer on other side, leaving the reader to make a decision.

Here is a possible timing of the events of that week. Sometime Friday evening or on Saturday during daylight, Nisan 10, Jesus arrives in Jerusalem. The crucifixion occurs Wednesday, Nisan 14, and the body is put into the tomb just before Sunset while it is still Wednesday Nisan 14. Wednesday, after sunset, begins Nisan 15, the first day of Unleavened Bread, an annual Sabbath. The resurrection occurs at Sunset on Saturday evening which is the end of Nisan 17.

These dates are compatible with a four-day inspection followed by three days and nights that the body is in the tomb. This timing also allows the women to prepare spices after the Sabbath and before the Sabbath. The only way this can happen is if there are two Sabbaths that week, an annual Sabbath on Thursday and a weekly Sabbath on Saturday. This means the women prepare the spices on Friday which is the only day the women can prepare spices on a single day that is both before a Sabbath and after a Sabbath.

Acknowledgments

John Reinhardt: "It will be my pleasure to help you get your book done, and done right." This is a direct quote from the first e-mail I received from John Reinhardt shortly after meeting him. John has been a book designer since the 1970s and I "just happened" to meet him in the community I live in as I was walking Teddy. John provided all the design work, including the great cover for this book. He also introduced me to Deb Strubel, my first editor. Without John's assistance this book would never have been finished. I am deeply grateful for all he did to make this book "done right."

Deb Strubel: Deb warned me that she would most likely not be able to finish editing my book, and that turned out to be the case. She taught me several things about writing that I needed to know and I am very grateful for her pointing these out to me. I still find myself leaving two spaces after a period occasionally, but it's not because Deb didn't tell me that is incorrect. When Deb had to stop the editing she referred me to Jim Watkins to do the editing.

Jim Watkins: The manuscript that Jim edited, which turned out to be my fifth version of this work, is entirely different than the first version Deb edited. This is due to the advice Jim gave me after he critiqued some chapters. Jim was a huge influence in the overall emphasis on humor in this book. He did an amazing job and I am so glad he got involved in this project. He also wrote a couple of paragraphs at the beginning of the introduction to the films about David. The term "LSD" was his invention. I love it.

ACKNOWLEDGMENTS

Richard Ritenbaugh: Richard is a minister in the "Church of the Great God" in Fort Mill, SC. He has been very helpful in answering questions about events in the Bible that I describe in the book. He was also very patient with me as we spent many hours on the phone. I have learned many things from him over the thirty years I have known him and his wife Beth.

Brad Scott: Brad is an expert in Hebrew thought and language who speaks all over the world. He has been very helpful to me in answering questions as I worked my way through this book. I learned a great amount of information reading his book and watching many of his videos. The timing of Jesus proclaiming his ministry is just one of many places where I received help from Brad. Brad also gave me permission to make a cameo appearance as an expert witness in the grand jury scene. I hope I did him justice, he is incredibly smart!

My neighbor Ann Smith: Ann generously agreed to proof my book after it was edited and found dozens of mistakes that were still there.

My Daughter Becky: Becky proofed my book, but also added some great humor. For example it was her idea to suggest that Moses separate his staff into two light sticks to guide the Israelites through the Red Sea at night.

My Wife Nancy: Nancy helped me in many ways on this project. In addition to proofing the final manuscript, she also listened to me for over three years as I talked about this book. She commented on my ideas, especially if they were stupid ideas. She also contributed material that is in the book. For example, the four kinds of snakes that Eve describes were Nancy's invention. I am heartbroken that she did not live to see the book in print, but I look forward to seeing her someday and thanking her again.

REFERENCES

Available online at:
holywoodbook.com

www.ingramcontent.com/pod-product-compliance
Lightning Source LLC
Chambersburg PA
CBHW071220290426
44108CB00013B/1231